Studies in Educational Leadership

Volume 23

Series Editor
Kenneth A. Leithwood, OISE, University of Toronto, Canada

Editorial Board
Christopher Day, University of Nottingham, United Kingdom
Stephen L. Jacobson, Graduate School of Education, Buffalo, U.S.A.
Bill Mulford, University of Tasmania, Hobart, Australia
Peter Sleegers, University of Nijmegen, The Netherlands

Scope of the Series
Leadership we know makes all the difference in success or failures of organizations. This series will bring together in a highly readable way the most recent insights in successful leadership. Emphasis will be placed on research focused on pre-collegiate educational organizations. Volumes should address issues related to leadership at all levels of the educational system and be written in a style accessible to scholars, educational practitioners and policy makers throughout the world.

The volumes – monographs and edited volumes – should represent work from different parts in the world.

More information about this series at http://www.springer.com/series/6543

Kenneth Leithwood • Jingping Sun
Katina Pollock
Editors

How School Leaders Contribute to Student Success

The Four Paths Framework

Springer

Editors
Kenneth Leithwood
University of Toronto
Ontario Institute for Studies in Education
 University of Toronto
Ontario, ON, Canada

Jingping Sun
University of Alabama
The College of Education University of
 Alabama
Tuscaloosa, AL, USA

Katina Pollock
Western University
Faculty of Education Western University
London, ON, Canada

Studies in Educational Leadership
ISBN 978-3-319-50979-2   ISBN 978-3-319-50980-8 (eBook)
DOI 10.1007/978-3-319-50980-8

Library of Congress Control Number: 2017931561

© Springer International Publishing AG 2017
This work is subject to copyright. All rights are reserved by the Publisher, whether the whole or part of the material is concerned, specifically the rights of translation, reprinting, reuse of illustrations, recitation, broadcasting, reproduction on microfilms or in any other physical way, and transmission or information storage and retrieval, electronic adaptation, computer software, or by similar or dissimilar methodology now known or hereafter developed.
The use of general descriptive names, registered names, trademarks, service marks, etc. in this publication does not imply, even in the absence of a specific statement, that such names are exempt from the relevant protective laws and regulations and therefore free for general use.
The publisher, the authors and the editors are safe to assume that the advice and information in this book are believed to be true and accurate at the date of publication. Neither the publisher nor the authors or the editors give a warranty, express or implied, with respect to the material contained herein or for any errors or omissions that may have been made. The publisher remains neutral with regard to jurisdictional claims in published maps and institutional affiliations.

Printed on acid-free paper

This Springer imprint is published by Springer Nature
The registered company is Springer International Publishing AG
The registered company address is: Gewerbestrasse 11, 6330 Cham, Switzerland

Contents

1 Introduction 1
Kenneth Leithwood, Jingping Sun, and Katina Pollock

Part I The Nature of Successful Leadership

2 A Model of Successful School Leadership from the International
Successful School Principalship Project 15
David Gurr

3 The Ontario Leadership Framework: Successful School Leadership
Practices and Personal Leadership Resources 31
Kenneth Leithwood

Part II The Rational Path

4 Leadership and Learning: Conceptualizing Relations Between
School Administrative Practice and Instructional Practice 49
James Spillane

5 Effects of Distributed Leadership on School Academic
Press and Student Achievement 69
John Malloy and Kenneth Leithwood

6 Towards Sustaining Levels of Reflective Learning:
How Do Transformational Leadership, Task Interdependence,
and Self-Efficacy Shape Teacher Learning in Schools? 93
Arnoud Oude Groote Beverborg, Peter J.C. Sleegers,
Maaike D. Endedijk, and Klaas van Veen

Part III The Emotional Path

7 Leadership Effects on Student Learning Mediated
by Teacher Emotions 137
Jingping Sun and Kenneth Leithwood

| 8 | Principals, Trust, and Cultivating Vibrant Schools | 153 |

Megan Tschannen-Moran and Christopher R. Gareis

| 9 | Generation X School Leaders as Agents of Care: Leader and Teacher Perspectives from Toronto, New York City and London | 175 |

Karen Edge, Katherine Descours, and Keren Frayman

Part IV The Organizational Path

| 10 | Complexity and Volume: An Inquiry into Factors That Drive Principals' Work | 209 |

Katina Pollock, Fei Wang, and David Cameron Hauseman

| 11 | Creating Communities of Professionalism: Addressing Cultural and Structural Barriers | 239 |

Joseph Murphy

| 12 | Effects of Principal Professional Orientation Towards Leadership, Professional Teacher Behavior, and School Academic Optimism on School Reading Achievement | 263 |

Roxanne Mitchell and John Tarter

| 13 | Leading Teacher Learning in China: A Mixed Methods Study of Successful School Leadership | 279 |

Shengnan Liu and Philip Hallinger

Part V The Family Path

| 14 | Effects of Family Educational Cultures on Student Success at School: Directions for Leadership | 311 |

William H. Jeynes

| 15 | Changing the Educational Culture of the Home to Increase Student Success at School | 329 |

Kenneth Leithwood and Penny Patrician

| 16 | Conclusion | 353 |

Kenneth Leithwood, Jingping Sun, and Katina Pollock

About the Editors

Dr. Kenneth Leithwood is emeritus professor at OISE/University of Toronto. His research and writing are about school leadership, educational policy and organizational change. He has published extensively on these topics. For example, he is the senior editor of both the first and second *International Handbooks on Educational Leadership and Administration* (Kluwer Publishers, 1996, 2003). His most recent books include *Linking Leadership to Student Learning* (2012, Jossey Bass), *Leading School Turnaround* (2010, Jossey Bass), *Distributed Leadership: The State of the Evidence* (2009, Routledge), *Leading With Teacher Emotions in Mind* (2008, Corwin), *Making Schools Smarter* (Corwin, 3rd edition, 2006) and *Teaching for Deep Understanding* (Corwin, 2006). With colleagues, he completed one of the largest studies of its kind about how state-, district- and school-level leadership influences student learning. Professor Leithwood is the inaugural recipient of the University of Toronto's *Impact on Public Policy award*, AERA's 2011 Outstanding Leadership Researcher Award and the 2012 *Roald F. Campbell Lifetime Achievement Award* from the University Council for Educational Administration. He is a *fellow of the Royal Society of Canada*.

Dr. Jingping Sun is an assistant professor in the Department of Educational Leadership, Policy and Technology Studies at the College of Education, University of Alabama. She obtained her PhD at the Ontario Institute for Studies in Education, University of Toronto. Her research is about educational leadership, policy evaluation and improvement, data-based decision making and research synthesis. Prior to joining the faculty at the University of Alabama, she worked at the Ontario Ministry of Education in Canada. Her policy experience at the provincial level was mainly about large-scale development of school and district leaders. Her work can be found in leading journals on educational leadership such as *Educational Administration Quarterly*.

Dr. Katina Pollock is associate professor of educational leadership and policy in Critical Policy, Equity and Leadership Studies at the Faculty of Education, Western University. Katina has been awarded a number of research grants and contracts with various funders. Her most recent grant (with Dr. Fei Wang) explores Secondary School Principals' Understanding of Work Intensification. In addition to her traditional scholarship efforts, Dr. Pollock has also been involved in large-scale knowledge mobilization initiatives that connect research to practice. She is currently co-director for the Knowledge Network for Applied Education Research (KNAER), an initiative supported by the Ontario Ministry of Education. Katina's most recent publication includes "The work of school leaders: North American similarities, local differences" (with Murakami and Swapp) and "Juggling multiple accountability systems: How three principals' manage these tensions in Ontario, Canada" (with Winton).

Chapter 1
Introduction

Kenneth Leithwood, Jingping Sun, and Katina Pollock

Using several different sources of evidence, we have argued over the past 10 years that among the wide array of school conditions influencing students, leadership is second only to classroom instruction (e.g., Leithwood et al. 2004; Scheerens et al. 1989; Reetzig and Creemers 2005). We have also pointed out that, to our knowledge, there are no documented cases of failing schools turning around in the absence of talented leadership (Leithwood et al. 2010). So leadership matters, although how much it matters often seems to depend on the nature of the evidence being reported. For the most part, large-scale quantitative leadership studies report modest but significant effects of leadership on student learning (Witziers et al. 2003), while more in-depth, qualitative leadership studies suggest much larger effects. Leadership also seems to contribute most to those schools struggling the hardest to serve their students well (Day et al. 2011).

Those in formal school leadership roles, of course, have many fewer opportunities to interact with students directly than do teachers or parents. So it not the direct relationship between an individual school leader and a student, or a group of students, that explains most of those significant leadership effects. Appreciating this common-sense fact of school leadership life has persuaded most of those doing research about leadership effects to design their studies to include both mediating and moderating variables. These designs are typically referred to as "indirect effects" leadership models (e.g., Hallinger and Heck 1998; Leithwood and Louis

---

K. Leithwood (✉)
Ontario Institute for Studies in Education, University of Toronto, Toronto, ON, Canada
e-mail: kenneth.leithwood@utoronto.ca

J. Sun
The College of Education, University of Alabama, Tuscaloosa, AL, USA
e-mail: jsun22@ua.edu

K. Pollock
Faculty of Education, Western University, London, ON, Canada
e-mail: kpolloc7@uwo.ca

© Springer International Publishing AG 2017
K. Leithwood et al. (eds.), *How School Leaders Contribute to Student Success*,
Studies in Educational Leadership 23, DOI 10.1007/978-3-319-50980-8_1

2012; Robinson et al. 2009) and evidence continues to grow about the extent to which selected mediators and moderators "explain" leadership effects on students.

Leaders, we have come to understand, are often not just the few individuals in a school holding formal administrative or leadership positions. Leadership is often widely shared or distributed with teachers, parents and students also assuming such a role from time to time. While those in formal leadership positions almost always perform essential leadership functions, the complexity and volume of challenges needing to be addressed in most schools most of the time far outstrip the capacities of the relatively small cadre of formal leaders in a school to address. With few exceptions, however, others in the school look to those in formal roles for clues about what will be considered important in the organization and the extent to which improvement efforts are likely to attract long-term support. Those with whom leadership is shared depends on the challenges faced by the school, the willingness of staff members to assume leadership on behalf of their colleagues and often the delegation of leadership by those in formal administration positions.

In sum, leadership matters a good deal to the success of students. It often matters most when and where it is most needed. Its' effects on students are typically indirect and it is almost always distributed throughout the organization. These claims about school leadership effects are the point of departure for this book. The book assumes that the case for leadership effects, while varying in strength across the large corpus of relevant evidence now available,[1] is sufficiently well documented and that the key question facing practicing leaders and leadership scholars at this point is about "how". How does school leadership influence student learning? The purpose for this book is to both broaden and deepen one approach to answering this key question and is, as Liu and Hallinger explain, part of "a broader global effort aimed at understanding the means by which leaders contribute to school improvement." (Chap. 13, this book); it extends the meaning attached to the now widely- used phrases "leadership for learning" (e.g., Hallinger 2011) and "learning-focused leadership" (e.g., Knapp et al. 2010).

The approach to answering this key "how" question explored in this book was initially developed in the context of a very large leadership development project in the Canadian province of Ontario (*Leading Student Achievement: Networks for Learning*). Faced with multiple forms of evidence about the value of a wide array project initiatives, many based on substantial independent research, the projects' directors and its' evaluator (Leithwood) developed a theory of action to guide their efforts. Figure 1.1, the framework for the book, summarizes this theory of action. This framework is premised on assumptions about leadership as the exercise of influence and recognition (Hallinger and Heck 1996, 1998) of such influence on students as indirect. As the figure indicates, leaders' influence "flows" along four "paths" to reach students – Rational, Emotional, Organizational and Family paths. Each of these paths is populated by key conditions or variables which (a) can be

---

[1] For a sample of high quality reviews of literature justifying this claim, see Hallinger and Heck (1998), Witziers et al. (2003), Marzano et al. (2005), Robinson et al. (2008) Leithwood and Sun (2012).

1 Introduction

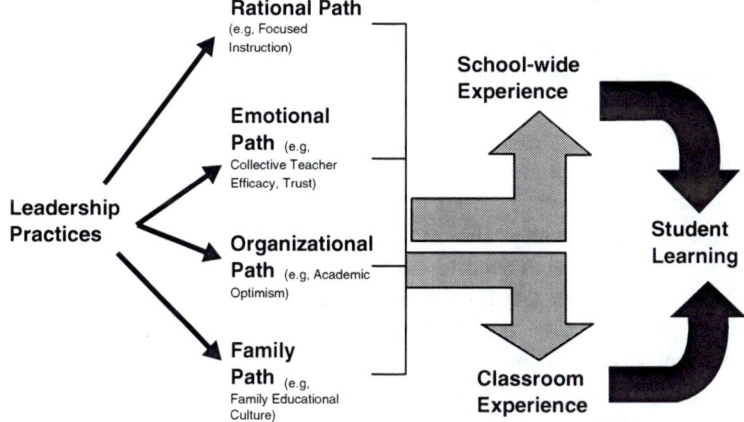

Fig. 1.1 Four paths of leadership influence on student learning

influenced by those exercising leadership and (b) have relatively direct effects on students.

Conditions or variables on the Rational Path are rooted in the knowledge and skills of school staff members about curriculum, teaching, and learning – the technical core of schooling. The Emotional Path includes those feelings, dispositions, or affective states of staff members (both individually and collectively) shaping the nature of their work, for example, teachers' sense of efficacy. Conditions on the Organizational Path include features of schools that structure the relationships and interactions among organizational members including, for example, cultures, policies, and standard operating procedures. On the Family Path are conditions reflecting family expectations for their children, their culture and support to students, and community orientations toward school and general education.

Selecting the most promising of these conditions – a task requiring knowledge of relevant research, as well as local context – and improving their status are among the central challenges facing leaders intending to improve student learning in their schools, according to this framework. As the status of conditions or variables on each Path improves through influences from leaders and other sources, the quality of students' school and classroom experiences is enriched, resulting in greater payoffs for students. Over an extended period of time, leaders should attend to conditions in their schools in need of strengthening on all Paths.

In sum, the job of school leaders, in collaboration with their colleagues, is to:

- Identify conditions not yet sufficiently developed to realize their potential contribution on students;
- Select from those conditions, which one or several ought to become a focus for the school's improvement efforts in light of the school's current goals, priorities and other features of the school's context;
- Plan and act to improve the status of those conditions selected for improvement.

This conception of how school leadership influences students is also an approach to school improvement, one which cedes considerable autonomy to school leaders and their colleagues about what is to be improved and how such improvement will take place. The accountability demands saturating much contemporary educational policy (e.g., *No Child Left Behind* (*NCLB*) and its' successor *Each Student Succeeds Act*) call for leaders who are *strategic* in making their efforts to meet the learning-needs of students, develop school conditions or cultures defined as continuous improvement, and to increase the organizational learning capacities of schools. To be strategic, school leaders need to know about those classroom, school and malleable family conditions that both contribute significantly to student learning and that they can influence; the approach outlined in this book makes a significant contribution to the strategic capacities of school leaders.

Approaching school improvement from the perspective described here also requires considerable "systems thinking" on the part of school leaders. While variables associated with each of the four paths are distinct, they also interact with variables on the other paths and failure to take such interaction into account will severely limit a school leader's influence. This means, for example, that if a school leader decides to improve the status of a school's Academic Press (a variable on the Rational Path), she will also need to consider what her teachers' feelings will be, in response. The leader will need to ensure that her teachers begin to feel, for example, efficacious about their role in fostering the school's academic press (a variable on the Emotional Path).

The need for alignment across paths seems to hugely complicate leaders' work. But, as this Academic Press example illustrates, picking only one or two powerful variables on a path, and planning for the most likely interactions makes the leadership task much more manageable. This way of thinking about the leadership task, however, does add weight to the argument that leaders' success will typically depends on devoting one's attention to a small number of priorities.

Aside from its surface reasonableness, the case for alignment of leadership influence across paths can be justified on both historical grounds as we have argued elsewhere:

> From an historical perspective, at some point over the past six decades, reformers have considered selected interventions on each of the four paths independently to be the solution to problems of student underachievement, and each has been found wanting. Post-Sputnik efforts to reform curriculum and instruction exemplified a preoccupation with the rational path but to little apparent effect. Disappointed reformers then began a journey along the emotional path, the most visible manifestation of which was the organizational development (OD) movement of the '80s and its efforts to improve working relationships in schools and districts. With OD's failure to live up to expectations, reformers switched to the organizational path during the late '80s and early '90s, setting off a wave of school restructuring which appeared to make little difference to student learning. Previous examples of efforts to exercise influence on the family path include both the community school and full-service school movements (Leithwood et al. 2010, p. 21).

Many different sources of evidence appear throughout the chapters of this book to justify the account of how leadership influences student learning summarized in Fig. 1.1. However, a brief description of the original study "testing" this account serves as an advanced organizer for these other, more recent sources. This original study (Leithwood et al. 2010) used evidence from teacher responses (1445) to an online survey which measured a small set of variables or conditions on each of the Four Paths, as well as a set of leadership practices enacted by those in many roles in their schools ($N = 199$). Grade 3 and 6 math and literacy achievement data were provided by the province's annual testing program (Ontario's Educational Quality and Accountability program). The 2006 Canadian Census data provided a composite measure of school socioeconomic status (used as a control variable).

Results of this initial study indicated that the Four Paths, as a whole, explained 43% of the variation in students' math and language achievement. Variables or conditions on the Rational, Emotional, and Family Paths explained similarly significant amounts of that variation, while variables on the Organizational Path were not as strongly related to student achievement. Leadership, as it was measured in this study, had its greatest influence on the Organizational Path and least influence on the Family Path.

Several important implications for practice emerged from the results of this study for practicing leaders.[2] The first of these implications was the extension of what it means to make evidence-informed decisions. Guided by the Four Paths model, such decisions would need to include considerations of research evidence about variables with demonstrable effects on student learning and how leaders influence the condition or status of those variables. Successful school improvement decisions cannot simply rest on evidence about student achievement, no matter the quality of such evidence and the care with which it is interpreted.

A second closely related implication for practicing leaders arises from identification, by the Four Paths, of largely neglected bodies of knowledge and skills that should be part of leadership preparation and ongoing professional development. Among variables associated with each of the Four Paths, some have been a common focus of attention by school leaders and those providing leadership development experiences for many years (primarily those on the Rational and Organizational Paths). Many variables on both the Emotional and Family Paths, however, have been largely neglected, even though results of this study and many others suggest that such variables are likely to have at least comparable effects on student learning.

Third, our results challenged the dominant narrative about ideal forms of school leadership, one that is saturated with the language of instruction. Evidence highlighted by the Four Paths suggests that even on the Rational Path some school-level variables (e.g., Academic Press and Disciplinary Climate) have impacts on student learning that actually rival the effects of those classroom-level instructional variables that principal leaders are now admonished to focus on but typically feel only moderately able to improve (e.g., specific instruction strategies, teachers' questioning techniques).[3]

---

[2] Some of the text in the next four paragraphs is adopted/adapted from Leithwood et al. 2010.

[3] Adding additional weight to this implication about the range of variables, other than just instruction, on which leaders might focus their improvement efforts, are the results of a recent meta-analytic review of evidence about the effects of interventions aimed at enhancing students' motivation to learn (Lazowski and Hulleman 2016). Results from this review suggest substantially larger effects on student performance indicators of efforts to improve their motivation to learn, as compared with comprehensive school reform programs, the majority of which are focused on classroom instruction (effect sizes of .52 and .11 respectively).

There is no doubt that teachers and students would benefit from a type of well-informed leadership heavily focused on classroom instructional. But it is fraught with difficulties as a model for the work at least of those in formal school leadership roles because it takes no account of the wide range of challenges the vast majority of those in such roles face in their administrative lives (e.g., see Chap. 10 this book) and often seems to point to the principal as the only person capable of helping teachers improve instruction. This focus also ignores the extremely important and largely overlooked leadership that schools need and that, in most schools, only those in formal leadership roles are able to deliver. Successful leaders improve learning in their schools in many ways. Improving instruction will always be important but it is by no means the only influence on student learning. Indeed, engaging the school productively with parents (Family Path), if this has not been a focus, may well produce larger effects on student learning, in the short run, than marginal improvements to already at least satisfactory levels of instruction.

1.1 Organization of the Book[4]

The book consists of five parts along with a concluding chapter. Each part begins with a brief overview of research relevant to the theme of the part written by the editors, followed by several chapters that provide an in-depth analysis or critique of some theme, topic or problem central to the substance of the part. A large proportion of the chapters in the book were written by others and their purpose is to provide independent perspectives on key features of the book's framework; these chapters serve to broaden, deepen or in several cases, reveal limitations of the book's framework. Chapters authored or coauthored by the editors provide more extensive evidence about Part themes than has previously been reported.

1.1.1 Part One: The Nature of Successful Leadership

The first of two chapters in this part, authored by David Gurr, synthesizes results of research about successful leadership carried out by he and his colleagues as part of the International Successful School Principalship Project (ISSPP), a project that has been underway since 2001. Building on Gurr, Drysdale and Mulford's earlier leadership model, the work of school leaders is described in this chapter as engaging within the school context to influence student and school outcomes through interventions in teaching and learning, school capacity building, and the wider context. The qualities a leader brings to their role, a portfolio approach to using leadership ideas, constructing networks, collaborations and partnerships, and utilising

---

[4] The brief description of chapters included in this part are based on, or adapted from, abstracts written by the authors of each chapter.

accountability and evaluation for evidence-informed improvement, are important additional elements. The model is applicable to all in leadership roles in schools.

The second chapter in this part provides a brief overview of the *Ontario Leadership Framework* (Leithwood 2012), a comprehensive description of those leadership practices and personal leadership resources the "best available evidence" suggests contribute either directly or indirectly to student learning and well-being. Developed for the Ontario Ministry of Education, the *Framework* outlines standards and expectations for educational leadership in the province and is widely used within the province as a guide for leadership selection, development and self-appraisal.

1.1.2 Part 2: The Rational Path

The first of the three chapter in this part, authored by Spillane, unpacks the range of possible ways in which leadership is related to changes in teachers' instruction, a key variable on the Rational Path. Spillane argues that one problem we face in understanding relations between school leadership and student learning is that core constructs in our work are often variably and weakly defined. Spillane begins by conceptualizing school administration and instruction from what he refers to as a distributed perspective, using theoretical work in distributed and situated cognition, activity theory, and micro sociology. This chapter shows how conceptualizing both leadership and instruction in particular ways shapes how we might frame and hypothesize relations among these phenomena.

Malloy and Leithwood, in the second chapter in this part, provide empirical evidence about distributed leadership effects on student achievement mediated by Academic Press, another potentially powerful variable on the Rational Path. This study began with a focus on Academic Optimism (see Mitchell and Tarter, Chap. 12, for an extended treatment of this variable), a composite variable including not only Academic Press but also Collective Teacher Efficacy and Teacher Trust. However, evidence from the study highlighted the disproportionate contribution to student learning of Academic Press. The study also inquired about four different forms of leadership distribution but found only one of these forms ("planful alignment") contributed indirectly to student achievement in mathematics through its effects on Academic Press.

The third chapter in this part by Oude, Beverborg, Sleegers, Endedijk and van Veen, reports the results of a longitudinal study about how selected transformational leadership practices, task interdependence, self-efficacy, and teachers' engagement in self-reflection mutually affect each other over time. Findings from this study point to the important role transformational leadership practices play in facilitating teamwork, and sustaining teachers' levels of learning in schools. Teacher self-reflection and task interdependence, this study found, reciprocally influence each other and these processes are fostered by considerate and stimulating transformational leadership practices.

1.1.3 Part 3: The Emotional Path

The two chapters in this part provide evidence about the contribution of four teacher emotions to student learning and leadership practices demonstrably useful in enhancing these emotions. The first of these chapters is a meta-analytic review of research by Sun and Leithwood. This chapter identifies four distinct teacher emotions with significant effects on student learning (collective teacher efficacy, teacher commitment, teacher trust in others, and Organizational Citizenship Behavior) and describes those leadership practices which foster productive forms of these four teacher emotions; most of those practices reflect a transformational approach to leadership.

The second chapter, authored by Tschannen-Moran and Gareis, is about teacher trust in leaders and how principals can cultivate trust by attending to five facets of trust, as well as the correlates of trust that mediate student learning, including Academic Press, Collective Teacher Efficacy, and Teacher Professionalism. This chapter argues that trust is not just relevant to leadership influence on the Emotional Path but plays a role in how leaders influence student learning through each of the four paths described in this book.

Authored by Edge, Descours and Frayman, the third chapter draws on evidence from a 3-year study of the lives, experiences and aspirations of Generation X (under 40 years of age) principals and vice-principals in London, New York City, and Toronto. More specifically, the paper examines a thin slice of interview evidence from nine school-based studies in which nine leaders and 54 teachers discuss their perspectives on the question: Is it the leader's role to care for his or her teachers? The evidence demonstrates that leaders and teachers both place a high level of importance on leaders' ability and willingness to be supportive, understanding, and approachable. Teachers also expect leaders to serve as advocates for and role models of good work/life balance. While the school-level studies take place in radically different city-based contexts, the expectation of leaders' care for teachers transcends different accountability and policy structures. Both groups focus their discussion on work/life balance and, more specifically, the need for leaders to understand that teachers are people with lives beyond school.

1.1.4 Part 4: The Organizational Path

The four chapters in this part are concerned, in general, with the circumstances or contexts in which leaders find themselves and how leaders are influenced by, and go about influencing, those contexts in ways that impact the learning of their students. The first of these chapters, by Pollock, Wang and Hauseman, unpacks evidence about how the work lives of principals (in the Canadian province of Ontario) is intensifying in terms of its complexity and volume. Many factors moderate and drive such work intensification and this chapter identifies what and how such factors interact to complicate principals' work. Using multiple forms of evidence, this chapter indicates that there are many key areas that moderate principals' work, such as administrative duties and responsibilities, jurisdictional policies, external influences, partnerships, and challenges and possibilities. School principals are experiencing increased expectations at work in terms of the number of tasks they are expected to undertake, the duration of time they are required to complete those tasks, and the many challenges they face at their work. Principals' choice of leadership approaches and practices is subject to factors that exist within and beyond schools. Such factors moderate the way that principals carry out their work and limit their choices in exercising their professional autonomy.

Murphy's chapter, based on an integrative review of research, is about how leaders help create a productive professional community in their schools. The chapter aims at better understanding the barriers and constraints that hinder or prevent growth of professional community, as well as how educators can be successful in meeting these challenges. Evidence from this review indicates that there are dynamic cultural and well-entrenched structural barriers that make the realization of professional community problematic. Some of these elements are visible while many others are deeply buried in the meta-narrative of school improvement. Absent direct attention to these conditions by school leaders, efforts to nurture professional community in schools will be seriously handicapped.

The third chapter by Mitchell and Tarter reports the results of a study testing the effects of the principal's professional orientation towards leadership on two mediating variables, Academic Optimism (which we consider to be part of a school's culture) and Professional Teacher Behavior on school reading achievement. Results of this study indicate that a path to reading achievement in which the principal's orientation to leadership was the immediate antecedent of Academic Optimism and Professional Teacher Behavior. Academic Optimism, these results indicate, is as an important influence on reading achievement and principals' leadership orientation is critical to the establishment of a context in which Academic Optimism and Professional Teacher Behavior can flourish.

The fourth and final chapter in this part about the Organizational Path is by Liu and Hallinger. This chapter explores the consequences for schools and leaders' work of broad national contexts, norms and values. This mixed methods study conducted in China uses quantitative evidence to describe leadership-teacher learning processes in a sample of 31 urban and rural schools. After establishing differences in the 'strength' of learning-centered leadership and teacher professional learning between the two groups of schools, qualitative case studies of an urban and a rural school are used as examples of how learning-centered leadership practices were enacted in the very different contexts. This chapter offers useful insights into a key policy issue in China and also contributes to our broader understanding of how context shapes the enactment of school leadership in different settings.

1.1.5 Part 5: The Family Path

The first chapter in this part is a meta-analytic review of evidence about the effects on students of family educational culture while the second chapter is an original empirical study on the same theme. William Jeynes authors the meta-analytic review of research. His chapter examines the overall impact on student success at school of parental involvement, as well as specific components of parental involvement. Four different measures of student success at school are used – an overall measure of all components of academic achievement combined, grades, standardized tests, and other measures that generally included teacher rating scales and indices of academic attitudes and behaviors. The differing effects of parental involvement by race and socioeconomic status are also part of this review. Results indicate that the influence of parental involvement, overall, is significant for secondary school children. Parental involvement as a whole had significant effects on all of the academic variables in the study (.50 to.55 of a standard deviation unit). The chapter also reviews evidence about school leader practices which assist parents to support the success of their children at school.

The second chapter, by Leithwood and Patrician, describes a quasi-experimental field study which explored the relative effects of alternative types of school interventions on parent engagement. All of these interventions aimed to further engage parents in the education of their children as a means of both improving student achievement and closing gaps in achievement for students living primarily in challenging social and economic circumstances. Initiatives by school staffs aimed at helping those families struggling to build productive educational cultures in their homes would appear to be a very promising strategy for closing achievement gaps between advantaged and disadvantaged students. The study provides eight lessons school and district leaders might take heed of as they embark on their own parent engagement interventions.

1.2 Conclusion

In the concluding chapter, the editors provide a summary of the results reported in the book's chapters along with some reflections on those results. Also provided is a unique approach to helping practicing school leaders use the results of relevant research to guide their own decision making; this approach is illustrated using a recent, large-scale data set not yet reported elsewhere. Implications are identified for school leadership development and associations are noted between the expectations for leadership development reflected in recent school leadership standards and the contents of the book as a whole.

References

Day, C. Sammons, P. Leithwood, K. Harris, A., Hopkins, D. Gu, Q., Brown, E., & Ahtaridou, E. (2011). *Successful school leadership: Linking with learning and achievement*. London: Open University Press.

Hallinger, P. (2011). Leadership for learning: Lessons from 40 years of empirical research. *Journal of Educational Administration, 49*, 125–142.

Hallinger, P., & Heck, R. (1996). The principal's role in school effectiveness: A review of methodological issues. In K. Leithwood (Ed.), *The international handbook of educational leadership and administration* (pp. 723–784). Dordrecht: Kluwer Publishers.

Hallinger, P., & Heck, R. (1998). Exploring the principal's contribution to school effectiveness, 1980–1995. *School Effectiveness and School Improvement, 9*, 157–191.
Knapp, M. S., Copland, M. A., Honig, M. I., Plecki, M. L., & Portin, B. S. (2010). *Learning focused leadership and leadership support: Meaning and practice in urban systems*. Seattle, WA: Center for the Study of Teaching and Policy, University of Washington.
Lazowski, R., & Hulleman, C. (2016). Motivation interventions in education: A meta-analytic review. *Review of Educational Research, 86*, 602–640.
Leithwood, K. (2012). *The Ontario leadership framework 2012 with a discussion of the research foundations*. Toronto: Institute for Educational Leadership.
Leithwood, K., & Louis, K. S. (2012). *Linking leadership to student learning*. San Francisco: Jossey-Bass.
Leithwood, K., & Sun, J. (2012). The nature and effects of transformational school leadership: A meta-analytic review of unpublished research. *Educational Administration Quarterly, 48*, 387–423.
Leithwood, K., Louis, K., Wahlstrom, K., & Anderson, S. (2004). *How leadership influences student learning: A review of research for the learning from leadership project*. New York: Wallace Foundation.
Leithwood, K., Anderson, S., & Mascall, B. (2010a). School leaders' influences on student learning: The four paths. In T. Bush, L. Bell, & D. Middlewood (Eds.), *The principles of educational leadership and management (Chapter 2)*. London: Sage.
Leithwood, K., Harris, A., & Strauss, T. (2010b). *Leading school turnaround: How successful leaders transform low-performing schools*. San Francisco: Jossey-Bass.
Leithwood, K., Patten, S., & Jantzi, D. (2010c). Testing a conception of how leadership influences student learning. *Educational Administration Quarterly, 46*, 671–706.
Marzano, R., Waters, T., & McNulty, B. (2005). *School leadership that works: From research to results*. Arlington: Association for Curriculum and Staff Development.
Reetzig, G., & Creemers, B. (2005). A comprehensive framework for effective school improvement. *School Effectiveness and School Improvement, 16*, 407–424.
Robinson, V., Lloyd, C., & Rowe, K. (2008). The impact of leadership on student achievement: An analysis of the differential effects of leadership types. *Educational Administration Quarterly, 44*, 635–674.
Robinson, V., Hohepa, M., & Lloyd, C. (2009). *School leadership and student outcomes: Identifying what works and why*. Auckland: University of Auckland.
Scheerens, J., Vermeulen, C., & Pelgrum, W. (1989). Generalizability of instructional and school effectiveness indicators across nations. *International Journal of Educational Research, 13*, 691–706.
Witziers, B., Bosker, R. J., & Kruger, M. L. (2003). Educational leadership and student achievement: The elusive search for an association. *Educational Administration Quarterly, 39*, 398–425.

Part I
The Nature of Successful Leadership

Introduction

The framework described and explored in this book argues that what leaders do contributes to students' success by improving the status or condition of selected variables associated with each of four paths. Clearly, however, not everything that leaders do has positive consequences. Some leadership practices, at best, make no demonstrable contribution to school improvement and student success while others are actually quite toxic – autocratic approaches to decision making, the pursuit of goals not shared by other stakeholders, emotional insensitivity, and showing favoritism among staff members are examples of such practices. So an important point of departure for unpacking the framework is to provide some clarification about those approaches to leadership likely to improve the condition of variables on the four paths.

As many of the chapters in this book demonstrate, there is a compelling case to be made that improving variables on each of the four paths places sometimes unique demands on leadership. Nonetheless, these unique demands typically entail more specific enactments of what we have termed elsewhere "core" leadership practices (e.g., Leithwood and Riehl 2005). The past 20 years of educational leadership research has identified an increasingly common set of core practices, often in the context of exploring the effects on schools, teachers and students of at least partly distinct models or approaches to leadership. By now, the bodies of evidence resulting from this research are large enough to attract significant systematic syntheses. This is the case, for example, for instructional leadership (e.g., Robinson et al. 2008), transformational school leadership (e.g., Leithwood and Sun 2012), inclusive leadership (Riehl 2000), learning-focused leadership (Knapp et al. 2010), leadership for learning (Hallinger 2011), as well as "integrated" approaches to leadership (Marks and Printy 2003). The different accounts of successful leadership exemplified by such models almost always include overlapping categories of practices; indeed, the labels of these models are often more distinct than the practices they include.

Policy makers and leadership developers have, by now, used the results of much of this research to create relatively comprehensive leadership standards and frameworks to help serve such practical purposes as leader selection, appraisal, and professional learning. A recent comparative synthesis of three such comprehensive leadership frameworks (Murphy et al. 2006; Leithwood 2012; Sebring et al. 2006), identified five domains of school leadership shared by these frameworks – Establishing and conveying the vision, Facilitating a high-quality learning experience for students, Building professional capacity, Creating a supportive organization for learning, and Connecting with external partners (Hitt and Tucker 2016). These five domains serve to define our meaning of "core" leadership practices for purposes of this section of the book.

Gurr's chapter in this section of the book offers a conception of how core practices influence students based on evidence collected across many countries. Leithwood's chapter summarizes one of the three comprehensive frameworks included in the comparative analysis by Hitt and Tucker (2016) describing in more detail some of the more specific features of that framework.

References

Hallinger, P. (2011). Leadership for learning: Lessons from 40 years of empirical research. *Journal of Educational Administration, 49*, 125–142.

Hitt, D., & Tucker, P. (2016). Systematic review of key leadership practices found to influence student achievement: A unified framework. *Review of Educational Research, 86*(2), 531–569.

Knapp, M. S., Copland, M. A., Honig, M. I., Plecki, M. L., & Portin, B. S. (2010). *Learning focused leadership and leadership support: Meaning and practice in urban systems*. Seattle: Center for the Study of Teaching and Policy, University of Washington.

Leithwood, K., (2012). *The Ontario Leadership Framework with a disccussion of its research foundations*. Toronto: Institute for Educational Leadership.

Leithwood, K., & Riehl, C. (2005). What we already know about successful school leadership. In W. A. Firestone & C. Riehl (Eds.), *A new agenda: Directions for research on educational leadership* (pp. 12–27). New York: Teachers College Press.

Leithwood, K., & Sun, J. (2012). The nature and effects of transformational school leadership: A meta-analytic review of unpublished research. *Educational Administration Quarterly, 48*(3), 387–423.

Marks, H. M., & Printy, S. M. (2003). Principal leadership and school performance: An integration of transformational and instructional leadership. *Educational Administration Quarterly, 39*, 370–397.

Murphy, J., Elliot, S., Goldring, E., & Porter, A. (2006). *Learning-centered leadership: A conceptual foundation*. New York: Wallace Foundation.

Riehl, C. J. (2000). The principal's role in creating inclusive schools for diverse students: A review of normative, empirical literature on the practice of educational administration. *Review of Educational Research, 70*, 55–81.

Robinson, V. M., Lloyd, C. A., & Rowe, K. J. (2008). The impact of leadership on student outcomes: An analysis of the differential effects of leadership types. *Educational Administration Quarterly, 44*, 635–674.

Sebring, P., Allensworth, E., Bryk, A., Easton, J., & Luppescu, S. (2006). *The essential supports for school improvement*. Chicago: Consortium on Chicago School Research.

Chapter 2
A Model of Successful School Leadership from the International Successful School Principalship Project

David Gurr

The International Successful School Principalship Project (ISSPP) has been actively conducting research about the work of successful principals since its initiation in 2001. Stimulated by the results of an earlier study, Day and his colleagues (Day et al. 2000) wanted to explore on a large scale the characteristics and practices of principals leading successful schools, and so assembled a group comprising of researchers from seven countries: Australia, Canada, China, Denmark, England, Norway, and Sweden. This group agreed to conduct multiple-perspective case studies focused on the leadership of principals in successful schools.

The rationale for the project was relatively simple. Up to that time what was known about principal leadership relied too much on studies that only used principals as the data source, and too much of the literature was derived from studies in North America and the United Kingdom. Gathering the opinions of others in the schools (school board members, teachers, parents, and students), and doing this across several countries, was a way to extend and enhance knowledge of the contribution of principals to school success.

The project continues today (2016) with active research groups in more than 20 countries, producing more than 100 case studies, and nearly as many papers, book chapters and books published, with four project books (Day and Gurr 2014; Day and Leithwood 2007b; Moos et al. 2011b; Ylimaki and Jacobson 2011b) and seven special journal issues. The project website is www.uv.uio.no/ils/english/research/projects/isspp, and concise published overviews of the project are contained in Leithwood and Day (2007a), Jacobson and Ylimaki (2011) Moos et al. (2011a), and Gurr and Day (2014a).

Most principals and schools included in this research have been selected using one or more of the following criteria:

D. Gurr (✉)
Melbourne Graduate School of Education, University of Melbourne, Melbourne, VIC, Australia
e-mail: d.gurr@unimelb.edu.au

- Evidence of student achievement beyond expectations on state or national tests, where this evidence exists.
- Principals' exemplary reputations in the community and/or school system. This could be gained through consultation with system personnel or other principals, school inspection reports, and so forth.
- Other indicators of success that are more context-specific, such as the overall reputation of the school, awards for exemplary programs, *etc.*

Data collection methods for the cases have included individual interviews with principals, senior staffs and school board members, group interviews with teachers, parents and students, and analysis of appropriate documents. Observation of the work of principals and the functioning of their schools was part of those case studies in which principals were revisited to explore the sustainability of success after 5 years. Further description of methodology can be found in many of the ISSPP research papers cited in this paper.

The intent of this chapter is to synthesize what has been learned through the project about how school leadership, primarily principal leadership, influences student learning. The chapter summarizes the findings of the project and offers a conception of the links between leadership and student learning partially built on earlier conceptualizations of project members. The paper is an unapologetically ISSPP self-referential paper which aims to help readers unfamiliar with this project to navigate their way through what has been described by Brian Caldwell (2014), in the forward to the fourth book, as "the most comprehensive and coherent international comparative study of the principalship ever undertaken" (p. xxi).

2.1 ISSPP Findings About the Nature of Successful Principal Leadership

The size of the ISSPP makes it a difficult project to understand. The fourth project book (Day and Gurr 2014) contains 15 stories of principal leadership success from 13 countries, with the final chapter (Gurr and Day 2014b) providing a synthesis of these stories. The eleven themes from this chapter provide a convenient way to synthesize the results of the whole project about the nature of successful principal leadership. The following section is adapted from Gurr (2014a).

2.1.1 High Expectations

ISSPP results consistently highlight the high expectations of successful principals. Indeed this is a consistent outcome of more than 50 years of evidence from effective schools research. These high expectations are manifest at both personal and collective levels; they are high yet reasonable, and constantly demonstrated and reinforced in the practice of the principals. The expectations are also individualised and very much about helping individuals to achieve their best, rather than focussed on meeting external accountability demands.

2.1.2 Pragmatic Approaches

ISSPP results indicate that no single model of leadership satisfactorily captures what successful principals do. To take what possibly remain the two dominant views of educational leadership, for example, these principals are neither just transformational nor just instructional leaders, but show elements of both, with the use of both styles especially important for schools in challenging contexts (Moos et al. 2011c). In essence, these principals develop approaches to leadership which enable them to lead a school community successfully; they are less concerned with the academic debates that rage about the impact of various leadership styles. They are concerned to motivate and to support and develop staff, and they are also concerned to ensure improvement in teaching and learning. Whilst they typically aren't the hands-on instructional leaders wished for in the eighties, and perhaps evident again, (see the work of John Fleming described in Hardy 2006; Gurr 2007; and Gurr et al. 2007, 2010b) they are very successful, ensuring improvement in curriculum, pedagogy and assessment, most often by working with other school leaders to influence teacher practice.

2.1.3 Leadership Distribution

For these successful school leaders, distributed leadership is almost assumed as they will openly say that the success of their school is due to the leadership of many, and they genuinely value the contribution of teachers, parent and students. The distribution of leadership was an important finding from the sustainability phase of the project described in the third project book (see Moos et al. 2011c). Indeed, developing leadership in others is a focus of their work. Successful leadership, then, is best thought of as layered and multidimensional, with, for example, instructional leadership influence distributed within a school, and having multiple foci such as academic improvement, satisfying accountability policies, and promoting democratic education (Leithwood et al. 2006; Ylimaki and Jacobson 2011a).

2.1.4 Core Leadership Practices

Whilst the principals are not easily labelled as adopting a particular leadership style, it is clear that across countries and contexts there is support for the four core practices of setting direction, developing people, leading change and improving teaching and learning, articulated in other research, (e.g., Gurr et al. 2007; also see Chap. 3) and confirmed throughout the ISSPP (see Leithwood and Day 2007b; Moos et al. 2011c); even in a remote village context in Kenya, these dimensions can be seen clearly in how a principal transformed a school (Wasonga 2014). There are also additional practices to these, such as use of strategic problem solving, articulating a set of core ethical values, building trust and being visible in the school, building a safe and secure environment, introducing productive forms of instruction to staff, coalition building, and the promotion of equity, care and achievement (Leithwood and Day 2007b).

2.1.5 Heroic Leadership

In many cases there is evidence of heroic leadership, for example, in the way principals challenge the status quo, fight for the best opportunities for their students, and have a positive and empowering view of what is possible for a school community, whatever the circumstances. But it is heroic leadership that is inclusive (see Day and Leithwood 2007a for the initial highlighting of this), and which has been described as post-heroic (Drysdale et al. 2011a, 2014). Whilst there is an obligation on principals and others in leadership roles to exercise leadership, leading a school requires collaborative and aligned effort by all. These leaders are often heroic, but they do not lead alone, and they are concerned to foster collaboration. For example, whilst they typically have important symbolic roles, and are generally the key story-tellers and sense-makers in their communities, they are careful to involve the school community in establishing a compelling shared vision. Ensuring the vision is lived is important, and typically the leaders act as both guardians of the vision and champions of change.

2.1.6 Capacity Development

Successful school leaders are people centred. They obviously get enormous satisfaction from seeing students develop, but they are also concerned to develop the adults in a school community, and core to this is their interest and ability in building the capacity of teaching and non-teaching staff to be better at what they do. This has been explained in a capacity building model of successful school leadership based on Australian cases (Drysdale and Gurr 2011) which emphases personal, professional, organisational and community capacity building. This approach to leadership is also clearly illustrated in the description of the leadership of Rick Tudor (Doherty et al. 2014).

2.1.7 Trust and Respect

A standout characteristic of the principals is the degree to which they are respected and trusted by their school communities (see, in particular, Day 2011; Moos 2014; Pashiardis and Savvides 2014; Wang et al. 2014). Acting with integrity and being transparent about their values, beliefs and actions, modelling good practice, being careful to ensure fairness in how they deal with people, involving many in decision making, are qualities and practices that engender respect and trust. Because of this, the school communities rarely challenge the principals if sometimes they have to make important decisions with little consultation; the foundation of respect and trust meant that top-down decisions can sometimes be accepted.

2.1.8 Continuous Learning

Successful leadership characteristics, dispositions and qualities are developed over time, and, as Ylimaki and Jacobson (2011a) observed, are socially constructed from the interaction of life experiences and the knowledge of principals with their work. Some of these principals had early leadership opportunities, but their success as principals is generally crafted through a blend of on-the-job learning, formal and informal professional learning, mentoring or sponsorship by significant others, and some serendipity in the pathways to leadership. All the principals were restless folk, seeking new ideas, new ways to do things, new opportunities for their schools, and so they are always developing as professionals. Development of successful principals was a focus of both ISSP books two and three which included several dedicated chapters (e.g., Gurr et al. 2011a, b; Jacobson et al. 2011; Johnson et al. 2011).

2.1.9 Personal Resources

There are many personal qualities, beliefs and values that help principals be successful leaders. Acumen, optimism, persistence, trust (behaving in a way that promotes the attribution of trust in the leader by others, and also displaying trust in others), tolerance, empathy, alertness (shown through high levels of physical and mental energy), curiosity, resilience, benevolence, honesty, openness, respectful, and humbleness were some of the traits on display. They have a strong ethic of care, empathy for others, value individuality and display the transformational leadership quality of individual consideration, believe in freedom and democracy, are good at balancing individual and collective care among other things. Above all they are driven by the desire to provide the best educational environment they can for all students. Even in the most challenging contexts, they view challenges as obstacles to overcome rather than problems that are insurmountable, and so they are always looking to improve the learning environment.

Perhaps using a spiritual, moral or social justice base, or more simply from an understanding of what is possible in education, they have the courage to what is right to help their students be the best they can. Chapters from the fourth book illustrate this courage well (Merchant et al. 2014; Minor-Ragan and Jacobson 2014; Raihani et al. 2014; Torres-Arcadia and Flores-Kastanis 2014; Wasonga 2014; Yaakov and Tubin 2014).

2.1.10 Context Sensitivity

Apart from these themes there are several other observations that can be made. Successful school leadership is context sensitive (Ylimaki and Jacobson 2011a), but it is not context driven. Using a range of common leadership practices that seem to promote success in most contexts, successful school leaders fine tune their responses to the context and culture in which they lead to optimise school success (Gurr 2014b). As Day (2007, p. 68) noted early in the story of the ISSPP, successful principals demonstrate the ability to:

> …not [be] confined by the contexts in which they work. They do not comply, subvert, or overtly oppose. Rather they actively mediate and moderate within a set of core values and practices which transcend narrowly conceived improvement agendas.

2.1.11 Sustaining Success

Moos et al. (2011c) found several factors which seemed to be important for principals to sustain their success. These factors included actively engaging with others to arrive at a consensus about what a school should do (what they termed as building the "better argument"); personal qualities and beliefs such as resilience, commitment to making a difference, and engaging the school and wider community; balancing discourses (e.g., social justice and high achievement); utilising both transformational and instructional leadership practices, such practices being especially important for schools in challenging contexts; continuing their own professional learning (whether it be through compulsory or voluntary programs); and, managing accountability expectations.

In some of this sustainability research, principals' attitudes to change had an impact on the level and type of school success. For example, Drysdale et al. (2011b) described contrasting attitudes toward change on the part of two principals. Both were successful but one principal had developed her school to a point where she became resistant to further change, and she sought to protect what had been achieved. The other principal, driven by a vision of creating a world-class special school, continued to seek new opportunities and new ways to further improve her school.

Having summarised findings from this large project, a helpful way to conceptualise how school leadership influences student learning is to consider the development of models or schematic representations of the findings. The next section develops a model, based on several models produced by research groups in the ISSPP, and takes into account the summary of findings just reported.

2.2 A Model of How Successful School Leadership Influences Student Learning

Over the life of the project there have been both individual and team attempts to model the influence of successful principal leadership on student learning. These models have been developed by two Australian groups, from doctoral research supervised by the Australian researchers in Singapore and Indonesia, and from the Cyprus research group. Full accounts of these models can be found in Gurr and Day 2014b; Drysdale et al. 2009, 2011b; Gurr and Drysdale 2007, 2013; Gurr et al. 2003, 2006, 2010a, b; Mulford and Edmunds 2009; Mulford and Johns 2004; Mulford and Silins 2011; Mulford et al. 2009; Pashiardis and Savvides 2011; Pashiardis et al. 2011; Raihani 2007, 2008; Raihani and Gurr 2006; and Wang 2010.

Across most of these models from the four countries, establishing collective direction, developing people and improving teaching and learning are common and explicit; implicitly, there is a sense of being able to lead change. All of these attributes are common to mainstream views of school leadership such as that developed by Leithwood and colleagues (e.g. Leithwood et al. 2006; see Chap. 3), and confirmed in the early phases of the ISSPP (e.g., Leithwood and Day 2007b). Nuanced differences in leadership are found in the emphasis on developing teacher capacity in the Australian models, on the development of self, acknowledgement of leadership legacy and engaging with the context in the Singapore model, the broad school outcomes and cultural values in the Indonesian model, and creative leadership needed to balance competing values within constrained contexts in Cyprus. Engaging with and influencing context seems important to most of these earlier ISSP models.

Figure 2.1 synthesizes and extends these ISSPP model-building efforts using, as its main point of departure, a model first described in Gurr et al. 2006. This model has two overarching organisers. One of these organizers is the distinction between the why, how and what of successful school leadership articulated by Mulford and Johns 2004. The second organizer is the three impact "levels" from Gurr et al. 2003; these levels moving from the least direct impact on learning outcomes (level 3, impact of the wider school context), to level 2 (impact of leadership in the school), and level 1 (impact of teaching and learning).

2.2.1 "What" Leadership Success Means for Students

Both organisers assume broad definitions of student learning, something that has been a consistent feature of the ISSPP research. Although the definition of success used to select schools was relatively narrow, those in selected schools were keen to emphasise the broad range of outcomes that successful schools have, outcomes for both student and others. For example, Mulford and Silins' (2011) analysis of teacher and principal survey data used three measures of student outcomes: student academic achievement, student social and development skills, and student empowerment. Drysdale and Gurr

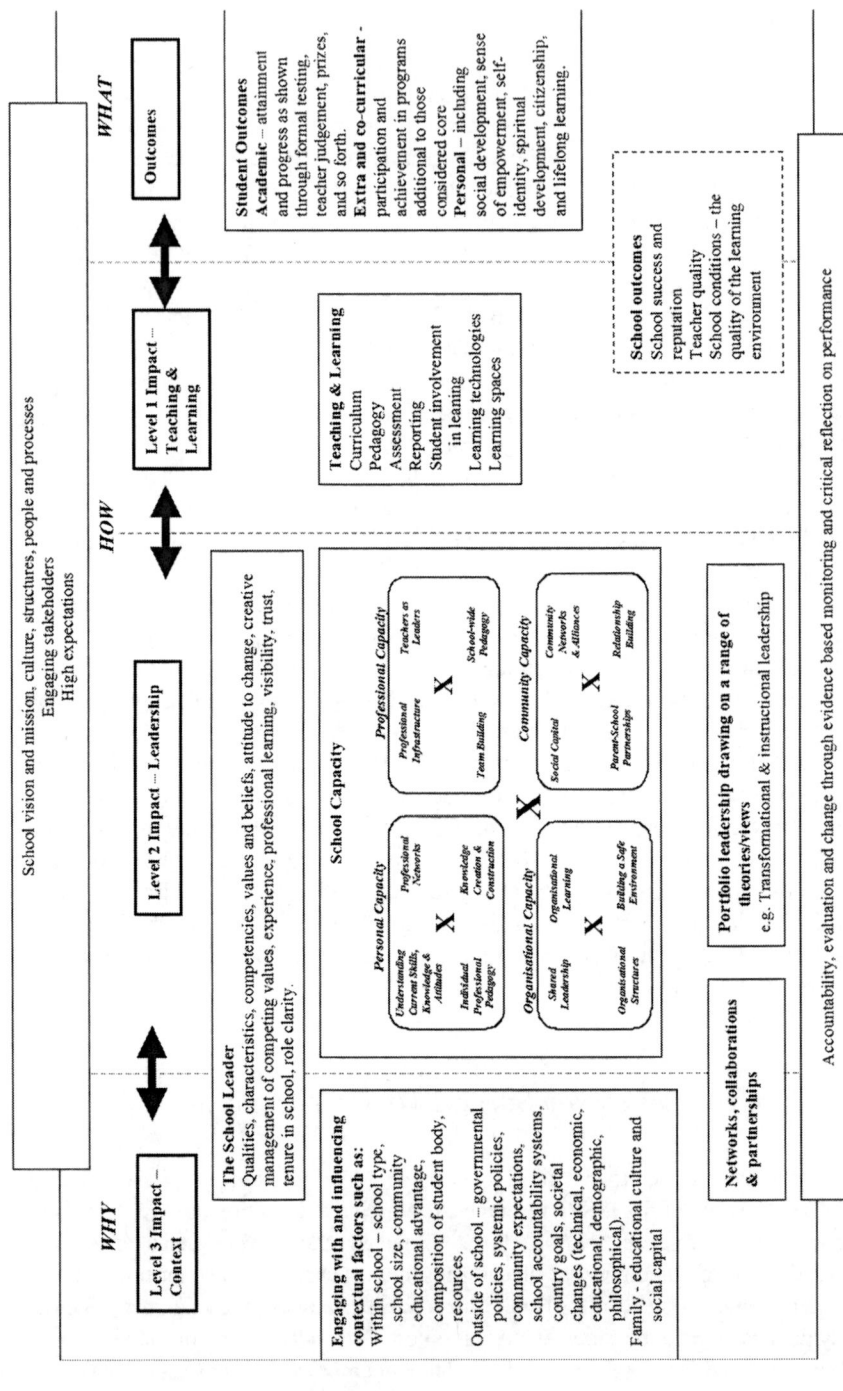

Fig. 2.1 An International Successful School Principalship Project (ISSPP) model of successful school leadership

(2011) included traditional (e.g., results on standardised tests and other contrived measures of attainment) and authentic (e.g., outcomes of learning that involve knowledge construction and disciplined inquiry) measures (see Newmann et al. (2007) of student learning. Wang's (Wang et al. 2014) Singapore cases included student and school outcomes, with the history and reputation of the school an important element of success. School reputation also featured as an outcome in Mulford and Silins' (2011) model, as this was shown to be a predictor of academic achievement. Raihani's (2007) Indonesian cases emphasised the academic achievement of students on national tests, the spiritual development of students, and the quality of the school and staff.

As these examples illustrate, in terms of the first organiser for the Fig. 2.1 model, the "what" element of the Fig. 2.1 model includes a broad range of student outcomes including academic attainment and progress, participation and achievement in extra and co-curricular programs, and personal aspects such as social development. Importantly, it also includes school outcomes such as the success and reputation of the school, the quality of the teachers, and the quality of the learning environment.

2.2.2 How and Why Leadership Success is Enacted

The "how" element in Fig. 2.1 includes areas of action associated with leadership and teaching and learning, and the "why" element is associated with the context in which schools operate, both of which are discussed in detail below.

The other organiser in the model is the level of impact on student outcomes, with three levels noted: impact from teaching and learning, from leadership, and from context. Note that this is not an organiser in terms of school outcomes as the impact on these comes mostly from the leadership and the teaching and learning levels, with relatively less influence from context and with this less controlled over this influence (for example, in community judgement on school reputation, or level of government funding assistance). It is also true that the school and student outcomes have a reciprocal effect (e.g., teacher quality influence student outcomes, and student outcomes influence reputation/success), and so school outcomes is placed between level 1/how and outcomes/what, with a dotted border used to indicate the specialness of this group.

Level 1 impact is focused on the work of teachers with students, and includes the usual areas of curriculum, pedagogy, assessment and reporting, plus student involvement in their learning, the use of learning technologies, and the provision of appropriate learning spaces. Leadership intervention in this area directly impacts on the work of teachers and so has the most direct leadership effect on student outcomes. Interventions could include: ensuring there is a guaranteed and viable curriculum, developing teaching expertise, developing assessment of student learning that informs the teaching program, developing greater student ownership of their learning, utilising current learning technologies, and ensuring learning spaces are inviting and conducive to good learning.

Level 2 emphases the role of school leaders in building the capacity of teachers and others adults in the school, what someone brings to the role of school leader, and utilisation by school leaders of various views of leadership. This capacity-building emphasis comes primarily from the Victorian cases (see Drysdale and Gurr 2011; Gurr and Drysdale 2007, 2013; Gurr et al. 2010a, b), and draws on the research of King and Newmann (2001) and Mitchell and Sackney (2001) to make sense of how successful school leaders focus much of their energy on developing people. School capacity is viewed as comprising four areas of personal, professional, organisational and community capacity, with each element having at least four areas. Whilst focussed on developing teachers, it includes development of other staff, parents, and community members. Capacity building is one of three teacher-level predictor variables in Mulford and Silins' (2011) model, and the only one that impacts on all three of the student outcomes (academic achievement, social development and empowerment).

The capacities and dispositions of schools leaders (as summarized in the previous section of this paper) that promote school success are part of all earlier models. For Mulford these are part of the "why" element. Mulford and Johns (2004) included principal values (good, passionate, equity and social justice focus, other-centered, hard-working and sense of humour), Drysdale and Gurr (2011) included the personal aspects of schools leaders as part of the leadership impact level and so they shifted from Mulford's emphasis on "why" to "how". In Fig. 2.1, the school leader box is drawn across the "why" and "how" boundary to indicate that these features might be drivers for what leaders do (the "why" element) as well as features that allow or enable them to be successful leaders (the "what" element).

The term school leader rather than principals is used in Fig. 2.1 deliberately. Although the ISSPP is focused on principal leadership, there is sufficient evidence from the project to broaden the model to apply to all school leaders (senior leaders, middle-level leaders, and perhaps teacher leaders). For principals, the model locates much of their work at level 2, helping to develop the adults in a school. They also often work at level 3 actively responding to and influencing the wider context, and sometimes at level 1, depending to a large extent on the school context, with school size a key determiner of the extent to which they work directly with teachers in classrooms (principals of smaller schools tend to work more closely with teachers directly).

The Fig. 2.1 model also applies to middle level leaders, and others with a leadership role. Depending on their role in terms of influencing teaching and learning, middle level leaders, in particular, are more likely to focus their work across levels 1 and 2 (Gurr and Drysdale 2013). An example would be a head of a curriculum area working in a coaching role with teachers to improve pedagogy. To date, however, the ISSPP has not done much to unpack the nature of successful middle level leadership although the research has consistently indicated that principals need to draw on a repertoire of leadership ideas, and, in particular, utilise the both instructional and transformational leadership styles. In Fig. 2.1 this has been termed a portfolio approach to leadership see Gurr (2001) in which wide knowledge about leadership helps develop characteristics and practices that can be drawn upon depending on need and circumstances.

The context identified in level 3 of the model includes the school organization, family and external contexts that leaders need to respond to and influence. Many of these aspects will moderate the impact of leadership behaviour if they are ignored, and so the title is "engaging with and influencing contextual factors". For example, the survey-based model from Tasmania illustrates the importance of being able to influence the home context (enhancing family educational culture and social capital as noted more than a decade ago by Leithwood and Steinbach 2003) with a supportive home educational environment showing positive impact on student empowerment and social skills. Bella Irlicht, a case principal from Australia, was renowned for the way she could influence the political and system context to benefit her school, and enable her to build a world-class specialist school (see Drysdale et al. 2011b; Gurr et al. 2006. Gurr (2014b) provides several examples from the ISSPP that show how successful principals are able to not only respond to internal and external contextual factors, but also to influence these so that they become part of the reason for school success.

Developing networks, collaborations and partnerships extends across levels 3 and 2. Often the availability of these is part of the context (for example, a system may construct school networks/partnerships) yet successful principals seem to be good at developing these associations to enhance their schools, and indeed seeking out new associations. Developing networks, collaborations and partnerships was a key feature of the success of many of the ISSPP principals. Examples include Irlicht's work mentioned previously, and the leadership of another case principal, Minor-Ragan, in transforming a failing school (Minor-Ragan and Jacobson 2014).

There are two elements that extend across the model. At the bottom of Fig. 2.1, the use of evidence-based monitoring and critical reflection to promote change reflects earlier modelling efforts by Mulford and Johns (2004), although the language has been adapted to *accountability, evaluation and change* to better address the need for performance review at individual and organisational levels that leads to positive change and improvement. Throughout the ISSPP cases successful principals have demonstrated considerable skill in collecting evidence to help inform the progress of their schools, and to help teachers and, in some cases, students to collect evidence to improve their individual practices (e.g., the instructional leadership of John Fleming [Hardy 2006; Gurr et al. 2003]).

An addition to earlier ISSPP models across levels is described in the box at the top of Fig. 2.1. This addition reinforces the importance of the school context and how school leaders actively influence this through developing a shared vision and mission and a positive culture, having appropriate structures, people and processes in the school, the active engagement of stakeholders within and outside the school, and the promotion of high expectations for all. This feature of the model builds on Drysdale and Gurr (2011), and reflects much of what is known about effective schools (Reynolds et al. 2011) and has sometimes been labeled as pre-conditions for school improvement (Zbar et al. 2007).

2.3 Conclusions

The model in Fig. 2.1, while largely encompassing and extending earlier ISSPP conceptual efforts, still needs more refinement, and ultimately verification through further research. In the next phase of the ISSPP, case studies are being collected of schools that are underperforming, as well as further collection of cases of successful schools. A new survey has been developed for principals, teachers, and students, with these surveys meant to be used within the cases rather than more widely within a system as in the Tasmanian survey Analyses of the cases through the conceptual lenses of the model in Fig. 2.1 will help test the power of the Fig. 2.1 model.

It is also possible to test the model using quantitative survey methods. This would allow the ISSPP to say more about variables that may moderate leader practices such as school size, type and location. The caution is that the survey would most likely be large and require the smaller scale of distribution and intense effort to collect responses demonstrated by the Tasmanian research group to achieve a worthwhile sample. The immediate task, though, is to consider this model in relation to other contemporary ideas about how leadership influences student learning; but this is a task for another paper.

References

Caldwell, B. J. (2014). Forward. In C. Day & D. Gurr (Eds.), *Leading schools successfully: Stories from the field* (pp. xxi–xxii). London: Routledge.
Day, C. (2007). Sustaining success in challenging contexts: Leadership in English schools. In C. Day & K. Leithwood (Eds.), *Successful principal leadership in times of change* (pp. 59–70). Dordrecht: Springer.
Day, C. (2011). Building and sustaining successful principalship in an English school. In L. Moos, O. Johansson, & C. Day (Eds.), *How school principals sustain success over time: International perspectives* (pp. 91–108). Dordrecht: Springer.
Day, C., & Gurr, D. (2014). *Leading schools successfully: Stories from the field*. London, UK: Routledge.
Day, C., & Leithwood, K. (2007a). *Successful principal leadership in times of change*. Dordrecht: Springer.
Day, C., & Leithwood, K. (2007b). Building and sustaining successful principalship. In C. Day & K. Leithwood (Eds.), *Successful principal leadership in times of change* (pp. 171–188). Dordrecht: Springer.
Day, C., Harris, A., Hadfield, M., Tolley, H., & Beresford, J. (2000). *Leading schools in times of change*. Buckingham: Open University.
Doherty, J., Gurr, D., & Drysdale, L. (2014). The formation and practice of a successful principal: Rick Tudor, Headmaster of Trinity Grammar School, Melbourne, Australia. In C. Day & D. Gurr (Eds.), *Leading schools successfully: Stories from the field* (pp. 85–97). London: Routledge.
Drysdale, L., & Gurr, D. (2011). The theory and practice of successful school leadership in Australia. *School Leadership Management, 31*, 355–368.
Drysdale, L., Goode, H., & Gurr, D. (2009). An Australian model of successful school leadership: Moving from success to sustainability. *Journal of Educational Administration, 47*, 697–708.
Drysdale, L., Goode, H., & Gurr, D. (2011a, September). *The heroic leader – Myth or reality: Findings from current research of successful school principals*. In Proceedings of the European Conference on Educational Research, Berlin, Germany.
Drysdale, L., Goode, H., & Gurr, D. (2011b). Sustaining school and leadership success in two Australian schools. In L. Moos, O. Johansson, & C. Day (Eds.), *How school principals sustain success over time: International perspectives* (pp. 25–38). Dordrecht: Springer.

Drysdale, L., Bennett, J., Murakami, E., Johansson, O., & Gurr, D. (2014). Heroic leadership in Australia, Sweden, and the United States. *International Journal of Educational Management, 28*, 785–797.

Gurr, D. (2001). Editorial: Views of leadership. *Leading and Managing, 7*, ii–iv.

Gurr, D. (2007). We can be the best. In P. Duignan & D. Gurr (Eds.), *Leading Australia's schools* (pp. 124–131). Sydney: ACEL/DEST.

Gurr, D. (2014a). Finding your leadership. *Perspectives in Education, 2*, 1–2.

Gurr, D. (2014b). Successful school leadership across contexts and cultures. *Leading and Managing, 20*, 75–88.

Gurr, D., & Day, C. (2014a). Leading schools. In C. Day & D. Gurr (Eds.), *Leading schools successfully: Stories from the field* (pp. 1–6). London: Routledge.

Gurr, D., & Day, C. (2014b). Thinking about leading schools. In C. Day & D. Gurr (Eds.), *Leading schools successfully: Stories from the field* (pp. 194–208). London: Routledge.

Gurr, D., & Drysdale, L. (2007). Models of successful school leadership: Victorian case studies. In C. Day & K. Leithwood (Eds.), *Successful principal leadership in times of change* (pp. 39–58). Dordrecht: Springer.

Gurr, D., & Drysdale, L. (2013). Middle-level school leaders: Potential, constraints and implications for leadership preparation. *Journal of Educational Administration, 51*, 55–71.

Gurr, D., Drysdale, L., di Natale, E., Ford, P., Hardy, R., & Swann, R. (2003). Successful school leadership in Victoria: Three case studies. *Leading and Managing, 9*, 18–37.

Gurr, D., Drysdale, L., & Mulford, B. (2006). Models of successful principal leadership. *School Leadership and Management, 26*, 371–395.

Gurr, D., Drysdale, L., & Mulford, B. (2007). Instructional leadership in three Australian schools. *International Studies in Educational Administration, 35*, 20–29.

Gurr, D., Drysdale, L., & Goode, H. (2010a). Successful school leadership in Australia: A research agenda. *International Journal of Learning, 17*, 113–129.

Gurr, D., Drysdale, L., & Mulford, B. (2010b). Australian principal instructional leadership: Direct and indirect influences. *Magis, 2*, 299–314.

Gurr, D., Drysdale, L., Ylimaki, R., & Moos, L. (2011a). Preparing instructional leaders. In R. Ylimaki & S. Jacobson (Eds.), *US and cross-national policies, practices, and preparation: Implications for successful instructional leadership, organizational learning, and culturally responsive practices* (pp. 125–152). Dordrecht: Springer.

Gurr, D., Ylimaki, R., Drysdale, L., & Jacobson, S. (2011b). Preparation for sustainable leadership. In L. Moos, O. Johansson, & C. Day (Eds.), *How school principals sustain success over time: International perspectives* (pp. 183–198). Dordrecht: Springer.

Hardy, R. (2006). Successful leaders. In *In Successful schools: A case study of a government primary school principal in Victoria, Australia*. Melbourne: University of Melbourne.

Jacobson, S., & Ylimaki, R. (2011). Comparative perspectives: An overview of seven educational contexts. In R. Ylimaki & S. Jacobson (Eds.), *US and cross-national policies, practices, and preparation: Implications for successful instructional leadership, organizational learning, and culturally responsive practices* (pp. 1–16). Dordrecht: Springer.

Jacobson, S. L., Johansson, O., & Day, C. (2011). Preparing school leaders to organisational learning and capacity building. In R. Ylimaki & S. Jacobson (Eds.), *US and cross-national policies, practices, and preparation: Implications for successful instructional leadership, organizational learning, and culturally responsive practices* (pp. 103–124). Dordrecht: Springer.

Johnson, L., Moller, J., Ottesen, E., Pashiardis, P., Savvides, V., & Vedoy, G. (2011). Leadership preparation for culturally diverse schools in Cyprus, Norway, and the United States. In R. Ylimaki & S. Jacobson (Eds.), *US and cross-national policies, practices, and preparation: Implications for successful instructional leadership, organizational learning, and culturally responsive practices* (pp. 153–178). Dordrecht: Springer.

King, M. B., & Newmann, F. M. (2001). Building school capacity through professional development, conceptual and empirical considerations. *International Journal of Educational Management, 15*, 86–94.

Leithwood, K., & Day, C. (2007a). Starting with what we known. In C. Day & K. Leithwood (Eds.), *Successful principal leadership in times of change* (pp. 1–16). Dordrecht: Springer.

Leithwood, K., & Day, C. (2007b). What we learned: A broad view. In C. Day & K. Leithwood (Eds.), *Successful principal leadership in times of change* (pp. 189–203). Dordrecht: Springer.

Leithwood, K., & Steinbach, R. (2003). Successful leadership for especially challenging schools. In B. Davies & J. West-Burnham (Eds.), *Handbook of educational leadership and management* (pp. 25–43). London: Pearson.

Leithwood, K., Day, C., Sammons, P., Harris, A., & Hopkins, D. (2006). *Seven strong claims about successful school leadership*. Nottingham: National College of School Leadership.

Merchant, B., Garza, E., & Ramalho, E. M. (2014). USA—Culturally-responsive leadership. In C. Day & D. Gurr (Eds.), *Leading schools successfully: Stories from the field* (pp. 174–183). London: Routledge.

Minor-Ragan, Y., & Jacobson, S. (2014). USA—Her own words: Turning around an underperforming school. In C. Day & D. Gurr (Eds.), *Leading schools successfully: Stories from the field* (pp. 9–18). London: Routledge.

Mitchell, C., & Sackney, L. (2001). Profound improvement: Building capacity for a learning community. *Journal of Educational Administration, 39*, 394–398.

Moos, L. (2014). Denmark—A strength of purpose: Building credibility and trust. In C. Day & D. Gurr (Eds.), *Leading schools successfully: Stories from the field* (pp. 61–69). London: Routledge.

Moos, L., Day, C., & Johansson, O. (2011a). Introduction to the international successful school principalship project. In L. Moos, O. Johansson, & C. Day (Eds.), *How school principals sustain success over time: International perspectives* (pp. 1–13). Dordrecht: Springer.

Moos, L., Johansson, O., & Day, C. (2011b). *How school principals sustain success over time: International perspectives*. Dordrecht: Springer.

Moos, L., Johansson, O., & Day, C. (2011c). New insights: How successful school leadership is sustained. In L. Moos, O. Johansson, & C. Day (Eds.), *How school principals sustain success over time: International perspectives* (pp. 223–230). Dordrecht: Springer.

Mulford, B., & Edmunds, B. (2009). *Successful school principalship in Tasmania*. Launceston: University of Tasmania.

Mulford, B., & Johns, S. (2004). Successful school principalship. *Leading and Managing, 10*, 45–76.

Mulford, B., & Silins, H. (2011). Revised models and conceptualisation of successful school principalship for improved student outcomes. *International Journal of Educational Management, 25*, 61–82.

Mulford, B., Johns, S., & Edmunds, B. (2009). *Successful school principalship in Tasmania: Case studies*. Launceston: University of Tasmania.

Newmann, F. M., King, M. B., & Carmichael, D. L. (2007). *Authentic instruction and assessment: Common standards for rigor and relevance in teaching academic subjects*. Des Moines: Iowa Department of Education.

Pashiardis, P., & Savvides, V. (2011). The interplay between instructional and entrepreneurial leadership styles in Cyprus rural primary school. *Leadership and Policy in Schools, 10*, 412–427.

Pashiardis, P., & Savvides, V. (2014). Cyprus—Trust in leadership: Keeping promises. In C. Day & D. Gurr (Eds.), *Leading schools successfully: Stories from the field* (pp. 129–139). London: Routledge.

Pashiardis, P., Savvides, V., Lytra, E., & Angelidou, K. (2011). Successful school leadership in rural contexts: The case of Cyprus. *Educational Management Administration and Leadership, 39*, 536–553.

Raihani. (2007). *Successful school leadership in Indonesia: A study of the principals' leadership in three successful senior secondary schools in Yogyakarta*. Doctoral thesis, University of Melbourne, Melbourne, Australia.

Raihani. (2008). An Indonesian model of successful school leadership. *Journal of Educational Administration, 46*, 481–496.

Raihani, & Gurr, D. (2006). Value-driven school leadership: An Indonesian perspective. *Leading and Managing, 12,* 121–134.

Raihani, Gurr, D., & Drysdale, L. (2014). Leading an Islamic school. In a multicultural setting in Indonesia. In C. Day & D. Gurr (Eds.), *Leading schools successfully: Stories from the field* (pp. 184–193). London: Routledge.

Reynolds, D., Sammons, P., de Fraine, B., Townsend, T., & van Damme, J. (2011). *Educational effectiveness research (EER): A state of the art review.* Paper presented at the annual meeting of the International Congress for School Effectiveness and Improvement, Cyprus. Retrieved from http://www.icsei.net/icsei2011/State_of_the_art/State_of_the_art_Session_A.pdf.

Torres-Arcadia, C., & Flores-Kastanis, E. (2014). Mexico—From fragmentation to community: A journey of change. In C. Day & D. Gurr (Eds.), *Leading schools successfully: Stories from the field* (pp. 31–43). London: Routledge.

Wang, L. H. (2010). *Successful school leadership in Singapore.* Doctoral thesis, University of Melbourne, Australia.

Wang, L. H., Gurr, D., & Drysdale, L. (2014). Working together with others. In C. Day & D. Gurr (Eds.), *Leading schools successfully: Stories from the field* (pp. 149–160). London: Routledge.

Wasonga, T. (2014). Kenya—From perdition to performance. In C. Day & D. Gurr (Eds.), *Leading schools successfully: Stories from the field* (pp. 44–58). London: Routledge.

Yaakov, O. B., & Tubin, D. (2014). Israel—The evolution of success. In C. Day & D. Gurr (Eds.), *Leading schools successfully: Stories from the field* (pp. 19–30). London: Routledge.

Ylimaki, R. M., & Jacobson, S. L. (2011a). Comparative perspective on organisational learning, instructional leadership, and culturally responsive practices: Conclusions and future directions. In R. Ylimaki & S. Jacobson (Eds.), *US and cross-national policies, practices, and preparation: Implications for successful instructional leadership, organizational learning, and culturally responsive practices* (pp. 179–190). Dordrecht: Springer.

Ylimaki, R. M., & Jacobson, S. L. (2011b). *US and cross-national policies, practices, and preparation: Implications for successful instructional leadership, organizational learning, and culturally responsive practices.* Dordrecht: Springer.

Zbar, V., Marshall, G., & Power, P. (2007). *Better schools, better teachers, better results: A handbook for improved performance management in your school.* Camberwell: ACER.

Chapter 3
The Ontario Leadership Framework: Successful School Leadership Practices and Personal Leadership Resources

Kenneth Leithwood

This chapter, in the section of our book about *The Nature of Successful Leadership*, provides a brief but relatively comprehensive account of the leadership practices and personal "resources" identified in the now-significant corpus of research about school-level educational leadership as described by the *Ontario Leadership Framework* (OLF). Now in its second revision, the OLF (Leithwood 2012) serves as a touchstone for the guidance the Ontario government provides to districts and other professional agencies engaged in leadership recruitment, selection, development and appraisal. These are purposes largely shared by numerous other leadership frameworks and standards developed and used in many other educational systems around the world, for example, the U.S. *Professional Standards for School Leaders* (NPBEL 2015), the UK *National Standards for School Leadership* (NCSL 2008) and the *Australian Standard for School Principals* (AITSL 2015).

In addition to what is provided in the OLF itself, a recent comparative analysis of evidence-based leadership frameworks by Hitt and Tucker (2016) provides substantial independent justification for the claim that the OLF is relatively comprehensive. Rather than adding further to that claim, therefore, this chapter provides an overview of selected assumptions on which the OLF is based, describes its key features and illustrates how the OLF responds to some of the more demanding challenges facing leadership framework developers.[1] While the OLF outlines successful practices for both school and district-level leaders, this chapter restricts itself to the school-level focus of the OLF.

---

[1] Some of the text in this chapter is based directly on the primary OLF reference (Leithwood 2012)

K. Leithwood (✉)
Ontario Institute for Studies in Education, University of Toronto, Toronto, ON, Canada
e-mail: kenneth.leithwood@utoronto.ca

3.1 Three Assumptions

The three assumptions underlying the OLF examined in this section, were selected from a larger set because they are among the more controversial and complex assumptions likely to be faced by most developers of leadership frameworks.

Assumption One: Successful leadership is better described as "practices" than "competences". The OLF describes successful leadership "practices" rather than "competencies", a concept widely used in the management development field. A competency is typically defined as "an underlying characteristic of an individual that is causally related to effective or superior performance in a job" (Carroll et al. 2008, p 364). The commonly cited weaknesses of efforts to define management and (especially) leadership competencies are many, but the most compelling for the OLF is the lack of empirical evidence linking competencies to improved organizational outcomes. Research about effective educational leadership is almost exclusively evident about successful practices.

A "practice" is a bundle of activities exercised by a person or group of persons which reflect the particular circumstances in which they find themselves and with some shared outcome(s) in mind. Conceptualizing leadership as a set of practices reflects both the adaptive qualities (e.g., Heifetz 1999) and expert problem-solving processes (e.g., Leithwood and Steinbach 1995) emphasized in some accounts of effective leadership. So a focus on practices overcomes many of the limitations associated with a focus on competencies. But not all and for good reasons.

First, a commitment to being evidence based means that OLF's practices necessarily are derived from research about what effective leaders have done in the past, not what they might do in the future. But since our ability to predict those leadership practices likely to be effective in the future is extremely tenuous, to say the least, encouraging leaders to enact what is known now about effective practices seems the most prudent and likely the most productive direction to take in the near term.

Second, in spite of appreciating the integrated nature of effective leadership practices, any attempt at a fuller account of them, as in the OLF, does provide some encouragement for a fragmented understanding of how leadership is exercised. The alternative, however, is to offer forms of guidance to existing leaders (for example, be an "instructional" or a "transformational" leader) which are so abstract as to have almost no practical value.

In addition, some have argued (e.g., English 2006) that any effort to codify either leadership practices or competencies in a set of "standards" or a "framework" promotes a static conception of effective leadership whereas knowledge in the field is decidedly dynamic and evolving. There is no denying the dynamic and evolving nature of research-based knowledge about leadership. Indeed, the field is more active now than it has ever been. But the solution is not to simply throw up one's hands in despair of capturing existing knowledge. A much more productive solution is to commit to periodic reviews of the field and revisions of previous understandings. While the leadership research field is very active now, it is not so active as to make a "static" description of the field unhelpful for at least a period of 5–7 years.

Assumption Two: The OLF should encompass successful practices, on the part of those exercising leadership, whether those practices are typically categorized as "leadership" or "management". School leadership has been described for many decades as hectic and fast paced. And it is common to hear many school leaders explain this feature of their jobs as a function of being overburdened with *management* tasks that take away from the time they would prefer to devote to *leadership*. The OLF assumes, however, that once organizations are clear about their goals, their next job is to identify the full array of practices (actions, behaviours or tasks) needed to accomplish those goals and to determine which people in the organization are best suited to be the primary adapters and enactors of those practices. When primary responsibility for enacting a set of practices has been determined, the label associated with that set of practices is irrelevant. Better to simply ask what is it that they (teachers, school administrators, parents, district staff, etc.) need to do to help achieve the organization's goals.

There are, in addition, several closely related reasons why the leadership/management distinction is not at all useful. First, many practices typically referred to as *management* contribute as much to student learning as many practices typically referred to as *leadership*. For example, Grissom and Loeb (2011) found that principals' Organizational Management skills had significant and consistently greater effects on student achievement than any of the other four categories of skills that were measured; this set of skills also consistently predicted teacher satisfaction and parents' ratings of school performance. Internal Relations and Administration skills also had significant but weaker effects on achievement, whereas the effects on achievement of Instructional Management and External Relations were not significant.

An additional reason for rejecting the leadership/management distinction is that many practices typically referred to as *management* are the foundation on which practices typically referred to as *leadership* are built. Those practices typically referred to as leadership are often the practices closest to, or most directly responsible for achieving the end goals of the school. However, whether the time and opportunity to engage in those practices are available often depends, for example, on developing productive timetables and aligning resources with priorities, neither practice jumping out of most conceptions of what "leaders" do.

Assumption Three: People in many roles in schools are able to exercise leadership. So the OLF should provide guidance about exercising leadership to those in many roles. A rapidly growing body of evidence has confirmed the widespread understanding of those who work in schools that many people in schools and school systems provide leadership as defined by the OLF; it is not the exclusive purview of those in formal positions of authority as, for example, principals, vice principals or teacher leaders. Nor is such leadership confined to professional educators in the school. For example, parents are able to exert considerable influence on the purposes to which schools aspire and the processes for realizing those purposes, particularly when they act collectively.

Many claims about the virtues of intentionally sharing leadership – rather than just "letting it happen" – can be found in the literature (Leithwood et al. 2009). It is argued, for example, that shared leadership creates a more democratic organization and provides greater opportunities for collective learning and for teacher development. Shared leadership, it is also argued, increases the school's capacity to respond intellig, ently to the many and complex challenges it faces.

While there is little evidence for most of these claims, some empirical support evidence has begun to suggest that some forms of shared leadership contribute to improved student achievement (Heck and Hallinger 2009; Louis et al.2010), assist schools to cope productively with rapid leader succession (Mascall and Leithwood 2010) and facilitate school improvement processes (Harris et al. 2003; Higgins and Bonne 2011).

An additional and especially compelling reason for sharing leadership in schools is rooted in Ontario's commitment, a commitment of many other jurisdictions as well, to educational equity and inclusion as well as safe schools with a positive school climate. Prominent theorists and researchers concerned with these elements of social justice (e.g., Ladson-Billings 1995; Ryan 2006) argue that providing equitable opportunities to influence the school and school system's decision making by those whose voices typically have not been heard will lead to significantly improved educational experiences for diverse and disadvantaged students. Such cultural responsiveness, these theorists and advocates argue, requires knowledge about students and their circumstances best acquired directly from those whose interests have been neglected in the past. Sharing leadership with those who possess this knowledge, especially the parents and guardians of diverse and disadvantaged students, is among the most likely ways of acquiring this knowledge.

3.2 Successful Leadership Practices: Three Level of Specification

The approach to school-level leadership outlined in the OLF does not align itself with any specific leadership model or theory. While leadership models and theories provide a conceptual coherence which can assist in building understanding, no existing individual theory or model captures a sufficient proportion of what leaders actually do to serve the purposes intended for the OLF. That said, the OLF does reflect most of the practices found in current models of both "instructional" and "transformational" leadership. Using a term that has become common in the educational leadership literature, it is an "integrated" model (for example, see Printy et al. 2010; Robinson et al. 2009) although a more fully developed one than appears in most the literature to date. This integrated model aims to capture the relatively direct efforts of successful leaders to improve the quality of teaching and learning in their schools (the primary focus of instructional leadership models), as well as their efforts to create organizational conditions which enable and support those improvement efforts (the primary focus of transformational leadership models).

As Table 3.1 indicates, the OLF consists of five domains of practices and each of these domains includes a handful of more specific practices. The 21 more specific practices are closely aligned to evidence about successful leadership whereas the domains are best thought of as conceptual organizers that aid framework users' sense-making and memory. In addition, each of the 21 specific practices is further

Table 3.1 What successful school leaders do

Domains of practice	Successful leadership practices
Set directions	Build a shared vision
	Identify specific, shared, short-term goals
	Create high-performance expectations
	Communicate the vision and goals
Build relationships and develop people	Stimulate growth in the professional capacities of staff
	Provide support and demonstrate consideration for individual staff members
	Model the school's values and practices
	Build trusting relationships with and among staff, students and parents
	Establish productive working relationships with teacher federation representatives
Develop the organization to support desired practices	Build collaborative cultures and distribute leadership
	Structure the organization to facilitate collaboration
	Build productive relationships with families and communities.
	Connect the school to its wider environment.
	Maintain a safe and healthy school environment
	Allocate resources in support of the school's vision and goals
Improve the instructional program	Staff the instructional program
	Provide instructional support.
	Monitor student learning and school improvement progress
	Buffer staff from distractions to their work
Secure accountability	Build staff members' sense of internal accountability
	Meet the demands for external accountability

illustrated, as in Table 3.2, using just two of the leadership practices. This level of specification is described for all 21 leadership practices in the OLF itself.

One of the more complex challenges facing those developing leadership frameworks and standards is to determine the appropriate level of specification. Where is the "sweet spot" between a level of specification that generalizes to almost all leaders' and their circumstances (e.g., all elementary and secondary school principals in a state or province) and one that is relevant for only one set of leaders and their circumstances (secondary school department heads working with urban students from economically disadvantaged families)?

Framework developers are rarely explicit about how they address this challenge and there is no formula to help. The recently revised U.S. standards (NPBEA 2015) include two levels of specification, for example, whereas the OLF includes three levels: domains of practice, successful leadership practices associated with each domain, and illustrations of how to use each of the successful leadership practices. Settling on three levels for the OLF was simply a matter of responding to many

Table 3.2 From what to how: Two examples

Domain	What	How
Set directions	*Build a shared vision*	Establish, with staff, students and other stakeholders, an overall sense of purpose or vision for work in their schools to which they are all strongly committed;
		Build understanding of the specific implications of the schools' vision for its' programs and the nature of classroom instruction;
		Encourage the development of organizational norms that support openness to change in the direction of that purpose or vision;
		Help staff and other stakeholders to understand the relationship between their schools' vision and board and provincial policy initiatives and priorities.
Build relations & develop people	*Stimulate growth in the professional capacities of staff*	Encourage staff to reflect on what they are trying to achieve with students and how they are doing it;
		Lead discussions about the relative merits of current and alternative practices
		Challenge staff to re-examine the extent to which their practices contribute to the learning and well-being of all of their students;
		Facilitate opportunities for staff to learn from each other;
		Are a source of new ideas for staff learning;
		Encourage staff to pursue their own goals for professional learning;
		Encourage staff to develop and review their own professional growth goals and their relationship to school goals and priorities;
		Encourage staff to try new practices consistent with their own interests.

rounds of feedback. This was feedback provided during the framework development process from practicing leaders and those who worked with them, about the need for greater clarity about what each practice entailed "on the ground".

3.2.1 Domains of Practice

The first level of specification describes domains or categories which encompass underlying theories or explanation for why the described leadership practices are successful. In addition to offering a conceptual explanation for successful leadership practices, identification of domains makes a framework memorable and adds considerable meaning to the framework for those who are its intended users. For most of these purposes, whether or not the domains can be empirically justified, as in the case of the factor analysis underlying McREL's framework (Waters and Cameron 2007), is not critical. Left at the level of 21 "responsibilities", the McCrel framework is decidedly not memorable and very difficult to make sense of.

Each of the leadership practices described in the OLF reflects one of five broad domains or categories: Setting Directions, Building Relationships and Developing People, Developing the Organization to Support Desired Practices, Improving the Instructional Program and Securing Accountability. The first three of these domains originate in two sources. One source is a corpus of empirical research accumulated over at least three decades identifying a set of practices that are core or essential across many organizational contexts and sectors (Leithwood 1994; Leithwood and Riehl 2005; Yukl 1994). The second source is what Rowan et al. (1997) describe as "Decades of research on teaching" which explains variation in teachers' contributions to student achievement (teachers' performance or P) as a function of their knowledge and skill (ability or A), their motivation (M), and the settings in which they work (S): this explanation is captured succinctly in the formula $P = f(A, M, S)$.

Both sources cited above point to key functions of leaders as assisting their teachers and other organizational colleagues to further develop their motivations (one of the primary purposes for Setting Directions) and abilities (the purpose for Building Relationships and Developing People) to accomplish organizational goals, as well as to create and sustain supportive work settings (the goal of Developing the Organization to Sustain Desired Practices). In addition, every organization has a unique "technology" for accomplishing its primary purposes and the fourth domain of practices included in the OLF, Improving the Instructional Program, reflects that "technology" for schools (teaching and learning). Finally, the fifth domain of OLF, Securing Accountability, is justified by the policy context in which contemporary public schooling finds itself, one which places unprecedented demands on leaders to publicly demonstrate the progress being made toward accomplishing the purposes established for their organizations.

3.2.2 Leadership Practices and How They Are Enacted

The second level of specification, appearing in the left column of Table 3.1, describes successful leadership practices within each of the five domain at, or close to, the detail used in the research identifying each of the practices. At this level, fidelity to the relevant empirical research is paramount. OLF's claim to be evidence-based is largely justified by the explicit nature of the links it makes between high-quality empirical evidence and each of the 21 successful leadership practices. For an explicit discussion of these links, see the original OLF document (Leithwood 2012).

The third level of specification, illustrated in Table 3.2 (and fully described in the OLF itself), outlines how each of the successful leadership practices could be enacted in some relevant context. Evidence for these illustrative enactments can be found in much of the qualitative educational leadership literature. The shift from "what" leaders do to "how" they do it, however, is much less distinct than such language seems to suggest. Every attempt to describe a leadership practice might be carried out could be followed by a request for ever more detail prompted by variation in leaders' contexts; one person's "how" is another person's "what". The value of OLF practices depends, finally, on leaders enacting the practices in ways that are sensitive to the specific features of the settings in which they work, the people with whom they are working and changes over time. So the OLF stops at three levels of specification arguing that those using the OLF are expected to bring considerable local knowledge and problem-solving expertise to the enactment of the successful leadership practices. This expectation acknowledges the necessarily contingent nature of leaders' work in the dynamic environments of schools.

3.3 Leaders' Personal Qualities

In addition to successful leadership practices, as summarized in Tables 3.1 and 3.2, the OLF includes a small but critical number of personal resources or qualities which leaders draw on as they enact effective leadership practices and which, in turn, are shaped by those enactment experiences. Considered together, these resources substantially overlap some of the leadership "traits" which preoccupied early leadership research and which lately have proven to be powerful explanations for leaders' success. Leadership traits have been defined broadly as relatively stable and coherent integrations of personal characteristics that foster a consistent pattern of leadership performance across a variety of group and organizational situations".

While many traits or personal characteristics have been associated with leaders and leadership (e.g., Zacarro et al. 2004), the OLF includes only those for which there is compelling empirical evidence suggesting that they are instrumental to leadership success. Entitled "personal leadership resources" in the OLF (and often referred to by Ontario leaders now as "PLRs"), they are of three types– cognitive, social and psychological as summarized in Table 3.3.

Table 3.3 OLF's personal leadership resources

Cognitive resources	Problem-solving expertise
	Domain-specific knowledge
Social resources	Perceiving emotions
	Managing emotions
	Acting in emotionally appropriate ways
Psychological resources	Optimism
	Self-efficacy
	Resilience
	Proactivity

3.4 Cognitive Resources

Considerable evidence collected over many decades suggests that leaders' effectiveness is partly explained by intelligence and experience. This would only be surprising if it was not the case, although some early evidence indicates that stressful and hectic environments (features of environments in which school leaders often find themselves) reduce the advantage of greater intelligence to near zero. Intelligence and experience, however, are "surface" traits of leaders offering little guidance to those selecting and developing leaders or to leaders and aspiring leaders themselves. Below the surface of what is typically referred to as leader's intelligence are problem-solving capacities and below the surface of "experience" is the "domain-specific" knowledge useful for such problem solving; the OLF includes both as "cognitive resources".

Problem-Solving Expertise The literature on expert problem solving processes includes some variation in component processes or skills. For example, one approach, based on research with school leaders (Leithwood and Steinbach 1995), includes such processes as problem interpretation, goal setting, weighing principles and values, clarifying constraints, developing solution processes and controlling one's mood (expertise within these processes is described in the OLF). Another approach, based on research largely in non-school sectors (Mumford et al. 2006), includes similar though fewer processes including identifying the causes of the problem, determining the resources available to solve the problem, diagnosing the restrictions on one's choice of actions, and clarifying contingencies.

Evidence about problem solving highlighted in the OLF is primarily concerned with how leaders solve "unstructured" problems, the non-routine problems requiring significantly more than the application of existing know-how, or what is sometimes referred to as "adaptive leadership". Results of this research offer powerful guidelines for how to deal productively with the truly thorny challenges faced by those exercising leadership.

Knowledge About Learning Conditions with Direct Effects on Student Learning Because school leaders' influence on student learning is largely indirect (a well-documented assumption of the OLF), knowledge about learning conditions with significant effects on students that can be influenced by school leaders is an extremely important aspect of what leaders need to know. Indeed, "leadership for learning" can be described relatively simply, but accurately, as the process of (a) diagnosing the status of potentially powerful learning conditions in the school and classroom, (b) selecting those learning conditions most likely to be constraining student learning in one's school, and (c) improving the status of those learning conditions. This book synthesizes a considerable amount of evidence about such learning conditions on each of four "paths" and reflects many of the variables identified by Hattie (2009).

3.4.1 Social Resources

The importance attached to leaders' social resources has a long history. Early efforts to theorize leadership carried out at Ohio and Michigan State universities in the 1950s and 1960s situated relationship building among the two or three most important dimensions of effective leadership. More recently, Goleman has claimed that empathy "represents the foundation skill for all social competencies important for work" (Salfi 2011, p. 819). Transformational leadership theory includes a focus on "individualized consideration" and leader-member exchange theory (Erdogan and Liden 2002) argues that leadership effectiveness depends on building differentiated relationships with each of one's colleagues, relationships that reflect their individual needs, desires and capacities.

Social resources encompass the leader's ability to understand the feelings, thoughts and behaviors of persons, including oneself, in interpersonal situations and to act appropriately on that understanding. The three sets of social resources included in the OLF (summarized in Table 3.3) are perceiving emotions, managing emotions, and acting productively in response to their own and others' emotions. Enacting these social resources helps build a positive emotional climate in the school, an important mediator of leaders' impacts on the performance of their organizations (e.g., Menges et al. 2011).

Perceiving Emotions includes the ability to detect, from a wide array of clues, one's own emotions (self-awareness) and the emotions of others. People with this social resource are able to recognize their own emotional responses and how those emotional responses shape their focus of attention and influence their actions. They are also able to discern the emotions being experienced by others, for example, from their tone of voice, facial expressions, body language and other verbal and non-verbal information.

Managing Emotions includes managing one's own and others' emotions, including the interaction of emotions on the part of different people in pairs and groups. People with this relational resources are able to understand the reasons for their own "intuitive" emotional responses and are able to reflect on the potential consequences of those responses; they are also able to persuade others to be more reflective about their own "intuitive" emotional responses and to reflect on the potential consequences of those responses.

Acting in Emotionally Appropriate Ways entails the ability to respond to the emotions of others in ways that support the purposes for the interaction. This social resource allows leaders to exercise a high level of cognitive control over which emotions are allowed to guide their actions and to assist others to act on emotions most likely to best serve their interests.

3.4.2 Psychological Resources

The three psychological resources included in the OLF are optimism, self-efficacy and resilience. While evidence suggests that each of these resources make significant contributions to leadership initiatives responsible for risk-taking and eventual success (e.g., Avey et al. 2008), a recent line of theory and research argues that when the three resources act in synergy, that is, when one person possesses all three resources, they make an especially large contribution to leadership success.

Optimism is the habitual expectation of success in one's efforts to address challenges and confront change now and in the future. Optimistic leaders habitually expect good things to result from their initiatives while pessimistic leaders habitually assume that their efforts will be thwarted, as often as not. When the expectations of optimistic leaders are not met, they pursue alternative paths to accomplish their goals. Optimistic leaders expect their efforts to be successful in relation to those things over which they have direct influence or control but not necessarily to be powerful enough to overcome negative forces in their organizations over which they have little or no influence or control; they are realistic as well as optimistic. Optimistic leaders are likely to take initiative and responsible risks with positive expectations regardless of past problems or setbacks.

Self efficacy is a belief about one's own ability to perform a task or achieve a goal. It is a belief about ability, not actual ability. That is, efficacious leaders believe they have the ability to solve whatever challenges, hurdles or problems that might come their way in their efforts to help their organizations succeed. Self-efficacy beliefs contribute to leaders' success through their directive effects on leaders' choices of activities and settings and can affect coping efforts once those activities are begun. Efficacy beliefs determine how much risk people will take, how much effort they will expend and how long they will persist in the face of failure or difficulty. The stronger the self-efficacy the longer the persistence. Leadership self-efficacy or confidence, it has been claimed, is likely the key cognitive variable regulating leader functioning in a dynamic environment and has a very strong relationship with a leaders' performance.

Resilience is the ability to recover from or adjust easily to misfortune or change. Resilience is significantly assisted by high levels of efficacy but goes beyond the belief in one's capacity to achieve in the long run. At the core of resilience is the ability to "bounce back" from failure and even move beyond one's initial goals while doing so. Resilient leaders or potential leaders have the ability to thrive in the challenging circumstances commonly encountered by school leaders.

3.5 Conclusion

The purpose for this chapter was to provide a relatively comprehensive account of leadership practices that considerable amounts of evidence suggest have the potential to improve the status of conditions or variables on each of the four paths serving as the focus for this book. As Hitt and Tucker's (2016) comparative analysis indicates, while the OLF does not include all of the practices found in two other comparably evidence-based frameworks, it does include most of them. It seems safe to conclude, then, that improving the status of specific variables on each of the four paths described in this book may well demand unique responses by leaders. However, these responses are likely to be variants on the dimensions and practices outlined in the OLF.

References

Australian Institute for Teaching and School Leadership (AITSL). (2015). *Australian professional standard for principals and the leadership profiles*. Victoria: Education Services Australia.

Avey, J., Wernsing, T., & Luthans, F. (2008). Can positive employees help positive organizational change? Impact of psychological capital and emotions on relevant attitudes and behaviors. *Journal of Applied Behavioral Science, 44*, 48–70.

Carroll, B., Levy, L., & Richmond, D. (2008). Leadership as practice: Challenging the competence paradigm. *Leadership, 4*, 364.

English, F. (2006). The unintended consequences of a standardized knowledge base in advancing educational leadership preparation. *Educational Administration Quarterly, 42*, 461–472.

Erdogan, B., & Liden, R. (2002). Social exchanges in the workplace: A review of recent developments and future directions in leader-member exchange theory. In L. Neider & C. Schriesheim (Eds.), *Leadership* (pp. 65–114). Greenwich: Information Age.

Goleman, D. (1998). *Working with emotional intelligence*. New York: Bantam.

Grissom, J., & Loeb, S. (2011). Triangulating principal effectiveness: How perspectives of parents, teachers, and assistant principals identify the central importance of managerial skills. *American Journal of Educational Research, 48*, 1091–1123.

Heck, R., & Hallinger, P. (2009). Assessing the contribution of distributed leadership to school improvement and growth in math achievement. *American Educational Research Journal, 3*, 659–689.

Harris, A., Muijs, D., Chapman, C., Stoll, L., & Russ, J. (2003). *Raising attainment in the former coalfield areas*. London: Department for Education and Skills.

Hattie, J. (2009). *Visible learning. A synthesis of over 800 meta-analyses related to achievement*. New York: Routledge.

Heifetz, R. (1999). *Adaptive change: What's essential and what's expendable?* Cambridge, MA: Harvard Kennedy School of Government.

Higgins, J., & Bonne, L. (2011). Configurations of instructional leadership enactments that promote the teaching and learning of mathematics in a New Zealand elementary school. *Educational Administration Quarterly, 47*(5), 794–825.

Hitt, D., & Tucker, P. (2016). Systematic review of key leadership practices found to influence student achievement: A unified framework. *Review of Educational Research, 86*, 531–569.

Ladson-Billings, G. (1995). Toward a theory of culturally relevant pedagogy. *American Educational Research Journal, 32*, 465–491.

Leithwood, K. (1994). Leadership for school restructuring. *Educational Administration Quarterly, 30*, 498–518.

Leithwood, K. (2012). *The Ontario leadership framework with a discussion of the research foundations*. Toronto: Institute for Educational Leadership.

Leithwood, K., & Riehl, C. (2005). What do we already know about school leadership. In W. Firestone & C. Riehl (Eds.), *A new agenda for research in educational leadership* (pp. 12–27). New York: Teachers College Press.

Leithwood, K., & Steinbach, R. (1995). *Expert problem solving: Evidence from school and district leaders*. New York: SUNY Press.

Leithwood, K., Mascall, B., & Strauss, T. (2009). *Leading school turnaround*. San Francisco: Jossey Bass.

Louis, K., Dretzkey, B., & Wahlstrom, K. (2010). How does leadership affect student achievement? Results from a national survey. *School Effectiveness and School Improvement, 21*(3), 315–336.

Mascall, B., & Leithwood, K. (2010). Investing in leadership: the district's role in managing principal turnover. *Leadership and Policy in Schools, 9*, 367–383.

Menges, J., Walter, F., Vogel, B., & Bruch, H. (2011). Transformational leadership climate: Performance linkages, mechanisms, and boundary conditions at the organizational level. *The Leadership Quarterly, 22*(5), 893–909.

Mumford, M., Bedell, K., Hunter, S., Espejo, J., & Boatman, P. (2006). Problem-solving – turning crises into opportunities: How charismatic, ideological and pragmatic leaders solve problems. In M. Mumford (Ed.), *Pathways to outstanding leadership: A comparative analysis of charismatic, ideological and pragmatic leaders* (pp. 108–137). Mahwah: Lawrence Erlbaum.

National College for School Leadership (NCSL). (2008). *The national standards for school leadership: Consultation paper*. London: Department for Children, Schools and Families.

National Policy Board for Educational Administration. (2015). *Professional standards for educational leaders 2015*. Reston: Author.

Printy, S., Marks, H., & Bowers, A. (2010). *Integrated leadership: How principals and teachers share transformational and instructional influences*. East Lansing: Michigan State University.

Robinson, V., Hohepa, M., & Lloyd, C. (2009). *School leadership and student outcomes: Identifying what works and why: Best evidence synthesis iteration*. Wellington: University of Auckland and the New Zealand Ministry of Education.

Rowan, B., Fang-Shen, C., & Miller, R. (1997). Using research on employees' performance to student the effects of teachers on student achievement. *Sociology of Education, 70*, 256–284.

Ryan, J. (2006). Inclusive leadership for social justice in schools. *Leadership and Policy in schools, 5*, 3–18.

Salfi, N. (2011). Successful leadership practices of head teachers for school improvement: Some evidence from Pakistan. *Journal of Educational Administration, 49*(4), 414–432.

Waters, T., & Cameron, G. (2007). *The balanced leadership framework: Connecting vision with action*. Denver: McCrel.

Yukl, G. (1994). *Leadership in organizations* (3rd ed.). Englewood Cliffs: Prentice Hall.

Zacarro, S., Kemp, C., & Bader, P. (2004). Leader traits and abilities. In J. Antonakis, A. Cianciolo, & R. Sternberg (Eds.), *The nature of leadership* (pp. 104–124). Thousand Oaks: Sage.

Part II
The Rational Path

Introduction

This section of the book includes three chapters which explore a selection of variables on the Rational Path; Chap. 4 is a conceptual exploration of the relationship between leadership and classroom instruction while Chaps. 5 and 6 are concerned with Academic Press, Teacher Learning and several variables examined in more detail in Part III.

The Rational Path, is populated by both classroom and school-level variables all of which are central to the "the technical core" of schooling – the knowledge and skills of school staffs about curriculum, teaching, and learning. There is now a considerable amount of evidence available about the effects on student learning of many variables on the Rational Path and school leaders are able to prioritize for their attention those both relevant in their own school contexts and known to have the greatest chance of improving their students' learning. In general, the "cognitive resources" described in Chapter Three are critical to leaders' efforts to improve the condition of these variables in their schools.

This introduction offers a brief but comprehensive summary of evidence related to three of the most powerful variables on the Rational Path along with approaches to leadership likely to improve their condition when such evidence is available.

Classroom Instruction

Hattie's (2009) synthesis of evidence implies that school leaders carefully consider the value of focusing their efforts on improving key aspects of their teachers' instruction as, for example, the extent to which teachers are providing students with immediate and informative feedback ($d = 0.73$), teachers' use of reciprocal teaching strategies ($d = 0.74$), teacher-student relations ($d = 0.72$), the management of classrooms ($d = 0.52$), and the general quality of teaching in the school. Those high-yielding instructional strategies identified by Marzano (2009) begin to explain what the quality of teaching in the classroom means.

In sum, effective instruction is explicitly guided by the goals that teachers intend to accomplish with their students and student progress is constantly monitored to make sure that students are actively engaged in meaningful learning. High quality teaching also entails providing students with prompt, informative feedback and is directed by analyses of achievement results often leading to the provision differentiated instruction. Effective forms of instruction enable students to construct their own knowledge and provide opportunities for students to learn collaboratively. Face-to-face instruction can be enhanced with technology-facilitated assignments reinforcing what has been learned in class.

Leadership practices likely to foster the development of classroom-level variables are those associated with the dimension "Improving the Instructional Program" as briefly described in Chap. 3: staffing the instructional program; providing instructional support; monitoring student learning and school improvement progress and; buffering staff from distractions to their work.

Academic Emphasis or Press

In schools with a well-developed Academic Emphasis, administrators and teachers set high but achievable school goals and classroom academic standards. They believe in the capacity of their students to achieve and encourage their students to respect and pursue academic success. School administrators supply resources, provide structures and exert leadership influence. Teachers make appropriately challenging academic demands and provide quality instruction to attain these goals. Students value these goals, respond positively, and work hard to meet the challenge.

Of the more than two dozen empirical studies which have been published since about 1989, by far the majority have reported significant, positive, and at least moderate relationships between Academic Emphasis and student achievement (e.g., Goddard et al. 2000). Most of this evidence suggests that a school's Academic Emphasis makes an especially valuable contribution to the achievement of disadvantaged children.

A small number of studies have identified leadership practices likely to increase a school's Academic Emphasis (e.g., Alig-Mielcarek 2003; Jacob 2004; Jurewicz 2004). Some are fundamentally *Direction Setting* in intent, for example: developing and communicating shared goals; establishing high expectations; and; helping to clarify shared goals about academic achievement. Other leadership practices identified by the evidence are about *Building Relationships and Developing People,* including the promotion of school-wide professional development. Yet others aim at *Developing the Organization to Support Desired Practices* as, for example: not burdening teachers with bureaucratic tasks and busy work; grouping students using methods that convey academic expectations; providing an orderly environment; and establishing clear homework policies. The remaining leadership practices emerging from research on how to foster Academic Emphasis are primarily about *Improving the Instructional Program* as summarized above.

Disciplinary Climate

This concept, has emerged over the last couple of decades in response to the shift in the focus on discipline from individual students to the school. Willms and Ma (2004), for example, argue that the traditional way of dealing with indiscipline, mainly at the classroom level, seems insufficient and that the Disciplinary Climate of the classroom and school has important effects on students. This climate is shaped by features of schools and the larger community; classroom disruption can be a direct reflection of the conflict or tension between teachers and students across the school, as a whole. Using a comprehensive U.S database, Willms and Ma (2004) developed a multi-dimensional conception of school Disciplinary Climate covering "… student discipline perceptions and experiences, school culture, teacher classroom management, student engagement and commitment, school prevention and intervention in response to indiscipline, and conflicts in the social and cultural values between schools and students" (p. 10). Research during the last decade, using large data sets and sophisticated statistical methods, has produced consistent evidence demonstrating the contribution of a school's Disciplinary Climate to the learning of its students.

Existing research offers very limited guidance about specifically what leaders might do to develop the Disciplinary Climate in their schools. What evidence there is (e.g., Benda 2000; Leithwood et al. 2004) recommends flexible rather than rigid responses by leaders to disciplinary events and engagement of staff and other stakeholders in developing school-wide behaviour plans. A broader body of evidence does indicate that "the principal is the most potent factor in determining school climate" and that "a direct relationship between visionary leadership and school climate and culture is imperative to support teacher efforts that lead to the success of the instructional [and disciplinary] program" (Rencherler 1991, cited in Benda 2000). Clearly, near-term insights about the further development of this condition in schools will need to come from the collective wisdom of one's colleagues and active experimentation in one's school.

References

Alig-Mielcarek, J. M. (2003). *A model of school success: Instructional leadership, academic press, and student achievement.* Unpublished doctoral dissertation. Ohio State University, Columbus.

Benda, S. M. (2000) *The effect of leadership styles on the disciplinary climate and culture of elementary schools.* Unpublished doctoral dissertation. Widener University, Chester.

Goddard, R., Hoy, W. K., & Woolfolk Hoy, A. (2000). Collective teacher efficacy: Its meaning, measure and impact on student achievement. *American Educational Research Journal, 37*, 479–507.

Hattie, J. (2009). *Visible learning: A synthesis of over 800 meta-analyses relating to student achievement.* New York: Routledge.

Jacob, J. A. (2004). *A study of school climate and enabling bureaucracy in select New York City public elementary schools.* Unpublished doctoral dissertation. University of Utah, Salt Lake City.

Jurewicz, M. M. (2004). *Organizational citizenship behaviors of middle school teachers: A study of their relationship to school climate and student achievement.* Unpublished doctoral dissertation. College of William and Mary, Williamsburg.

Leithwood, K., Louis, K. S., Anderson, S., & Wahlstrom, K. (2004). *How leadership influences student learning: A review of the evidence linking leadership to student learning.* New York: Wallace Foundation.

Marzano, R. (2009). *On excellence in teaching.* Denver: Solution Tree Publishers.

Willms, J. D., & Ma, X. (2004). School disciplinary climate: Characteristics and effects on eighth grade achievement. *Alberta Journal of Educational Research, 50*, 169–188.

Chapter 4
Leadership and Learning: Conceptualizing Relations Between School Administrative Practice and Instructional Practice

James Spillane

Research studies, research syntheses, and meta-analyses show that school leadership and management are important in maintaining instructional quality, leading instructional improvement, and realizing valued student outcomes. Though establishing strong causal inferences has proven difficult, an ever-expanding empirical knowledge base suggests that school leadership and management matter for classroom instruction and student learning (Bryk et al. 2009; Grisson and Loeb 2011; Hallinger and Heck 1996; Heck and Hallinger 1999; Leithwood et al. 2004; Louis and Kruse 1995; Newmann and Wehlage 1995; Purkey and Smith 1983; Robinson et al. 2008; Rosenholz 1989; Silins and Mulford 2002). Still, there is work to be done not only in establishing stronger causal inferences about these relations but, equally if not more important, explicating *how* school leadership and management actually influence instruction and student learning. Opening up the black box between school leadership and management (henceforth referred to as school administration) and student learning is essential if research knowledge is to inform practice in schools and school systems.

In this paper, I focus on one critical challenge to better understand relations between school administration and student learning. I argue that one problem we face is that core constructs in our work are often variably and weakly defined. While variability is inevitable and indeed potentially generative for scholarship, it is problematic when coupled with poorly defined constructs. Loose constructs pose problems for all of us contributing to fuzzy research, especially if constructs such as school leadership, management, or even instruction are weakly (or never explicitly) defined and operationalized. Fuzzy conceptualization makes comparing across studies, essential to the development of a robust empirical knowledge base, difficult if not impossible. Fuzzy conceptualizations can also contribute to a false sense of

---

J. Spillane (✉)
Institute for Policy Research, Northwestern University,
60208-0001 Evanston, IL, USA
e-mail: j-spillane@northwestern.edu

agreement among practitioners and policymakers as they use the same words (e.g., leadership, teaching) to denote distinctly different understandings of these phenomena. Hence, I argue that a critical but often overlooked challenge in studying relations between school administration and student learning is conceptual in nature.

Even when scholars use similar conceptual frameworks, such as a distributed framework, there are often substantial differences in how they define constructs and operationalize them. Transparency enables us as a field to compare and contrast the findings from separate studies. Consider three different studies by way of example, all using a distributed framework and all exemplifying the explicitness and transparency I am arguing for in this paper with respect to conceptualization and study operations. First, Leithwood and colleagues, building on Gronn's (2002) work on "holistic forms" of distributed leadership, conceptualize how leadership is distributed in schools by focusing on the extent to which the performance of leadership functions is consciously aligned across different sources of leadership and propose four study operations: planful alignment, spontaneous alignment, spontaneous misalignment, and anarchic misalignment (Leithwood et al. 2007). Second, to model distributed leadership effects on student learning, Heck and Hallinger (1999) conceptualize leadership as forms of collaboration practiced by the principal, teachers, and members of the school's improvement team. They developed study operations to tap into three aspects of distributed leadership in schools and measured these using survey items focused on teachers' perceptions of leadership as exercised by different sources—collaborative decision-making about educational improvement; the extent to which school leadership emphasized school governance that empowered staff and students; emphasis school leaders placed on participation in efforts to evaluate the school's academic development. Third, Camburn et al. (2003) surveyed teachers and formally designated school leaders in 120 elementary schools using a distributed framework, operationalizing leadership as a set of organizational functions. The study asked participants about leadership functions that fell into one of three categories—instruction, building management, and boundary spanning—and examined how responsibility for different leadership functions was arrayed by formally designated leadership position. These three studies exemplify the sort of transparency in conceptual and study operation work that is essential for comparing across studies in efforts to measure and explicate the "how" of relations between administrative practice and student learning. They also underscore how merely invoking a conceptual framework in our research is necessary but insufficient; it is also essential that we specify our constructs and our study operations for these constructs.

In this paper, I show how conceptualizing phenomena under study in particular ways shapes how we might frame and hypothesize relations among these phenomena. Conceptual (and practical) frameworks are similar to scaffolding that builders use to repair a building in that they give us access to particular aspects of phenomena while leaving other aspects in the background and often inaccessible (Lester 2005). By drawing on work in different theoretical traditions, conceptual frameworks serve as "a skeletal structure of justification" (rather than "structure of explanation") enabling us to frame and focus our exploration of phenomena such as school administrative practice and instruction (Eisenhart 1991). It is not surprising that studies conceptualizing the same phenomena in different ways can reach different or even conflicting conclusions about the nature of relations among these phenomena. Hence, explicitly defining and operationalizing core constructs in our research is essential so that we can systematically compare empirical findings in time and across time.

Rather than focusing on student achievement and/or attainment, I focus on instruction, as it is the most proximal cause of students' opportunities to learn that schools and school systems can manipulate. Student learning is critical, but teachers and school leaders cannot learn for students; students must do the learning themselves (Cohen 2011). What school leaders and teachers can do is create more or less rich opportunities for students to learn through instruction. Some readers may disagree pointing to, among other things, a strong association between students' achievement/attainment and their socio-economic circumstances and/or cultural backgrounds. Or, readers might point to empirical evidence suggesting that the effect sizes of school level variables such as school norms and climate (e.g., academic press) rival the effect size of classroom instructional approach. But, these objections are a function of conceptualizing instruction too narrowly, confined to classrooms and/or focused exclusively on cognitive or academic matter. However, instruction extends beyond the classroom to students' experience in schools more broadly in the hallways, lunchrooms, and before and after school start and end times. Further, as most school leaders and teachers will attest, instruction is about more than academic or cognitive matters; it is also fundamentally about social, emotional and affective matters. It involves how children's ideas and ways of being are treated inside schools. While schools and school systems cannot directly create more equitable societies (that being a matter for other public policy sectors such as taxation policy), how they treat students through *instruction* inside and outside the classroom do matter for student learning and by extension their achievement and attainment (Becker 1952; Gonzalez et al. 2005; Gutierrez and Vossoughi 2009; López et al. 2010; Moll 1988; Rosenthal and Jacobson 1968). In short, how we conceptualize instruction has fundamental entailments for studying relations between school administration and student learning: Conceptualizing instruction narrowly as purely a classroom or cognitive matter necessitates different research designs than conceptualizations that attempt to capture the multi-facet and multi-place nature of instruction.

I begin my argument by conceptualizing school administration and instruction from what I refer to as a distributed perspective, using theoretical work in distributed and situated cognition, activity theory, and micro sociology. I contrast a distributed conceptualization with more conventional, individually focused conceptualizations of both phenomena. I see this work as essential to developing a conceptual (or practical) framework for studying relations between these two social phenomena. Next, based on my conceptualization of school administrative practice and instructional practice, I sketch a framework for thinking about relations among them. To do so, I draw on social theory from several traditions and consider the entailments of taking a distributed perspective for developing a framework to focus empirical observation and measurement of relations between school administration and instruction. Third, I briefly discuss moving beyond conceptualization to developing study operations in order that we might observe and measure relations between school administration and instruction in the world under experimental (including quasi experimental) or "natural" conditions. I conclude with some reflections on the importance of conceptual work for research that purports to examine the strength and nature of relations between school administration and student learning.

4.1 Conceptualizing School Leadership and Management: A Distributed Perspective

For readability purposes, I use school administration or administrative practice to refer to school leadership and management. Leadership involves a social influence interaction in an effort to initiate change and transform existing ways of working in order to achieve some goal (Bass 1990; Cuban 1988). Definitions of leadership are abundant in the literature (Bass 1990). The onus is on researchers to be clear about our "working" definitions of leadership. This is not purely an academic or theoretical matter, but a very practical matter indeed whether we are researchers or practitioners. In my working definition, leadership refers to activities tied to the core work of an organization that are designed to influence the motivation, knowledge, affect, or practice of organizational members or that are understood by organizational members as intended to influence their motivation, knowledge, affect, or practice (Spillane and Diamond 2007). Though often portrayed as different and sometimes even as opposites, management and leadership are close relatives. Management is about maintaining current ways of doing things (Cuban 1988). Though analytically distinguishable, management and leadership work in tandem in day-to-day practice in organizations. School leaders are expected not only to lead improvement in instruction in their schools but also maintain the quality of instruction over time. Hence, it is critical to attend to both leadership and management referred to in this paper as school administrative practice.

For over a decade, several scholars have advanced a distributed perspective that re-conceptualizes school administration for research and development work (Gronn 2000; Spillane et al. 2001). Based on theoretical work on distributed and situated cognition, activity theory, and micro sociology, these scholars argue for attention to leadership and management *as practice* (Spillane 2006). Scholars of human activity working in several traditions argue for attention to activity systems that take into account people interacting with one another and their environment. Hutchins (1995), for example, argues for understanding the task of landing a plane by taking the cockpit rather than the pilot's mind as the unit of analysis. The cockpit, what Hutchins' terms a "socio-technical system," includes not only the pilot and co-pilot but also the instrumentation and tools (e.g., several instruments that measure speed) that enable them in the activity of landing the plane. These features of the situation are not merely "aides" to the pilots' cognition; rather, human activity is "stretched over" actors and aspects of their situation because what the pilots *notice*, how they *interpret* what they notice, and how they *negotiate* with one another the meanings of what they noticed is not only a function of their individual mental scripts but also their interactions and the tools that enable (and constrain) their joint work. Hutchins' notion of a "socio-technical system" suggests that in studying school administrative practice we must attend not simply to school leaders' intra-mental models and behavior but also to inter-mental models—models or representations of learning, teaching, and achievement contained in the material and abstract tools that school staff use to interact with one another. Scholars from various traditions use different constructs in shifting the unit of analysis from individual activity to people interacting with one another in a system including (but not limited to) "communities of practice" (Lave and Wenger 1991; Rogoff 2003), "activity systems" (Cole and Engeström 1993; Wertsch 1991), "social worlds" and "social forms" (Simmel 1955).

Framed from a distributed perspective, school administrative practice is the key unit of analysis (Spillane 2006; Spillane and Diamond 2007). Researchers have studied leadership behavior for a half-century or more (Fiedler 1967; Hemphill 1949), usually observing what individual leaders (typically the school principal) do, and identifying more or less efficacious behaviors. From a distributed perspective, however, framing practice as behavior fails to recognize its distributed nature because practice is constituted in the interactions rather than in the action of an individual. A distributed perspective, then, conceptualizes practice in a very particular way: practice is not just about the actions of individual leaders, though they are clearly relevant; it is fundamentally about *interactions* among leaders and among leaders and followers (Spillane 2006). And, leaders not only influence followers but followers also influence leaders in these interactions (Cuban 1988; Dahl 1961). Actions, though necessary, are insufficient in the study of administrative practice because practice is framed as a product of the interactions among leaders and followers. In this framing, school staff (e.g., principal, curriculum specialist or teacher), and indeed school stakeholders more broadly (e.g., parents, students, community members), can move in and out of the leader role depending on the activity or situation (see Fig. 4.1). In this paper I use the term practice to refer to social interactions, *not* individual behavior.

As evidenced in Hutchins' (1995) "socio-technical system", the situation also matters because people don't interact directly with one another; their interactions are made possible by "social structure"—everyday, often taken for granted, aspects of the situation including, but not limited to, language, social norms, organizational routines, work procedures, rules, and tools. Aspects of the situation frame and focus interactions among school staff and stakeholders thereby enabling and constraining school administrative practice. In this way, the situation *defines* school practice from the inside; it is internal to practice as depicted in Fig. 4.1.

Some readers will note that scholars have long taken the situation into account in scholarship on organizational administration. While this is correct, scholars more often than not treat aspects of the situation as *external* to practice, not as core constituting or defining elements of practice. In doing so, aspects of the situation are cast as independent variables that influence practice by muting or enhancing the effects of administrative practice on an outcome or dependent variable (e.g., student achievement) or by strengthening or weakening the influence of a leader's behavior on followers. In treating the situation as one of the three core constituting elements of administrative practice (along with leaders and followers), aspects of the situation do not simply affect what

Fig. 4.1 School administration practice

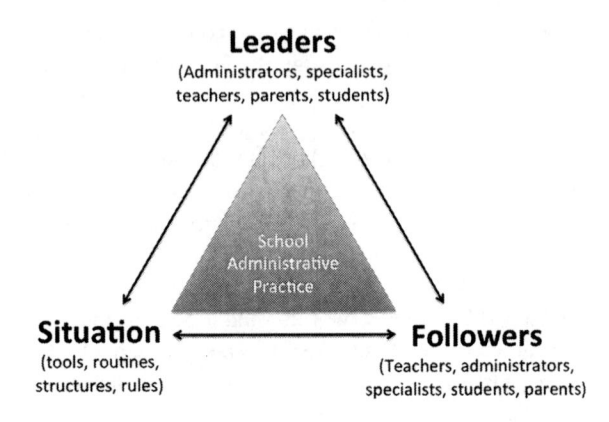

Leaders
(Administrators, specialists, teachers, parents, students)

School Administrative Practice

Situation ←⎯⎯⎯⎯⎯→ **Followers**
(tools, routines, structures, rules)   (Teachers, administrators, specialists, students, parents)

people do or plan to do but rather define practice from inside, enabling and constraining social interactions among people. Aspects of the situation are the *medium* for human interactions framing and focusing *how* leaders and followers interact and thereby defining administrative practice. In this view, aspects of the situation do not simply enhance or mute the effects of administrative practice on some outcome nor simply strengthen or weaken the influence of leaders' behavior: Rather, aspects of the situation are the vehicle for interacting and thereby *define* practice. Figure one captures the core constituting nature of the situation by affording it a position equivalent to leaders and followers rather than casting it in some secondary role (Spillane 2006; Suchman 1987).

Framing school administrative practice from a distributed perspective allows for the fact that multiple individuals in addition to the school principal are involved with the work (Camburn et al. 2003; Harris 2005; Leithwood et al. 2007; MacBeath et al. 2005; Spillane and Diamond 2007). In addition to other formally designated school leaders, a distributed perspective allows for the possibility that individuals without any formal leadership designation may be responsible for and engaged in leading and managing practice. Taking a distributed perspective involves understanding how different configurations of school staff and school stakeholder in interaction, by design or default, constitute the practice of leading and managing instruction. Such considerations press us to examine various factors, from the division or duplication of school administrative responsibilities to whether and how those who have a hand in the work do or do not complement one another.

4.2 Conceptualizing Instruction as a Collective, Situated, and Distributed Practice

As noted above, instruction is the most proximal means that schools have for influencing students' opportunities to learn and by extension student learning. Instruction is often conceptualized as what the teacher does, a *solo* practice, roughly equivalent to a teacher's behavior in the classroom. Indeed, there is a long tradition of research that examines the relations between teacher or teaching behaviors and students' learning, one of the most prominent being the process-product research tradition (Dunkin and Biddle 1974; Mitzel 1960). Process-product research examined relations between what teachers do and student learning, mostly measured in terms of student performance on standardized achievement tests. Scholars observed and measured discrete teaching behaviors (e.g., teachers use of praise, the length of wait time teachers allowed for a student to answer), summed variables across situations, and then correlated teaching behaviors with student achievement. While acknowledging its contribution to our understanding of teaching, process-product research has been criticized on several levels, including its often a-theoretical approach (Brophy 2001; Dunkin and Biddle 1974; Gage 1978; Gage and Giaconia 1981; Good et al. 1983).

Other scholars have conceptualized instruction differently, recognizing and foregrounding its distributed, situated, and collective nature as a practice (Cohen 2011; Cohen and Ball 1999; Delpit 1995; Doyle 1983; Hawkins 1967; Jackson 1968). Ball and Cohen's conceptual work on instruction is particularly informative here: They argue for conceptually framing teaching as a practice that is coproduced by teachers *and* their students on and with particular intellectual (e.g., mathematics, language arts) and physical material such as curriculum and texts (Cohen 2011; Cohen and Ball 1999). Framing instruction this way, it is no longer *just* a function of the teachers' skill and knowledge but also a function of students' knowledge and skill and indeed key aspects of the situation such as the intellectual material being taught and learned and the materials that are being used for instruction. Teachers and students in interaction with, and about, particular material co-produce teaching; Cohen and Ball (1999) refer to these three core constituting elements together as the instructional unit (Fig. 4.2).

Framed in terms of the three constituting elements of the instructional unit, instruction is not equivalent to a teacher's behavior or a function of her/his knowledge and skill. Instead, instruction takes form in the interaction of teachers and students about particular intellectual material and with aspects of the situation. All three elements—teachers, students, and materials—are mutually constitutive of instruction. Accordingly, instructional capability "is a function of the interaction among elements of the instructional unit, not the sole province of any single element" (Cohen and Ball 1999). By extension, then, instructional capability is not fixed but dependent on the particular instance of instruction. Conceptualizing instruction as a distributed practice acknowledges that the nature of practice and indeed the quality of practice is a function not simply of any one element but of these elements *in interaction*. The nature of instructional practice can look quite different even with the same teacher but different students and/or different materials.

As depicted in Fig. 4.2, context is also a key consideration with respect to instructional practice. Specifically, aspects of the situation, especially the immediate school situation, beyond those captured by the material/technologies element of the instructional unit influence instructional practice. Students' experiences outside the classroom around whether and how their peers and school staff respect their ideas influence how they interact in the classroom. Similarly, teachers' experiences outside the classroom, including whether and how they interact with colleagues, influence their classroom interactions with students. For example, teachers can learn about instruction from their peers

Fig. 4.2 The internal dynamics of instructional units (Adapted from Cohen and Ball (2009))

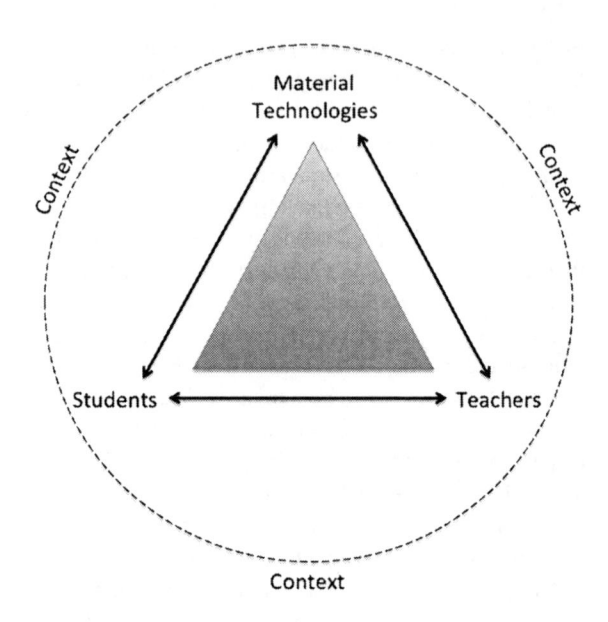

but whether they do depends on things such as school norms (e.g., academic press, relational trust, collective responsibility) and organizational arrangements (e.g., organizational routines, scheduling, etc.) (Jackson and Bruegmann 2009; Sebring et al. 2006).

My goal here is not to anoint any one theoretical tradition as the chosen way, but rather to illustrate the importance of conceptual work to our empirical investigations and show how tools from various theoretical traditions *might* be used to frame research on relations between school administration and classroom instruction.

4.3 Conceptualizing Relations Between School Administrative Practice and Instructional Practice

Conceptualizing both school administration and instruction from a distributed perspective, underscoring that practice is stretched over people and their situation, constrains how we frame research to investigate relations between them in several ways. In Fig. 4.3 and below, I sketch a conceptual framework for thinking about these relations. I say sketch because while my particular conceptualizations of administrative practice and instructional practice constrain how we might frame relations among them, they do not determine it. A sketch provides a rough description, outlining the contours of these relations while allowing for specification in future work. It is suggestive rather than prescriptive.

To begin with, in conceptualizing school administration and instruction as distributed practices, it follows that efforts to understand relations between the two phenomena are fundamentally about examining relations among two core school practices or

School Administrative Practice   **Instructional Unit**

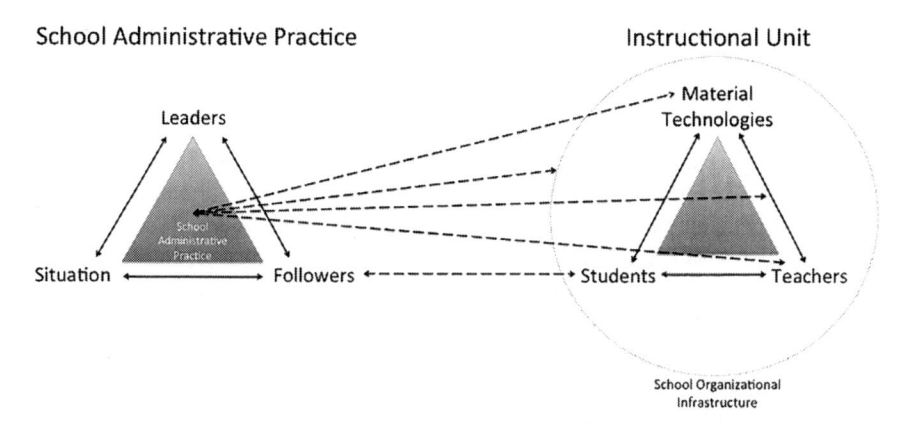

Fig. 4.3 Relationship between school administrative practice and instructional practice

systems of practice. Further, these two practices are not independent of one another. Key elements of the instructional unit, especially teachers and students, are also key constituting elements of school administrative practice. As several readers will appreciate, this interdependence poses particular challenges for scholars interested in estimating the effects of school administrative practice on instructional practice. Further, relations between school administrative and instructional practice are bidirectional rather than unidirectional as captured in the two-way arrows in Fig. 4.3. On the one hand, the three key elements of the instructional unit are the object or outcome of interest when studying the influence of school administration on instruction.

At the same time, elements of the instructional unit are key constituting elements of school administrative practice. For example, depending on the situation teachers are key constituting elements of both instructional practice and of school administrative practice.

Mindful of these observations, I organize my discussion of conceptualizing relations between instructional practice and school administrative practice below around two themes. First, I consider direct and indirect pathways between administrative practice and instructional practice. Second, I outline a framework for thinking about how administrative practice might influence instructional practice through these pathways attending to what dimensions of practice might be influenced and the social mechanisms that might be at play.

4.4 Administrative Practice and Instructional Practice Relations

Keeping in mind the core constituting elements of both administrative practice and instructional practice, we can sketch several possible pathways by which administration and instruction might relate (Leithwood et al. 2007). First, school administrative practice might relate chiefly to any one element of the instructional unit. For example, school administrative practice as captured in the performance of a school organizational routine such as a school assembly might focus on motivating students to take their mathematics learning seriously by recognizing exemplary academic performance or improvement in performance over time. Similarly, school administrative practice might encourage and reward teacher performance by recognizing and praising particular staff for exemplary classroom work. Second, school administrative practice might relate directly to two, rather than one, elements of the instructional unit, attending simultaneously to teacher and student, teacher and materials, and student and materials. For example, a lesson plan review routine where the school principal or grade level team regularly reviews the lesson plans teachers purport to use, which is common in some schools and school systems, focuses mostly on teacher and materials.

Third, school administrative practice might relate directly to all three elements of the instructional unit, attending simultaneously to teacher, students, and materials. Consider by way of example the Writing Folder Review Routine at Hillside Elementary in Chicago (Coldren 2007; Spillane and Coldren 2011). This organizational routine, designed to improve the quality of writing instruction at Hillside, involved a monthly review of students' writing folders. Each month, teachers sent students' writing folders along with their evaluations of the students' work to their principal for that month. The principal read the folders, providing written feedback to both students and teachers, recognizing exemplary work, identifying areas in need of improvement and offering suggestions for addressing these improvement needs. In the design and performance of the Writing Folder Review routine, we observe school administrative practice relating to all three elements of the instructional unit simultaneously. Specifically, the Writing Folder Review Routine connected administrative practice with teachers, students, and material simultaneously as the principal provided students with feedback on their writing and teachers with feedback about their writing instruction.

Similarly, teacher evaluation or supervision routines can, depending on their design and performance, address all three elements of the instructional unit. If the observer attends to not only what the teacher does, but also what students do, and the material under discussion. Learning Walk and Lesson Study routines also tend to focus on all three elements of the instructional unit together though the extent to which they do depends in important measure on their design and ultimately on their performance on the ground: Some elements of the instructional unit such as what the teacher does, the quality of the students' intellectual work, or the academic content can be privileged over other aspects in design and/or in performance of organizational routines such as lesson study, learning walks, and teacher supervisions.

We might hypothesize that school administrative practice that engages more elements of the instructional unit are likely to have a stronger influence on instructional practice than administrative practice that engages fewer elements (Cohen and Ball 1999). Motivating students and teachers about the same intellectual material, for example, more than likely increases the influence of the writing folder routine on instruction than if the routine had targeted only one element of the instructional unit.

Imagine if school leaders had designed a different organizational routine, such as regularly reviewing teacher lesson plans for writing; administrative practice would have focused mostly on teachers and materials, just two elements of the instructional unit.

Acknowledging these different pathways, we might conceptualize the directness of relations between school administrative practice and instructional practice in at least two ways. First, we might consider relations that involve more elements of the instructional unit as being more direct as they simultaneously engage more constituting elements of instruction. We might hypothesize then that administrative practice that related to all three elements (*i.e.*, teacher, student, and materials) of the instructional unit simultaneously and coherently are likely to have a more potent influence on instruction than administrative practice that focuses on a single element. Second, we might argue that administrative practice that relates directly to the actual performance of instruction by directly observing it (e.g., Learning Walks, teacher supervision or evaluation) involve a more direct relation than administrative practice that relates indirectly (e.g., reviewing teachers' lesson plans). Framing relations between school administration and instruction in this way underscores that direct relations between school administration and instruction can take multiple forms and that the degree of directness is not simply a function of being up close and in the classroom.

My discussion to this point has focused on direct relations between administrative practice and instructional practice. Relations between the two practices, however, may also be indirect in that they focus on what is referred to in the depiction of the instructional unit in Fig. 4.2 as "context". In Fig. 4.3, I use "school organizational infrastructure" instead of context and confine my discussion to the school infrastructure rather than the school system infrastructure more broadly (Cohen and Moffitt 2009; Cohen et al. 2013). Figure 4.3 frames administrative practice that focuses on designing, redesigning, and maintaining the school organizational infrastructure as having an indirect relationship with instructional practice. These indirect relations may be just as influential on instruction as direct relations in that they can create conditions that enable teachers to improve their teaching practice by learning from one another, among other things.

4.5 Influencing What, by What Means

Identifying the various pathways through which relations between school administrative practice and instructional practice might operate get us only so far, especially if we are intent on doing something more than measuring the effects of administrative practice on instructional practice. To better specify relations between school administrative practice and instructional practice, it is necessary to elaborate both on what *aspects of practice* are being influenced and the *mechanisms* through which this influence is (intended to and actually) exercised.

To begin, we can think about social practice in terms of four interrelated analytical dimensions—cognitive, affective, motivational, and behavioral. Though analytically separate, in practice these dimensions work in interaction (Marris 1974). Conceptualizing relations between administrative practice and instructional practice, then, we can examine what combination of cognitive, affective, motivational, and behavioral dimensions is the focus. Teachers' will or motivation and skill are critical to the quality of instructional practice. Similarly, students' motivation and their knowledge and skill fundamentally shape the quality of instructional practice. But the affective and behavioral dimensions are also key. If teachers and students are unable to put their will and skill into practice, it curtails the quality of instructional practice. At the same time, if teachers or students are afraid or feel threatened it curtails the quality of instructional practice.

Some administrative practice, for example, such as publicly recognizing exemplary work on the part of students or teachers foregrounds the motivational dimension, though it might also attend to the cognitive dimension by letting other students see what good work looks like. Similarly, the Writing Folder Review routine described above focuses mostly on motivational and cognitive dimensions of instructional practice by encouraging teachers to teach writing, motivating students to write well, and providing teachers with feedback on what to teach. Other administrative practice such as the performance of a professional learning community routine might simultaneously focus cognitive, motivational, and affective dimensions of instructional practice by providing teachers with opportunities to learn from colleagues, being motivated to improve through interactions with peers, and creating a sense of security among teachers especially as they engage in instructional change.

Here again it is important to acknowledge the bidirectional nature of relations between school administrative practice and instructional practice. Specifically, the affective, motivational, and cognitive dimensions of instructional practice can shape administrative practice. When teachers or students are not motivated to learn and improve the nature of school administrative practice is likely to look different than in situations when they are motivated to learn and improve. Similarly, when teachers and students feel secure, the nature of administrative practice is likely to be different than in situations where they feel threatened.

A second issue concerns what mechanism (or combination of mechanisms) are mobilized through these pathways and might account for school administrative practice influencing instructional practice. It is one thing to show a relationship between school administrative practice and instructional practice and to identify possible pathways for this relationship, but another matter to explain what brought about the association. A key challenge involves explicating the social mechanisms that account for observed associations between administrative practice and instructional practice. How does administrative practice influence (enable and constrain) instructional practice? Addressing this challenge is essential for research intent on establishing causal links as well as identifying the mechanisms at work.

One way (there are others) to conceptualize the means by which school administrative practice influences instructional practice is to borrow from new institutional theorists who identify three ways in which institutions structure practice—regulative, normative, and cultural-cognitive (Scott 2008). The regulative dimension refers to procedures, guidelines, and rules specifying what school leaders and teachers are required to do. School policy or rules might require that teachers to attend weekly grade level meetings to plan instruction. Rules, guidelines, and procedures (both school and school system) for instructional practice are created, enacted and enforced through school administrative practice. These regulations are designed to structure instructional practice, help maintain instructional quality, and lead instructional improvement. The regulative dimension can address any combination of elements of the instructional unit such as what content should be taught to students of a particular age, who can teach, and even how to engage students with particular subjects (e.g., instructional strategies). School administrative practice can involve the use of formal authority (e.g., positional authority) but also other means such as persuasion to manage instructional quality and lead instructional improvement.

The normative dimension refers to norms and values that create expectations and obligations for particular roles such as teacher, student, and school principal among organizational members and school stakeholders. The normative dimension, for example, might include norms that value (or not) collaboration and the exchange of instructional information among teachers. The normative dimension can establish expectations and obligations for both in classroom and out of classroom practice related to instruction. In some schools and school systems, for example, a norm of privacy prevails with the expectation that the classroom is the teacher's domain. In contrast, in other schools and school systems instruction is a public practice with the expectation that teachers share instructional ideas and knowledge with one another. School administrative practice can both maintain norms and work to transform them through various means including hiring and socializing new school staff members.

The cultural-cognitive dimension centers on sense making, including the scripts and belief systems organizational members construct and use for everyday practice. "A cultural cognitive conception of institutions stresses the central role played by the socially mediated construction of a common framework of meanings" (Scott 2014, p. 59). It centers on school leaders', teachers', and students' (along with school stakeholders') schema for understanding key aspects of their work including instruction, instructional improvement, learning, and achievement. For example, schemas for understanding academic performance may be predominantly ability-based or effort-based and, depending on which conceptualization prevails, have a profound influence on instructional practice as well as efforts to improve that practice.

Regulative, normative, and cultural-cognitive dimensions work in interaction rather than in isolation (Scott 2014). For example, teachers, school leaders, and students negotiate and interpret rules and regulations as they implement them so the influence of these rules cannot be explained entirely by the regulative dimension; it also necessitates attention to the cultural-cognitive dimension that influences the sense-making process and indeed the normative aspect that legitimates whose meanings carry weight.

Using the regulative, normative, and cultural-cognitive framework, we can begin to specify the mechanisms at work in the various pathways between administrative practice and instructional practice. These mechanisms operate in at least one of two ways. First, participants in administrative practice can marshal norms, regulations, and cultural-cognitive beliefs in an effort to influence one another. A coach or teacher leader, for example, might appeal to shared values or norms to persuade colleagues of the merit of a new curriculum, using a particular mathematics pedagogical strategy, or an approach to building pedagogical content knowledge among school staff.

Similarly, a school principal might directly or indirectly appeal to rules and regulations such as the positional authority of the principal position or some external agent or agency (e.g., school district, state)—as she/he negotiates with school staff about changing current practice (e.g., participating in weekly meetings to discuss instructional practice, getting students to justify their answers to mathematical problems).

We might think about these uses of norms, regulations, and beliefs in practice as social tactics (Fligstein 2001). Based on the literature on strategic social action (Gould 1993; Lukes 1974; Padgett and Ansell 1992), Fligstein (2001) theorizes a range of tactics that "socially skilled actors" use to persuade others and gain cooperation. These include: telling people what to do; agenda-setting; capitalizing on ambiguities and uncertainties; convincing others that what was possible was preferable; brokering; giving the impression of neutrality; joining groups to reorder preferences; getting others to believe that they are in control (even if they are not); and creating alliances and outliers. This list is not meant to be exhaustive, but to give a sense of the tactics that school leaders (e.g., including formal and informal teacher leaders) might use to gain cooperation of colleagues (Spillane and Anderson 2013).

While norms, regulations, and cultural-cognitive beliefs might be deployed directly in administrative practice in an effort to persuade school staff to change their instructional practice and maintain instructional quality, they can also be used indirectly to influence instructional practice. Specifically, school administrative practice might work to influence instructional practice by transforming the school's normative, regulative, and cultural-cognitive dimensions. By working to transform school norms (e.g., building norms of collaboration about instruction to replace norms of privacy), school administrative practice can influence instructional practice as teachers are more likely to learn from their peers when norms of collaboration, rather than norms of privacy, prevail in a school. Similarly, school administrative practice can transform school regulations and monitor their implementation so that teachers interact with one another about instruction regularly. In turn, these changes can potentially over time result in teachers learning from their peers and improving their practice.

To summarize tentatively, identifying the pathways between school administrative practice and instructional practice gets us only so far. We also need to conceptualize what *aspects of practice* are being influenced and the intended and actual *mechanisms* at play in practice.

4.6 From Conceptualizing Relations to Study Operations and Measures

This paper has focused chiefly on conceptualizing relations among school administrative practice and instructional practice, a key variable populated on the Rational Path (Leithwood et al. 2010). This is of course just the first step in designing research to examine relations between school administration and instruction, though an essential and necessary first step because absent careful conceptualization our empirical observations are fatally flawed. While some recent work has attended explicitly to study operations when using a distributed perspective, more work is necessary (Camburn et al. 2003; Spillane et al. 2007, 2009). At the same time, we have to move beyond conceptualization work to consider study operations and develop measures. I briefly address the issue in this section.

Developing study operations is especially critical for translating theoretical and analytical ideas into measures for data collection and analysis, enabling the distributed framework to be used systematically in research studies. By "study operation" we mean the definition and specification of an aspect of a conceptual or analytical framework so that it can be measured based on observations in the field. For example, the operationalization of theoretical or analytical ideas in the distributed perspective on school administration has received limited attention to date, with a handful of exceptions. This work will involve developing study operations and "measures" of different aspects of school leadership and management when viewed through a distributed perspective (Spillane and Healey 2010; Spillane et al. 2010). Such work is essential so that the field moves beyond relying chiefly on repackaging or re-labeling existing measures to fit with a distributed perspective. While we can, and indeed should, salvage existing measures where possible in applying a distributed perspective, an exclusive focus on salvaged measures runs the risk of a distributed perspective becoming simply a new label for old and familiar constructs. The same holds for conceptualizing instructional practice from a distributed perspective.

4.7 Discussion and Conclusion

Conceptualization work, along with developing study operations and measures, and instrument development will determine to a great extent the ultimate quality of any effort to study relations between school administrative practice, framed from a distributed perspective, and instructional practice, the most proximal cause of student achievement. Fancy statistical methods, or even random assignment study designs, cannot compensate for loose constructs, weak study operations and invalid and unreliable measurement. I focused my conceptual work on practice; that is, school administrative practice *and* instructional practice. I do so for two reasons. First, practice is ultimately where school administration and instruction connect. Second, if our research is to be useful and usable for policymakers and practitioners, it has to speak more directly to practice.

A key argument in this paper is that our conceptualization of both administrative practice and the instructional practice will (should) fundamentally shape how we study relations between the two. Though this is research design 101, it is something that is too frequently ignored or left implicit in the dialogue about how best to study the effects of school administration on classroom instruction and by extension student learning, where questions of study design (e.g., randomization or regression discontinuity study design), measurement (e.g., the stability of Value Added Measures), and statistical models garner most of the attention. Such matters are of fundamental importance but they all *ultimately* depend on good measurement of the phenomena under study and in turn that depends on careful conceptualization of the phenomena and how they might relate to one another.

While I believe that conceptualizing both administration and instruction from a distributed perspective has several affordances, my point is not that the distributed conceptualization advanced here is the one best way to conceptualize the phenomena. It is one way, and a way that I think has several affordances, especially if practice is a central consideration. More broadly, my argument is that conceptualization work in general is critical to conducting more rigorous theory building and theory testing research on relations between school administration, instruction, and student outcomes. Let's rise to the occasion as a field.

Acknowledgements This paper has benefited tremendously from several collaborative writing projects over the past decade. In particular papers with Kaleen Healey, Karen Seashore Louis, and Mary Kay Stein (Spillane and Healey 2010; Spillane and Louis 2002; Stein and Spillane 2005).

Work on this article was supported by the Distributed Leadership Studies (http://www.distributedleadership.org) funded by research grants from the National Science Foundation (REC–9873583, RETA Grant # EHR–0412510), the Institute for Education Sciences (Grant # R305E040085), and the Spencer Foundation (200000039). Northwestern University's School of Education and Social Policy and Institute for Policy Research supported this work. All opinions and conclusions expressed in this article are those of the authors and do not necessarily reflect the views of any funding agency.

References

Bass, B. M. (1990). *Bass & Stogdill's handbook of leadership: Theory, research, and managerial applications*. New York: Free Press.

Becker, H. S. (1952). Social-class variations in the teacher-pupil relationship. *Journal of Educational Sociology, 25*, 451–465.

Brophy, J. E. (2001). *Advances in research in teaching: Subject-specific instructional methods and activities* (Vol. 8). Oxford: Elsevier Science.

Bryk, A. S., Sebring, P., Allensworth, E., Luppescu, S., & Easton, J. Q. (2009). *Organizing schools for improvement: Lessons from Chicago*. Chicago: University of Chicago Press.

Camburn, E. M., Rowan, B., & Taylor, J. E. (2003). Distributed leadership in schools: The case of elementary schools adopting comprehensive school reform models. *Educational Evaluation and Policy Analyis, 25*, 347–373.

Cohen, D. K. (2011). *Teaching and its predicaments*. Cambridge, MA: Harvard College.

Cohen, D. K., & Ball, D. L. (1999). *Instruction, capacity, and improvement*. Philadelphia: Consortium for Policy Research in Education.

Cohen, D. K., & Moffitt, S. L. (2009). *The ordeal of equality: Did federal regulation fix the schools?* Cambridge, MA: Harvard University Press.

Cohen, D. K., Peurach, D., Glazer, J. L., Gates, K. E., & Goldin, S. (2013). *Improvement by design: The promise of better schools*. Chicago: University of Chicago Press.

Coldren, A. F. (2007). Spanning the boundary between school leadership and classroom instruction at hillside elementary school. In J. P. Spillane & J. B. Diamond (Eds.), *Distributed leadership in practice* (pp. 16–34). New York: Teachers College Press.

Cole, M., & Engeström, Y. (1993). A cultural-historical approach to distributed cognition. In G. Salomon (Ed.), *Distributed cognitions: Psychological and educational considerations* (pp. 1–46). Cambridge, UK: Cambridge University Press.

Cuban, L. (1988). *The managerial imperative and the practice of leadership in schools*. Albany: SUNY Press.

Dahl, R. A. (1961). *Who governs? Democracy and power in an American city*. New Haven: Yale University Press.

Delpit, L. (1995). *Other people's children: Cultural conflict in the classroom*. New York: New Press.

Doyle, W. (1983). Academic work. *Review of Educational Research, 53*, 159–199.

Dunkin, M. J., & Biddle, B. (1974). *The study of teaching*. New York: Rinehart and Winston.

Eisenhart, M. (1991, October). Conceptual frameworks for research circa 1991: Ideas from a cultural anthropologist, implications for mathematics education researchers. In Proceedings of the 13th annual meeting of the North American chapter of the international group for the psychology of mathematics education (Vol. 1, pp. 202–219). Blacksburg, VA.

Fiedler, F. E. (1967). *A theory of leadership effectiveness* (Vol. III). New York: McGraw-Hill.

Fligstein, N. (2001). *The architecture of markets*. Princeton: Princeton University Press.

Gage, N. (1978). *The scientific basis of the art of teaching*. New York: Teachers College Press.

Gage, N., & Giaconia, R. (1981). Teaching practices and student achievement: Causal connections. *New York University Education Quarterly, 12*, 2–9.

Gonzalez, N., Moll, L. C., & Amanti, C. (2005). *Funds of knowledge: Theorizing practices in households, communities, and classrooms*. Mahwah: Lawrence Erlbaum.

Good, T., Grouws, D., & Ebmeier, H. (1983). *Active mathematics teaching*. New York: Longman.

Gould, R. (1993). Collective action and network analysis. *American Sociological Review, 58*, 182–196.

Grissom, J. A., & Loeb, S. (2011). Triangulating principal effectiveness: How perspectives of parents, teachers, and assistant principals identify the central importance of managerial skills. *American Educational Research Journal, 48*, 1091–1123.

Gronn, P. (2000). Distributed properties: A new architecture for leadership. *Educational Management Administration and Leadership, 28*, 317–338.

Gronn, P. (2002). Distributed leadership as a unit of analysis. *Leadership Quarterly, 13*, 423–451.

Gutierrez, K. D., & Vossoughi, S. (2009). Lifting off the ground to return anew: Mediated praxis, transformative learning, and social design experiments. *Journal of Teacher Education, 61*, 100–117.

Hallinger, P., & Heck, R. H. (1996). The principal's role in school effectiveness: A review of methodological issues. In K. A. Leithwood (Ed.), *The international handbook of educational leadership and administration* (pp. 723–784). Dordrecht: Kluwer.

Harris, A. (2005). Leading or misleading? Distributed leadership and school improvement. *Journal of Curriculum Studies, 37*, 255–265.

Hawkins, D. (1967). I, thou, and it. In D. Hawkins (Ed.), *The informed vision: Essays on learning and human nature* (pp. 48–62). New York: Agathon.

Heck, R. H., & Hallinger, P. (1999). Next generation methods for the study of leadership and school improvement. In J. Murphy & K. S. Louis (Eds.), *Handbook of research on educational administration* (pp. 141–162). San Francisco: Jossey-Bass.

Hemphill, J. K. (1949). The leader and his group. *Educational Research Bulletin, 28*, 225–229.

Hutchins, E. (1995). How a cockpit remembers its speeds. *Cognitive Science, 19*, 265–288.

Jackson, P. W. (1968). *Life in classrooms*. New York: Holt, Rinehart, and Winston.

Jackson, K., & Bruegmann, E. (2009). Teaching students and teaching each other: The importance of peer learning for teachers. *American Economic Journal: Applied Economics, 1*, 85–108.

Lave, J., & Wenger, E. (1991). *Situated learning: Legitimate peripheral participation*. New York: Cambridge University Press.

Leithwood, K., Patten, S., & Jantzi, D. (2010). Testing a conception of how leadership influences student learning. *Educational Administration Quarterly, 46*(5), 671–706.

Leithwood, K. A., Louis, K. S., Anderson, S., & Wahlstrom, K. (2004). *How leadership influences student learning: A review of research for the learning from leadership project*. New York: Wallace Foundation.

Leithwood, K. A., Mascall, B., Strauss, T., Sacks, R., Memon, N., & Yashkina, A. (2007). Distributing leadership to make schools smarter: Taking the ego out of the system. *Leadership and Policy in Schools, 6*, 37–67.

Lester, F. K. (2005). On the theoretical, conceptual, and philosophical foundations for research in mathematics education. *ZDM, 37*, 457–467.

López, A., Correa-Chávez, M., Rogoff, B., & Gutierrez, K. D. (2010). Attention to instruction directed to another by us Mexican-heritage children of varying cultural backgrounds. *Developmental Psychology, 46*, 593–601.

Louis, K. S., & Kruse, S. D. (1995). *Professionalism and community: Perspectives on reforming urban schools*. Newbury Park: Corwin.

Lukes, S. (1974). *Power: A radical view*. London: Macmillan.

MacBeath, J., Oduro, G. K. T., & Waterhouse, J. (2005). *Distributed leadership in action: A study of current practice in schools*. Nottingham: National College for School Leadership.

Marris, P. (1974). *Loss and change*. London: Routledge & Kegan Paul.

Mitzel, H. E. (1960). Teacher effectiveness. In C. W. Harris (Ed.), *Encyclopaedia of educational research* (3rd ed., pp. 1481–1486). New York: Macmillan.

Moll, L. C. (1988). Some key issues in teaching Latino students. *Language Arts, 65*, 465–472.

Newmann, F. M., & Wehlage, G. G. (1995). *Successful school restructuring: A report to the public and educators*. Madison: Center on Organization and Restructuring of Schools.

Padgett, J., & Ansell, C. (1992). Robust action and the rise of the Medici. *American Journal of Sociology, 98*, 1259–1320.

Purkey, S. C., & Smith, M. S. (1983). Effective schools: A review. *Elementary School Journal, 83*, 426–452.

Robinson, V. M. J., Lloyd, C. A., & Rowe, K. J. (2008). The impact of leadership on student outcomes: An analysis of the differential effects of leadership types. *Educational Administration Quarterly, 44*, 635–674.

Rogoff, B. (2003). *The cultural nature of human development*. New York: Oxford University Press.

Rosenholtz, S. J. (1989). Workplace conditions that affect teacher quality and commitment: Implications for teacher induction programs. *Elementary School Journal, 89*, 421–439.

Rosenthal, R., & Jacobson, L. (1968). Pygmalion in the classroom. *The Urban Review, 3*, 16–20.

Scott, W. R. (2008). Approaching adulthood: The maturing of institutional theory. *Theory and Society, 37*, 427–442.

Scott, W. R. (2014). *Institutions and organizations: Ideas, interests, and identities* (4th ed.). Thousand Oaks: Sage.

Sebring, P., Allensworth, E., Bryk, A. S., Easton, J. Q., & Luppescu, S. (2006). *The essential supports for school improvement*. Chicago: Consortium on Chicago School Research.

Silins, H., & Mulford, B. (2002). Schools as learning organisations: The case for system, teacher and student learning. *Journal of Educational Administration, 40*, 425–446.

Simmel, G. (1955). *Conflict and the web of group affiliations*. New York: Free Press.

Spillane, J. P. (2006). *Distributed leadership*. San Francisco: Jossey-Bass.

Spillane, J. P., & Anderson, L. M. (2013). Administration des écoles, respect des normes gouvernementales, et obligation de résultats à forts enjeux: Changement politique et pédagogique aux états-unis. *Education et sociétiés, 32*, 53–73.

Spillane, J. P., & Coldren, A. F. (2011). *Diagnosis and design for school improvement: Using a distributed perspective to lead and manage change*. New York: Teachers College Press.

Spillane, J. P., & Diamond, J. B. (2007). *Distributed leadership in practice*. New York: Teachers College Press.

Spillane, J. P., & Healey, K. (2010). Conceptualizing school leadership and management from a distributed perspective. *Elementary School Journal, 111*, 253–281.

Spillane, J. P., & Louis, K. S. (2002). School improvement processes and practices: Professional learning for building instructional capacity. *Yearbook of the National Society for the Study of Education, 101*, 83–104.

Spillane, J. P., Halverson, R., & Diamond, J. B. (2001). Investigating school leadership practice: A distributed perspective. *Educational Researcher, 30*, 23–28.

Spillane, J. P., Camburn, E. M., & Pareja, A. S. (2007). Taking a distributed perspective to the school principal's workday. *Leadership and Policy in Schools, 6*, 103–125.

Spillane, J. P., Hunt, B., & Healey, K. (2009). Managing and leading elementary schools: Attending to the formal and informal organisation. *International Studies in Educational Administration, 37*, 5–28.

Spillane, J. P., Healey, K., & Kim, C. M. (2010). Leading and managing instruction: Using social network analysis to explore formal and informal aspects of the elementary school organization. In A. J. Daly (Ed.), *Social network theory and educational change* (pp. 129–156). Cambridge, MA: Harvard Education Press.

Stein, M. K., & Spillane, J. P. (2005). What can researchers on educational leadership learn from research on teaching? Building a bridge. In W. A. Firestone & C. Riehl (Eds.), *A new agenda for research in educational leadership* (pp. 28–45). New York: Teachers College Press.

Suchman, L. A. (1987). *Plans and situated actions: The problem of human-machine communication*. Cambridge, MA: Cambridge University Press.

Wertsch, J. V. (1991). A sociocultural approach to socially shared cognition. In L. B. Resnick, J. M. Levine, & S. D. Teasley (Eds.), *Perspectives on socially shared cognition* (pp. 85–100). Washington, DC: American Psychological Association.

Chapter 5
Effects of Distributed Leadership on School Academic Press and Student Achievement

John Malloy and Kenneth Leithwood

This study inquired about the effects of distributed leadership (Mascall et al. 2009) on teachers' academic optimism and students' math and language achievement. While leadership practices exercise a significant influence on student achievement, considerable evidence now indicates that such influence is mediated by internal school processes. (Hallinger and Heck 1996; Leithwood 2006; Robinson et al. 2008; Robinson and Timperley 2007). A growing body of evidence also argues for the increased impact of leadership practices enacted in a distributed fashion (Harris 2008).

Academic optimism is a composite variable including three factors, each of which has been associate positively with student achievement, including teacher commitment (e.g., Tschannen-Moran and Barr 2004; Ross and Gray 2006), teacher trust in clients (e.g., Bryk and Schneider 2002; Goddard et al. 2001) and academic emphasis or press (e.g., Lee and Smith 1999). Not surprisingly in light of such evidence, a growing body of research about academic optimism has also reported significant associations with achievement (Bevel and Mitchell 2012; Boonen et al. 2014; Hoy et al. 2006, 2008; Kirby and DiPaola 2011; Mitchell and Tarter in press; Smith and Hoy 2007; Wu et al. 2013). Distributed leadership is one plausible expression of the "enabling school structures" reported to be significant antecedents of academic optimism (Mitchell and Tarter in press; Tschannen-Moran 2009).

This study aimed to address three research questions. Do some patterns of distributed leadership have greater effects on academic optimism than others? To what extent does academic optimism mediate the effects of distributed leadership on student achievement? Which patterns of distributed leadership have the greatest effects on academic optimism and academic achievement?

J. Malloy
Toronto District School Board, 5050 Yonge Street, Toronto, ON M2N 5N8, Canada
e-mail: John.Malloy@tdsb.on.ca

K. Leithwood (✉)
Ontario Institute for Studies in Education, University of Toronto, Toronto, ON, Canada
e-mail: kenneth.leithwood@utoronto.ca

5.1 Framework

Summarizing the framework guiding the study, Fig. 5.1 proposes that four different patterns of distributed leadership (DL) each have direct effects on academic optimism (AO) and AO has direct effects on both the math and language achievement of students. The average socio-economic status (SES) of a school's students influence the status of each of the three primary variables in the study as well as moderate their relationships.

5.1.1 Patterns of Distributed Leadership

The bulk of research on distributed leadership in schools describes what such leadership amounts to in practice (Bennett et al. 2003; Gronn 2002; Harris et al. 2007; Harris and Spillane 2008; Leithwood et al. 2008; MacBeath 2005; Spillane 2006; Timperley 2005a). Distributed leadership is leadership practice shared by many (Harris 2003; Heller and Firestone 1995; O'Day 2002; Plowman et al. 2007; Spillane et al. 2007; Spillane and Diamond 2007; Timperley 2005b, 2008) and practiced in the "interactions between leaders, followers and their situation" (Spillane 2006, p. 26). Distributed leadership focuses attention on the expertise that individuals possess rather than the formal position they may hold (Anderson et al. 2008; Bennett et al. 2003; Heller and Firestone 1995; Leithwood and Jantzi 2006) and on how those providing leadership interact to provide such leadership to their organizations.

Distributed leadership is not simply a different form of delegation (Penlington et al. 2008). Delegated leadership typically means that the full array of leadership tasks that need to be performed are assigned to others, each of whom will typically enact them independently of others. Distributed leadership is not about people working independently on tasks that the formal leader has requested. Distribution of leadership implies that a network of individuals is working more or less interdependently to enact leadership practices toward a common goal. This network is strengthened through processes that focus their collective work and their learning (Halverson

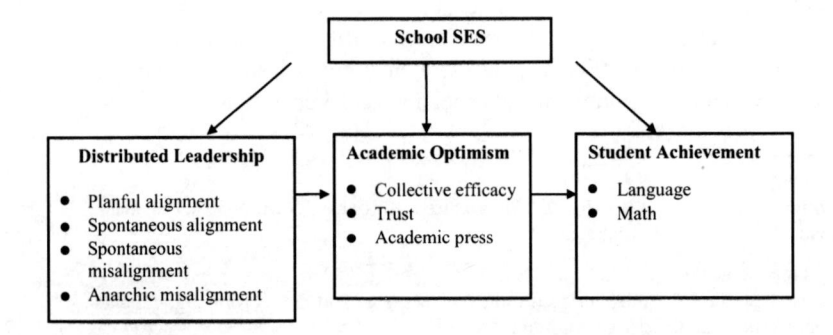

Fig. 5.1 Conceptual framework

2007) such as inquiry processes between teachers that enhance teacher capacity (Copeland 2003).

Leadership practices are distributed in distinctly different ways in schools, so identifying these different patterns is a critical part of research on distributed leadership effects. Different patterns may have different effects. There is, however, little consensus about how best to classify and describe such variation in leadership distribution. For example, one review (Leithwood et al. 2008) found .that patterns identified in the literature to date focused variously on five different classifications of patterns based on:

- the range of organizational members to whom leadership is distributed
- the degree to which distributed forms of leadership are coordinated
- the extent of interdependence among those to whom leadership is distributed
- the extent to which power and authority accompany the distribution of leadership responsibilities
- the stimulus for leadership distribution (Leithwood et al. 2008).

This study explored the effects[1] of four patterns identified during the first stage of a larger project within which this study is a subset, patterns based on the degree to which the distribution of leadership practices is coordinated. These patterns are labeled planful alignment, spontaneous alignment, spontaneous misalignment, and anarchic misalignment (for the evidence used to identify these patterns see Leithwood et al. (2007) and Mascall et al. (2009). The evidence used to identify these four patterns also found positive effects on teachers and students of only one of the patterns, planful alignment; the other three patterns actually had negative effects.

Planfully aligned distributed leadership exists when reflection and dialogue are the basis for decision making, when trust in the motivations and capacities of one's colleagues is present, when everyone understands their own and each other's role in the organization and when cooperation rather than competition described how people work together (Leithwood et al. 2007). When distributed leadership is planfully aligned, "the various sources of leadership consider which leadership practices or functions are best carried out by which source" (Mascall et al. 2009, p. 7). This study was also part of the second stage of this multi-step study which examined which patterns of distributed leadership matter most to student achievement

Planfully aligned distributed leadership relies on clear role clarification, effective communication, a defined understanding of the accountabilities that exist, and an understanding of who on staff possesses various expertise (Day and Leithwood 2007). A coherent vision must be maintained in the schools (Mayrowetz et al. 2008) and a common culture is needed to promote effective practice (Elmore 2000). Planfully aligned distributed leadership means that those who are the sources of leadership in the school determine which leadership practices and functions are

---

[1] The terms "effects" and "impacts" are used throughout the study even though evidence from the study is correlational in nature, supporting only weak causal claims. The study's use of the terms "effects" and "impacts" is consistent with widely accepted reporting conventions for analyses such as those included in this study

needed and who will exercise these functions and practices at any given time (Leithwood et al. 2007; Mascall et al. 2009).

5.1.2 Academic Optimism

A small but compelling line of research has found that when teachers a) possess a strong sense of collective efficacy, b) trust parents, students, their fellow educators and leaders, and c) believe that all students have the potential to succeed (academic press), a significant contribution is made to student achievement (Hoy et al. 2006; McGuigan and Hoy 2006; Smith and Hoy 2007). These three factors, collective efficacy, trust and academic press, considered together, form the variable Hoy et al. (2006) have labeled academic optimism.

Collective Efficacy The concept of collective efficacy is based in social cognitive theory about self-efficacy (Bandura 1986). Self-efficacy, a form of self-reflection which Bandura believes mediates knowledge and action, is defined as "people's beliefs in their capabilities to mobilize the motivation, cognitive resources and courses of action needed to exercise control over events in their lives" (Wood and Bandura 1989, p. 364). When people experience self-efficacy, they engage in challenging activities for a longer period of time and persevere more often when facing challenges compared to those who may have the knowledge and skills but lack this belief in their own capability (Wood and Bandura 1989).

Self-efficacy and collective efficacy are closely related (Goddard et al. 2000a) and the sources of collective efficacy are the same as the sources of self-efficacy: mastery experience, vicarious experience, verbal persuasion and physiological states of arousal (Goddard et al. 2000b). Learning takes place in different ways: through mastery experiences in which the learner engages directly; through vicarious experience which usually involves modeling by someone with greater capacity in a certain area; through verbal persuasions which are verbal judgments that must be perceived by the learner as authentic and the goals communicated through these persuasions must be perceived as attainable; and through physiological states which may be characterized as anxiety, stress, fatigue, satisfaction and calm (to name a few examples) which impact the environments in which we live (Bandura 1986; Wood and Bandura 1989).

Potentially, in a school with a strong sense of collective efficacy, teachers model for each other. In these schools, the norm is to share responsibility, to make commitments based upon shared beliefs and to learn from each other (Goddard et al. 2000a; Tschannen-Moran and Barr 2004). The perception teachers hold of themselves and of their colleagues will influence their actions. These actions will be judged by the group relative to group norms. In this way, collective efficacy impacts personal perceptions and group norms and these perceptions and norms impact actions (Goddard et al. 2000a, b). High-quality teaching must be internalized in the professional culture of schools. In other words, where collective efficacy exists, teachers may exhibit the ability to persevere and together they accept the challenges they face to improve student achievement for all students. Where there is a strong sense of collective efficacy, evidence suggests that teachers are more likely to maintain high standards, to concentrate on academic instruction, to monitor on-task behaviour and to build friendly, non-threatening relationships with students (Ashton et al. 1983).

Trust There is a positive correlation between teachers' sense of efficacy and trust between teachers and teachers, teachers and students, and teachers and parents (Tschannen-Moran and Barr 2004). Hoy et al. (2006) define trust as "one's vulnerability to another in terms of the belief that the other will act in one's best interest" (p. 429). When trust in schools means that staff is willing to be vulnerable to each other based on the belief that everyone in the community is benevolent, reliable, competent, honest, and open (McGuigan and Hoy 2006). Where there is a significant sense of trust, teachers report that they feel supported, they feel their interests are reflected, and they are involved in decision making (Louis 2007). The relationship between distributed leadership and trust is mutual and dynamic (Smylie et al. 2007).

Trust is a necessary component for school improvement (Bryk and Schneider 2002; Tschannen-Moran and Hoy 1998) because without it, teachers would not feel compelled to work together to bring about change (Louis 2007), nor would there be the ability to challenge existing structures where necessary (Regine and Lewin 2000). Systemic change is not possible without trust (Louis 2007). Schools with relational trust are more likely to implement changes that might be attributed to improved student achievement. By examining 400 Chicago elementary schools over a 10-year period, Bryk and Schneider (2002) concluded that relational trust consists of respect, competence, personal regard for others and integrity and that the success of any reform that is needed in schools hinges upon the degree of relational trust that exists in these schools.

Evidence suggests that trust impacts teacher commitment (Bryk et al. 1999) and where trust is present, teachers are more willing to engage in vicarious learning (Goddard et al. 2000a, b). Vicarious learning is an effective way to build collective efficacy because teachers are willing to learn from the expertise of others. This is another indicator of the explicit connection between trust and collective efficacy. Trust is also a foundational element for professional learning communities. Trust is developed when teachers share ideas with one another and through this experience, the members of the professional learning community gain the reputation as being trustworthy (Halverson 2007). Trust and cooperation are products of common learning goals shared by students, parents and teachers, and teaching and learning improve when trust exists (Hoy et al. 2006).

Trust in schools may improve student achievement. According to Hoy et al. (2006), "trust and cooperation among students, teachers and parents influenced regular student attendance, persistent learning, and faculty experimentation with new practices" (p. 430). Trust is a necessary ingredient that assists teachers to learn from one another about how to meet the needs of each student in the school. Trust between teachers and especially elementary students, which is highly correlated with the trust between teachers and parents, allows teachers to be innovative without worrying about parental response because cooperation between parents and teachers for the sake of the students is so strong (Hoy et al. 2006). Trust between teachers and teachers, teachers and students, and teachers and parents, potentially allows common learning goals to be created and achieved, leading to improved student achievement.

Academic Press Academic press, the third component of academic optimism, includes high expectations that are communicated by teachers to students about their academic efforts. Academic press is evident when schools make academic achievement their central purpose (McGuigan and Hoy 2006), and when teachers believe that students are capable of academic success regardless of their learning styles and needs (Anderson 2008). Further, academic press is evident when high yet achievable goals are set for students, students work hard and the culture in the schools assists students to respect academic achievement (Hoy et al. 2006).

Academic press or emphasis is associated with improved student achievement even when controlling for socio-economic status (Hoy et al. 2006). Indeed, some evidence indicates that "academic emphasis, rather than instructional leadership [is] the critical variable explaining achievement" (2006, p. 427). According to Bandura, there is a reciprocal relationship between academic press and student achievement (Bandura 1997). As student achievement improves, teachers increase academic press which further enhances student achievement.

Collective efficacy, trust and academic press together form the variable academic optimism. Evidence suggests that high levels of academic optimism contribute to student achievement across schools serving students with widely varying family backgrounds (Hoy et al. 2006) This variable has a cognitive function (collective efficacy) which speaks to how teachers perceive their own skills; an affective function (trust) which speaks to the important relationships between teachers and parents, students, others teachers and administrators; and a behavioral function (academic press) which speaks to the way teachers demonstrate their expectations for students to achieve (Smith and Hoy 2007). These three components, Hoy et al. (2006) claim, enhance each other to create effective conditions for learning in schools.

Three studies provide evidence to support the claim that a significant correlation exists between academic optimism and student achievement. (Hoy et al. 2006; McGuigan and Hoy 2006; Smith and Hoy 2007). Hoy et al.'s study (Hoy et al. 2006) was conducted with a sample of 96 high schools in a Midwestern U.S. state. Results of this study suggested that academic optimism was strongly related to a student achievement at the organizational level. Smith and Hoy (2007) explored the relationship between academic optimism and student achievement in elementary schools using a sample of 99 urban elementary schools in Texas. This study found significant relationships between improvement of student achievement in mathematics and academic optimism (Smith and Hoy 2007). The authors contend that "Academic optimism is a powerful motivator because it focuses on potential with its strength and resilience rather than pathology with its attendant weakness and helplessness" (p. 567).

McGuigan and Hoy (2006) explored the enabling structures that enhance academic optimism in a school. Teachers in 40 elementary schools in Ohio were surveyed to measure the levels of academic press, trust and collective efficacy in a school. The results of this study suggest that academic optimism is an organizational variable that improves student achievement and that enabling structures support the enhancement of academic optimism (McGuigan and Hoy 2006).

Students' Socio-economic Status Poor student achievement has often been attributed to low socio-economic status (SES). The Coleman report (Coleman et al. 1966) spoke about the negative consequences of low SES on student achievement citing that the characteristics of the school had a minimal effect on student achievement in the face of socio-economic challenges. Researchers have attempted to disprove this theory for decades and the research on academic optimism has contributed to this body of research (Hoy et al. 2006; McGuigan and Hoy 2006).

Boonen et al. (2014) "school mean socioeconomic status and school mean prior achievement are mainly indirectly associated with student achievement through academic optimism".

Wu et al. (2013) SES not related to student achievement in this study conducted in Taiwan but it was negatively related to academic optimism.

Bevel and Mitchell (2012) SES negatively related to all variables in the study including academic optimism and its components , as well as student achievement.

Kirby and DiPaola (2011) Academic optimism is negatively related to academic optimism ("teacher attitudes about students from low SES homes affects the academic optimism of a faculty" page554. 74% of the variance in student achievement explained by academic optimism

Hoy et al. (2006) Academic optimism made a significant contribution to student achievement after controlling for demographic variables and previous achievement. Effects on achievement were approximately the same for SES and Academic optimism

5.2 Methods

5.2.1 Sample

The population for this study was all 4450 teachers in 165 elementary schools in an Ontario school district with a long standing commitment to distributed leadership. Because of this commitment, there could be a greater chance that distributed leadership in some form would have been experienced by the survey respondents. This school district served students in urban, suburban and rural areas and the socio-economic demographic of the families served by this school district varied widely. The district served more than 70,000 elementary students. This study was part of the second phase of a distributed leadership research project conducted in this district over 3 years.[2]

Those schools in which at least six teachers responded to the survey were included so the achieved sample for the study was 2122 (47% response rate) elementary teachers located in 113 schools (68% response rate). The school was the unit of analysis used for answering all research questions.

5.2.2 Instruments

Data for this study were collected through a survey instrument administered to teachers, as well as evidence about student achievement data provided by Ontario's Education Quality and Accountability Office test (EQAO). Socio-economic status (SES) data for each school were provided by Statistics Canada and further refined by the district itself.

The teacher survey requested information about academic optimism, patterns of leadership distribution in their schools and factors assumed to influence such distribution. Items on the survey, using a seven-point response scale, were adapted from: the measure of academic optimism used by Hoy and his colleagues (Hoy et al. 2006; Hoy and Fedmen 1987; McGuigan and Hoy 2006; Smith and Hoy 2007); the measures of trust in leaders developed by both Podsakoff et al. (1990) and Bryk and Schneider (2002); the measure of trust between teachers developed by Bryk and Schneider (2002); the measure of collective efficacy by Ross et al. (2004); and the measure of distributed leadership used by Mascall et al. (2009). Specific items measuring academic optimism are described in Table 5.1.

One statement on the survey was used to measure each of four patterns of leadership distribution: planfully aligned, spontaneously aligned, spontaneously misaligned and anarchically misaligned distributed leadership. For planfully aligned distributed leadership the statement was: Leaders across this school collectively plan who should perform which leadership functions and they tend to follow the arrangements. For spontaneous alignment the statement was: Leadership tasks in this school are distributed with little or no planning. This distribution, however, is usually productive. For spontaneous misalignment the question was: Leadership tasks in this school are distributed with little or no planning. This distribution is not productive and often leads to confusion. For anarchical misalignment the statement was: Leaders coordinate their work carefully within their sub-units (divisions, departments, teams) but they do not coordinate their work with other sub-units.

The survey also requested demographic information about each respondent: including grade(s) taught, number of years in the present school, years of experience in education, grades included in the respondents' schools and the enrolment in

---

[2] This study is a secondary analysis of evidence collected by a study of distributed leadership led by Dr. Ken Leithwood. I was part of the team that designed the study and the analyses in this thesis extends beyond the analysis completed as part of the original project.

Table 5.1 Survey questions for academic optimism and each of its components

Academic optimism

Trust in leaders

1. I feel quite confident the leaders at my school always try to treat me fairly
2. I feel a strong loyalty to our school leaders
3. I would support the leaders at my school in almost any emergency
4. It's ok in this school to discuss feelings, worries and frustrations with school leaders
5. Leaders in our school look out for the personal welfare of teachers in this school

Trust in teachers

6. Teachers in this school really care about each other
7. Teachers in this school really trust each other
8. It's OK in this school to discuss feeling, worries and frustrations with other teachers
9. Teachers in this school respect colleagues who take the lead in school improvement efforts

Collective efficacy

10. If a student doesn't learn something the first time, teachers in this school will try another way.
11. Teachers in this school really believe every student can learn
12. If a student doesn't want to learn, most teachers here give up (R)
13. Teachers in my school need more training to know how to deal with the students who aren't learning.(R)
14. Teachers in my school don't have the skills needed to produce meaningful student learning. (R)

Academic press

15. My school sets high standards for academic success
16. Students respect others who get good grades
17. Students seek extra work so that they can be successful
18. Students try hard to improve on previous work
19. Academic achievement is recognized and acknowledged at my school
20. The learning environment in my school is orderly and focused

the school. The full survey was field-tested and refined prior to administration by inviting 16 teachers, representing four geographic areas in the school district to respond to the survey and provide feedback about the clarity and intention of individual survey statements.

Student achievement data used for this study were collected by the province's Educational Quality and Accountability Office (EQAO) in 2008. The mean for student achievement in English was determined by averaging the Grade 3 and Grade 6 reading and writing scores for those schools where six or more of the teachers participated in the survey. The mean for math was determined by averaging the Grade 3 and Grade 6 math scores for those schools which were included in this study. This mean represents the average number of students who achieved a level 3 or 4 on this test in 2008; the province has set level 3 as an acceptable standard of achievement for all students.

School socio-economic status was estimated using evidence provided by Statistics Canada for each school area about average family income and percentage of parents who had not graduated from high school The two variables were combined to create a measure of socio-economic status (SES) for each school 2006 Census date were merged with geographic data from student records. The smallest geographic area for which data were available from the Census was the dissemination area (DA), which is a neighborhood made up of 400 to 700 people. Student postal codes were linked with their corresponding dissemination areas, which allowed for assignment of Census data to individual students based on where they lived. This was the best option available, given that Statistics Canada does not release data that identifies individual households.

5.2.3 Analysis

Means and standard deviations of each item and scale were calculated. The internal reliability of each scale was tested using Cronbach's alpha. Correlations between variables were estimated and Structural Equation Modeling (SEM) was used for hypotheses testing. In this study, the relationship between different patterns of distributed leadership and each component of academic optimism was examined and then the relationship between each component of academic optimism and math and language achievement was examined. Academic optimism as a single variable was also examined in relation to different patterns of distributed leadership and both math and language achievement.

5.2.4 Results and Discussion

Table 5.2 shows the mean and standard deviation of teachers' responses to the survey using a Likert scale for four statements about leadership patterns and 20 statements about academic optimism. This table also includes mean SES data for the 113 sample schools, r the reliability of the multi-item scales used to measure academic optimism, and student achievement averages in both language and math.

Table 5.2 indicates that the scale for academic optimism and each of its components is reliable (Cronbach's alpha), exceeding .7.

5.2.5 Patterns of Distributed Leadership

Evidence in Table 5.2 indicates that teachers agreed that Planfully Aligned form of distributed leadership were evident in their schools to a greater extent (4.63) than either Anarchic Misalignment (3.82), Spontaneous Alignment (3.25), or Spontaneous Misalignment (2.73). The standard deviations for all four patterns fell in a narrow

Table 5.2 Means, standard deviations, scale reliabilities and number of items for variables in studies

	Mean	SD	Reliability	Number
Leadership patterns:			NA	
Planful alignment	4.63	.54		1
Spontaneous alignment	3.25	.53		1
Spontaneous misalignment	2.73	.65		1
Anarchic misalignment	3.82	.47		1
Academic optimism	5.27	.41	.74	20
Collective efficacy	5.42	.46	.91	5
Trust in leaders	5.44	.60	.96	5
Trust among teachers	5.31	.63	.96	4
Academic press	4.92	.48	.86	6
Student achievement in language	.73	.11	NA	NA
Student achievement in Mathematics	.73	.13	NA	NA
Collective school SES	.04	.92	NA	NA

N=113 schools [2122 teachers]

range (.41–.65) suggesting approximately similar distribution of responses by teachers to items measuring each of the four patterns.

5.2.6 Academic Optimism

The results for academic optimism as an aggregate variable, as well as the results for each component of academic optimism, suggested relatively high levels of academic optimism in these schools. As Table 5.2 indicates, the measures of component variables were found to be more reliable (.91, .96, .96, .86) then the reliability of the aggregate variable (.74). even though the number of items is much greater for the aggregate variable.

Table 5.3 reports the means and standard deviations of responses (using a seven-point scale) to the 20 items measuring academic optimism. The mean of 5.27 for academic optimism as an aggregate was relatively high and teachers did not differ widely in their perceptions (SD .41). Of the components of Academic Optimism, ratings of Collective Efficacy were 5.42 (SD .46), Trust in Leaders 5.44 (SD .60), Trust among Teachers 5.31 (SD .63) and Academic Press 4.92 (SD .48). These data suggest moderately high levels of academic optimism and its four components but with academic press rated lowest. Table 5.3 also indicates considerable consistency in teacher responses to the statements. The mean for most of the responses exceeded 5, meaning that the teachers agreed that each aspect of academic optimism was present in their school. Standard deviation fell in a relatively narrow (and low) range (.41 to .74). A reverse scale was used for three statements (12, 13 and 14) determining teachers' perceptions of collective efficacy.

Table 5.3 Mean and standard deviation for each survey question

	Mean	SD
Academic optimism	5.27	0.41
Trust in leaders	5.44	0.60
1. I feel quite confident the leaders at my school always try to treat me fairly	5.44	0.63
2. I feel a strong loyalty to our school leaders	5.29	0.67
3. I would support the leaders at my school in almost any emergency	6.06	0.51
4. It's ok in this school to discuss feelings, worries and frustrations with school leaders	5.18	0.68
5. Leaders in our school look out for the personal welfare of teachers in this school	5.22	0.74
Trust in teachers	5.31	0.63
6. Teachers in this school really care about each other	5.54	0.66
7. Teachers in this school really trust each other	5.14	0.70
8. It's OK in this school to discuss feeling, worries and frustrations with other teachers	5.24	0.65
9. Teachers in this school respect colleagues who take the lead in school improvement efforts	5.32	0.66
Collective efficacy	5.42	0.46
10. If a student doesn't learn something the first time, teachers in this school will try another way	5.86	0.45
11. Teachers in this school really believe every student can learn	5.74	0.50
12. If a student doesn't want to learn, most teachers here give up (R)	5.77	0.54
13. Teachers in my school need more training to know how to deal with the students who aren't learning (R)	3.91	0.59
14. Teachers in my school don't have the skills needed to produce meaningful student learning (R)	5.81	0.55
Academic press	4.92	0.48
15. My school sets high standards for academic success	5.63	0.60
16. Students respect others who get good grades	5.03	0.57
17. Students seek extra work so that they can be successful	3.75	0.64
18. Students try hard to improve on previous work	4.37	0.51
19. Academic achievement is recognized and acknowledged at my school	5.40	0.57
20. The learning environment in my school is orderly and focused	5.35	0.65

Table 5.3 also indicates relatively low ratings (below 4.0) for two items. The two statements were "Teachers in my school need more training to know how to deal with the students who are not learning" and "Students seek extra work so that they can be successful". Because the first statement is a reverse scored statement, the lower mean suggests that a significant number of teachers agree with this statement. This desire or willingness to engage in professional training in order to meet the needs of students who are not learning actually indicates a quality of collective efficacy in which teachers will persevere until they have found the solutions to assist each student's learning. The second statement refers to the perception teachers hold

about their students and this mean suggests many of their students do not seek extra work in order to be successful.

It is important to note that similar to the statement "Teachers in my school need more training to know how to deal with the students who are not learning", which was mentioned above, two more statements were also reverse scored statements. The two statements were "If a student doesn't want to learn, most teachers here give up" and "Teachers in my school don't have the skills needed to produce meaningful student learning". For these three statements a higher response means that teachers did not agree with the statement and obviously a lower response would mean more agreement. Though there was moderate agreement that teachers may need more training to deal with students who are not learning, there was disagreement that teachers give up on students who do not wish to learn (5.77) and teachers do not have the skills to produce meaningful student learning (5.81).

5.2.7 Socio-economic Status

SES was measured using median family income and the proportion of working age population with less than a high school education. As was previously described, this number is a school-based SES score determined from the individual score of each student in the school. Since these two variables have different units of measurement (i.e., $ for income and % for education), the standardized scores (also referred to as Z scores) were computed for each variable. For each school, Z scores were calculated for both income and education. This allowed for the combination of income and education into a single value because they were now measured using the same unit (i.e., number of standard deviations from the mean). By standardizing values in this way, the resulting distribution of values is always normal, with a mean of 0 and standard deviation of 1. For example, School A might have a Z score of 0.215 for income and −0.125 for education. This means that the median income of School A is 0.215 standard deviation units above the mean and the % of adults with less than high school is 0.125 standard deviation units below the mean.

To compute SES, the two values (income and education) for each school were averaged. Because the average of the two values was computed (as opposed to just adding them together), a mean of 0 and a standard deviation of 1 was retained for the distribution of SES scores. So, for School A, SES is computed as .045 standard deviation units above the mean of 0. Because the data from this school district were created to determine the schools with the lowest SES, a reverse code was used. In other words, positive numbers refer to schools with lower SES and negative numbers refer to schools with higher SES. The SES values in this district ranged from 2.671 (the school with the lowest SES) and −2.229 (the school with the highest SES) with a mean of 0 and a standard deviation of 1; therefore, a mean of .040 and a standard deviation of .92 would suggest that these 113 schools represent socio-economic diversity but serve a slightly lower SES demographic when compared to the rest of the district.

5.2.8 Student Achievement

To determine the mean for student achievement (Table 5.2), the 2008 EQAO Assessment for Grade 3 and Grade 6 students was used for the 113 schools where at least six teachers participated in the survey. This assessment determines student proficiency in reading, writing and math. A student is considered to be at standard when they score a level 3 or 4 (out of 4) on this assessment. The language score is the average of the reading and writing results and the numeracy score is the math result. For both scores, the average of Grade 3 and Grade 6 was determined. For example, if the score in Grade 3 reading was 68, in Grade 3 writing was 72, in Grade 6 reading was 74 and in Grade 6 writing was 71, the student achievement score in language for this school was calculated in the following way: (68+72+74+71= 285/4 = 71.25).

The mean for student achievement in language was .73 (SD .11). The mean for student achievement in math was .73 (SD .13). The mean for both math and language indicates the percentage of students who achieved level 3 and 4 on these assessments in the 113 schools. The 113 schools participating in this study would be considered similar to all of the schools in this district because the district average in math and language was also .73 in both subjects. The relatively small standard deviation in language (.11) and math (.13) indicates that most students in these 113 schools performed successfully. Compared to the Ontario provincial EQAO average in 2008 which was .65 for both language and math, these 113 schools performed above the province average in 2008.

5.3 The Relationship Between Leadership Patterns and Academic Optimism

Table 5.4 reports the correlations between the four patterns of distributed leadership and academic optimism including its component variables. These data begin to address one research question "Do some patterns of distributed leadership have greater effects on academic optimism than others?"

Planfully aligned distributed leadership is significantly and positively related to academic optimism as well as each of its components. Spontaneous alignment is negatively, (though not significantly) related to academic optimism and each of its components with one exception; the correlation between spontaneous alignment and academic press is positive yet insignificant. Spontaneous misalignment is negatively and significantly related to academic optimism and each component, while anarchic misalignment has a negative correlation to academic optimism and its components, with the exception of the correlation between anarchic misalignment and academic press where there is a positive yet insignificant correlation similar to spontaneous misalignment. The negative correlation is only significant between anarchic misalignment and academic optimism, trust in leaders and trust in teachers.

Table 5.4 Relationships between SES, Leadership patterns and academic optimism

	Academic optimism	Collective efficacy	Trust in leaders	Trust in teachers	Academic press	SES
Planful alignment	.54[a]	.40[a]	.52[a]	.32[a]	.38[a]	−.07
Spontaneous alignment	−.04	−.08	−.06	−.07	.09	−.04
Spontaneous misalignment	−.50[a]	−.31[a]	−.57[a]	−.34[a]	−.24[b]	.10
Anarchic misalignment	−.26[a]	−.18	−.30[a]	−.34[a]	.11	.00
Collective school SES	−.31[a]	−.12	−.26[a]	−.21[b]	−.32[a]	1.00[a]

Correlation Coefficients, N = 113
[a]Correlation is significant at the 0.01 level (2-tailed)
[b]Correlation is significant at the 0.05 level (2-tailed)

The correlation between SES and academic optimism and SES and each aspect of academic optimism is negative. This correlation is significant for the relationship between SES and academic optimism as a whole and between trust in leaders, trust in teachers and academic press. These results indicate less incidence of academic optimism in schools serving students with lower socio-economic status. SES has a negative correlation to each pattern of distributed leadership with the exception of spontaneous misalignment. None of these correlations are significant.

Planfully aligned distributed leadership is the only leadership pattern that has a positive and significant correlation to academic optimism and it components - collective efficacy, trust and academic press. Planfully aligned forms of distributed leadership have similar relationships with each component of academic optimism. The strength of the relationship between planfully aligned distributed leadership and each component of academic optimism is a moderate one ranging from .32 to .54.

5.3.1 The Relationship Between Academic Optimism and Student Achievement

Table 5.5 reports the correlations between SES and student achievement and academic optimism and student achievement in the 113 schools in this study. These results do not replicate previous findings (Hoy et al. 2006; McGuigan and Hoy 2006; Smith and Hoy 2007). The correlation between aggregate academic optimism and language achievement is a non-significant .13 and between aggregate academic optimism and mathematics achievement a non-significant .11. In contrast, some previous studies have reported a statistically significant relationship between academic optimism and math and language achievement of .21 and .27 respectively (Hoy et al. 2006), .54 for math and .50 for language (McGuigan and Hoy 2006) and .34 for math (Smith and Hoy 2007).

Table 5.5 Relationships between SES, Academic optimism and student achievement on 2008 EQAO tests

	Grades 3 & 6 Achievement		
	Language	Mathematics	SES
Academic optimism	.13	.11	−.31[a]
Collective efficacy	.04	.03	−.12
Trust in leaders	.06	.06	−.26[a]
Trust in teachers	−.14	−.16	−.21[b]
Academic press	.52[a]	.50[a]	−.32[a]
Collective school SES	−.38	−.32[a]	1.00[a]

Correlation Coefficients, N = 113
[a]Correlation is significant at the 0.01 level (2-tailed)
[b]Correlation is significant at the 0.05 level (2-tailed)

Though this study does not show a statistically significant correlation between academic optimism and student achievement in language and math, there is a statistically significant and positive correlation between academic press and language achievement of .52 and between academic press and math achievement of .50. Correlations between student math and language achievement and any other component of academic optimism are not significant.

5.3.2 Planfully Aligned Distributed Leadership and Academic Press

Path models were calculated using planfully aligned distributed leadership as the independent variable, academic press as a mediating variable, and students' math and language achievement as the dependent variable. Results of testing these two models are described in Figs. 5.1 and 5.3 which also demonstrate the effects of SES, treated as a moderator.

Figure 5.1 illustrates the effects of planfully aligned distributed leadership and academic press on language achievement. In this figure, the regression coefficient between planfully aligned distributed leadership and academic press is .36. This effect is statistically significant as is the regression coefficient between academic press and student language achievement which is .44. Collective school SES has a negative but statistically insignificant effect on planfully aligned distributed leadership (−.07) and a negative but statistically significant effect on academic press (−.30). The effect of collective school SES on student language achievement is negative and statistically significant (−.24) as would be expected from previous research (Fig. 5.2).

Figure 5.2 indicates a statistically significant and moderately strong direct effect (regression coefficient = .36) of planfully aligned distributed leadership on academic press and a slightly stronger significant direct effect (regression coefficient = .44) of academic press on students language achievement. Collective school SES

Fig. 5.2 SES, Planful alignment, and academic press effect on language achievement

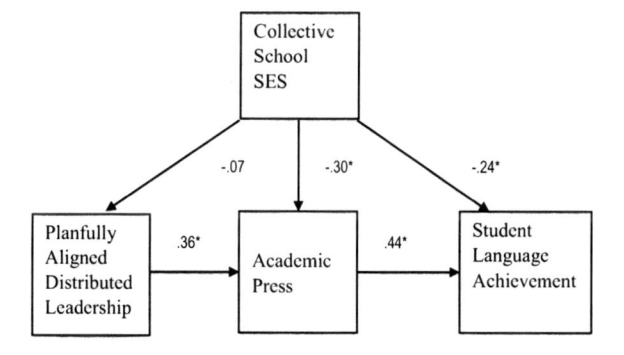

```
                        Collective
                        School
                        SES
                  -.07    -.30*         -.24*
        ┌──────────┐  .36*  ┌────────┐  .44*  ┌──────────┐
        │ Planfully│───────▶│Academic│───────▶│ Student  │
        │ Aligned  │        │ Press  │        │ Language │
        │Distributed│       │        │        │Achievement│
        │Leadership│        └────────┘        └──────────┘
        └──────────┘
```

Explained Variance:	
Leadership	.00
Academic Press	.24
Student Language Achievement	.32

Fit Indices		Standardized Total Effects of:	Student Achievement
RMSEA	.00	SES	-.38*
RMR	.02	Leadership: Planful Alignment	.16*
AGFI	.96	Academic Press	.44*
NFI	.99		
X2 = .93, df= 1, p= 0.33			

has negative direct effects on all three of the other variables in this model; this effect is statistically significant in the case of both academic press (−.30) and student language achievement (− .24).

The Fig. 5.1 model, as a whole, explains 24% of the variation in academic press and 32% of the variation in student language achievement. Of the 32% of variation in student language achievement accounted for by this model (Standardized Total Effects data) academic press explains a statistically significant 44% while planfully aligned distributed leadership explains a statistically significant 16%. Most of the remaining variation is accounted for by collective school SES (−.38).

Witziers et al. reported a direct effect size of .02 when studying the direct effects of leadership on student achievement. This conclusion was drawn from the meta-analysis of 37 multinational studies (Witziers et al. 2003). According to Marzano et al. (2005) who studied the direct and indirect effect of leadership on students' achievement, the effect that was determined from this meta-analysis was .40. Since the standardized total effect of planfully aligned distributed leadership and academic press is .60, this result exceeds the effect concluded from previous studies.

Fig. 5.3 SES, Planful alignment, and academic press effect on mathematics achievement

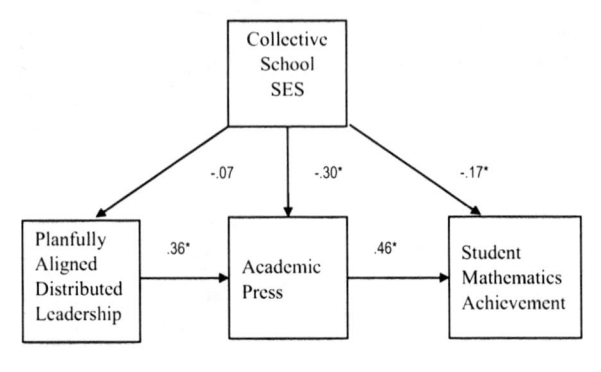

```
                        ┌─────────────┐
                        │ Collective  │
                        │   School    │
                        │    SES      │
                        └──┬───┬───┬──┘
                     -.07  │   │-.30*  -.17*
              ┌────────────┘   │       └──────────┐
              ▼                ▼                  ▼
      ┌────────────┐   ┌────────────┐    ┌────────────┐
      │ Planfully  │   │            │    │  Student   │
      │  Aligned   │.36*│  Academic │.46*│Mathematics │
      │Distributed │──▶│   Press   │───▶│Achievement │
      │ Leadership │   │            │    │            │
      └────────────┘   └────────────┘    └────────────┘
```

Explained Variance:	
Leadership	.00
Academic Press	.24
Student Mathematics Achievement	.29

Fit Indices		Standardized Total Effects of:	Student Achievement
RMSEA	.11	SES	-.32*
RMR	.04	Leadership: Planful Alignment	.17*
AGFI	.89	Academic Press	.46*
NFI	.97		
$X2 = 2.41$, df= 1, p= 0.12			

Therefore, this model supports the positive effect planfully aligned distributed leadership and academic press together have on student achievement.

Figure 5.3 illustrates the effects of planfully aligned distributed leadership and academic press on math achievement. In this figure, the effect of planfully aligned distributed leadership on academic press is .36. This effect is statistically significant. The effect of academic press on student math achievement is .46; again this is a statistically significant effect. The collective school SES has a negative yet insignificant effect on planfully aligned distributed leadership (−.07) and a negative and significant effect on academic press (−.30). The effect of collective school SES on student math achievement is negative and significant (−.17). Figure 5.3 indicates a statistically significant and moderately strong direct effect (regression coefficient = .36) of planfully aligned distributed leadership on academic press and a slightly stronger significant direct effect (regression coefficient = .46) of academic press on students' mathematics achievement. Collective school SES has negative direct effects on all three of the other variables in this model; this effect is significant in the case of both academic press (−.30) and student language achievement (− .17).

The Fig. 5.3 model, as a whole, explains 24% of the variation in academic press and 29% of the variation in student mathematics achievement. Of the 29% of variation in student mathematics achievement accounted for by this model (Standardized Total Effects data) academic press explains a significant 46% while planfully aligned distributed leadership explains a significant 17%. Most of the remaining variation is accounted for by collective school SES (−.32). Since the standardized total effect of planfully aligned distributed leadership is .17, this effect is significant compared to direct leadership effects concluded from previous studies.

These findings vary from previous studies which concluded that the proportion of between-school variance in student math and language achievement explained by collective efficacy was .53 and .69 respectively (Goddard et al. 2000a, b), and the proportion of between-school variance explained by trust was .81 for both math and reading achievement (Goddard et al. 2001). Similar findings were found previously for academic press: the proportion of between- school variance in math achievement explained by academic press was .47 and in reading achievement .50. These results also challenge previous findings that academic optimism has a significant direct effect on student achievement. Academic press alone had a significant and positive impact on student achievement.

5.4 Conclusions and Implications

Three significant features of the study limit the robustness of its findings. First, evidence for the study came from only one large school district, a district with long-standing commitments to improving achievement by encouraging the development of distributed leadership in schools. This context is by no means representative of districts at large. Second, each pattern of distributed leadership was measured using only one survey item, whereas multi-item scales measuring each pattern would be likely to produce more reliable evidence about the status of each pattern in schools. Third, the evidence used to estimate student achievement was 1-year school averages; longitudinal evidence of changes in achievement would have allowed for a more direct test of the impact on improvements in achievement of the independent and mediating variables of interest in the study.

Notwithstanding these limitations, evidence from this study challenge the results of some previous research about both the contributions of academic optimism to student achievement and the widespread support for undefined concepts of "shared leadership. Among the components included in our aggregate measure of academic optimism, only academic press demonstrated significant effects on student achievement. Prior evidence does indicate that academic press, considered by itself, has a significant impact on achievement (e.g., Goddard et al. 2000a, b). Perhaps the other two components of academic optimism (trust and efficacy) contribute to student achievement only in so far as they enable the development of academic press in schools. Conceptually, academic press seems to be the closest of these three components to the expectations teachers and parents hold for student learning and that students hold for themselves. Perhaps high levels of efficacy and trust encourage both students and teachers to risk the effort and commitment required to achieve beyond previous expectations. Using research designs that encompass all three components of academic optimism, future research testing that possibility would be useful.

There is some research on changing the attitudes and beliefs of teachers that hinder the development of high levels of academic press (Timperley and Robinson 2002), as well as the types of instructional decisions teachers make and the classroom environments they create based upon their attitudes about their students (Rubie-Davis et al. 2011). However, given the substantial contribution to student achievement of high academic press, additional research aimed at determining what school leaders might do to develop it in their schools is clearly warranted.

While all four patterns of distributed leadership included in the study are legitimate manifestations of "shared leadership", only the "planfully aligned" pattern had positive relationships with academic optimism and its components, as well as with student math and language achievement; the three other patterns actually had negative relationships with these variables. These results, should they be confirmed through subsequent research, are a call for much more discriminating approaches to sharing leadership, whether such sharing is across those in administrative roles or with teachers, parents and students. Unless such sharing is well coordinated and intentional, these results suggest, the outcome is likely to be confusion or conflict about organizational directions and strategy. Future research (using multi-scale measures of distributed leadership patterns) is needed to confirm or disconfirm findings about the need for carefully coordinated forms of shared leadership if it is make any positive contribution to student achievement and the conditions in schools which mediate such achievement. Qualitative studies unpacking in much more detail the nature of such coordinated patters would also be very useful.

Further study is also needed about how planfully aligned distributed leadership is implemented in schools and what those in formal leadership positions must do to support this type of leadership.

References

Anderson, S. E. (2008). *Atlas public schools: Case study differentiated district support for school improvement*. Toronto: Ontario Institute for Studies in Education.

Anderson, S. E., Moore, S., & Sun, J. (2008). Positioning the principals in patterns of school leadership distribution. In K. Leithwood, B. Mascall, & T. Strauss (Eds.), *Distributed leadership according to the evidence*. New York: Routledge.

Ashton, P., Webb, R., & Doda, N. (1983). *A study of teachers' sense of efficacy: Gainesville*. Gainesville: University of Florida.

Bandura, A. (1986). *Social foundations of thought and action*. Englewood Cliffs: Prentice-Hall.

Bandura, A. (1997). *Self-efficacy: The exercise of control*. New York: Freeman.

Bennett, N., Harvey, J., Wise, C., & Woods, P. (2003). Distributed leadership: A review of literature. National College for School Leadership Retrieved from www.ncsl.org.uk/literaturereviews

Bevel, R., & Mitchell, R. (2012). The effects of academic optimism on elementary reading achievement. *Journal of Educational Administration, 50*(6), 773–787.

Boonen, T., Pinxten, M., Van Damme, J., & Onghena, P. (2014). Should schools be optimistic? An investigation of the association between academic optimism of schools and student achievement in primary education. *Educational Research and Evaluation, 20*, 3–24.

Bryk, A., & Schneider, B. (2002). *Trust in schools*. New York: Russell Sage Foundation.

Bryk, A., Camburn, E., & Louis, K. S. (1999). Professional community in Chicago elementary schools: Facilitating factors and organizational consequences. *Educational Administration Quarterly, 35*(5), 751–781.

Coleman, J. S., Campbell, E. Q., Hobson, C. J., McPartland, J., Mood, A. M., & Weinfeld, F. D. (1966). *Equality of Educational Opportunity*. Washington, DC: US Department of Health, Education & Welfare. Office of Education.

Copeland, M. A. (2003). Leadership of inquiry: Building and sustaining capacity for school improvement. *Educational Evaluation and Policy Analysis, 25*(4), 375–395.

Day, C., & Leithwood, K. (2007). *Successful principal leadership in times of change*. Dordrecht: Springer.

Elmore, R. (2000). *Building a new structure for school leadership*. Washington, DC: Albert Shanker Institute.

Goddard, R. D., Hoy, W. K., & Woolfolk Hoy, A. W. (2000a). Collective teacher efficacy: Its meaning, measure, and impact on student achievement. *American Educational Research Journal, 37*(2), 479–507.

Goddard, R. D., Sweetland, S., & Hoy, W. (2000b). Academic emphasis of urban elementary schools and student achievement in reading and mathematics: A multilevel analysis. *Educational Administration Quarterly, 36*(5), 683–702.

Goddard, R. D., Tschannen-Moran, M., & Hoy, W. K. (2001). A multilevel examination of the distribution and effects of teacher trust in students and parents in urban elementary schools. *Elementary School Journal, 102*(1), 3–17.

Gronn, P. (2002). Distributed leadership. In K. Leithwood & P. Hallinger (Eds.), *Second international handbook of educational leadership and administration* (pp. 653–696). Dordrecht/Boston: Kluwer Academic.

Hallinger, P., & Heck, R. H. (1996). Reassessing the principal's role in school effectiveness: A review of empirical research, 1980-1995. *Educational Administration Quarterly, 32*(1), 5–44.

Halverson, R. (2007). Systems of practice and professional community: The adams case. In J. P. Spillane (Ed.), *Distributed leadership in practice* (pp. 35–62). New York: Teachers College Press.

Harris, A. (2003). Teacher leadership as distributed leadership: Heresy, fantasy or possibility? *School Leadership & Management, 23*(3), 313–324.

Harris, A. (2008). Distributed leadership and knowledge creation. In K. Leithwood, B. Mascall, & T. Strauss (Eds.), *Distributed leadership according to the evidence* (pp. 253–266). New York: Routledge.

Harris, A., & Spillane, J. (2008). Distributed leadership through the looking glass. *Management in Education, 22*(1), 31–34.

Harris, A., Leithwood, K., Sammons, P., & Hopkins, D. (2007). Distributed leadership and organizational change. *Journal of Educational Change, 8*(4), 337–347.

Heller, M. F., & Firestone, W. A. (1995). Who's in charge here? Sources of leadership for change in eight schools. *Elementary School Journal, 96*(1), 65.

Hoy, W. K., & Fedmen, J. A. (1987). Organizational health: The concept and its measure. *Journal of Research and Development in Education, 20*(4), 30–37.

Hoy, W., Tarter, J. C., & Woolfolk Hoy, A. W. (2006). Academic optimism of schools: A force for student achievement. *American Educational Research Journal, 43*(3), 425–446.

Hoy, A. W., Hoy, W. K., & Kurz, N. (2008). Teachers' academic optimism: The development and test of a new construct. *Teaching and Teacher Education, 24*, 821–835.

Kirby, M., & DiPaola, M. (2011). Academic optimism and community engagement in urban schools. *Journal of Educational Administration, 49*, 542–562.

Lee, V., & Smith, J. (1999). Collective responsibility for learning and its effects on gains in achievement for early secondary school students. *American Journal of Education, 104*(2), 103–147.

Leithwood, K. (2006). *Teacher working conditions that matter.* Toronto: Elementary Teachers' Federation of Ontario.

Leithwood, K., & Jantzi, D. (2006). Transformational school leadership for large-scale reform: Effects on students, teachers, and their classroom practices. *School Effectiveness and School Improvement, 17*(2), 201–227.

Leithwood, K., Mascall, B., Strauss, T., Sacks, R., Memon, N., & Yashkina, A. (2007). Distributing leadership to make schools smarter: Taking the ego out of the system. *Leadership and Policy in Schools, 6*(1), 37–67.

Leithwood, K., Mascall, B., & Strauss, T. (2008). *Distributed leadership according to the evidence.* New York: Routledge.

Louis, K. (2007). Trust and improvement in schools. *Journal of Educational Change, 8*(1), 1–24.

MacBeath, J. (2005). Leadership as distributed: A matter of practice. *School Leadership & Management, 25*(4), 349–366.

Marzano, R. J., Waters, T., & McNulty, B. A. (2005). *School leadership that works.* Alexandria: Association for Supervision and Curriculum Development.

Mascall, B., Leithwood, K., Strauss, T., & Sacks, R. (2009). The relationship between distributed leadership and teachers' academic optimism. In A. Harris (Ed.), *Distributed leadership: Different perspectives* (pp. 81–100). New York: Springer.

Mayrowetz, D., Murphy, J., Louis, K. S., & Smylie, M. A. (2008). Conceptualizing distributed leadership as a school reform: Revisiting job redesign theory. In K. Leithwood, B. Mascall, & T. Strauss (Eds.), *Distributed leadership according to the evidence* (pp. 167–196). New York: Routledge.

McGuigan, L., & Hoy, W. K. (2006). Principal leadership: Creating a culture of academic optimism to improve achievement for all students. *Leadership and Policy in Schools, 5*(3), 203–229.

Mitchell, R., & Tarter, J. (in press). Chapter 12: Effects of principal professional orientation toward leadership, professional teacher behavior and school academic optimism on school reading achievement. In K. Leithwood, J. Sun, & K. Pollock (Eds.), *How school leaders contribute to student success: The four paths framework.* The Netherlands: Springer.

O'Day, J. (2002). Complexity, accountability, and school improvement. *Harvard Educational Review, 72*(3), 293.

Penlington, C., Kington, A., & Day, C. (2008). Leadership in improving schools: A qualitative perspective. *School Leadership & Management, 28*(1), 65–82.

Plowman, D. A., Solansky, S., Beck, T. E., Baker, L., Kulkarni, M., & Travis, D. V. (2007). The role of leadership in emergent, self-organization. *Leadership Quarterly, 18*(4), 341–356.

Podsakoff, P., Mackenzie, S., Moorman, R., & Fetter, R. (1990). Transformational leaders behaviour and their effects on followers' trust in leader satisfaction and organizational leadership behaviours. *Leadership Quarterly, 1*(2), 107–142.

Regine, B., & Lewin, R. (2000). Leading at the edge: How leaders influence complex systems. *Emergence, 2*(2), 5–23.

Robinson, V. M. J., & Timperley, H. S. (2007). The leadership of the improvement of teaching and learning: Lessons from initiatives with positive outcomes for students. *Australian Journal of Education, 51*(3), 247–262.

Robinson, V. M. J., Lloyd, C. A., & Rowe, K. J. (2008). The impact of leadership on student outcomes: An analysis of the differential effects of leadership types. *Educational Administration Quarterly, 44*(5), 635–674.

Ross, J. A., & Gray, P. (2006). School leadership and student achievement: The mediating effects of teacher beliefs. *Canadian Journal of Education, 29*(3), 798–822.

Ross, J. A., Hogaboam-Gray, A., & Gray, P. (2004). Prior student achievement, collaborative school processes, and collective teacher efficacy. *Leadership and Policy in Schools, 3*(3), 163–188.

Rubie-Davis, C., Flint, A., & McDonald, L. G. (2011). Teacher beliefs, teacher characteristics, and school contextual factors: What are the relationships? *British Journal of Educational Psychology, 82*(Pt 2), 1–19.

Smith, P., & Hoy, W. (2007). Academic optimism and student achievement in urban elementary schools. *Journal of Educational Administration, 45*(5), 556–568.

Smylie, M. A., Mayrowetz, D., Murphy, J., & Louis, K. S. (2007). Trust and the development of distributed leadership. *Journal of School Leadership, 17*, 465–503.

Spillane, J. P. (2006). *Distributed leadership* (1st ed.). San Francisco: Jossey-Bass.

Spillane, J. P., & Diamond, J. B. (2007). *Distributed leadership in practice.* New York: Teachers College.

Spillane, J. P., Camburn, E. M., & Pareja, A. S. (2007). Taking a distributed perspective to the school principal's workday. *Leadership and Policy in Schools, 6*(1), 103–125.

Timperley, H. S. (2005a). Distributed leadership: Developing theory from practice. *Journal of Curriculum Studies, 37*(4), 395–420.

Timperley, H. S. (2005b). Instructional leadership challenges: The case of using student achievement information for instructional improvement. *Leadership and Policy in Schools, 4*(1), 3–22.

Timperley, H. S. (2008). Distributing leadership to improve outcomes for students. In K. Leithwood, B. Mascall, & T. Strauss (Eds.), *Distributed leadership according to the evidence* (pp. 197–222). New York: Routledge.

Timperley, H. S., & Robinson, V. M. J. (2002). Achieving school improvement through challenging and changing teachers' schema. *Journal of Educational Change, 2*, 281–300.

Tschannen-Moran, M. (2009). Fostering teacher professionalism: The role of professional orientation and trust. *Educational Administration Quarterly, 45*, 217–247.

Tschannen-Moran, M., & Barr, M. (2004). Fostering student learning: The relationship of collective teacher efficacy and student achievement. *Leadership and Policy in Schools, 3*(3), 189–209.

Tschannen-Moran, M., & Hoy, W. (1998). Trust in schools: A conceptual and empirical analysis. *Journal of Educational Administration, 36*(4), 334.

Witziers, B., Bosker, R. J., & Kruger, M. L. (2003). Educational leadership and student achievement: The elusive search for an association. *Education and Administration Quarterly, 39*(3), 398–425.

Wood, R., & Bandura, A. (1989). Social cognitive theory of organizational management. *The Academy of Management Review, 14*(3), 361–384.

Wu, J., Hoy, W., & Tarter, J. (2013). Enabling school structure, collective responsibility and a culture of academic optimism. *Journal of Educational Administration, 51*(2), 176–193.

Chapter 6
Towards Sustaining Levels of Reflective Learning: How Do Transformational Leadership, Task Interdependence, and Self-Efficacy Shape Teacher Learning in Schools?

Arnoud Oude Groote Beverborg, Peter J.C. Sleegers, Maaike D. Endedijk, and Klaas van Veen

During the past decade, teachers and schools over the globe have been confronted with all kind of changes, including changes in students' demographics, large-scale educational reforms, and accountability policies aimed at improving the quality of education. Building school-wide capacity by promoting teachers' individual and collective learning is considered an important prerequisite for school's ability to change and sustain improvement.

To be able to understand the mechanisms underlying sustained improvement, researchers have started to examine how teacher learning is embedded in schools and linked with building school–improvement capacity (Clarke and Hollingsworth 2002; Geijsel et al. 2009; Sleegers et al. 2005; Stoll 2009; Stoll et al. 2009). In line with this focus, empirical studies into the interplay between leadership, workplace conditions, and psychological factors in teacher learning have been conducted (Kwakman 2003; Richardson and Placier 2001; Smylie et al. 1996). Findings from these studies indicate that both psychological (e.g., self-efficacy, motivation) and organizational factors (e.g., transformational leadership, an open and trustful

A.O.G. Beverborg (✉)
Johannes Gutenberg University, Mainz, Germany
e-mail: a.oudegrootebeverborg@uni-mainz.de

P.J.C. Sleegers
BMC Consultancy, Amersfoort, The Netherlands
e-mail: petersleegers@bmc.nl

M.D. Endedijk
Department of Educational Science, Faculty of Behavioural, Management and Social Sciences, University of Twente, P.O. Box 217, 7500 AE Enschede, The Netherlands
e-mail: m.d.endedijk@utwente.nl

K. van Veen
Department of Teacher Education, Faculty of Behavioural and Social Sciences, University of Groningen, Grote Kruisstraat 2/1, 9712 TS Groningen, The Netherlands
e-mail: klaas.van.veen@rug.nl

climate, task and goal interdependence) affect teacher learning such as self-reflection (Geijsel et al. 2009; Kwakman 2003; Runhaar et al. 2010; Thoonen et al. 2011; Van Woerkom 2004). Moreover, the impact of transformational leadership practices on self-reflection seems to be mediated by both teamwork and teacher motivational factors, including teachers' self-efficacy beliefs (Geijsel et al. 2009; Kwakman 2003; Smylie et al. 1996; Thoonen et al. 2011). More specifically, a recent cross-sectional study has shown how transformational leadership, perceived task interdependence, and self-efficacy are positively related to teachers' engagement in reflective learning activities (Oude Groote Beverborg et al. 2015). Additionally, research has found that teachers' engagement in professional learning activities contributes to changing teachers' instructional practices with the ultimate goal of increasing student achievement (Thoonen et al. 2011; Desimone 2009; Sleegers et al. 2014; Yammarino et al. 2008).

Although this research has contributed to a deeper understanding of mechanisms underlying educational change and teacher learning in schools, most of the studies are cross-sectional in nature, limiting valid and reliable claims about the direction of influence of the relations found. As cross- sectional estimates may generate misleading interpretations of mediation, longitudinal research can make stronger claims about causality (Cole and Maxwell 2003; Eschleman and LaHuis 2013; Maxwell et al. 2011; McArdle 2009). Moreover, longitudinal studies can make an important contribution to a complete understanding of the nature and dynamics of teacher learning as an important catalyst to foster sustained school improvement. Modeling the influences of transformational leadership, task interdependence, and self-efficacy on teachers' reflective learning over time will enable us to both validate previous findings from cross-sectional studies, and investigate possible reciprocal relations undetected by cross sectional models (e.g., Heck and Hallinger 2010; Salanova et al. 2006; Xanthopoulou et al. 2009). For example, sustained engagement in self-reflection, as one of the key professional learning activities of teachers, may help teachers to discover how to benefit from workplace conditions such as being task interdependent. Coming to understand how their team members' knowledge and skills can function as resources, in turn, can then be beneficial to further their own learning (e.g., Horn and Little 2010; Nonaka 1994; Spillane et al. 2002). Additionally, longitudinal research also provides opportunities to investigate the type of change of teachers' engagement in professional learning activities and its antecedents. Levels may be enhanced or declined or sustained, as the result of a variable's (e.g., self-reflection) own dynamics or a coupling with other variables (e.g., transformational leadership and self-efficacy), and change rates may differ for individual teachers depending on their previous levels (e.g., Ferrer and McArdle 2010). Exploration of these dynamics yields valuable insights in how teacher learning in schools, and its organizational and psychological antecedents, changes over time and what drive their changes. Although different scholars have emphasized the need for using more longitudinal designs in school improvement research (Feldhoff et al. 2014; Hallinger and Heck 2011; Heck and Hallinger 2014; Sleegers et al. 2014; Thoonen et al. 2012) there is still little systematic evidence for how organizational and psychological factors shape teacher learning in the context of the school *over time*. More longitudinal research is thus needed to increase our understanding of the nature and dynamics of these relationships and how change in schools occurs over time. This study aimed to make a significant contribution to this line of research by conducting a longitudinal study into the nature and dynamics of the paths that link transformational leadership practices, task interdependence, teachers' self-efficacy beliefs, and, consequently, their engagement in self-reflective learning activities (e.g., Geijsel et al. 2009; Leithwood et al. 2002).

The study was conducted within the context of Vocational Education and Training (VET) colleges in the Netherlands. During the past decade, VET colleges have become massive educational institutions due to many mergers and have also been involved in large educational reforms aimed at stimulating students' self-regulated and competence-based learning. One prominent issue in the implementation of these reforms is the reorganization of teachers' working conditions into multidisciplinary teams. Teachers from different disciplines and different subjects are called to collaborate for imparting the competences students need to become strong professionals and thus be better prepared for occupational participation in continuously changing labor market (Kwakman 2003; Poortman 2007; Truijen 2012). As a consequence, individual VET teachers are challenged to learn how to work effectively in teams directed at strengthening their professional expertise and, in turn, fostering student learning. The study builds on earlier, cross-sectional, work in which we examined the influence of transformational leadership practices (e.g., vision building, stimulation and consideration), task and goal interdependence as aspects of teamwork, and self-efficacy on teachers' engagement in professional learning activities (e.g., self-reflection, asking for feedback) in Dutch VET colleges (Oude Groote Beverborg et al. 2015). The findings showed two clearly differentiated paths to explain the variation of teachers' engagement in learning activities of which one path leads from a transformational leader that shares a vision, through teachers' perceptions of being goal interdependent, to teachers asking for feedback. As such, asking for feedback seems to be situated in a context of immediate interaction towards a common goal and can be cultivated when a transformational leader keeps sharing the school's vision. The second path leads from a transformational leader who shows consideration for teachers individually, through teachers' perceptions of working together on tasks and their senses of self-efficacy, to teacher self-reflection. These findings suggest that teachers' engagement in self-reflective activities is situated in a context of past experiences of collaboration and can be cultivated through a leader's consideration of needs and individual support. The purpose of this longitudinal study was to investigate whether this latter path that links the relations between transformational leadership practices, task interdependence, self-efficacy, and teacher self-reflection can still be found when assessed *over time*, thereby validating and extending previous models and findings from cross-sectional research. We also use the added value of a longitudinal design to explore reciprocal relations between these variables, and assess the dynamics of change that occur.

The main research question that guided our research was: How do transformational leadership practices, task interdependence, self-efficacy, and teacher self-reflection mutually shape each other over time?

6.1 Theoretical Framework

An important contribution of our study lies in our attempts to examine changes in transformational leadership practices, task interdependence, teachers' self-efficacy beliefs and their engagement in professional learning activities and how the relationships among these variables evolve over time, by using Latent Difference Score modeling (LDS; see for a more detailed elaboration, below). To understand these relationships, we draw on theories on adult learning, teacher motivation, teamwork and transformational leadership, and use previous findings from cross-sectional research on the interplay between teachers' psychological states and organizational conditions in teacher learning. The model that guided our inquiry is depicted in Fig. 6.1. To test this model, we used data from a sample of 655 Dutch VET teachers. We discuss the variables of our study more fully, and the expected relationship among them in further detail below.

6.1.1 Professional Learning Through Engagement in Self-Reflection

Inspired by adult learning theories and situated cognitive perspective on teacher learning, we conceptualized professional learning as an on-going informal learning process that is embedded within the school and that takes place during the entire career (Jarvis 1987; Kwakman 2003; Marsick and Watkins 1990; Putnam and Borko 2000; Sleegers et al. 2005; Smylie and Hart 1999). In line with this perspective, the focus of teacher learning in the context of the school is on teachers' engagement in

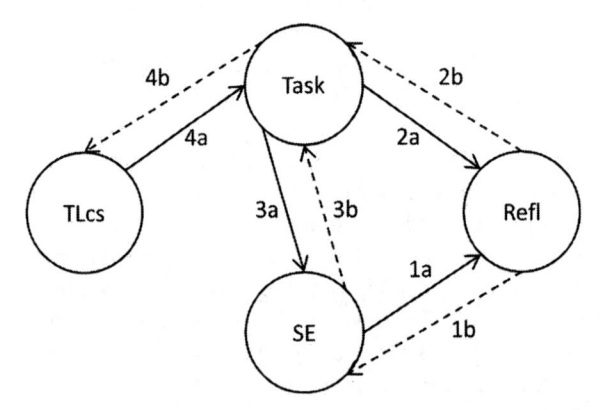

Fig. 6.1 Theoretical framework of how self-reflection (Refl) is influenced by self-efficacy (SE), perceived task interdependence (Task) and the transformational leadership practices individualized consideration and intellectual support (TLcs; *solid arrows*), as well as the reciprocal relations that will be explored (*dashed arrows*). The numbers 1a–4b represent the hypotheses

a variety of professional learning activities aimed at stimulating their own professional development and the development of the school as a whole.

Although scholars have studied a variety of different professional learning activities to capture the content of professional learning (e.g., Kwakman 2003; Meirink et al. 2009), a distinction between individual and social professional learning activities can be depicted from the literature (Kwakman 2003; Lohman 2005; Schön 1983; Van Woerkom 2004). Individual learning activities refer to activities aimed to explore and reflect on one's own values, interests, abilities, and career goals, and are carried out individually without any assistance from colleagues or supervisors. Examples of individual learning activities are reflecting on past performances, reading professional material, and focusing on future career goals. Social learning activities refer to activities aimed at acquiring new knowledge, skills, information and ideas that are acquired in social interaction with others. Examples of social learning activities are sharing knowledge, asking for feedback and challenging groupthink. Although both types of learning activities are ways to discover the proper script for future actions and are nested in a social context, the sources and thereby the nature of these learning activities thus differ. As indicated, in this study we focus on self-reflection as one of the most important individual learning activities teachers are engaged in during their daily practice (Jarvis 1987; Van Woerkom 2003).

Self-reflection is an introspective activity and refers to a person recreating the experience of acting in a given situation. In "reliving" this experience a person supplements the memory of the experience with new ideas that can either be self-generated or based on information gained from others. This creates an altered and thus new experience, which can then serve as the basis for future action (e.g., Barsalou 2008). Self-reflection allows teachers to broaden their teaching repertoire, generate new knowledge, and make knowledge explicit aimed at discovering a workable script for adaptation to changing circumstances (Jarvis 1987; Van Woerkom 2003). These adaptations may in turn fuel continuance of individual teachers' own reflections (Clarke and Hollingsworth 2002), and can be of value for team members (Van Woerkom 2004), as knowledge gained through self-reflection can be made explicit and shared. Moreover, as circumstances continuously change old solutions expire, and hence sustained levels of engagement in self-reflection are important for maintaining high levels of craftsmanship (Klarner et al. 2008; Korthagen and Vasalos 2005). Newly generated knowledge can be experimented with to fit to changed circumstances (Eraut 2004; McArdle and Coutts 2010). Research has shown that self-reflection contributes to changing instructional practices, and in turn improved student performance (Desimone 2009; Korthagen 2001; Kwakman 2003; Sleegers et al. 2014; Thoonen et al. 2011). The importance of teacher reflection for improving the quality of education therefore leads to the question how to facilitate reflection, and how to sustain sufficient levels of learning over time (Giles and Hargreaves 2006; Timperley and Alton-Lee 2008).

6.1.2 Self-Efficacy Beliefs

Self-efficacy represents the level of competence a person expects to display in a given situation. Self-efficacy develops, for instance, from coping with various difficult and complex situations successfully as the experience of mastery is one of the most important sources of self-efficacy, next to modeling or vicarious experiences, social persuasion, and physiological and emotional states (Bandura 1997). In addition, repeatedly perceiving team members resolving problems can facilitate the development of a teacher's own self-efficacy through vicarious learning or modeling. Persons with higher levels of self-efficacy will persist in the face of difficulties, feel empowered, are less constraint by doubts, and will thus arrive quicker at a satisfying solution (Bandura 1993; Caprara et al. 2008).

Cross-sectional research has shown that teachers who have higher levels of self-efficacy are more engaged in learning activities (e.g., self-reflection) that may challenges existing knowledge, beliefs, and classroom practices than their colleagues with lower levels of self-efficacy (Geijsel et al. 2009; Katz-Navon and Erez 2005; Runhaar 2008; Thoonen et al. 2011; Walumbwa et al. 2005). Additionally, longitudinal research indicates that self-efficacy has predictive power over time on levels of vigor and dedication of teachers (Simbula et al. 2011, as well as on changing instructional practices (Sleegers et al. 2014). Interestingly for the present study, empirical evidence suggests that self-efficacy is not a stable phenomenon: it grows in primary school children (Phan 2012), declines in adolescents (Caprara et al. 2008), and fluctuates in teachers (Thoonen et al. 2012). To what extent teachers' beliefs in their self-efficacy changes, and the manner in which these changes relate over time to engagement in self-reflection, has yet to be addressed. It seems however likely that increases in beliefs about their own effectiveness motivate teachers to meet challenges, and thereby may positively affect their engagement in professional learning activities over time. Additionally, reflection may also impact self-efficacy. Generating knowledge to adapt to changing circumstances helps to resolve problems and come to satisfying solutions. Sustained levels of self-reflection can therefore lead to mastery experiences, and thus help to develop beliefs of self-efficacy, which makes it worthwhile to explore whether a bidirectional link between these variables can be found. As only a few available studies have examined this reciprocal relationship (Bandura 1997; Malmberg et al. 2014), more research is needed. Based on previous cross-sectional studies, we expect that higher reported levels of self-efficacy will increase teachers' engagement in self-reflection (Hypothesis 1a). In line with the outcomes of the few available studies studying the reciprocal relationship (Bandura 1997; Malmberg et al. 2014), we also hypothesize that as teachers' engagement in self-reflection increases over time, their self-efficacy beliefs will also increase (Hypothesis 1b).

6.1.3 Perceived Task Interdependence

Task interdependence refers to the perceived degree of interaction between team members required to complete tasks. Thus, task interdependence can be seen as providing the infrastructure needed to stimulate teacher interaction as well as the exchange of information and resources for successful task completion (Campion et al. 1993; Cummings 1978; De Jong et al. 2007; Van der Vegt et al. 2000). Research on the role of collaboration between teachers for promoting professional learning has provided evidence for the positive impact of teacher interaction on teacher learning, and, in turn, enhance team effectiveness (Truijen 2012; Wageman 1995). Because teachers can use knowledge that team members have made explicit as input for their own reflection, interacting with team members facilitates teacher engagement in self-reflective activities (Meirink et al. 2009, 2010; Runhaar 2008). In addition, teachers' self-efficacy beliefs have been shown to mediate the effect of teacher interaction on professional learning and vigor and dedication of teachers (Geijsel et al. 2009; Thoonen et al. 2011; Simbula et al. 2011) by removing uncertainty and ambiguity (Staples and Webster 2008). Collaboration and teacher interaction can thus offer teachers an "efficacy boost" (Hoy and Spero 2005), thereby facilitating their engagement in professional learning activities. Although these findings make it likely that perceptions of task interdependence have a positive impact on engagement in self-reflection and self-efficacy beliefs, we know little about how interactions with peers who are directly engaged in the same task affect teachers' sense of self-efficacy and their self-reflective activities over time.

As teachers need time to come to understand how to interact with colleagues to complete tasks, generating knowledge to adapt to changing circumstances might help (Mulford 2010; Scribner et al. 2002). When teachers find adequate ways to interact with each other, obtained knowledge from colleagues can be beneficial to further promote their own learning (Desimone 2009; Horn and Little 2010; Nonaka 1994; Spillane et al. 2002). Additionally, enhanced efficacy beliefs about resolving conflict in teams through vicarious team experience have been found to positively affect expected outcomes of teams (Stone and Bailey 2007). Therefore, self-efficacy may also influence change in perceptions of task interdependence: having a more positive view of intra-team conflict and having confidence that conflicts will be resolved may lead to more frequent and more positive interactions. Teachers may thus come to value more interdependence in working on tasks. In this study, we therefore hypothesize that higher levels of perceived task interdependence will increase teachers' engagement in self-reflection (Hypothesis 2a). Based on a more dynamic representation of the assumed associations between these variables, we also expected that as teachers' engagement in self-reflection increases over time, perceived task interdependence would also increase (Hypothesis 2b). In addition, we hypothesize the time-based dynamic relations between self-efficacy and task interdependence as follows: as teachers perceive higher levels of perceived task interdependence, higher level beliefs about their own self-efficacy are expected to follow (Hypothesis 3a) and vice versa (Hypothesis 3b).

6.1.4 Transformational Leadership

Leadership is widely assumed to play a major role in the promotion of school improvement efforts and educational change, particularly when the leadership is characterized as what is called "transformational leadership" (Leithwood et al. 1999). A transformational leader aims at development in a context of organizational change and is committed to the empowerment of individual teachers and teacher teams as a whole (Avolio et al. 2004; Leithwood et al. 2002; Leithwood and Sleegers 2006; Yammarino et al. 2008). Three transformational leadership dimensions have been found critical for the enhancement of individual learning activities (McArdle and Hamagami 2001). The first dimension of initiating and identifying a vision refers to a leader who works on the development of shared goals and priorities by inspiring teachers to formulate shared goals, connect to these, commit to them, and try to attain them. The second dimension of individualized consideration refers to support and attention for individual needs and feelings. Teachers should feel empowered by a considerate transformational school leader and—as a consequence—seek to interact with other teachers and coordinate responsibility in the tasks they share (Geijsel et al. 1999, 2009). Intellectual stimulation as the third dimension of transformational leadership involves the encouragement of teachers to continuously calibrate the adequacy of their knowledge and instructional practices. It tries to incite a critical attitude towards oneself and one's team members through the idea that not one solution is absolute, that there are alternatives to problems, and that conflict can be functional for effective teamwork. As such, it can improve team-work by enhancing teachers' abilities to solve individual, group and organizational problems (Geijsel et al. 2009; Dionne et al. 2007).

Whereas the three dimensions of transformational leadership would appear to directly influence self-efficacy and teacher learning (e.g., Geijsel et al. 2003; Sleegers et al. 2014; Yost 2006), empirical research that addressed these effects did not consistently find these effects, however (e.g., Nielsen and Munir 2009; Tims et al. 2011). Instead of a direct link, it seems more likely that the relation between transformational leadership on the one hand, and self-efficacy and self-reflection on the other hand, is mediated by perceptions of workplace conditions (e.g., Geijsel et al. 2009; Korek et al. 2010; Nir and Kranot 2006; Thoonen et al. 2011). Previous studies have indeed found that transformational leadership practices are related to various workplace conditions and have an initiating role in enhancing these conditions (e.g., Sun and Leithwood 2012).

In addition, it has recently been shown that transformational school leadership can enhance the prerequisites for perceiving interdependence—including teacher collaboration and trust (Moolenaar et al. 2012; Thoonen et al. 2011). In our previous cross-sectional research on the impact of transformational leadership practices on teamwork, self-efficacy and teacher learning in VET colleges, we have found that individualized consideration and intellectual stimulation affect task interdependence directly, while vision building did not. Moreover, it appeared that the influence of transformational leadership on teachers' efficacy beliefs and self-reflection was mediated by perceived task interdependence (Oude Groote Beverborg et al. 2015). Although the few available studies provide some evidence for the relationship between teamwork processes, especially perceived task interdependence, and two of the three dimensions of transformational leadership, including individualized consideration and intellectual stimulation, more research is needed to assess how these transformational leadership practices affect perceptions of task interdependence over time, thereby validating and expanding previous findings.

Furthermore, a bi-directional link between transformational leadership and task interdependence seems likely. In the long term, building teacher craftsmanship, may distribute the sources of leadership in a school from one (or few) to many sources. Leadership may diffuse first through the team, and finally through the organization (Day et al. 2010; Hallinger and Heck 2011). Interacting and collaborating with colleagues might contribute to this process, because it elevates levels of potentially useful knowledge individual teachers and teacher teams may use to become more proficient. Based on the aforementioned, we therefore hypothesize that as transformational leadership practices (e.g., individual consideration and intellectual stimulation) increase over time, teachers' perceptions of their task interdependence would also increase (Hypothesis 4a). In addition, as interacting and collaborating with colleagues might contribute to more distributive forms of leadership, we expected that higher levels of perceived task interdependence would lead to slow changes in transformational leadership over time (Hypothesis 4b).

6.2 The Present Study

The aim of the present study is to longitudinally assess the mutual relations between transformational leadership (*i.e.*, individualized consideration and intellectual stimulation), perceived task interdependence, self-efficacy, and teachers' engagement in self-reflection over time.

On the basis of findings from previous studies, we formulated four hypotheses regarding the reciprocal relations between self-reflection, self-efficacy, task interdependence and the transformational leadership practices individualized consideration and intellectual support. These hypotheses are visualized in Fig. 6.1. We tested these assumed dynamic associations between our variables, using data gathered on three yearly-based measurement occasions from 655 Dutch Vocational Education and Training teachers. As such, this study will make a unique contribution to a deeper understanding of the dynamics and complexities underlying sustainable school improvement.

6.3 Method

In order to assess the time-based dynamics of the relationship between these variables, we used Latent Difference Score (LDS) modeling (Ferrer and McArdle 2010; McArdle 2009; McArdle and Hamagami 2001). LDS modeling, derived from dynamic system theory (Ferrer and McArdle 2010), is a form of Structural Equation

Modeling (SEM), and combines cross-lagged regression analysis and latent growth curve modeling. This allows for the modeling of dynamic intra-individual change. Dynamic modeling of this nature provides opportunities to explore and test the hypothesized reciprocity of the relationships amongst the variables examined in our study by illustrating how changes in one variable (e.g., self-reflection) over time depend on the state of another variable (e.g., self-efficacy, and task interdependence) and any prior change in the system as a whole. Details regarding sample, measures and analytic strategy are described below.

6.3.1 Sample

Data were collected from teachers of interdisciplinary teams from the various departments of six VET colleges (e.g., a technology department, an economics and business department, a health and welfare, department, an education department). The interdisciplinary teams within these departments were responsible for the coaching of a specific group of students, the guidance of their learning processes, the planning of the curricula for the group and assessment of their progress.

We used convenience sampling to obtain a sample as large as possible. The six VET colleges were contacted via their boards of directors. For two of the colleges, the teachers were contacted directly to invite them to participate in the present study. For the other four colleges, the team leaders were asked if their teams would be willing to participate. Questionnaires were sent to the teachers of the teams that were willing to participate. To maximize responding, we informed each team about the goals of our research, told them about the content of the questionnaire and offered to give a presentation on the main findings once the study was completed.

The questionnaires were administered using the online program "survey monkey". During 3 years (from 2010 to 2012), questionnaires were sent to more than 800 teachers. On each measurement occasion about 400 returned the questionnaire, with response rates of 53%, 52%, and 47% for the three sequential occasions. Not all returned questionnaires could be used for further analysis, because, for example, respondents did not fill out the questionnaire completely. Subsequent analyses are based on the data of 655 unique respondents, of which 144 responded on all three occasions, 181 responded on two occasions, and 330 responded on only one occasion. Moreover, Mplus, the software we used to analyze the data with, provides maximum likelihood estimation for missing data, and it computes the standard errors for the parameter estimates using the observed information matrix (Muthén and Muthén 1998–2010). See Appendix 1 for a more detailed description of the responses.

Over three measurement occasions with 1 year intervals and of all the teachers who responded, the average age was 48 years (standard deviation of 10). The majority of the respondents worked more than 32 h per week (about 60%). Many of the respondents had worked as a teacher for more than 20 years (32%); a sizeable percentage had worked around 10 years as a teacher (21%). Most of the teachers had a bachelor's degree (72%); 16% had a master's degree; and 12% had completed only a secondary level of education. See Appendix 2 for a more detailed description of the sample on the three measurement occasions.

6.3.2 Measures

The following variables were assessed using already existing, well-validated measurement scales: transformational leadership individualized consideration and intellectual stimulation (11 items) (Geijsel et al. 2009; Oude Groote Beverborg et al. 2015; Thoonen et al. 2011), task interdependence (4 items) (Oude Groote Beverborg et al. 2015; Runhaar 2008; Runhaar et al. 2010; Van der Vegt et al. 2000), occupational self-efficacy (6 items) (Oude Groote Beverborg et al. 2015; Schyns and Von Collani 2002; Runhaar 2008; Runhaar et al. 2010), and self-reflection (5 items) (Oude Groote Beverborg et al. 2015; Runhaar 2008; Runhaar et al. 2010). Teachers indicated the extent to which the item content applied to them on five-point scales (1 = strongly disagree, 2 = partially disagree, 3 = do not disagree, do not agree, 4 = partially agree, 5 = strongly agree). The items in the questionnaire referred to the above mentioned concepts (see Appendix 3 for an overview of the scaled variables and related items).

As mentioned earlier, two dimensions of transformational leadership, including individualized consideration and intellectual stimulation, were measured based on previous cross-sectional research (Geijsel et al. 2009; Oude Groote Beverborg et al. 2015; Thoonen et al. 2011). Individualized consideration was defined as the extent to which the school leader acknowledges teachers' efforts, provides individualized support for teachers and was measured using five items. The second scale, providing intellectual stimulation, consisted of six items and concerned the degree to which the school leader provides teachers with intellectual stimulation. The reliability of these subscales has been found to be satisfactory (Geijsel et al. 2009; Oude Groote Beverborg et al. 2015; Sleegers et al. 2014; Thoonen et al. 2011): Cronbach's alpha coefficients for individualized consideration varied from 0.87 to 0.93 and for intellectual stimulation from 0.88 to 0.94.

Task interdependence refers to the extent to which teachers perceive that the interaction and coordination of team members is required to complete tasks (four items). Cronbach's alpha coefficients, ranging from 0.70 to 0.79, have been reported in literature (Oude Groote Beverborg et al. 2015; Runhaar 2008; Van der Vegt et al. 2000).

Occupational self-efficacy was defined as the extent to which teachers have a future-oriented belief about their level of competence that they expect to display in a given situation. This scale consists of six items. The reliability of this scale has been found to be satisfactory (Oude Groote Beverborg et al. 2015; Runhaar 2008; Runhaar et al. 2010): Cronbach's alpha coefficients for occupational self-efficacy varied from 0.75 to 0.80.

Teachers engagement in self-reflection refers to the extent to which teachers are engaged in individual activities aimed at making implicit knowledge explicit (5 items). Cronbach's alpha coefficients, ranging from 0.72 to 0.82 have been reported in the literature (Oude Groote Beverborg et al. 2015; Runhaar 2008; Runhaar et al. 2010).

In preliminary analysis we first conducted confirmatory factor analysis per variable on all three measurement occasions, using Mplus 7.1 (Muthén and Muthén 1998–2010). The findings showed that, for all three measurement occasions, the items loaded well on their factors.

Second, we investigated whether the variables were longitudinally valid by testing models with unrestraint factor loading per item on each of the three measurement occasions, *versus* models in which each item's factor loading was constraint to be equal over time (McArdle and Prindle 2013). The findings showed that our measures were invariant, and the latent or true scores of the variables could be separated from the random error of measurement. Moreover, all variables significantly predicted themselves over time, indicating that they were stable (see Appendix 4).

Finally, we constructed a measurement model to assess whether the theoretical constructs (factors) such as we measured them fitted well to the data in relation with one another. To obtain factor means we had to apply the assumption of measurement error with means of 0. The findings showed an acceptable fit of the model to the data, $\chi^2(2977) = 6055.275$ ($p = 0.000$), RMSEA = 0.040, CFI = 0.838, SRMR = 0.073. The items and their parameter estimates (*i.e.*, factor loadings and residual variances) are presented in Appendix 3, and the means, standard errors of the means, and the correlations between all variables at all measurement occasions are presented in Appendix 5.

6.3.3 Analytic Strategy

As indicated above, we analyzed the data from this study using Latent Difference Score (LDS) structural equation modeling programmed in Mplus 7.1 (Muthén and Muthén 1998–2010). The key elements of an LDS approach are the variables' latent difference factors, which specify the variable's change score at each time point (see for instance McArdle and Prindle 2008; Sbarra and Allen 2009). Unique in the LDS approach is that this change score consists of two components:

1. A constant change component, which is a constant underlying growth parameter or the underlying constant slope (latent slope);
2. A proportional change component, which is the autoregressive coefficient (Ferrer and McArdle 2010).

Together they form the so-called dual change score model, in which both components together model the intra-individual change. Changes in the LDS model accumulate over subsequent time points (Ferrer and McArdle 2010; McArdle 2009; McArdle et al. 2000). For the reader's complete understanding, a bivariate dual change Latent Difference Score (LDS) model, is visualized and discussed briefly in Appendix 6.

The dual change model (constant change and proportional change) might not be the model that fits best to the intra-individual change present. For example, if the variables do not show a constant increase (or decline) within the timeframe that was measured, a model including only the proportional change component will fit the data better than the full dual change model. As a first step in our analysis we, therefore, tested for every variable separately (univariate LDS model) which type of change model fitted the data best. We tested three versions of the univariate LDS models against each other (Eschleman and LaHuis 2013):

1. an LDS model with invariant autoregressions and a latent slope (dual change model) against an
2. LDS model with freed autoregressions and without a latent slope (proportional change model);
3. an LDS model with invariant autoregressions and a latent slope (dual change model) against an LDS model without autoregressions and with a latent slope (constant change model);
4. an LDS model without autoregressions and with a latent slope (constant change model) against an LDS model with freed autoregressions and without a latent slope (proportional change model).

The models were compared using the Chi-square difference ($\Delta\chi^2$) test with degrees of freedom (df) equal to the difference in numbers of parameters left free for estimation. Additionally, a good fit of a model to the data is indicated by a Chi-square (χ^2 (df)) that is not significant, an RMSEA (Root Mean Square Error of Approximation) ≤ 0.06, a CFI (Comparative Fit Index) >0.95, and an SRMR (Root Mean Square Residual) ≤ 0.08 (Hu and Bentler 1999). After selection of the best fitting models we performed subsequent analyses to see whether better fits were obtained by freeing or constraining other parameters.

In the second step we extended the best fitting univariate change score model to multivariate LDS models. As multiple variables are included, the initial factors and slope factors of different variables will also be correlated. More interesting however are the coupling parameters (γ's, see Appendix 6) between difference factors at time t and measurement occasion factors at time t-1. These coupling parameters may be in one direction, but the coupling may also be bidirectional, such that reciprocity between variables becomes a testable property of the model. The couplings relate variables on all occasions, that is, they are now dynamically related. This means that a variable's change depends on the variable's level at a previous time point and on a systematic growth rate, as well as, when coupled with another variable, on the level of the other variable at a previous time point. Change patterns therefore depend on the presence of these parameters, and even when parameter values are constant over time non-linear trajectories may be obtained (see for an example Sbarra and Allen 2009). The parameters are interpreted together, because they jointly bring about the dynamics of the system (Ferrer and McArdle 2010. For testing our hypotheses, the coupling parameters are studied because they test for the prediction (over time) of one variable (e.g., self-efficacy) on another (e.g., self-reflection), and therefore strengthen claims of causality, and provide a strong basis for claims of mediation

(Eschleman and LaHuis 2013; McArdle 2009). Moreover, these predictions are independent of outcome variables' histories.

In order to explain the multivariate LDS model we used Mplus 7.1 (Muthén and Muthén 1998–2010) to test the dynamics of the assumed paths that link the variables in our study (see Fig. 6.1). The multivariate model was assessed in three steps. First, the variables were modeled in a "straightforward" causal manner, based on findings from our previous cross-sectional research. Second, corresponding "reversed causal" coupling parameters were added to assess the reciprocal relations between variables. Third, on the basis of the principle of parsimony, non-significant effects were removed from the model. More detailed information about the Mplus codes used, are available on request by the first author.

6.4 Results

6.4.1 Univariate Model Selection

We started our data analysis with examining which univariate LDS models fitted best the intra-individual change of each variable in our study. As mentioned earlier, we tested three versions of the univariate LDS models against each other. These tests indicated for all variables that the proportional change models (model with freed autoregressions and without a latent slope) fitted the data best (see for Model selection and $\Delta\chi^2$ tests Appendix 7). This means that overall the variables did not show a constant increase (or decline) within the timeframe that we measured.

Subsequent tests to assess whether the models would fit the data better if their proportional change parameters were held invariant (Eschleman and LaHuis 2013), indicated this to be the case for self-reflection, self-efficacy, and task interdependence. Subsequent tests showed that levels of self-reflection declined between occasion 1 and 2 ($\mu_{Refl2} - \mu_{Refl1} = -0.072, p = 0.015$), after which its level was sustained, self-efficacy increased between occasion 1 and 2 ($\mu_{SE2} - \mu_{SE1} = 0.057, p = 0.045$), after which its level was sustained, task interdependence remained constant, and that consideration and support increased between occasion 1 and 2 ($\mu_{TLcs2} - \mu_{TLcs1} = .123, p = 0.024$), as well as between occasion 2 and 3 ($\mu_{TLcs3} - \mu_{TLcs2} = 0.088, p = 0.041$).[1] But despite that the values of consideration and stimulation appear

---

[1] Because proportional change models were selected (and not dual change models), the equation to calculate difference scores with is the following:

$$Yit = ..._1 + \beta Y * Yit - 1$$

where $\mu_{\Delta t}$ is the estimated intercept of the difference score at a certain occasion. To test whether measurement occasion scores significantly differ from occasion to occasion, measurement occasion scores are compared. Measurement occasion scores are calculated by adding an occasion's difference score and its previous measurement occasion score.

incremental they are not constant enough to prefer a model with a constant change factor (*i.e.*, a dual change model) over a proportional change model (as indicated by the results of the model comparisons). Univariate proportional change models, their values, fit measures, as well as their corresponding trajectories, are presented in Appendix 8.

6.4.2 Testing the Multivariate Model

Based on these findings, we subsequently examined the dynamic relationships between the variables of our study with a multivariate proportional change model. The coupling parameters are of primary interest, as they provide the evidence for causal relations.

A four-variable proportional change model was fit to the data. The included variables were consideration and stimulation, perceived task interdependence, self-efficacy, and self-reflection. In this first model only those unidirectional coupling parameters were included that had been found in our previous cross-sectional study, resulting into a path that led from a transformational leader who shows consideration for teachers individually and stimulate teachers intellectually, through teachers' perceived task interdependence (Hypothesis 4a), to self-efficacy (Hypothesis 3a), and self-reflection (Hypothesis 1a and 2a). The fit of the model to the data was acceptable: $\chi^2(3028) = 6222.830$ ($p = 0.000$), RMSEA = 0.040, CFI = 0.832, SRMR = 0.084. In the second model reciprocal relations were included. We therefore added the "reversed causal" coupling parameters from task interdependence to consideration and stimulation (Hypothesis 4b), from self-efficacy to task interdependence (Hypothesis 3b), from self-reflection to task interdependence (Hypothesis 2b), and from self-reflection to self-efficacy (Hypothesis 1b). The fit of this second, modified, model to the data was acceptable: $\chi^2(3024) = 6207.606$ ($p = 0.000$), RMSEA = 0.040, CFI = 0.832, SRMR = 0.082, and this less restraint model fitted the data better than the first model: $\Delta \chi^2(4) = 15.224$ ($p = 0.004$). Based on the principal of parsimony, we removed the following non-significant coupling parameters from the second model: from self-efficacy to self-reflection (Hypothesis 1a), from self-efficacy to task interdependence (Hypothesis 3b), from task interdependence to self-efficacy (Hypothesis 3a), and from task interdependence to consideration and stimulation (Hypothesis 4b). This resulted in a third model with an acceptable fit: $\chi^2(3028) = 6213.389$ ($p = 0.000$), RMSEA = 0.040, CFI = 0.832, SRMR = 0.083, and this more parsimonious model fitted the data as well as the less restrained second model: $\Delta\chi^2(4) = 5.783$ ($p = 0.216$). Allowing the coupling parameters to be variant did not improve the fit of the model to the data. Parameter values of the third, parsimonious multivariate LDS model are presented in Table 6.1. For complete understanding, the correlations between the initial factors and the coupling parameters of this third model are presented in Fig. 6.2.

Values in the figure are significant. TLcs = transformational leadership consideration and stimulation; Task = task interdependence; SE = self-efficacy; Refl = self-reflection. TLcs[t] represents its measurement occasion factor at time t. Δ[#]TLcs

Table 6.1 Parameter estimates from the final multivariate latent proportional change score model.

Parameter	TLcs	Task	SE	Refl
Autoregression (proportion) β_1	−0.570	−0.592	−0.383	−0.335
Autoregression (proportion) β_2	−0.255	==	==	==
Initial mean μ_1	3.676	4.551	4.087	4.346
Difference factor1 intercept $\mu_{\Delta 1}$	2.216	1.634	1.112	0.768
Difference factor2 intercept $\mu_{\Delta 2}$	1.058	1.621	1.064	0.820
Coupling γ TLcs[t−Δt]→ΔTask[t]		0.073		
Refl[t−Δt] →ΔTask[t]		0.171		
Refl[t−Δt] →ΔSE[t]			0.117	
Task[t−Δt] →ΔRefl[t]				0.135
Initial variance ϕ_1^2	1.051	0.259	0.261	0.236
Difference factor1 variance $\omega_{\Delta 1}^2$	0.574	0.182	0.097	0.136
Difference factor1 variance ω_{Δ}^2	0.316	0.221	0.169	0.132
Correlations ρ	I TLcs	I task	I SE	I refl
I TLcs	1			
I task	0.126	1		
I SE	0.119	0.089	1	
I refl	0.063	0.099	0.122	1

represents its latent difference factors for subsequent occasions. The black single headed arrows are the invariant couplings from one variable to another (the γ's) with their values. The double equality signs represent invariance. The bold grey arrows are the autoregressions (β's) with their values. The grey arrows without values are fixed at 1. TLcs does not have invariant autoregressions, Task, SE, and Refl do. The model is simplified to stress the influences over time and to ease interpretation.

As can be seen in Fig. 6.2, the most parsimonious model indicates:

- a leading role of consideration and stimulation on perceived task interdependence (Hypothesis 4a);
- reciprocity between task interdependence and self-reflection (Hypothesis 2a and 2b);
- a peripheral role of self-efficacy, as only the level of self-reflection influenced the levels of self-efficacy, but not vice versa.

This final model explained 37.3% of the variance of the first latent difference score of consideration and stimulation, and 13.6% of its second, 28.8% of task interdependence's first and 27.5%, of its second, 23.8% of self-efficacy's first, and 14.5% of its second, and 14.0% of self-reflection's first, and 17.3% of the variance of its second latent difference score.

Values in the table are significant. Double equality signs indicate that this parameter was held invariant. $N = 655$, number of free parameters = 131. TLcs = transformational leadership consideration and stimulation; task = task interdependence; SE = self-efficacy; Refl = self-reflection. Factor loadings from the measurement occasion factors are not listed. See therefor Appendix 3. Error variances are not listed.

Fig. 6.2 Simplified representation of the parsimonious multivariate proportional change Latent Difference Score (LDS) model.

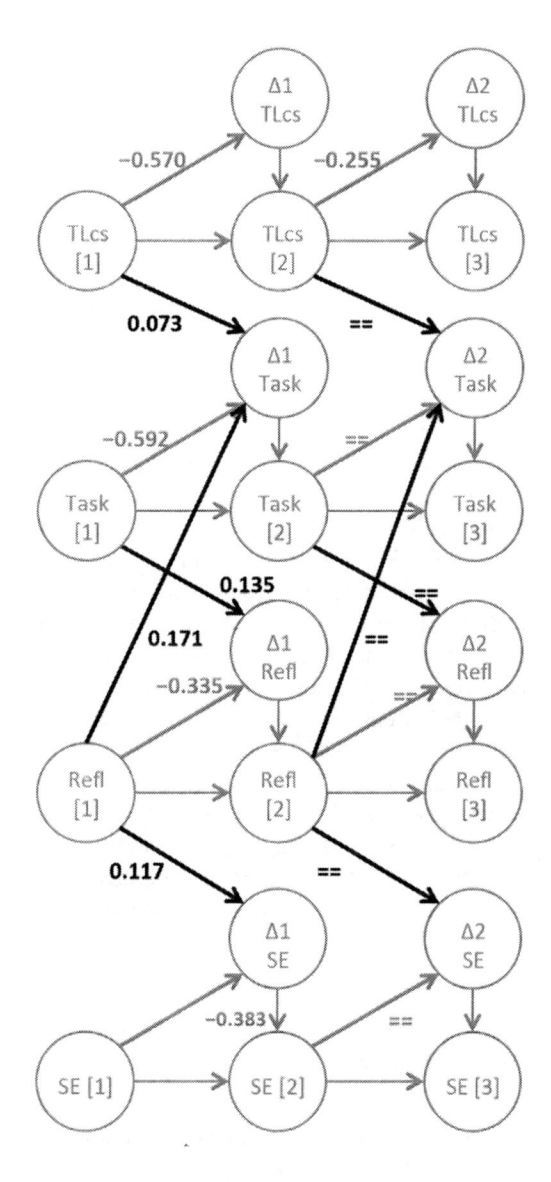

See for an approximation Appendix 3. Error variances from the final structural model deviate from those in the measurement model with a maximum of 0.004, 0.003, 0.006, and 0.007 for TLcs, Task, SE, and Refl, respectively.

We will elaborate on the most important findings from the parsimonious multivariate LDS model by first giving interpretations of the initial levels from each variable, followed by our interpretations of the parameters relating the variables (following the order of the parameters in Table 6.1). Change of the separate variables was already discussed in the univariate model selection section (see autoregressions and difference factors intercepts in Table 6.1 and Appendix 8).

All initial factor means were significant (see μ_1 in Table 6.1). Consideration and stimulation's initial factor mean was above average (about 3.7 on a 5-point scale). Self-efficacy's initial factor mean was high, and task interdependence's and self-reflection initial factor means were very high (all above 4 on a 5-point scale).

All initial mean factors were significantly and positively correlated (see ρ's in Table 6.1), suggesting that higher perceptions of consideration and stimulation of the transformational leader co-occurred with higher perceptions of task interdependence, higher beliefs in efficacy, and higher engagement in self-reflective activities, at the onset of the study (first measurement *occasion*).

The variables were related over time in the parsimonious multivariate LDS model through four significant, and invariant, coupling parameters (see Fig. 6.2, and γ's in Table 6.1). The first coupling parameter is from consideration and stimulation to task interdependence. Intra-individual increases in a transformational leader's consideration and stimulation practices lead to intra-individual increases in perceptions of the need to interact to complete tasks. This supports our Hypothesis 4a. The second coupling parameter is from task interdependence to self-reflection, and the third is from self-reflection to task interdependence. Intra-individual increases in perceptions of the need to interact to complete tasks lead to intra-individual increases in engagement in self-reflective actions, as well as vice versa. As we hypothesized (Hypotheses 2a and 2b), task interdependence and self-reflection are thus reciprocally related. The fourth coupling parameter is from self-reflection to self-efficacy. Intra-individual increases in engagement in self-reflective actions lead to intra-individual increases in beliefs of competence (Hypothesis 1b).

Overall these results show a leading role of the transformational leadership practices consideration and stimulation. Task interdependence was found to be directly influenced by consideration and stimulation. Task interdependence and self-reflection were found to have reciprocal roles in sustaining each other's levels. Surprisingly, self-efficacy was only coupled to self-reflection, and levels of self-efficacy were sustained by levels of self-reflection.

6.5 Discussion

The present investigation tested the longitudinal effects of transformational leadership practices (*i.e.*, consideration and stimulation), perceptions of task interdependence, and self-efficacy beliefs, on VET teachers' engagement in self-reflection. In addition, possible reciprocal relations between these variables were explored. Data of three measurement occasions with yearly intervals from a total of 655 participants were used for the analyses. Each variable was analyzed with univariate LDS models to assess their change. To analyze the time-based dynamic relations between the variables, a multivariate LDS model was tested. As the LDS approach enables us to represent dynamic relations between our variables over time, this approach can be considered as a strong and innovative approach for examining the role teacher learning may play in building school's capacity to change and sustained improvement.

None of the variables showed systematic constant change. Interestingly reflection declined between measurement occasion 1 and 2, after which its (still high) level was sustained. The decline on the second measurement occasion might indicate that teachers had become more critical on their own levels of reflection. However, such a critical attitude did not result in sustained decline. To understand more about the process through which self-reflection progresses, future studies must address self-reflection not only in terms of an activity, but also in terms of the content that is reflect on, to distinguish reflection on reflection from reflection to improve, for instance, instructional practices. Levels of self-efficacy were found to increase between occasion 1 and 2, after which they remained stable. These findings partly concur with findings from previous studies into the variability of teacher self-efficacy (Raudenbush et al. 1992; Ross et al. 1996; Thoonen et al. 2012). These findings showed variability in teacher-self-efficacy according to contextual (*i.e.*, student groups) and person (*i.e.*, teacher) effects as well as quite stable effects over time. More research is needed to increase our knowledge on the variability of teacher self-efficacy, using more time-intense intervals; for example monthly or weekly-based time intervals instead of yearly-based. Task interdependence did not change. This may be the most surprising finding of this study, as we expected that teachers' perceptions of task interdependence would have increased after the implementation of multidisciplinary teams in VET colleges. However, the finding that initial levels of task interdependence were already very high might indicate that teachers had welcomed an infrastructure that facilitated more contact with colleagues (e.g., Scribner et al. 2002; Stoll et al. 2009). Although consideration and stimulation increased over time, we did not find a systematic constant change factor. Apparently, after the initiation of teams, and over the course of the study, school leaders seem to attend to individual teachers' needs and feelings more, and challenged their beliefs, values, and practices more.

All four variables' initial factors were significantly and positively correlated. This suggests that those teachers scoring higher on any one variable tend to score higher in all other variables at the onset of the study. This means that people who reflect more, have higher levels of self-efficacy, perceive more interaction with team members to complete tasks, and also perceive their leader to be more considerate and more stimulating. Thus, higher personal and organizational resources that are assumed to be beneficial to take charge of change tend to go together.

Variables were sustained by the influence of other variables, but not all our hypotheses were confirmed. First, contrary to our hypothesis (Hypothesis 1a), self-efficacy did not influence self-reflection: the coupling parameter from self-efficacy to self-reflection was not significant This finding is not in line with previous cross-sectional findings which have suggested that self-efficacy beliefs are a critical component for self-reflection (Geijsel et al. 2009; Sleegers et al. 2014). Furthermore, it contrasts with the claim that self-efficacy has a pivotal role as a psychological lever between leadership and performance (Schyns 2004), at least when performance consists of the generation of new knowledge. As such, the assumed causal influence of self-efficacy on self-reflection seems not to withstand the test of time. One explanation may be that teachers with high sustained levels of self-efficacy are less motivated to learn. As they already feel excessively confident, they may think that they have nothing left to learn. However, we did find the reversed effect (Hypothesis 1b): self-reflection had a positive influence on self-efficacy. Teachers who generate more knowledge and try to find better workable scripts for changing circumstances through engagement in self-reflective practices also strengthen their beliefs of competence to overcome future obstacles. Given that under changing circumstances, one must continuously experience small successes that add up in order to sustain levels of self-efficacy (Bandura 1986; Caprara et al. 2008), it thus seems that generating new knowledge to improve one's functioning leads to such small successes. This finding can therefore be seen as indirect evidence of the beneficial role of self-reflection in adapting teaching practices to the circumstances at hand (e.g., Thoonen et al. 2012). So, rather than that beliefs of competence motivate teachers to learn, does learning generate beliefs of competence.

Secondly, we found evidence for the assumed relationship between task interdependence and self-reflection (Hypotheses 2a and 2b). Teachers' perceptions of needing to interact to complete tasks positively influenced their engagement in self-reflective activities. This finding adds to the existing evidence regarding the beneficial role of collaboration for teachers' engagement in learning activities (Meirink et al. 2010; Runhaar et al. 2010; Sleegers et al. 2014; Staples and Webster 2008). Exploration of the dynamic relations between perceived task interdependence and self-reflection pointed towards the reversed effect: Apparently, self-reflection significantly contributes to sustain teachers' perceptions of task interdependence. Together, these effects indicate that perceptions of task interdependence and engagement in self-reflection are reciprocally related. While teachers are reflecting on how to interact with team members, they discover workable scripts for possible future interactions. Thus when enacting their newly developed scripts, teacher are able to discover that team members provide them with new information, given that they perceive these interactions with team members as beneficial to complete the tasks at hand. In turn, they can then use this information to further reflect on how to improve. As such, self-reflection and perceptions of task interdependence co-develop (e.g., Clement and Vandengerghe 2000; Horn and Little 2010; Little 1990; Somech and Bogler 2002). Their co-development implies that change in either one of these processes can initiate change in the other, given that there is potential to interact.

Thirdly, with respect to the relations between self-efficacy and task interdependence (Hypotheses 3a and 3b), we did not find time-based dynamic relations between task interdependence and self-efficacy, Apparently, levels of beliefs in one's own competence stem both from previous levels of those beliefs as well as from levels of engagement in self-reflection, rather than from perceptions of task interdependence. This finding contrasts with claims about the mediational role collaboration, or more generally, workplace conditions play in the relation between leadership practices and self-efficacy beliefs (e.g., Geijsel et al. 2009; Nir and Kranot 2006; Thoonen et al. 2011; Tims et al. 2011).

Fourthly, as assumed in hypothesis 4a, consideration and stimulation positively influenced task interdependence: a leader who considers the needs and feelings of a teacher more, and challenges that teacher to calibrate the adequacy of knowledge more, positively influences teacher's perception of task interdependence. This suggest that when teachers feel more supported by their leader, they also feel more empowered to interact with their team members to complete tasks (e.g., Jung and Sosik 2002; Maynard et al. 2013; Scribner et al. 2002), validating the impact of leadership practices on collaboration, and more generally, working conditions in schools as found in previous studies (Dionne et al. 2007; Nir and Kranot 2006). Given the effects of task interdependence on self-reflection as found in this study, this finding substantiates claims of the indirect effect of leadership on teacher learning as mediated by teacher collaboration (Geijsel et al. 2009; Thoonen et al. 2011). A leader who enacts, and also grows into, a transformational role is in an indirect way beneficial for teachers to become more engaged in self-reflection. Additionally, exploration of the opposite effect (Hypothesis 4b) gave no signs that the fit of the model could be strengthened by adding the influence from task interdependence to consideration and stimulation. This indicates that, at least within the short timeframe that we measured, collaboration on tasks does not lead to more distributed forms of leadership, nor does it offer an explanation of the increase in transformational leadership that we found. Subsequent longitudinal research using data collected over a longer period of time might capture such processes better.

In sum, our longitudinal study provides some strong evidence for causality and time-based dynamic relations. The findings contradict the central role of self-efficacy in elevating teacher engagement in learning activities (Runhaar et al. 2010; Yost 2006). It did however corroborate the initiating role of transformational leadership practices (Leithwood et al. 1999; Leithwood and Sleegers 2006) in affecting teacher collaboration. More specifically, its increase helped to sustain levels of task interdependence. Additionally, we were able to provide some initial evidence for the reciprocity between task interdependence and self-reflection in sustaining each other on the one hand, and the subsequent positive influence of self-reflection on sustaining levels of self-efficacy on the other hand. This provides some evidence for the beneficial role of working in teams to foster teacher learning, and shows that, after teams have been formed, teachers' engagement in knowledge generating activities helps to sustain their perceptions of being interdependent to complete tasks successfully. This suggests that teachers co-create their own learning environment through collaboration and engagement in reflective learning, while being supported by a considerate and stimulating leader. Important to note, this investigation does not only provide evidence for the fact *that* variables are causally related, but it sheds some light on *how* variables are related, as the multivariate LDS model allows tracking the mutual influences of the variables from occasion to occasion. In our opinion, this is only an intermediate step in moving from understanding which variables cause change in, ultimately, teaching practices and student learning, to understanding how changing organizational and psychological factors interact to build school-wide capacity for sustained improvement (Giles and Hargreaves 2006; Stoll et al. 2009).

6.5.1 Limitations

In this study we made use of a versatile model type for longitudinal data: the Latent Difference Score model (McArdle 2009). It allowed to model change in a way similar to latent growth curve models but extended on them by adding proportional change to constant change. Change is thereby defined in a precise way, which makes interpretations of influences on change more robust.

Despite this benefit, a model without constant change factors fitted better to the data than a model with constant change factors. Given the high initial means of task interdependence, self-efficacy, and self-reflection, little systematic constant positive change might have been expected after the first measurement occasion. That is, finding growth of these variables may have been hindered by a ceiling effect. This issue might be resolved by using different instruments, such as 7-point questionnaires that can capture more variation. However, measurement instruments may not be the main problem. The little systematic constant change found may also be explained by the differences in the frames of reference respondents may have when answering the questionnaires, resulting in "response shift". (Oort et al. 2009). With response shift, observed changes in respondents' test scores at different measurement occasions may reflect something other than true changes in the attributes that we want to measure. Over a period of time teachers may have changed their internal standards or redefined their targets. For example, VET teachers may become more critical about team work, their own competence and their motivation to learn, due to institutional policy (formation of multidisciplinary teams) and the social settings in which they are embedded. The measurement of changed teachers' perceptions of task interdependence, their self-efficacy beliefs and engagement in self-reflective learning activities can bring about the additional problem that teachers may also change their frame of reference, rendering scores from different measurement occasions incomparable. On the other hand, it also may be that these variables are already beneficial for teachers' improvements when they remain constant. For instance, self-reflection stimulates teachers to remain proficient employees, now and in the future. Whereas professional learning is a core competence of teachers, their productivity lies at the knowledge and skills they can teach their pupils (e.g., Timperley and Alton-Lee 2008). Moreover, most of the participants had many years of service, and seem to experience a high level of competence in their profession. For experienced teachers sustaining high levels of self-reflection may be important for adapting effectively to the (changing) circumstances at hand. Their development, in this sense, would be similar to the innovation of new services as found in other organizations and industries (Nonaka 1994). Future research must establish whether a sustained level of self-reflection can continuously generate solutions to challenges at the moments the challenges present themselves.

A second caution for interpreting our findings, however, is the fit of the model to the data. Although the RMSEA value was good and the SRMR value was acceptable, the CFI value indicated a weak fit (Hu and Bentler 1999). This could at first sight leave some suspicions about whether other types of models may fit the data better, such as a cross-lagged model without a mean structure (Eschleman and LaHuis 2013). Focussing only on explaining variance in this way would however have meant to forgo a model that explicitly assesses the change in levels of the variables, and thus to abandon our aim of assessing whether, and when, any change occurred. Moreover, a series of $\Delta\chi^2$ tests indicated that the parsimonious multivariate proportional change model fitted the data best, and that none of the variables was spurious. An additional analytic caution for interpreting our findings is that data were collected from teachers who were nested in teams. We were unable to correct for this dependency in the data, because we did not have enough power to do so: the amount of parameters vastly exceeded the amount of teams. Future research must establish to what extent being a member of a team affects the coupling of reflective activities to and from other variables.

Lastly, despite the benefits of a longitudinal design, inferring causality must still be done with caution, as unmeasured variables may account for the found effects better than the measured variables (Eschleman and LaHuis 2013; McArdle 2009). Although we used variables which were shown to be important to elevate self-reflection, we used only a small set of variables that make up a school's capacity for change (*i.e.*, teachers' learning activities, personal and structural resources, and directive influences such as leadership). Additionally, self-reflection's initial level and changes were not fully explained by the variables in the model. Inclusion of variables tapping into such concepts as the sharing of information, teacher commitment, functional team conflict, distributed leadership practices, and shared focus on teacher learning, would validate and expand our findings (Fullan 2007; Hallinger and Heck 2011; Johnson and Johnson 2009; Spillane et al. 2012; Thoonen et al. 2012; Tjosvold et al. 2004). Investigating whether these relations also hold over time using data gathered from principals and students, or in other organizations or industries, would be a fruitful endeavor for future research (e.g., Edmondson et al. 2007).

6.6 Conclusion

All in all, an image rises from this longitudinal study that, in a Dutch VET context, educational improvements are driven by the reciprocity between self-reflective activities and perceptions of task interdependence. Interacting with team members to complete tasks provides input for teachers' reflections about one's functioning, which in turn provide input for subsequent interactions, and so on. Sustained engagement in self-reflection then results in sustained beliefs in self-efficacy, which suggests that the reciprocity between interaction and reflection can thus continuously offer teachers mastery experiences. Finally, a considerate and stimulating transformational leader can furthermore facilitate this process. Together, the present findings point to the important role transformational leadership practices play in facilitating teamwork and sustaining teachers' levels of reflection.

Acknowledgments The authors would like to thank Barbara Müller for her invaluable advice in the preparation of the manuscript. This work was supported by the NWO Programming Council for Educational Research (PROO) [grant number 411-07-302].

Appendices

Appendix 1: Response Rates per Occasion

Questionnaires:	t1	t2	t3
Send	853	857	822
Returned	454	449	389
Response rate	53%	52%	47%
Dropped	−16	−87	−65
Unique responses on measurement occasions:			
Occasions 1&2&3		144	
Occasions 1&2 or 1&3 or 2&3	82	45	54
Occasion 1 or 2 or 3	167	82	81
Total unique responses in the data set		655	

Note: cases could be dropped, for instance, because not all returned questionnaires were filled out completely

Appendix 2: Sample Descriptives per Occasion

		t1	t2	t3
Gender (men)		66%	68%	60%
Age (years)	Mean	48	48	48
	sd	9	10	10
	Min	22	20	21
	Max	62	63	65
Job size	>32 h	61%	62%	58%
Tenure	>20 years	33%	32%	32%
	10 years	20%	22%	22%
	<½ year	4%	2%	0%
Education	Master	16%	16%	14%
	Bachelor	72%	74%	79%
	2nd education	12%	10%	7%

Note: Years and percentages have been rounded

Appendix 3: Variables and Their Scales

All scales were responded to as follows: (1) disagree much, (2) partially disagree, (3) do not disagree, do not agree, (4) partially agree, (5) agree much.

Transformational Leadership: Individual Consideration and Intellectual Stimulation

Includes attending to the needs and feelings of individual teachers, support of professional development of teachers and challenging teachers to constantly evaluate their current knowledge and daily practices (Geijsel et al. 2009; Oude Groote Beverborg et al. 2015; Thoonen et al. 2011).

My leader	Invariant factor loadings	Residual variances t1	t2	t3
...takes the opinions of individual teachers seriously	1.000	0.507	0.325	0.418
...shows appreciation when a teacher takes the initiative for educational improvement	0.998	0.443	0.386	0.436
...listens carefully to the ideas of team members	0.955	0.434	0.362	0.383
...has an eye and an ear for problems being experienced by teachers with policy implementation	0.930	0.387	0.349	0.325
...helps teachers to express their emotions	0.839	0.548	0.475	0.542
...encourages teachers to try new things in line with their own interests	0.940	0.335	0.369	0.332
...stimulates teachers to reflect on how to improve in the department	0.949	0.298	0.328	0.275
...encourages teachers to seek and discuss new information and ideas which are relevant to the direction in which the department is developing	0.914	0.303	0.279	0.321
...engages individual teachers in discussion of personal and professional goals	0.847	0.325	0.331	0.393
...encourages teachers to experiment with new teaching methods	0.833	0.532	0.596	0.614
...creates sufficient opportunities for teachers to work on their professional development	0.913	0.646	0.474	0.545

Cronbach's alphas are at: t1=.956; t2=.947; t3=.943

Task Interdependence

Refers to the degree to which interaction and coordination of team members are required to complete tasks (Oude Groote Beverborg et al. 2015; Runhaar 2008; Runhaar et al. 2010).

	Invariant factor loadings	Invariant residual variances
For the conduct of our jobs, the members of my team need information from each other	1.000	0.128
To do our jobs well, we have to work together as a team	1.012	0.087
The work of one team member influences the conduct of the tasks of other team members	0.880	0.623
To do our work well, we have to coordinate our work as a team	0.987	0.169

Cronbach's alphas are at: t1=.783; t2=.779; t3=823

Occupational Self-Efficacy

A future-oriented belief about the level of competence person expects to display in a given situation (Oude Groote Beverborg et al. 2015; Runhaar 2008; Runhaar et al. 2010; Schyns and von Collani 2002).

	Invariant factor loadings	Residual variances		
		t1	t2	t3
I can remain calm when confronted with difficulties in my work because I know that I can fall back on my competences	1.000	0.421	0.363	0.299
When I am confronted with a problem in my work, I can usually find different solutions	0.999	0.352	0.242	0.243
Whatever happens in my work, I can usually manage	1.005	0.277	0.292	0.220
My past experiences have prepared me well for my current work	1.024	0.411	0.315	0.391
In my work, I achieve the goals which I have set for myself	0.937	0.413	0.321	0.283
I am adequately equipped to face the demands of my work	0.966	0.330	0.287	0.265

Cronbach's alphas are at: t1=.801; t2=.800; t3=850

Reflection

An individual learning activity aimed at making implicit knowledge explicit (Oude Groote Beverborg et al. 2015; Runhaar 2008; Runhaar et al. 2010; van Woerkom 2003).

	Invariant factor loadings	Residual variances		
		t1	t2	t3
I ponder what I find important in my work	1.000	0.140	0.181	0.141
I monitor progress with regard to the goals of my work	0.935	0.255	0.210	0.219
I reflect on the manner in which I do my work	0.985	0.147	0.197	0.180
I compare my performance with how I performed one year ago	0.921	0.526	0501	0.425
I think about my communication with colleagues	0.976	0.277	0.256	0.212

Cronbach's alphas are at: t1=.823; t2=.815; t3=854

Appendix 4: Chi-square Difference (ΔX^2) Tests of Invariance and Stability

		TLcs	Task	SE	Refl
Factor loadings λ's	Equal – unequal	24.143(20)	8.061(6)	9.658(10)	4.758(8)
Residual variances ψ's	Equal – unequal	36.889(22)†	4.380(8)	55.265(12)*	23.961(10)*
Autoregressions ß's	Absent – free	183.144(2)*	88.125(2)*	154.481(2)*	163.616(2)*

* $p < .01$, † $p < .05$, degrees of freedom (df) in parentheses
TLcs = transformational leadership consideration and stimulation; task = task interdependence; SE = self-efficacy; Refl = self-reflection

ΔX^2 tests of the autoregressions include the assumption of measurement error with a mean of 0, and TLcs, SE, and Refl had variant residual variances, Task had invariant residual variance

A significant ΔX^2 test indicates a worsening through restraint. The more restraint model is listed first in the second column. Thus, significance indicates to select the second listed model, and vice versa.

Appendix 5: Correlation Table

Means, Standard Errors of the means, and Correlations from the measurement model

Variables	Mean	S.E.	1	2	3	4	5	6	7	8	9	10	11
1. TLcs [1]	3.680	.051											
2. TLcs [2]	3.804	.047	.415*										
3. TLcs [3]	3.884	.048	.471*	.574*									
4. Task [1]	4.556	.027	.116*	.064†	.034								
5. Task [2]	4.505	.029	.107*	.113*	.083*	.113*							
6. Task [3]	4.467	.032	.118*	.106*	.106*	.100*	.139*						
7. SE [1]	4.088	.031	.115*	.002	.034	.085*	.059*	.060*					
8. SE [2]	4.147	.030	.071†	.032	.004	.046*	.080*	.026	.164*				
9. SE [3]	4.126	.034	.076	.032	.037	−.025	.053*	.047†	.132*	.155*			
10. Refl [1]	4.350	.026	.049	.055	.015	.094*	.080*	.046†	.116*	.080*	.056*		
11. Refl [2]	4.271	.029	.055	.067*	.055	.080	.111	.047†	.072*	.109*	.078*	.140*	
12. Refl [3]	4.261	.030	.132*	.108*	.097*	.091*	.092*	.105*	.112*	.084*	.100*	.151*	.188*

* p<.01, † p<.05

TLcs = Transformational Leadership consideration and stimulation; Task = task interdependence; SE = self-efficacy; Refl = self-reflection; [1], [2], [3] indicate measurement occasions 1, 2, 3, respectively

Appendix 6: Latent Difference Score Models

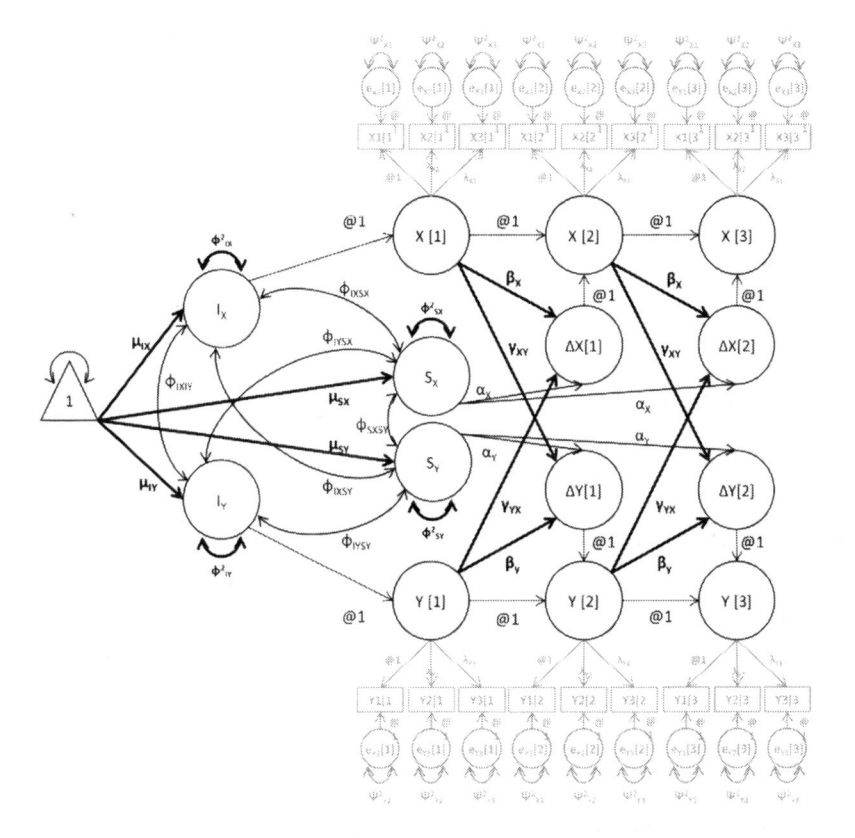

Bivariate dual change Latent Difference Score model. This model may appear complicated, but because a number of constraints are typically applied there are few parameters that are estimated. Roughly from middle left to bottom right: Bold and grey are used to create contrast to make the graph easier to read. The triangle represents a constant with a mean of 1 and variance of 1, circles represent factors, squares represent observations. Y and X represent variables. I represents an initial factor with a mean μ_I and variance ϕ_I^2. S stands for slope and represents a systematic constant change factor (or intra-individual constant growth), also with a mean and variance. ϕ's represent covariances between initial and slope factors. Δ stands for difference. [1], [2], and [3] indicate measurement occasions. ΔY[1] represents thus the first latent difference score of variable Y, and is the most important parameter; hence the name of the model. It represents intraindividual change proportional to the levels of its influences on the previous time point. The Δ values are a function of slope factor loadings (α's), autoregressive effects (β's), and regressions on other variables (γ's, or couplings). α's are typically set at one when measurement occasions are equidistant. The values of Δ's may differ over time, even when their influences are invariant (which they are in the figure, which is indicated by equal labels).

They are created from measurement occasion factors (e.g., Y[2]), by fixing their factor loading at one (@1). Furthermore, Y[1] represents the factor of measurement occasion 1 of variable Y, Y1[1] represents the first item of variable Y on the first measurement occasion, $e_{y1}[1]$ represent the measurement error of the first item, and ψ^2 is its variance. Measurement occasion factor loadings (λ's) must be held invariant. Measurement error variance can be held invariant (and it is in the figure). The model in the figure is termed a dual change model because change stems from both a constant change factor (S), and autoregressions (β's). The model can be changed into a constant change model by fixing the autoregressions at zero, and into a proportional change model by removing the slope factor and freeing the autoregressions.

Appendix 7: Model Selection and Optimization Chi-square Difference (ΔX^2) Tests

		TLcs	Task	SE	Refl
Change model	dual – proportional	461.382(2)*	269.723(2)*	71.610(2)*	109.127(2)*
Change model	constant – dual	348.621(1)*	1.351(1)	2.249(1)	17.969(1)*
Change model	constant – proportional	810.003(3)*	271.074(3)*	73.859(3)*	127.096(3)*
Proportional change model optimization autoregressions β's equal – unequal		20.688(1)*	.606(1)	1.123(1)	2.026(1)

* $p<.01$, degrees of freedom (df) in parentheses
TLcs = transformational leadership consideration and stimulation; task = task interdependence; SE = self-efficacy; Refl = self-reflection
TLcs, SE, and Refl had variant residual variances, Task had invariant residual variance
A significant ΔX^2 test indicates a worsening through restraint. The more restraint model is listed first in the second column. Thus, significance indicates to select the second listed model, and vice versa

Appendix 8: Univariate Latent Proportional Change Models, Their Trajectories, and Their Fit Measures

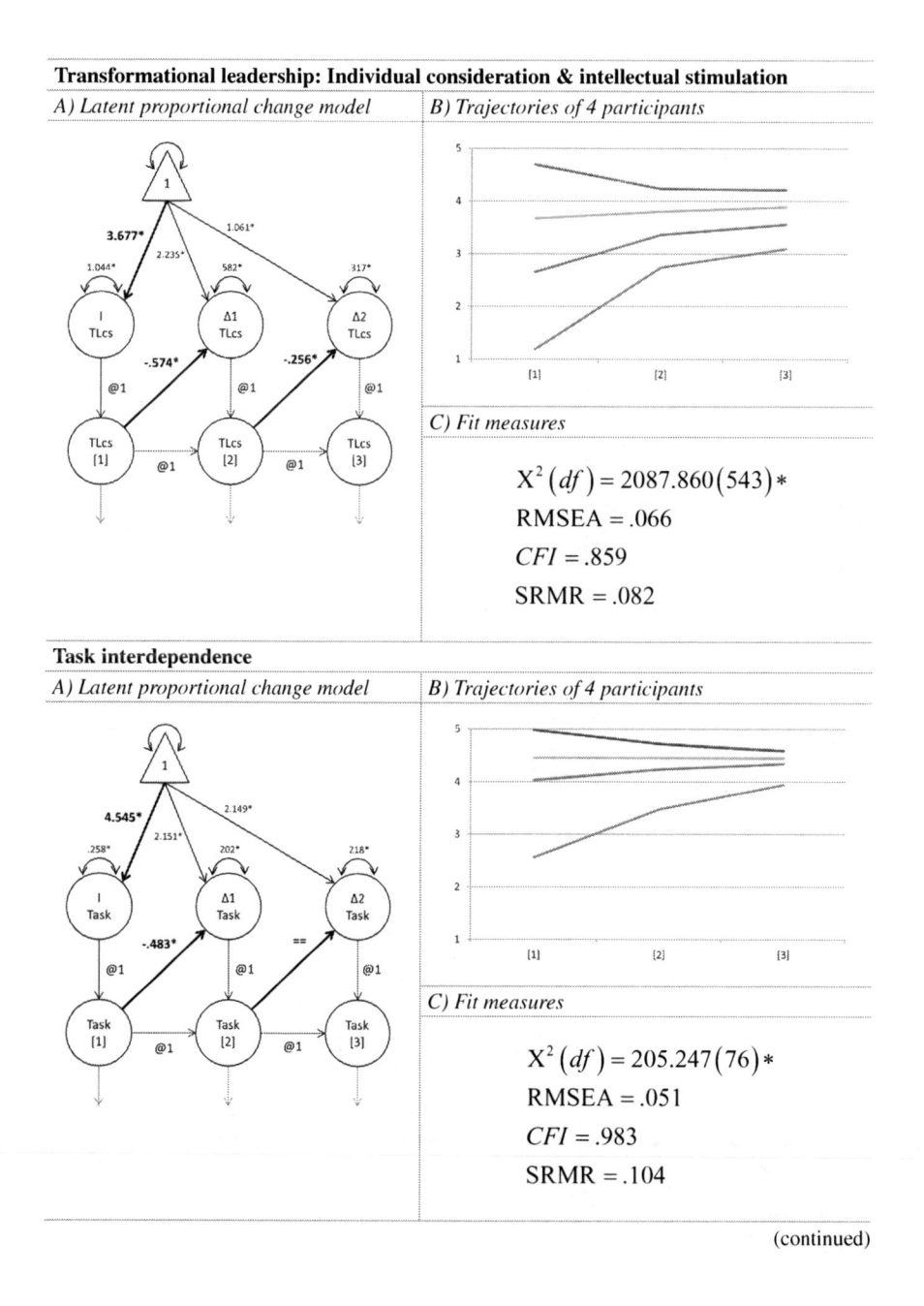

Transformational leadership: Individual consideration & intellectual stimulation

A) Latent proportional change model

B) Trajectories of 4 participants

C) Fit measures

$$X^2(df) = 2087.860(543)*$$
$$RMSEA = .066$$
$$CFI = .859$$
$$SRMR = .082$$

Task interdependence

A) Latent proportional change model

B) Trajectories of 4 participants

C) Fit measures

$$X^2(df) = 205.247(76)*$$
$$RMSEA = .051$$
$$CFI = .983$$
$$SRMR = .104$$

(continued)

Self-efficacy

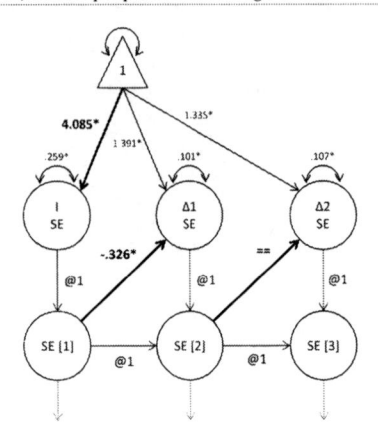

A) Latent proportional change model	B) Trajectories of 4 participants

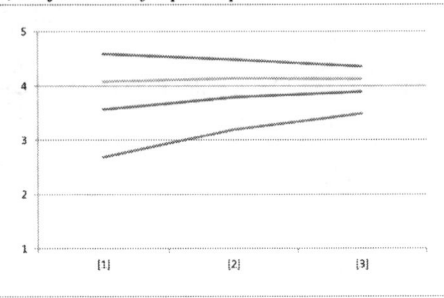

C) Fit measures

$$X^2(df) = 508.794(159)*$$
$$RMSEA = .058$$
$$CFI = .852$$
$$SRMR = .119$$

Self-reflection

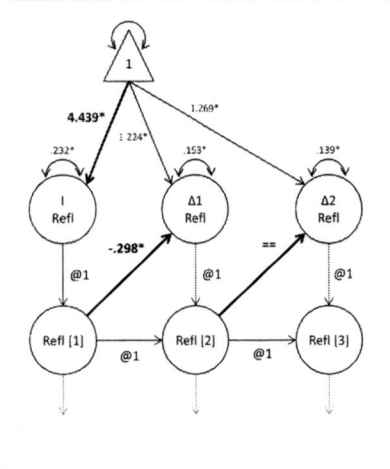

A) Latent proportional change model	B) Trajectories of 4 participants

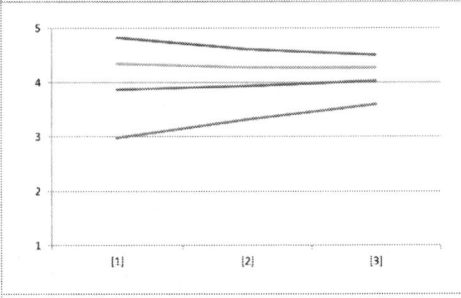

C) Fit measures

$$X^2(df) = 329.371(109)*$$
$$RMSEA = .056$$
$$CFI = .906$$
$$SRMR = .125$$

*$p < .01$
A)'s: Double equality signs indicate that this parameter is contraint to be equal over time
Observations, measurement occasion factor loadings, and measurement errors are not shown, but their inclusion is referred to by the gray arrows
B)'s: Trajectories per variable are based on model estimated values, derived from initial values of 4 randomly selected participants.

References

Avolio, B. J., Zhu, W., Kho, W., & Bhata, P. (2004). Transformational leadership and organizational commitment: Mediating role of psychological empowerment and moderating role of structural distance. *Journal of Organizational Behavior, 25*, 951–968.

Bandura, A. (1986). *Social foundations of thought and action: A social cognitive theory.* Englewood Cliffs: Prentice Hall.

Bandura, A. (1993). Perceived self-efficacy in cognitive development and functioning. *Educational Psychologist, 28*, 117–148.

Bandura, A. (1997). *Self-efficacy: The exercise of control.* New York: Freeman.

Barsalou, L. W. (2008). Grounded cognition. *Annual Review of Psychology, 58*, 617–645.

Campion, M. A., Medsker, G. J., & Higgs, A. C. (1993). Relations between work groups characteristics and effectiveness: Implications for designing effective work groups. *Personnel Psychology, 46*, 823–847.

Caprara, G. V., Fida, R., Vecchione, M., del Bove, G., Vecchio, G. V., Barbaranelli, C., & Bandura, A. (2008). Longitudinal analysis of the role of perceived self-efficacy for self-regulated learning in academic continuance and achievement. *Journal of Educational Psychology, 100*, 525–534.

Clarke, D. J., & Hollingsworth, H. (2002). Elaborating a model of teacher professional growth. *Teaching and Teacher Education, 18*, 947–967.

Clement, M., & Vandenberghe, R. (2000). Teachers' professional development: A solitary or collegial (ad)venture? *Teaching and Teacher Education, 16*, 81–101.

Cole, D. A., & Maxwell, S. E. (2003). Testing mediational models with longitudinal data: Questions and tips in the use of structural equation modeling. *Journal of Abnormal Psychology, 112*, 558–577.

Cummings, T. G. (1978). Self-regulating work groups: A socio-technical analysis. *Academy of Management Review, 3*, 625–634.

Day, C., Sammons, P., Leithwood, K., Hopkins, D., Harris, A., Gu, Q., & Brown, E. (2010). *Ten strong claims about successful school leadership.* Nottingham: NCLS.

De Jong, S. B., van der Vegt, G. S., & Molleman, E. (2007). The relationships among asymmetry in task dependence, perceived helping behavior, and trust. *Journal of Applied Psychology, 92*, 1625–1637.

Desimone, L. M. (2009). Improving impact studies of teachers' professional development: Toward better conceptualizations and measures. *Educational Researcher, 38*, 181–199.

Dionne, S. D., Yammarino, F. J., Atwater, L. E., & Spangler, W. D. (2007). Transformational leadership and team performance. *Journal of Organizational Change Management, 17*, 177–193.

Edmondson, A. C., Dillon, J. R., & Roloff, K. S. (2007). 6 three perspectives on team learning: Outcome improvement, task mastery, and group process. *Academy of Management Annals, 1*, 269–314.

Eraut, M. (2004). Informal learning in the workplace. *Studies in Continuing Education, 26*, 247–273.

Eschleman, K. J., & LaHuis, D. (2013). Advancing occupational stress and health research and interventions using latent difference score modelling. *International Journal of Stress Management, 21*, 112–136.

Feldhoff, T., Radisch, F., & Klieme, E. (2014). Methods in longitudinal school improvement: State of the art. *Journal of Educational Administration, 52*, 565–736.

Ferrer, E., & McArdle, J. J. (2010). Longitudinal modeling of developmental changes in psychological research. *Current Directions in Psychological Science, 19*, 149–154.

Fullan, M. (2007). *The new meaning of educational change* (4th ed.). New York: Teachers College Press.

Geijsel, F. P., Sleegers, P. J. C., & van den Berg, R. M. (1999). Transformational leadership and the implementation of large-scale innovation programs. *Journal of Educational Administration, 37*, 309–328.

Geijsel, F., Sleegers, P., Leithwood, K., & Jantzi, D. (2003). Transformational leadership effects on teachers' commitment and effort toward school reform. *Journal of Educational Administration, 41*, 228–256.

Geijsel, F. P., Sleegers, P. J., Stoel, R. D., & Kruger, M. L. (2009). The effect of teacher psychological and school organizational and leadership factors on teachers' professional learning in Dutch schools. *The Elementary School Journal, 109*, 1–22.

Giles, C., & Hargreaves, A. (2006). The sustainability of innovative schools as learning organizations and professional learning communities during standardized reform. *Educational Administration Quarterly, 42*, 124–156.

Hallinger, P., & Heck, R. (2011). Exploring the journey of school improvement: Classifying and analyzing patterns of change in school improvement processes and learning outcomes. *School Effectiveness and School Improvement, 22*, 149–173.

Heck, R. H., & Hallinger, P. (2010). Collaborative leadership effects on school improvement: Integrating unidirectional-and reciprocal-effects models. *The Elementary School Journal*, 226–252.

Heck, R. H., & Hallinger, P. (2014). Modelling the longitudinal effects of school leadership on teaching and learning. *Journal of Educational Administration, 52*, 653–681.

Horn, I. S., & Little, J. W. (2010). Attending to problems of practice: Routines and resources for professional learning in teachers' workplace interactions. *American Educational Research Journal, 47*, 181–217.

Hoy, A. W., & Spero, R. B. (2005). Changes in teacher efficacy during the early years of teaching: A comparison of four measures. *Teaching and Teacher Education, 21*, 343–356.

Hu, L., & Bentler, P. M. (1999). Cutoff criteria for fit indexes in covariance structure analysis: Conventional criteria versus new alternatives. *Structural Equation Modeling, 6*, 1–55.

Jarvis, P. (1987). *Adult learning in the social context*. London: Croom Helm.

Johnson, D. W., & Johnson, R. T. (2009). Energizing learning: The instructional power of conflict. *Educational Researcher, 38*, 37–51.

Jung, D. I., & Sosik, J. J. (2002). Transformational leadership in work groups: The role of empowerment, cohesiveness, and collective-efficacy on perceived group performance. *Small Group Research, 33*, 313–336.

Katz-Navon, T. Y., & Erez, M. (2005). When collective-and self-efficacy affect team performance the role of task interdependence. *Small Group Research, 36*, 437–465.

Klarner, P., Probst, G., & Soparnot, R. (2008). Organizational change capacity in public services: The case of the World Health Organization. *Journal of Change Management, 8*, 57–72.

Korek, S., Felfe, J., & Zäpernick-Rothe, U. (2010). Transformational leadership and commitment: A multilevel analysis of group-level influences and mediating processes. *European Journal of Work and Organizational Psychology, 19*, 364–387.

Korthagen, F. (2001, April). *Linking practice and theory: The pedagogy of realistic teacher education*. In Proceedings of the Annual Meeting of the American Educational Research Association, Seattle, WA.

Korthagen, F., & Vasalos, A. (2005). Levels in reflection: Core reflection as a means to enhance professional growth. *Teachers and Teaching, 11*, 47–71.

Kwakman, K. (2003). Factors affecting teachers' participation in professional learning activities. *Teaching and Teacher Education, 19*, 149–170.

Leithwood, K., Sleegers, P. (Eds.), (2006). Transforming school leadership [Special issue]. *School Effectiveness and School Improvement, 17*.

Leithwood, K., Jantzi, D., & Steinbach, R. (1999). *Changing leadership for changing times*. Buckingham: Open University.

Leithwood, K., Jantzi, D., & Mascall, B. (2002). A framework for research on large-scale reform. *Journal of Educational Change, 3*, 7–33.

Little, J. (1990). The persistence of privacy: Autonomy and initiative in teachers' professional relations. *Teachers College Record, 91*, 509–536.

Lohman, M. C. (2005). A survey of factors influencing the engagement of two professional groups in informal workplace learning activities. *Human Resource Development Quarterly, 16*, 501–527.

Malmberg, L. E., Hagger, H., & Webster, S. (2014). Teachers' situation-specific mastery experiences: Teacher, student group and lesson effects. *European Journal of Psychology of Education, 29*, 429–451.

Marsick, V. J., & Watkins, K. (1990). *Informal and incidental learning in the workplace*. New York: Routledge.

Maxwell, S. E., Cole, D. A., & Mitchell, M. A. (2011). Bias in cross-sectional analyses of longitudinal mediation: Partial and complete mediation under an autoregressive model. *Multivariate Behavioral Research, 46*, 816–841.

Maynard, M. T., Mathieu, J. E., Gilson, L. L., O'Boyle, E. H., & Cigularov, K. P. (2013). Drivers and outcomes of team psychological empowerment a meta-analytic review and model test. *Organizational Psychology Review, 3*, 101–137.

McArdle, J. J. (2009). Latent variable modeling of differences and changes with longitudinal data. *Annual Review of Psychology, 60*, 577–605.

McArdle, J. J., & Hamagami, F. (2001). Latent difference score structural models for linear dynamic analyses with incomplete longitudinal data. *Learning and Individual Differences, 12*, 53–79.

McArdle, J. J., & Prindle, J. J. (2008). A latent change score analysis of a randomized clinical trial in reasoning training. *Psychology and Aging, 23*, 702–719.

McArdle, K., & Coutts, N. (2010). Taking teachers' continuous professional development (CPD) beyond reflection: Adding shared sense-making and collaborative engagement for professional renewal. *Studies in Continuing Education, 32*, 201–215.

McArdle, J. J., & Prindle, J. J. (2013). Basic issues in the measurement of change. In *APA handbook of testing and assessment in psychology: Test theory and testing and assessment in industrial and organizational psychology* (pp. 223–243). Washington, DC: American Psychological Association.

McArdle, J. J., Hamagami, F., Meredith, W., & Bradway, K. P. (2000). Modeling the dynamic hypotheses of Gf-Gc theory using longitudinal life-span data. *Learning and Individual Differences, 12*, 53–79.

Meirink, J. A., Meijer, P. C., Verloop, N., & Bergen, T. C. (2009). How do teachers learn in the workplace? An examination of teacher learning activities. *European Journal of Teacher Education, 32*, 209–224.

Meirink, J. A., Imants, J., Meijer, P. C., & Verloop, N. (2010). Teacher learning and collaboration in innovative teams. *Cambridge Journal of Education, 40*, 161–181.

Moolenaar, N. M., Sleegers, P. J. C., & Daly, A. J. (2012). Teaming up: Linking collaboration networks, collective efficacy, and student achievement. *Teaching and Teacher Education, 28*, 251–262.

Mulford, B. (2010). Recent developments in the field of educational leadership: The challenge of complexity. In A. Hargreaves, A. Lieberman, M. Fullan, & D. Hopkins (Eds.), *Second international handbook of educational change* (pp. 187–208). Dordrecht: Springer.

Muthén, L. K., & Muthén, B. O. (2010). *Mplus user's guide* (6th ed.). Los Angeles: Author.

Nielsen, K., & Munir, F. (2009). How do transformational leaders influence followers' affective wellbeing? Exploring the mediating role of self-efficacy. *Work and Stress, 23*, 313–329.

Nir, A. E., & Kranot, N. (2006). School principal's leadership style and teachers' self-efficacy. *Planning and Changing, 37*, 205–218.

Nonaka, I. (1994). A dynamic theory of organizational knowledge creation. *Organization Science, 5*, 14–37.

Oort, F. J., Visser, M. R. M., & Sprangers, M. A. G. (2009). Formal definitions of measurement bias and explanation bias clarify measurement and conceptual perspectives on response shift. *Journal of Clinical Epidemiology, 62*(11), 29–1137.

Oude Groote Beverborg, A., Sleegers, P. J. C., & van Veen, K. (2015). Fostering teacher learning in VET colleges: Do leadership and teamwork matter? *Teaching and Teacher Education, 48*, 22–33.

Phan, H. P. (2012). The development of English and mathematics self-efficacy: A latent growth curve analysis. *Journal of Educational Research, 105*, 196–209.

Poortman, C.L. (2007). Workplace learning processes in senior secondary vocational education. Ph.D. thesis, University of Twente, Enschede, The Netherlands. Retrieved from http://doc.utwente.nl/57877/1/thesis_Poortman.pdf

Putnam, R. T., & Borko, H. (2000). What do new views of knowledge and thinking have to say about research on teacher learning? *Educational Researcher, 29*, 4–15.

Raudenbush, S. W., Rowan, B., & Cheong, Y. F. (1992). Contextual effects on the self-perceived efficacy of high school teachers. *Sociology of Education, 65*, 150–167.

Richardson, V., & Placier, P. (2001). Teacher change. In *Handbook of research on teaching* (pp. 905–947). Washington, DC: American Educational Research Association.

Ross, J. A., Cousins, J. B., & Gadalla, T. (1996). Within-teacher predictors of teacher efficacy. *Teaching and Teacher Education, 12*, 386–400.

Runhaar, P.R. (2008). Promoting teachers' professional development. Ph.D. thesis, University of Twente, Enschede, The Netherlands. Retrieved from http://doc.utwente.nl/60129/1/thesis_Runhaar,_P.pdf

Runhaar, P., Sanders, K., & Yang, H. (2010). Stimulating teachers' reflection and feedback asking: An interplay of self-efficacy, learning goal orientation, and transformational leadership. *Teaching and Teacher Education, 26*, 1154–1161.

Salanova, M., Bakker, A. B., & Llorens, S. (2006). Flow at work: Evidence for an upward spiral of personal and organizational resources. *Journal of Happiness Studies, 7*, 1–22.

Sbarra, D. A., & Allen, J. J. (2009). Decomposing depression: On the prospective and reciprocal dynamics of mood and sleep disturbances. *Journal of Abnormal Psychology, 118*, 171–182.

Schön, D. A. (1983). *The reflective practitioner: How professionals think in action*. New York: Basic.

Schyns, B. (2004). The influence of occupational self-efficacy on the relationship of leadership behavior and preparedness for occupational change. *Journal of Career Development, 30*, 247–261.

Schyns, B., & Von Collani, G. (2002). A new self-efficacy scale and its relation to personality constructs and organizational variables. *European Journal of Work and Organizational Psychology, 11*, 219–241.

Scribner, J. P., Hager, D. R., & Warne, T. R. (2002). The paradox of professional community: Tales from two high schools. *Educational Administration Quarterly, 38*, 45–76.

Simbula, S., Guglielmi, D., & Schaufeli, W. B. (2011). A three-wave study of job resources, self-efficacy, and work engagement among Italian schoolteachers. *European Journal of Work and Organizational Psychology, 20*, 285–304.

Sleegers, P., Bolhuis, S., & Geijsel, F. (2005). School improvement within a knowledge economy: Fostering professional learning from a multidimensional perspective. In N. Bascia, A. Cumming, A. Datnow, K. Leithwood, & D. Livingstone (Eds.), *International handbook of educational policy* (pp. 527–543). Dordrecht: Kluwer.

Sleegers, P. J. C., Thoonen, E. E. J., Oort, F. J., & Peetsma, T. T. D. (2014). Improving classroom practices: The role of school-wide capacity for sustainable improvement. *Journal of Educational Administration, 52*, 617–652.

Smylie, M. A., & Hart, A. W. (1999). School leadership for teacher learning and change: A human and social capital development perspective. In J. Murphy & K. S. Louis (Eds.), *Handbook of research on educational administration* (pp. 421–441). San Francisco: Jossey-Bass.

Smylie, M. A., Lazarus, V., & Brownlee-Conyers, J. (1996). Instructional outcomes of school-based participative decision making. *Educational Evaluation and Policy Analyis, 18*, 181–198.

Somech, A., & Bogler, R. (2002). Antecedents and consequences of teacher organizational and professional commitment. *Educational Administration Quarterly, 38*, 555–577.

Spillane, J. P., Reiser, B. J., & Reimer, T. (2002). Policy implementation and cognition: Reframing and refocussing implementation research. *Review of Educational Research, 72*, 387–431.

Spillane, J. P., Kim, C. M., & Frank, K. A. (2012). Instructional advice and information providing and receiving behavior in elementary schools exploring tie formation as a building block in social capital development. *American Educational Research Journal, 49*, 1112–1145.

Staples, D. S., & Webster, J. (2008). Exploring the effects of trust, task interdependence and virtualness on knowledge sharing in teams. *Information Systems Journal, 18*, 617–640.

Stoll, L. (2009). Capacity building for school improvement or creating capacity for learning? A changing landscape. *Journal of Educational Change, 10*, 115–127.

Stoll, L., Bolam, R., McMahon, A., Wallace, M., & Thomas, S. (2009). Professional learning communities: A review of the literature. *Journal of Educational Change, 7*, 221–258.

Stone, R. W., & Bailey, J. J. (2007). Team conflict self-efficacy and outcome expectancy of business students. *Journal of Education for Business, 82*, 258–266.

Sun, J., & Leithwood, K. (2012). Transformational leadership effects on student achievement. *Leadership and Policy in Schools, 11*, 418–451.

Thoonen, E. E. J., Sleegers, P. J. C., Oort, F. J., Peetsma, T. T. D., & Geijsel, F. P. (2011). How to improve teaching practices: The role of teacher motivation, organizational factors, and leadership practices. *Educational Administration Quarterly, 47*, 496–536.

Thoonen, E. E., Sleegers, P. J. C., Oort, F. J., & Peetsma, T. T. (2012). Building school-wide capacity for improvement: The role of leadership, school organizational conditions, and teacher factors. *School Effectiveness and School Improvement, 23*, 441–460.

Timperley, H., & Alton-Lee, A. (2008). Reframing teacher professional learning: An alternative policy approach to strengthening valued outcomes for diverse learners. *Review of Research in Education, 32*, 328–369.

Tims, M., Bakker, A. B., & Xanthopoulou, D. (2011). Do transformational leaders enhance their followers' daily work engagement? *The Leadership Quarterly, 22*, 121–131.

Tjosvold, D., Yu, Z. Y., & Hui, C. (2004). Team learning from mistakes: The contribution of cooperative goals and problem-solving. *Journal of Management Studies, 41*, 1223–1245.

Truijen, K. (2012). Teacher teaming: Exploring factors that influence effective team functioning in a vocational education context. Ph.D. thesis, University of Twente, Enschede, The Netherlands, Retrieved from http://doc.utwente.nl/80028/1/thesis_K_Truijen.pdf

Van der Vegt, G., Emans, B., & van de Vliert, E. (2000). Team members' affective responses to patterns of intragroup interdependence and job complexity. *Journal of Management, 26*, 633–655.

Van Woerkom, M. (2003). Critical reflection at work: Bridging individual and organisational learning. Ph.D. thesis, University of Twente, Enschede, The Netherlands.

Van Woerkom, M. (2004). The concept of critical reflection and its implications for human resource development. *Advances in Developing Human Resources, 6*, 178–192.

Wageman, R. (1995). Interdependence and group effectiveness. *Administrative Science Quarterly, 40*, 145–180.

Walumbwa, F. O., Lawler, J. J., Avolio, B. J., Wang, P., & Shi, K. (2005). Transformational leadership and work-related attitudes: The moderating effects of collective and self-efficacy across cultures. *Journal of Leadership and Organizational Studies, 11*, 2–16.

Xanthopoulou, D., Bakker, A. B., Demerouti, E., & Schaufeli, W. B. (2009). Reciprocal relationships between job resources, personal resources, and work engagement. *Journal of Vocational Behavior, 74*, 235–244.

Yammarino, F. J., Dionne, S. D., Schriesheim, C. A., & Dansereau, F. (2008). Authentic leadership and positive organizational behavior: A meso, multi-level perspective. *The Leadership Quarterly, 19*, 693–707.

Yost, D. S. (2006). Reflection and self-efficacy: Enhancing the retention of qualified teachers from a teacher education perspective. *Teacher Education Quarterly, 33*, 59–76.

Part III
The Emotional Path

Introduction

The three chapters in this section explore conditions or variables on the Emotional Path. Chapter 7 is a meta-analytic review of the effects on students of both individual and collective teacher efficacy, teacher commitment, organizational citizenship behavior and teacher trust in colleagues, parents, and students. Chapter 8 outlines the factors that contribute to trust building among leaders and their colleagues. Evidence reported in Chap. 9 indicates that teachers award considerable importance to leaders' ability and willingness to care about their staff and model good work/life balance.

Conditions on the Emotional Path are distinct feelings, dispositions, and affective states of teachers, both individually and collectively, about school-related matters. There are a large handful of consequential teacher emotions (Leithwood 2006; Leithwood and Beatty 2007). This section introduction, illustrates and summarizes the nature and effects on students of three especially powerful emotions- Collective Teacher Efficacy, Teacher Trust in others and Organizational Citizenship Behavior. This introduction also describes approaches to leadership that available evidence suggests have a positive influence on each of these conditions

Collective Teacher Efficacy (CTE)

Collective Teacher Efficacy is the level of confidence a group of teachers feels about its ability to organize and implement whatever educational initiatives are required for students to achieve high standards of achievement. The effects of efficacy or collective confidence on performance is indirect through the persistence it engenders in the face of initial failure and the opportunities it creates for a confident group to learn its way forward rather than giving up (Tschannen-Moran et al. 1998).

In highly efficacious schools, evidence suggests that teachers accept responsibility for their student's learning. Learning difficulties are not assumed to be an inevitable by-product of low socio-economic status, lack of ability, or family background. CTE creates high expectations for students as well as the collectively confident teachers. Evidence suggests that high levels of CTE encourage teachers to set challenging benchmarks for themselves, engage in high levels of planning and organization, devote more classroom time to academic learning. High CTE teachers are more likely to engage in activity-based learning, student-centered learning, and interactive instruction. Among other exemplary practices high CTE is associated with teachers adopting a humanistic approach to student management, testing new instructional methods to meet the learning needs of their students and the provision of extra help to students who have difficulty and display persistence and resiliency in such cases; reward students for their achievements; believe their students can reach high academic goals; display more enthusiasm for teaching; commit to community partnerships; and have more ownership in school decisions

While the total number of well-designed studies inquiring about CTE effects on students is still modest, their results are both consistent and impressive. This relatively recent evidence demonstrates a significant positive relationship between collective teacher efficacy and achievement by students in such areas of the curriculum as reading, math and writing. Furthermore, and perhaps more surprising, several of these studies have found that the effects on achievement of CTE exceed the effects of students socio-economic status (e.g., Goddard et al. 2000), a variable that typically explains by far the bulk of achievement variation across schools, usually in excess of 50%. High CTE schools also are associated with lower suspension and dropout rates as well as greater school orderliness (Tschannen-Moran and Barr 2004).

There are two sources of insight about how leaders might improve the collective efficacy of their teaching colleagues. One source is the theoretical work of Bandura (1993), clearly the major figure in thinking about CTE. His work, by now widely supported empirically, identifies a number of conditions which influence the collective efficacy of a group: opportunities to master the skills needed to do whatever the job entails; vicarious experiences of others performing the job well, and beliefs about how supportive is the setting in which one is working. Leaders have the potential to influence all of these conditions, for example, by:

- sponsoring meaningful professional development,
- encouraging their staffs to network with others facing similar challenges in order to learn from their experiences;
- structuring their schools to allow for collaborative work among staff,

A second source of insight about how leaders might improve the collective efficacy of their teaching colleagues is the small number of studies that have inquired about the leadership practices which improve CTE. For the most part, these have been studies of transformational leadership practices on the part of principals (e.g., Ross and Gray 2006; Leithwood 1994). Evidence from these studies demonstrates significant positive effects on CTE when principals:

- clarify goals by, for example, identifying new opportunities for the school, developing (often collaboratively), articulating and inspiring others with a vision of the future, promoting cooperation and collaboration among staff towards common goals;
- offer individualized support by, for example, showing respect for individual members of the staff, demonstrating concern about their personal feelings and needs, maintaining an open door policy, and valuing staff opinions;
- provide appropriate models of both desired practices and appropriate values ("walking the talk").

Teacher Trust in Colleagues, Parents and Students

Trust is conceptualized in many different specific ways. But almost all efforts to clarify the nature of trust include a belief or expectation, in this case on the part of most teachers, that their colleagues, students and parents support the schools' goals for student learning and will reliably work toward achieving those goals. Transparency, competence, benevolence, and reliability are among the qualities persuading others that a person is trustworthy.

Teacher trust is critical to the success of schools and nurturing trusting relationships with students and parents is a key element in improving student. Dimensions of trust shown to be related to positive outcomes in school include:

- Benevolence: a person's confidence that their well-being and/or things they hold dear to them will not be harmed;
- Reliability; a person's belief that individuals will act consistently in ways that are beneficial those who commit their trust;
- Competence: beliefs in the ability of a person to perform consistently and up to a well-known standard;
- Honesty: including beliefs about a person's truthfulness, integrity and authenticity
- Openness.

Trust remains a strong predictor of student achievement even after the effects of student background, prior achievement, race and gender have been taken into account in some studies of trust in schools. Goddard (2003) argues that when teacher-parent, and teacher-student relationships are characterized by trust, academically supportive norms and social relations have the potential to move students toward academic success. Results of a second study by Goddard et al. (2001) provide one of the largest estimates of trust effects on student learning. In this study trust explained 81% of the variation between schools in students' math and reading achievement.

Principal leadership has been highlighted as a critical contributor to trust among teachers, parents and students (e.g., Bryk and Schneider 2003). This evidence suggests that principals engender trust with and among staff and with both parents and students when they:

- recognize and acknowledge the vulnerabilities of their staff;
- listen to the personal needs of staff members and assist as much as possible to reconcile those needs with a clear vision for the school;
- create a space for parents in the school and demonstrate to parents that they (principal) are reliable, open, and scrupulously honest in their interactions;
- buffer teachers from unreasonable demands from the policy environment or from the parents and the wider community;
- behave toward teachers in a friendly, supportive, and open manner; set high standards for students and then follow through with support for teachers.

Evidence suggests a significant positive relationship between several transformational leadership practices and collective teacher efficacy including inspiring group purpose, providing individualized support, modeling, and holding high performance expectations (e.g., Ross and Gray 2006; Podsakoff et al. 1990).

Organizational Citizenship Behavior (OCB)

Organizational Citizenship Behavior (OCB) refers to individual behavior that is discretionary, not directly or explicitly recognized by the formal reward system, and that, in the aggregate, promotes the effective functioning of the organization. While OCB is overtly about behavior not emotion, it is included as part of the Emotional Path because of its' conceptual relationship to commitment. Indeed, OCBs seem likely to be at least one set of explicit manifestations of organizational commitment.

Organ (1988) and Podsakoff and his colleagues (e.g., Podsakoff et al. 2000) proposed five types of OCBs that improve the work environment: Altruism, Conscientiousness, Sportsmanship, Courtesy, and Civic Virtue. In schools, however, they converge into one dimension. The small number of empirical studies about the impact of OCB on student learning report a significant positive correlation between the OCB of faculty and student achievement in both reading and mathematics (e.g., $r = 0.30$ and 0.34), the same magnitude of relationship as between teacher's OCB and students' socio-economic status (SES).

Being flexible, nurturing, informal, encouraging novel solutions to problems, and limiting the use of formal organizational procedures are considered best practices for cultivating teachers' OCB in schools. School leaders who focus on enforcing the rules and regulations will not be successful in motivating teachers to "go the extra mile". While formality breeds rule-oriented behavior and rigidity, modeling, informal praise, and supportiveness are all practices that nurture the development of OCB.

References

Bandura, A. (1993). Perceived self-efficacy in cognitive development and functioning. *Educational Psychologist, 28*, 117–148.

Bryk, A., & Schneider, B. (2003). *Trust in schools: A core resource for school reform. Educational leadership*. Alexandria: Association for Supervision and Curriculum Development.

Goddard, R. D. (2003). Relational networks, social trust, and norms: A social capital perspective on students' chances of academic success. *Educational Evaluation and Policy Analyis, 25*, 59–74.

Goddard, R. D., Hoy, W. K., & Hoy, A. W. (2000). Collective teacher efficacy: Its meaning, measure, and impact on student achievement. *American Educational Research Journal, 37*, 479–507.

Goddard, R. D., Tschannen-Moran, M., & Hoy, W. K. (2001). A multilevel examination of the distribution and effects of teacher trust in students and parents in urban elementary schools. *The Elementary School Journal, 102*, 3–17.

Leithwood, K. (1994). Leadership for school restructuring. *Educational Administration Quarterly, 30*, 498–518.

Leithwood, K. (2006). *Teacher working conditions that matter: Evidence for change*. Toronto: Elementary Teachers' Federation of Ontario.

Leithwood, K., & Beatty, B. (2007). *Leading with teacher emotions in mind*. Thousand Oaks: Corwin.

Organ, D. W. (1988). *Organizational citizenship behavior: The good soldier syndrome*. Lexington: D.C. Heath.

Podsakoff, P. M., MacKenzie, S. B., Moorman, R. H., & Fetter, R. (1990). Transformational leader behaviors and their effects on followers' trust in leader, satisfaction, and organizational citizenship behaviors. *Leadership Quarterly, 1*, 107–142.

Podsakoff, P. M., MacKenzie, S. B., Paine, J. B., & Bachrach, D. J. (2000). Organizational citizenship behaviors: A critical review of the theoretical and empirical literature and suggestions for future research. *Journal of Management, 26*, 513–563.

Ross, J. A., & Gray, P. (2006). Transformational leadership and teacher commitment to organizational values: The mediating effects of collective teacher efficacy. *School Effectiveness and School Improvement, 17*, 179–199.

Tschannen-Moran, M., & Barr, M. (2004). Fostering student learning: The relationship of collective teacher efficacy and student achievement. *Leadership and Policy in Schools, 3*, 189–209.

Tschannen-Moran, M., Hoy, A. W., & Hoy, W. K. (1998). Teacher efficacy: Its meaning and measure. *Review of Educational Research, 68*, 202–248.

Chapter 7
Leadership Effects on Student Learning Mediated by Teacher Emotions

Jingping Sun and Kenneth Leithwood

This chapter assumes readers' familiarity with the overall framework for the book (see Chap. 1): in brief, school leadership influences student learning indirectly by improving key learning conditions on each of four "paths" – Rational, Emotional, Organizational and Family paths. Concerned only with the Emotional Path, this paper reviews evidence about the effects on student achievement of four teacher emotions or dispositions and those leadership practices likely to help improve the condition of each. While evidence indicates that leaders' attention to variables on all four paths can improve student learning (e.g. Leithwood et al. 2010; Sun and Leithwood 2015), teacher emotions are especially critical since they "seep across paths" thus shaping leaders' success in improving most variables on the other three paths.

A narrative review by the second author (Leithwood and Beatty 2008) of more than 90 empirical studies of teacher emotions and their consequences for classroom practice and student learning pointed to a large handful of teacher emotions with significant effects on teaching and learning including both individual and collective teacher efficacy, job satisfaction, organizational commitment, morale, stress/burnout, engagement in the school or profession, and teacher trust in colleagues, parents, and students. Based on a series of meta-analyses by us, teacher trust in others, teacher commitment, teacher collective efficacy and Organizational Citizenship Behavior or OCB (reasons for classifying OCB as an emotion appear below) were selected as most significant and the focus of this chapter.

J. Sun (✉)
The College of Education, University of Alabama, Tuscaloosa, AL, USA
e-mail: jsun22@ua.edu

K. Leithwood
Ontario Institute for Studies in Education, University of Toronto, Toronto, ON, Canada
e-mail: kenneth.leithwood@utoronto.ca

7.1 Teacher Trust in Others

Common across the many different definitions of trust, either explicitly or implicitly, is one party's willingness to be vulnerable to another party based on the belief that the latter party is (a) competent, (b) reliable, (c) open, and (d) concerned (Mishra 1996). Tschannen-Moran and Hoy (1998) claim that the two overarching elements of trust that must be established in schools are: Teachers' trust in the principal (teachers have confidence in the principal keeping his or her word and acting in the best interest of the teachers) and teachers' trust in colleagues (teachers believe that teachers can depend on each other in difficult situations and that teachers can rely on the integrity of their colleagues). In addition, Goddard's (2003) finding also indicate that when teacher-parent, and teacher-student relationships are characterized by trust, the academically supportive norms and social relations that result help move students toward academic success.

Faculty trust in colleagues, the principal, students and parents has been linked to school effectiveness (Goddard et al. 2001; Hoy et al. 1990; Tarter et al. 1995; Tschannen-Moran and Hoy 1998), positive school climate (Hoy et al. 1996; Tarter et al. 1989) and improved student achievement (Leithwood et al. 2010); these associations remain significant even when socioeconomic status and other student demographics factors (prior achievement, school SES, race, and gender) are accounted for (Goddard et al. 2001). In addition, three correlates of trust, namely academic press, teacher collective efficacy, and teacher professionalism, are also indicative of the centrally important role that trust plays in how leadership influences student learning (Tschannen-Moran and Gareis 2015b). In Chap. 8 (this book), Tschannen-Moran and colleagues explore the role that faculty trust in the principal plays in student learning, how principals can cultivate trust by attending to the five facets of trust, as well as the correlates of trust that mediate student learning.

Bryk and his colleagues (Bryk et al. 2010) point out that principals play an important role in developing, nurturing, and maintaining relational trust (trust in others) in schools. Principals establish respect and personal regard by recognizing and acknowledging the vulnerabilities of their staff. They build trustful relationships with teachers by listening to their needs and assisting as much as possible to reconcile those needs with a clear vision for the school. Demonstrating collegial leadership (e.g., being friendly, supportive, and open) is a way of trusting teachers' decision making abilities and providing support and constructive criticism as opposed to constant monitoring and micro managing (Tschannen-Moran and Hoy 1998).

Parents are encouraged to become partners in the educational process when principals create a space for them and when principals' interactions with parents are perceived by parents to be reliable, open, and scrupulously honest. If parents fail to respond, school personnel need to respond with understanding rather than disdain in order to foster mutual respect and trustworthiness (Goddard et al. 2001).

A stable community of students directly affects the relational trust between teachers and parents. When there is a high turnover in the student population, teachers find it difficult to maintain positive relationships with parents. Similarly, parents who are new to a school community often find it difficult to build new relationships constantly and fall back on an element of distrust as opposed to trust (Bryk et al. 2010). Principals should take extra measures to respond to an unstable community.

7.1.1 Teacher Commitment

In the last three decades, various dimensions of teacher commitment have been extensively studied including commitment to teaching, to students, to the school organization, and to change. Commitment to teaching encompasses a handful of more specific objects of commitment such as exercising a craft, dedication to the teaching profession and to the subject specialty, enjoyment and quality of teaching, and professional development (Billingsley and Cross 1992; Firestone and Rosenblum 1998; Gordon 1999; Menzies 1995). Commitment to students includes teachers' caring about students, making extra efforts to help them succeed academically, and fostering the social integration of students in the classroom (Firestone and Rosenblum 1998; Nir 2002). Teachers who are committed to students believe in the value of life-long learning, build connection with them, and value their feedback, (Cain 2001; Nir 2002;). Organizational commitment has been conceptualized and measured as a mainly individual's strong belief in the organization, identification and involvement in the organization, and a strong desire to remain a part of the organization (Freeston 1997; Leithwood et al. 1999; Porter et al. 1974). Commitment to change includes elements of motivation, a more fundamental psychological state (Leithwood et al. 1999). Motivational processes are qualities of a person oriented toward the future and aimed at helping the person to evaluate the need for change or action (Leithwood et al. 1999).

Teacher commitment to teaching, students and schools, (but not commitment to change) all contribute to student learning both independently and collectively (Glaze 2001; Griessler 2001; Housego 1999; Langer 2000; Strahan et al. 2001). The "ingredients" of teacher commitment, which could be teachers' feelings/emotions, attitudes, capacity, values, beliefs, motivations, overt commitment behaviours and sincerity (or insincerity) (Sun 2004), are reported as being positively associated with successful learning (Gill and Reynolds 1999; Janisch and Johnson 2003), teachers' instruction (Langer 2000; Hendel 1995), student moral growth (Williams 1993), and students' academic achievements (Harvey et al. 1998; Housego 1999). The majority of the studies examining teacher commitment and student outcomes are qualitative.

A leader's values, motives, personality, understanding and attitudes play a role in influencing teacher commitment (Sun 2004). If a teacher likes the leader's personality, has a similar value orientation and agrees with or accepts the leader's motives, he or she is likely to be influenced positively by the principal. When a teacher understands a leader's background experiences, he or she is more inclined to accept the leader's influence (Sun 2004). Principals' authenticity (consistency between words and actions) or in-authenticity (inconsistency between values and behaviors) significantly increases or decreases teacher commitment. A good relationship increases teacher enjoyment and heightens the teacher's desire to make extra effort and to remain a part of the school team, while a negative relationship decreases teachers' commitment to school (Russell 2003).

Holistic leadership, characterized by supportive relationships, participation in the school shared governance, a culture of collaboration, connectedness and commitment to community (Beattie 2002), also contribute positively to teacher commitment, and student learning. School leaders can also influence teacher commitment by fostering shared governance and a culture of collaboration (Beattie 2002), professional learning communities (Stein and Burger 1999), school-based management (Nir 2002), collaborative professional development activities (Mantle-Bromley 1998), and participatory decision-making (Reames and Spencer 1998).

7.1.2 Collective Teacher Efficacy

Collective Teacher Efficacy (CTE) is the level of confidence a group has in its capacity to organize and execute the tasks required to reach desired goals (Bandura 1993; Goddard et al. 2004). Correlations between measures of CTE and student learning range from .38 to .99, with an average r of .61 based on the effect size averaging of six studies (Barr 2002; Eells 2011; Garcia 2004; Hoy et al. 2002; Hylemon 2006; Tschannen-Moran and Barr 2004). For example, Goddard and his colleagues' (Goddard et al. 2000) study showed that collective teacher efficacy was a significant predictor of elementary student achievement in both mathematics and reading with the effects of CTE larger than those of SES. This relationship was moderated by the ethnicity of students; strongest correlations are associated with Caucasian students followed by African American and Hispanic students (Garcia 2004).

Ross and Gray's (2006) study of 3074 teachers in 218 Canadian elementary schools in two Ontario districts found that transformational leadership had a significant positive impact on the collective teacher efficacy of the school ($r = .45$; path analysis coefficient = .42, $p<.01$). Armstrong-Coppins (2003) explored what principals do to increase collective teacher efficacy in Midwest US urban high schools using a mixed method. A relationship was found between the principals' transformational leadership, as measured by the Nature of Leadership instrument (Hipp 1995 & Leithwood 1994, cited in Armstrong-Coppins 2003), and CTE. Schools with higher levels of transformational leadership had higher levels of CTE (path analysis coefficient = .48, $p<.01$).

7.1.3 Organizational Citizenship Behavior (OCB)

Organizational Citizenship Behavior (OCB) refers to individual behavior that is discretionary, not directly or explicitly recognized by the formal reward system, and that, in the aggregate, promotes the effective functioning of the organization. While OCB is overtly about behavior not emotion, it is included in this analysis because of its' conceptual relationship to commitment. Indeed, OCBs seem likely to be at least one set of explicit manifestations of organizational commitment. Organ (1988) and Podsakoff and his colleagues (Podsakoff et al. 2000) have proposed five types of OCBs that improve the work environment: Altruism, Conscientiousness, Sportsmanship, Courtesy, and Civic Virtue. In schools, however, they converge into one dimension (Tschannen-Moran 2001).

Empirical studies about the impact of OCB on student learning are few, though emerging; they suggest a significant and positive correlation between the OCB of faculty and student achievement in both reading and mathematics [e.g., r = .30 and .34 in 83], the same as the relationship between teacher's OCB and students' socio-economic status (SES). Being flexible, nurturing informal organization, encouraging novel solutions to problems, and limiting the use of formal rules and regulations are best practices for cultivating teachers' OCB in schools. Principals who focus on enforcing the rules and regulations will not be successful in motivating teachers to go the extra mile. Formality breeds rule-oriented behavior and rigidity. Modeling, informal praise, and supportiveness are all effective leadership practices.

7.2 Methods

Current empirical research falls short in estimating the indirect influence of school leadership on student learning because the majority of existing studies examine either the impact of leadership on learning or the effect of some (mediating) variable on student learning instead of both at the same time. Even large-scale studies using more sophisticated statistical modelling to examine mediating effects, the type of methods not often employed in the field of educational leadership, can only enter several variables into their models due to the lack of power and other statistical limits. Employing meta-analytical techniques complemented by an innovative effect size summation method, this study calculated and compared the effectiveness of multiple "critical paths" thus exploring propositions that cannot be answered by single studies.

Three methods were used in this study: standard meta-analysis, narrative review, and effect size summation and averaging. Standard meta-analysis techniques were used to assess the magnitude of school leadership's impacts on each of the path variables and the impacts of the each of the path variables on student learning outcomes. Narrative review method were used to identify school leadership practices effective in improving each of the path variables, and to identify and describe the key variables or constructions populated on the Emotional Path. Effect size summation and averaging techniques were used to calculate an "effectiveness" or "power" index for leadership practices effective in influencing each of the four Emotional Path variables. Since narrative review methods are well-known to most scholars, this section is limited to a description of the meta-analytic review techniques used in this review. Meta-analysis is a systematic set of methods for synthesizing the results of empirical studies. Despite considerable variation in execution, scholars generally agree that the basic procedures involved in meta-analysis (and in this study[1]) include:

1. An exhaustive search for related literature & the selection of a body of studies to be analyzed using appropriate inclusion criteria;
2. Systematic coding of the characteristics of studies, effect sizes and related statistics;
3. Calculation of the mean effect size;
4. Conducting homogeneity and heterogeneity analysis of the effect size distribution variances and moderators testing.

These are the major steps used to conduct the series of meta-analyses reported in this paper.[2] Pearson correlation coefficient r was chosen because it is the most suitable type of effect size for meta-analyzing results of the studies that examine correlational relationships (Rosenthal 1991). This study focused on the examination of correlational relationship, (i.e. to what extent do school leaders influence teachers' inner states; to what extent these inner states influence student learning outcomes). As well, most of the studies involved in meta-analytic calculations report correlational coefficients rs. Thus the use of r s as the effect sizes reduces variances in effect size distributions. Sample sizes of the studies were coded for calculating inverse variance weight ω'. This value is required to calculate the weighted mean of effect sizes as a way to eliminate sampling error (Lipsey and Wilson 2001).

If various statistics other than Pearson r were reported by the original studies, such as t or F, as the results of statistical analyses such as T-test or ANOVA, then ES r's were calculated based on the converting formulae provided by Fox and Tracy when the related statistics reported by the original studies permitted for doing the calculations. Fisher z transformations were conducted to adjust the effect sizes. The achieved sample of schools was used as the sample size for each study. Weighted means (Lipsey and Wilson 2001) were calculated to reduce sampling error. Internal and external validity was enhanced by exhaustive, appropriate, inclusion of sampled studies, studies using appropriate inclusion criteria, systematic coding of study characteristics and effect sizes, calculating mean effect size, and reducing publication bias to a minimum by including both published and unpublished studies. Macros for SPSS written by Wilson (Wilson 2009; Lipsey and Wilson 2001)

---

[1] Step 4 was not used in this study due to the limited numbers of the studies involved in the series of the meta-analyses in this review.

[2] Step 4 was not used in this study due to the limited numbers of the studies involved in the series of the meta-analyses in this review.

were used to perform meta-correlation computations. Fixed effects models (FEM) were used.

To identify promising variables on the Emotional Path, we first identified a list of variables that significantly contribute to student learning and estimated[3] the extent of this contribution. Then we identified from this list those variables that our meta-analytical review suggested are malleable to school leadership influence. Next we combined these two estimates. This combined magnitude of "extent of influence" is considered a power index (the strength of the path from school leadership through the selected emotional variable to student learning) denoting the *indirect* influence of school leadership.

Meta-analysis is usually used to calculate direct effects between two variables. However, the addition of effect sizes denoting the impacts of significant producers of student learning and the impact of school leadership on those variables provides a way to compare the relative power of the critical paths using meta-analysis with second-hand data. Path analytical techniques or structural equation modeling are generally considered standard methods for examining indirect influence in original studies. However, these techniques require a large data sets and place limits on the number of variables entered into the equation. The use of effect size summation in this study provides an alternative way to portray the *indirect* influence of school leadership revealing patterns only evident in accumulations of research.

The evidence included in this review was provided by two bodies of literature: studies that examined the relationship between teachers' emotions and student learning, and studies that examined the relationship between school leaders and teachers' emotions.

7.2.1 Evidence About Variables on the Emotional Path

To be included as a variable on the Emotional Path in this paper, a variable had to (a) contribute to student learning as measured by standardized tests, to a similar or greater extent than Socioeconomic Status (SES) and (b) be malleable to school leadership. The average correlation coefficient between SES and student learning is about .30 based on Hattie's 2009 meta-analysis. So previous evidence about variables selected for attention in this paper had to demonstrate a correlation of at least .30 with student achievement.

With this inclusion criterion, published studies were searched through the Scholar's Portal, which covers the major journals in the field of educational administration[3] and data bases (e.g., Eric, ProQuest Dissertation) in the field of education. Additional sources of evidence were located through the reading of reference lists as we reviewed the initial studies. We dropped variables that had weaker relationships

---

[3] We estimate the "extent" or impact by averaging effect sizes (i.e., in most cases, the correlational coefficients reported by the studies). If the effect sizes reported are in different nature, we will convert them into correlational coefficients when possible.

with student learning and variables for which insufficient data were available to calculate effects on student learning or calculate how malleable they were to transformational leadership. This process identified the 12 studies involved in the calculation of effect sizes and an additional dozen studies that demonstrated a positive impact on student learning of selected variables but did not report sufficient data for calculating meta-correlations (e.g., these studies only reported path regression coefficients). These studies were conducted mainly in North America in a range of rural, urban and suburban public schools (e.g., Kentucky, New Jersey; Ohio; Ontario) including elementary, middle and high schools in diverse geographic areas.

7.2.2 Evidence About Leadership Practices

The source of the evidence about leadership practices relevant for improving variables on the Emotional Path was unpublished theses or dissertations on transformational school leadership (TSL). This body of evidence was used to examine the impact of school leadership on each of the four emotional variables. Studies on TSL were chosen because TSL (e.g., Leithwood 1992) and instructional leadership (e.g., Hallinger and Murphy 1985) have been the two most frequently studied models of school leadership and the only school leadership models that have been empirically measured and tested.

Our review was restricted to the evidence about TSL because motivating and inspiring colleagues are central goals of TSL. As well, evidence about TSL provides a manageable size data base since the search for studies that examined the relationship between instructional leadership and teachers' emotional variables did not result in enough evidence from which to draw data for this meta-analytical review.

There were not sufficient numbers of published studies on TSL that could be used to conduct the meta-analyses intended in this study. Dissertations were reviewed to reduce publication bias, to mine insights yet unreported in the published literature, and to provide evidence of a standard, high quality. The biggest on-line database for doctoral dissertations, the Proquest Dissertation & Theses, was searched for all dissertations that inquired about transformational leadership in education with a completion time between 1996 and 2014. In order to be selected for review, a thesis had to be based on quantitative data; use at least one of the following types of statistical analyses: correlation, regression, ANOVA and T-Test; investigate the effects[4] of TSL on at least one of the four emotions of interest in this paper; and be conducted in more than two schools. Thirty-two theses were identified that met all of these criteria. These studies were conducted primarily in North America, but also in Europe, Asia and Africa. Most were conducted in a range of rural, urban and suburban public schools. A small number took place in private schools, Catholic schools, or vocational schools.

---

[4]While we use the phrase transformational leadership *effects* repeatedly throughout our descriptions of results, the relationships reported in this study are all correlational.

To complement our interpretation of results from this body of unpublished research, we also took account of the results of some especially well-known published studies as, for example, about instructional leadership (e.g., Hallinger and Murphy 1985), transformational leadership (e.g., Leithwood and Sun 2012), and learner-centered leadership (Robinson 2011). The studies included in this review are not inclusive, though we tried to be exhaustive.

7.3 Results

7.3.1 Teacher Trust in Others

Based on the meta-analysis of three studies (Kerley 2014; Tarter et al. 1989; Tschannen-Moran and Gareis 2015a; Zeinabadi 2014), we estimate the correlation between trust in others and student achievement to be .28 (weighted mean effect size r). Our meta-analysis of three studies (Kindel 2011; Mannion 1999; Marks 2002) indicated that TSL practices had significant effects on teachers' trust in others (weighted mean effect size, $r = .37$). Collegial, shared leadership is strongly related to faculty trust in the principal [Beta = 0.677, $p < 0.01$ in Tschannen-Moran and Hoy 1998; $r = .92$ in 27]. The authenticity of principal behavior also makes a significant contribution to school climate with trust being a key component [Beta = 0.828, $p < 0.01$ in 9]. Thus, the power for the path from leadership to student learning through teacher trust is 0.65 (.37 +.28).

Teacher trust in principals is most influenced by leadership practices which teachers interpret as indicators of vulnerability, understanding, benevolence, competence, consistency and reliability, openness, respect and integrity (Handford and Leithwood 2013; Tschannen-Moran and Gareis 2015b). For example, principals must distinguish their positional, evaluative responsibilities from their collaborative, formative efforts when drawing upon their creative expertise to make positive changes in schools. They must not create a sense that taking a risk as a teacher – whether by sharing ideas or attempting innovative practices – will result in punitive outcomes for them. Principals can also earn the trust of their faculties by demonstrating goodwill and genuine concern for teachers' well-being through their interpersonal interactions, formal communications and decisions (Tschannen-Moran and Gareis 2015b). As well, principals can build teacher trust by fostering collaboration in schools. Collaboration and trust are reciprocal processes (Bryk et al. 2010). Collaboration requires time, energy, and sharing resources which in turn develops trust. The greater the collaboration between co-workers the greater the trust that is developed between individuals in a workplace. Principals' collaboration with teachers can also foster teachers' collaboration with parents, which in turn adds to teachers' trust in the principal (Tschannen-Moran 2001).

Environmental press (positive pressure from the parents and community to change school policy) can make or break a school environment. Principals need to help teachers cope in such an environment through support and by maintaining the integrity of the school's programs. Principals build trust with their staff when they protect them from unreasonable community demands. (Tschannen-Moran and Hoy 1998).

7.3.2 Teacher Commitment (TC)

Based on our meta-analysis of two quantitative studies uncovered in our search (Nicklaus and Ebmeier 1995; Solomon 2007), we estimated the correlations between teacher commitment and students' achievement to be $r = .30$. Park's (2005) two-level hierarchical linear modeling indicates a significant impact on student achievement of teacher commitment to the profession as $b = .123; p < .05$).

A meta-analysis of 24 dissertations that examined the relationship between TSL and teachers' commitment reported a strong association between the two (weighted mean $r = .61$) (Sun 2015). The addition of new evidence published between 2010 and 2014 (Boberg 2013; Kieres 2013; Kindel 2011) did not alter this result. Similar findings were found in studies that involved other leadership models (Billingsley and Cross 1992; Ebmeier 2003; John and Taylor 1999; Reames and Spencer 1998; Sun 2004). Nicklaus and Ebmeier (1995), for example, suggest that supervision can play a major role in increasing teachers' commitment (commitment to the core values of the school and the teaching profession), and other affective variables (.30) and these variables, in turn, are linked directly to student achievement $(r = .30)$. We estimate the power index for this path to be .92 (.62 +.30).

The following leadership practices are reported to make positive contributions to teacher commitment, in general:

- support (Billingsley and Cross 1992; Ebmeier 2003; John and Taylor 1999), or individual supports (Leithwood et al. 1999; Leithwood and Sun 2012),
- collaborative supervision (Ebmeier 2003),
- principals' control and empowerment strategies (Blasé Blase 1993),
- direction-setting (i.e., building a shared vision and developing consensus about goals creating high performance expectations) (Leithwood et al. 1999),
- modeling (Leithwood et al. 1999; Sun 2010) [41, 61],
- intellectual stimulation (Leithwood et al. 1999),
- encouragement of innovation and risk taking (Reames and Spencer 1998),
- consideration (John and Taylor 1999), and
- emphasis on teaching (Sheppard 1996).

7.3.3 Collective Teacher Efficacy (CTE)

Our meta-analysis of three unpublished studies of TSL indicated a positive relationship (weighted mean $r = .30$) between principals' TSL and collective teacher efficacy (Nicholson 2003; Rutledge 2010; Solomon 2007). Other published studies report larger impacts. For example, transformational school leadership made a small but practically important contribution to overall student achievement through the mediating effects of collective teacher efficacy and teacher commitment (Ross and Gray 2006). Thus, the power index for the path linking leadership to student learning through CTE is 0.91 (.61 +.30).

Particularly influential with CTE are four transformational leadership practices including:

- *Inspiring group purpose*: principals identify new opportunities for the school while developing (often collaboratively), articulate and inspire others with a vision of the future, promote cooperation and collaboration among staff towards common goals (Leithwood and Sun 2012; Robinson 2011).
- *Providing individualized support*: School leaders listen and attend to individual teachers' opinions and needs, respect them, mentor or coach them or provide them with professional development opportunities, maintain an open door policy, develop positive relationships with teachers, provide resource and financial support, build trust, positively integrate teachers into the school organization and the implementation of school programs, and foster a sense of belonging and stability (Leithwood and Sun 2012; Sun 2015).
- *Providing appropriate models*: school leaders provide a model of high ethical behavior, instill pride, symbolize success, and walk the talk (Leithwood and Sun 2012).
- *Holding high expectations*: Expecting a high level of professionalism from staff; holding high expectations for students; expecting staff to be effective innovators (Leithwood et al. 1999).

7.3.4 Organizational Citizenship Behavior (OCB)

Based on our meta-analysis of two studies (DiPaola and Hoy 2005; Zeinabadi 2014), we estimated the correlation between teachers' OCB and student achievement to be .41. Our meta-analysis of three studies (Boberg 2013; Mannion 1999; Marks 2002) indicated that transformational leadership practices had a significant, close to large, impact on OCB (the weighted mean effect size, $r = .48$). The power index for the path from leadership to student achievement through OCB is .89 (.48 + .41).

To enhance teachers' OCB in schools principals can:

- Encourage teachers to experiment and make important decisions about teaching and learning.
- Provide mentors to socialize new teachers, who routinely demonstrate organizational citizenship behaviors.
- Protect teachers from administrative trivia – unnecessary meetings, too much paper work, silly rules, busy work, etc.
- Try not to make the teaching contract too specific in terms of what teachers can and cannot do. If the contract is specific, work with the union leadership to enhance flexibility.
- Develop high levels of academic success with teachers, and then support and help teachers achieve those goals (DiPaola and Hoy 2005).

In sum, this review of evidence about variables on the Emotional Path indicates that each of four emotions has significant effects on student achievement and can be improved by leaders enacting practices generally associated with transformational approaches to leadership. All other things equal, does it matter which of the four variables leaders chose to act on? The power indices calculated as a means of answering this question indicate that leadership practices mediated by three of the four emotions have similar effects (ranging from .89 to .91). The power index for teacher trust was much lower, .65. However, the potential for leadership to influence the four variables differs considerably; teacher commitment and CTE appear to be more malleable to leadership influence than either OCB or teacher trust. This discrepancy at least raises an important question for school leaders planning their improvement efforts. The question for leaders is not just about which emotions stand the greatest chance of improving student learning, it is also a question about which emotions they have the greatest chance of influencing? We explore the uses of power indices further in Chap. 16.[5]

7.4 Conclusion

The limitations of the study described in this chapter are related to the small sample of the studies used in meta-correlation analyses (though we did cover about dozens of hundred studies in our narrative review to compliment the meta-analytical review), the use of only one type of school leadership model to calculate the leadership impacts on teacher emotions, and the use of unpublished evidence for calculating school leadership impacts.

This chapter has provided partial justification for leaders' attention to four variables on the Emotional path – Collective Teacher Efficacy, Teacher Commitment, Organizational Citizenship Behavior, and Teacher Trust in Others. Results of our

---

[5] The power indices calculated in this chapter were based on estimates of effects or impacts across multiple studies, many of which were unpublished. So these power indices may be different than those based on an original large-scale data set as used, for example, in Chap. 16.

review of evidence suggest approximately similar potential effects of leaders' working to improve three of the four emotional variables but somewhat weaker effects of a focus on teacher trust in others.

References

Armstrong-Coppins, D. R. (2003). *What principals do to increase collective teacher efficacy in urban schools*. (Order, 3119769). Available from ProQuest dissertations & theses global. (305232461).
Bandura, A. (1993). Perceived self-efficacy in cognitive development and functioning. *Educational Psychologist, 28*, 117–148.
Barr, M. F. (2002). *Fostering student achievement: A study of the relationship of collective teacher efficacy and student achievement*. Unpublished doctoral dissertation, College of William and Mary, VA.
Beattie, M. (2002). Educational leadership: Modeling, mentoring, making and re-making a learning community. *European Journal of Teacher Education, 25*, 199–221.
Billingsley, B. S., & Cross, L. H. (1992). Predictors of commitment, job satisfaction, and intent to stay in teaching: A comparison of general and special educators. *Journal of Special Education, 25*, 453–471.
Blase, J. (1993). The micropolitics of effective school-based leadership: Teachers' perspectives. *Educational Administration Quarterly, 29*, 142–163.
Boberg, J. E. (2013). *High school principal transformational leadership behaviors and teacher extra effort during educational reform: The mediating role of teacher agency beliefs*. (Order, 3596758). Available from ProQuest dissertations & theses global. (1449841530).
Bryk, A. S., Sebring, P. B., Allensworth, E., Luppescu, S., & Easton, J. Q. (2010). *Organizing schools for improvement*. Chicago: University of Chicago Press.
Cain, M. S. (2001). Ten qualities of the renewed teacher. *Phi Delta Kappan, 82*, 702–705.
DiPaola, M. F., & Hoy, W. K. (2005). Organizational citizenship of faculty and achievement of high school students. *High School Journal, 88*, 35–44.
Ebmeier, H. (2003). How supervision influences teacher efficacy and commitment: An investigation of a path model. *Journal of Curriculum and Supervision, 18*, 110–141.
Eells, R. J. (2011). *Meta-analysis of the relationship between collective teacher efficacy and student achievement*. Unpublished doctoral dissertation, Loyola University Chicago, IL.
Firestone, W. A., & Rosenblum, S. (1998). Building commitment in urban high schools. *Educational Evaluation and Policy Analysis, 10*, 285–299.
Freeston, K. R. (1997). Leader substitutes in educational organizations. *Educational Administration Quarterly, 23*, 45–59.
Garcia, H. (2004). *The impact of collective efficacy on student achievement: Implications for building a learning community*. Unpublished doctoral dissertation, Loyola University, Chicago, IL.
Gill, S., & Reynolds, A. J. (1999). Educational expectations and school achievement of urban African American children. *Journal of School Psychology, 37*, 403–424.
Glaze, A. E. (2001). ACCESS: One school district's response to expelled students. *Education Canada, 40*(4), 44–45.
Goddard, R. D. (2003). Relational networks, social trust, and norms: A social capital perspective on students' chances of academic success. *Educational Evaluation and Policy Analysis, 25*, 59–74.
Goddard, R. D., Hoy, W. K., & Hoy, A. W. (2000). Collective teacher efficacy: Its meaning, measure, and impact on student achievement. *American Educational Research Journal, 37*, 479–507.

Goddard, R. D., Tschannen-Moran, M., & Hoy, W. K. (2001). A multilevel examination of the distribution and effects of teacher trust in students and parents in urban elementary schools. *Elementary School Journal, 102*(1), 3–17.

Goddard, R., Hoy, W. K., & Hoy, A. W. (2004). Collective efficacy beliefs: Theoretical developments, empirical evidence, and future directions [Electronic version]. *Educational Researcher, 33*, 3–13.

Gordon, G. L. (1999). Teacher talent and urban schools. *Phi Delta Kappan, 81*, 304–307.

Griessler, M. (2001). The effects of third language learning on second language proficiency: An Austrian example. *International Journal of Bilingual Education and Bilingualism, 4*, 50–60.

Hallinger, P., & Murphy, J. (1985). Assessing the instructional management behavior of principals. *Elementary School Journal, 86*, 217–247.

Handford, V., & Leithwood, K. (2013). Why teachers trust school leaders. *Journal of Educational Administration, 51*, 194–212.

Harvey, B. Z., Sirna, R. T., & Houlihan, M. B. (1998). Learning by design: Hands-on learning. *American School Board Journal, 186*, 22–25.

Hattie, J. A. C. (2009). *A synthesis of over 800 meta-analyses relating to achievements.* New York: Routledge.

Hendel, C. (1995). Behavioral characteristics and instructional patterns of selected music teachers. *Journal of Research in Music Education, 43*, 182–203.

Housego, B. E. J. (1999). Outreach schools: An educational innovation. *Alberta Journal of Educational Research, 45*, 85–101.

Hoy, W. K., Tarter, C. J., & Bliss, J. R. (1990). Organizational climate, school health, and effectiveness: A comparative analysis. *Educational Administration Quarterly, 26*, 260–279.

Hoy, W. K., Sabo, D., & Barnes, K. (1996). Organizational health and faculty trust: A view from the middle level. *Research in Middle Level Education Quarterly, 19*(Spring), 21–39.

Hoy, W. K., Sweetland, S. R., & Smith, P. A. (2002). Toward an organizational model of achievement in high schools: The significance of collective efficacy. *Educational Administration Quarterly, 38*, 77–93.

Hylemon, L. V. (2006). *Collective teacher efficacy and reading achievement for Hispanic students in reading first and non-reading first schools in southwest Florida.* Unpublished doctoral dissertation, University of Central Florida, Orlando, FL.

Janisch, C., & Johnson, M. (2003). Effective literacy practices and challenging curriculum for at-risk learners: Great expectations. *Journal of Education for Students Placed at Risk, 8*, 295–308.

John, M. C., & Taylor, V. J. W. (1999). Leadership style, school climate, and the institutional commitment of teachers. *Feature, 2*, 25–57.

Kerley, D. (2014). *Exploring connections among relational trust, teachers efficacy and student achievement.* Unpublished doctoral dissertation, University of Kentucky. Lexington, KY.

Kieres, K. H. (2013). *A study of the value added by transformational leadership practices to teachers' job satisfaction and organizational commitment.* (Order, 3579651). Available from ProQuest dissertations & theses global. (1509821371).

Kindel, D. (2011). *Teacher commitment to the implementation of ninth grade academies and their perceptions of school leadership.* (Order, 3449690). Available from ProQuest dissertations & theses global. (863480237).

Langer, J. A. (2000). Excellence in English in middle and high school: How teachers' professional lives support student achievement. *American Educational Research Journal, 37*, 397–439.

Leithwood, K. (1992). The move towards transformational leadership. *Educational Leadership, 49*(5), 8–12.

Leithwood, K., & Beatty, B. (2008). *Leading with teacher emotions in mind.* Thousand Oaks: Corwin.

Leithwood, K., & Sun, J. (2012). The nature and effects of transformational school leadership: A meta-analytic review of unpublished research. *Educational Administration Quarterly, 48*, 387–423.

Leithwood, K., Jantzi, D., & Steinbach, R. (1999). *Changing leadership for changing times*. Philadelphia: Open University Press.

Leithwood, K., Patten, S., & Jantzi, D. (2010). Testing a conception of how leadership influences student learning. *Educational Administration Quarterly, 46*, 671–706.

Lipsey, M. W., & Wilson, D. B. (2001). *Practical meta-analysis*. Thousand Oaks: Sage.

Mannion, P. T. (1999). The relationship of principal transformational leadership characteristics to principal trust characteristics, colleague trust characteristics, and organization trust characteristics. *Dissertation Abstracts International, 60*(05) A, AAI9929712.

Mantle-Bromley, C. (1998). 'A day in the life' at a professional development school. *Educational Leadership, 55*(5), 48–51.

Marks, D. E. (2002). A study of two leadership styles and school cultural norms in small middle schools. *Dissertation Abstracts International, 63*(02) A, AAI3041397.

Menzies, T. V. (1995). *Teacher commitment in colleges of applied arts and technology: Sources, objects, practices and influences*. Unpublished doctoral dissertation, OISE/University of Toronto, ON, Canada.

Mishra, A. K. (1996). Organizational responses to crisis: The centrality of trust. In R. Kramer & T. Tyler (Eds.), *Trust in organizations* (pp. 261–287). Thousand Oaks: Sage.

Nicholson, M. R. (2003). Transformational leadership and collective efficacy: A model of school achievement. *Dissertation Abstracts International, 64*(06) A, AAI3093682.

Nicklaus, J., & Ebmeier, H. (1995). The impact of peer and principal collaborative supervision on teachers' trust, commitment, desire for collaboration, and efficacy. *Journal of Curriculum and Supervision, 14*, 351–378.

Nir, A. E. (2002). School-based management and its effect on teacher commitment. *International Journal of Leadership in Education, 5*, 323–341.

Organ, D. W. (1988). *Organizational citizenship behavior: The good soldier syndrome*. Lexington: Lexington/D.C. Heath.

Park, I. (2005). Teacher commitment and its effects on student achievement in American high schools. *Educational Research and Evaluation, 11*, 461–485.

Podsakoff, P. M., MacKenzie, S. B., Paine, J. B., & Bachrach, D. J. (2000). Organizational citizenship behaviors: A critical review of the theoretical and empirical literature and suggestions for future research. *Journal of Management, 26*, 513–563.

Porter, L. W., Steers, R. M., Mowday, R. T., & Boulian, P. V. (1974). Organizational teacher commitment, job satisfaction and turnover among psychiatric technicians. *Journal of Applied Psychology, 59*, 603–609.

Reames, E. H., & Spencer, W. A. (1998, April). *Teacher efficacy and commitment: Relationships to middle school culture*. Paper presented at the annual meeting of the American Educational Research Association, San Diego, CA. (ERIC Document Reproduction Service, ED419793).

Robinson, V. (2011). *Student-centered leadership*. San Francisco: Jossey Bass.

Rosenthal, R. (1991). *Meta-analytic procedures for social research* (Rev ed.). Thousand Oaks: Sage.

Ross, J. A., & Gray, P. (2006). School leadership and student achievement: The mediating effects of teacher beliefs. *Canadian Journal of Education, 29*, 798–822.

Russell, M. (2003). Leadership and followership as a relational process. *Educational Management Administration and Leadership, 31*, 145–157.

Rutledge, R. D., II. (2010). *The effects of transformational leadership on academic optimism within elementary schools*. (Order, 3439841). Available from ProQuest dissertations & theses global. (851889192).

Sheppard, B. (1996). Exploring the transformational nature of instructional leadership. *Alberta Journal of Educational Research, 42*, 325–344.

Solomon, C. (2007). The relationships among middle level leadership, teacher commitment, teacher collective efficacy, and student achievement. *Dissertation Abstracts International, 69*(06) A. AAT3322742

Stein, B. B., & Burger, C. (1999). A community for learning. *Teacher Librarian, 27*, 32–35.

Strahan, D., Smith, T. W., McElrath, M., & Toole, C. M. (2001). Profiles in caring: Teachers who create learning communities in their classrooms. *Middle School Journal, 33*, 41–47.

Sun, J. (2004). Understanding the impact of perceived leadership styles on teacher commitment. *International Studies in Educational Administration, 32*(2), 17–30.

Sun, J. (2010). *A review of transformational leadership research: A meta-analytic approach*. Unpublished doctoral dissertation. OISE/University of Toronto, ON, Canada.

Sun, J. (2015). Conceptualizing the critical path linked by teacher commitment. *Journal of Educational Administration, 53*, 597–624.

Sun, J., & Leithwood, K. (2015). Direction-setting school leadership practices: A meta-analytical review of evidence about their influence. *School Effectiveness and School Improvement, 26*(4), 499–523. doi:10.1080/09243453.2015.1005106.

Tarter, C. J., Bliss, J. R., & Hoy, W. K. (1989). School characteristics and faculty trust in secondary schools. *Educational Administration Quarterly, 25*, 294–308.

Tarter, C. J., Sabo, D., & Hoy, W. K. (1995). Middle school climate, faculty trust and effectiveness: A path analysis. *Journal of Research and Development in Education, 29*, 41–49.

Tschannen-Moran, M. (2001). Collaboration and the need for trust. *Journal of Educational Administration, 39*, 308–331.

Tschannen-Moran, M., & Barr, M. (2004). Fostering student learning: The relationship of collective teacher efficacy and student achievement. *Leadership and Policy in Schools, 3*, 189–209.

Tschannen-Moran, M., & Gareis, C. R. (2015a). Faculty trust in the principal: An essential ingredient in high-performing schools. *Journal of Educational Administration, 53*, 66–92.

Tschannen-Moran, M., & Gareis, C. R. (2015b). Principals, trust, and cultivating vibrant schools. *Societies, 5*, 256–276. doi:10.3390/soc5020256.

Tschannen-Moran, M., & Hoy, W. K. (1998). Trust in schools: A conceptual and empirical analysis. *Journal of Educational Administration, 36*, 334–352.

Williams, M. M. (1993). Actions speak louder than words: What students think. *Educational Leadership, 51*, 22–23.

Wilson, D. B. (2009). *Meta-analysis stuff*. Retrieved from http://mason.gmu.edu/~dwilsonb/ma.html

Zeinabadi, H. R. (2014). Principal–teacher high-quality exchange indicators and student achievement: Testing a model. *Journal of Educational Administration, 52*, 404–420.

Chapter 8
Principals, Trust, and Cultivating Vibrant Schools

Megan Tschannen-Moran and Christopher R. Gareis

Principals are charged with providing hands-on leadership to one of the most significant institutions in our society, the schoolhouse. Our society is well served when schools function at their highest level. Students develop the skills, values, and habits of mind that will allow them to become productive and engaged citizens of our democracy. The well-being of our society suffers when schools fail to adequately fulfill our hopes for them, when the learning of both students and faculty alike are impaired by a lack of safety, low morale, or unresolved conflict. There are a myriad of responsibilities placed on the shoulders of principals in order to foster the kinds of learning environments we hope for. A growing body of research suggests that primary among these is earning the trust of their teachers and exercising the requisite skills to cultivate a pervasive culture of trust between teachers and students (Tschannen-Moran and Gareis 2002).

Trust is increasingly recognized as an essential element in vibrant, well-performing schools. This is, in part, because trust undergirds the cooperative behavior necessary for cultivating high performance. Trust becomes salient when people enter into relationships of interdependence, where the outcomes one desires cannot be met without the involvement and contribution of others. Once trust is established, the confidence one holds in the intentions and capacity of the other person to fulfill one's expectations results in feeling a greater sense of ease in the interdependence and a willingness to take risks. Trust also is a dynamic construct in that it can change over the course of a relationship, as the nature of the interdependence between two people changes, and as expectations are either fulfilled or disappointed. Although trust occurs between individuals, it also occurs *among* individuals within complex human organizations, such as schools. Without trust, organizational effectiveness

---

M. Tschannen-Moran (✉) • C.R. Gareis
Educational Leadership, School of Education, College of William and Mary, Williamsburg, VA, USA
e-mail: Mxtsch@wm.edu

and efficiency are hampered (Bryk and Schneider 2002; Tschannen-Moran 2014b; Uline et al. 1998).

Trust is a multifaceted construct, meaning that people assess many elements simultaneously when making judgments of trust. These elements, or facets, may vary somewhat depending on the context or nature of the trust relationship. Specifically, trust is defined as the willingness to be vulnerable to another party based on the confidence that the other party is benevolent, honest, open, reliable, and competent (Tschannen-Moran 2014b; Tschannen-Moran and Hoy 1998). Although most educators acknowledge the importance of trust in their work, these qualities too often get squeezed out with the pressures of accountability. Such pressures can drive school leaders to impatience and anxiety, resulting in a climate of tension and fear that interferes with the learning of both children and adults alike. These schools are likely to be dreary and discouraging places rather than the joyful learning communities we long for. Cultivating a climate of trust, in contrast, allows the members of a school community to amplify their school's strengths and create environments where curiosity and love of learning abide. Student learning is facilitated by equipping school leaders and teacher leaders to more fully realize their positive intentions for their professional relationships resulting in strong relationships of trust. In so doing, the learning of teachers and students is enhanced.

A school principal is charged with a wide array of responsibilities, including the development of a shared vision for the school and stewardship of that vision, fostering an environment conducive to student learning, engaging all members of the school community, managing the organization, ensuring the effectiveness of the faculty, and doing these things with integrity and fairness (Council of Chief State School Officers 2008). In enacting these various duties, they have both a direct and an indirect influence on student learning (Leithwood et al. 2010; Hallinger and Heck 1996). Although principals are ultimately held accountable to student learning in their buildings, the most consistent research results have suggested that their impact on student achievement is largely indirect (Leithwood et al. 2010; Tschannen-Moran and Gareis 2002; Zeinabadi 2014). The purpose of this special issue is to examine the mediating variables through which those indirect effects function, and among those variables trust is certainly among the strongest. In this paper, we will explore the evidence that points to the role that faculty trust in the principal plays in student learning, how principals can cultivate trust by attending to the five facets of trust, as well as the correlates of trust that mediate student learning.

8.1 Trust and Student Achievement

School leaders who create bonds of trust help create the conditions that inspire teachers to move to higher levels of effort and achievement (Chugtai and Buckley 2009; Forsyth and Adams 2014; Handford and Leithwood 2013; Notman and Henry 2011; Salfi 2011; Tschannen-Moran 2003, 2009; Zeinabadi 2014). In contrast, when teachers and principals do not trust one another, each seeks to minimize their vulnerability and risk by adopting self-protective stances. The result can be disengagement that consequently diminishes student learning (Bryk and Schneider 2002). Few other variables examined by educational researchers come close to the level of predictive power of trust on student achievement.

Because of the nature of interdependence between teachers and principals, and the authority that principals exercise in relations to them, teachers tend to pay particular attention to the trustworthiness of their principals. In a study that included elementary, middle, and high school levels in both urban and suburban settings, Tschannen-Moran (2014a) found that the level of trust teachers held for the principal set a tone for the building. Faculty trust in the principal was related to their trust in colleagues, students and parents, as well as the level of parent trust in the school. Student trust in teachers was not directly related to faculty trust in the principal; however, it was indirectly related to the overall climate of trust in the schools through intercorrelations with the remaining faculty and parent trust measures. Each of these five types of trusting relationships in schools was moderately to strongly related to student achievement. Moreover, 78% of the variance in student achievement was explained by the combined influence of these five trust variables. This is powerful evidence that trust is an essential element of productive schools. The correlation between faculty trust in principal and faculty trust in colleagues speaks to a tone set by administrators that influences the climate of the school (Tschannen-Moran 2009). Where the principal has established high trust relationships, teachers are more likely to perceive that they can trust their colleagues as well. Conversely, where trust in the administrator is low, trust in colleagues is likely to suffer as well. In schools where principals, teachers, students, and parents trust each other, a climate of success is more likely. These schools are better positioned to accomplish the essential educational goals of fostering student achievement and equipping students for citizenship. It is interesting and important that both faculty trust in the principal and trust in colleagues are related to faculty trust in students (Tschannen-Moran 2014a). Where the adults trust one another, they are more likely to extend trust to their students as well. In contrast, where distrust characterizes the relationships among the adults in a school, the trust between teachers and students is likely to suffer as well.

In a related study, Tschannen-Moran and Gareis (2002) found both a direct relationship between principal trustworthiness and student achievement, as well as evidence of an indirect influence of this trustworthiness on student achievement through elements of school climate, including teacher professionalism, academic press, and community engagement. This suggests that when principals are trustworthy, they set a tone that influences how teachers relate to one another, to students, and to the community at large. These, in turn, were individually and collectively related to student achievement (Tschannen-Moran and Gareis 2002). The findings of this study reflect both current and evolving conceptions of school leadership, which explicitly include the fostering and use of trust as a professional responsibility of school leaders (Council of Chief State School Officers 2008, 2014). We explore below the principal behaviors that cultivate trust as well as three correlates of trust in schools.

8.1.1 Vulnerability

Trust is most relevant when two or more parties are dependent on one another for something they need or care about. The goals that educators aspire to are far beyond what any individual alone can accomplish. Therefore, educators are necessarily interdependent, and with interdependence comes vulnerability. Trust is characterized by the extent to which one is willing to rely upon and make oneself vulnerable to another and to do so with a certain sense of ease or comfort (Baier 1994; Bigley and Pearce 1998). The uncertainty concerning whether the other intends to and will act appropriately, however, entails taking a risk (Rousseau et al. 1998; Solomon and Flores 2001). The person extending trust recognizes the potential for betrayal and harm from the other. Taking that leap of faith requires trust. This leap may, in turn, create the conditions for the development of even deeper trust when the expected behavior becomes manifest.

Trust has been defined as a willingness to make oneself vulnerable to someone else in the belief that your interests or something that you care about will not be harmed (Tschannen-Moran 2014b). For a school leader, this can mean being trustworthy to others in the sense of acknowledging, allowing, and protecting others' demonstrations of vulnerability toward her- or himself. It can also mean extending trust by demonstrating some degree of vulnerability to others. In either case, the facets of benevolence, honesty, openness, competence, and reliability constitute the behaviors that potentially foster trust among principals, teachers, students, and others in school communities.

8.1.2 Benevolence

A starting point for the development of trust is a sense of caring or benevolence. For principals to earn the trust of their teachers, they must demonstrate genuine care for teachers, students, and parents alike. Benevolence is characterized by a generalized spirit of good will and a willingness to extend oneself in support of the well-being of the other. School leaders can promote trust through exhibiting benevolent behaviors, such as showing consideration and sensitivity for employees' needs and interests, acting in a way that protects employees' rights, and refraining from exploiting others for personal gain. This creates the confidence in teachers that their well-being or something they care about will be protected and not harmed by the person they have trusted (Baier 1994; Zand 1997).

Trust rests on the assurance that one can count on the good will of another person to act in one's best interest and to refrain from knowingly or willingly doing one harm. In an ongoing relationship, the future actions or deeds required for continued trust are typically not specified; there is simply the assumption of an attitude of mutual good will (Putnam 2000). The sense of care for the person and the relationship are so strong that one can rest assured that the other person would not capitalize on an opportunity to enhance their outcomes and willingly forego personal gain if it would bring potential harm to the trusting party if such an opportunity were to come at the expense of the trusting partner (Cummings and Bromily 1996). Principals who hope to earn the trust of their faculties need to demonstrate good will and genuine concern for teachers' well-being.

Akin to benevolence is respect or the recognition of the inherent worth or value of another person and the contributions they make to the collective. In a situation in which one is dependent upon and consequently vulnerable to another, faith in the caring intentions or altruism of the other is particularly important. Teachers want to feel assured that they will be treated fairly and with respect. This aspect of a perception of benevolence suggests an affective or emotional element to trust. Indeed, Leithwood et al.(2010) classify trust as one factor in a construct labeled the Emotions Path of School Leadership. However, the perception of benevolence also involves cognitive judgment of the behaviors of others and one's experiences with them. Although there is an emotional element to trust, it is not primarily an emotional process. There is an important distinction between trust and affection. For example, it is possible to like someone you do not trust, as well as to trust someone you do not especially like (McAllister 1995). The perception of benevolence, therefore, is oftentimes anchored in judgments of the behaviors of principals in the daily enterprise of leading and managing the school.

8.1.3 Honesty

Honesty is a fundamental facet of trust (Bird et al. 2012; Butler and Cantrell 1984; Cummings and Bromily 1996; Rotter 1967). To be trusted, principals must also be honest in their interactions with teachers (Tschannen-Moran and Hoy 1998). Honest behavior is anchored in moral principles and is cultivated through behaviors that demonstrate integrity of character, authenticity, and accountability for one's actions. When teachers begin to perceive a discrepancy between their principal's words and actions, suspicion is the likely result. The revelation of dishonest behavior may be more damaging to trust than lapses in other facets because it is read as an indictment of the person's character. Once a principal has been caught in a lie and the faculty has lost faith in the word of their principal, it will be hard for them to earn or regain trust because language is an essential tool leaders must use to lead and inspire people.

Honesty entails not only to the conventional sense of telling the truth, but it also includes a sense of integrity and authenticity of behavior (Bird et al. 2012, 2009; Hoy and Henderson 1983; Hoy and Kupersmith 1985; Tschannen-Moran and Hoy 1998). Correspondence between a person's statements and deeds characterizes integrity. Integrity is the perceived match between a person's values as expressed in words and those expressed through action (Simons 1999). People earn a reputation of integrity from telling the truth and keeping promises (Dasgupta 1988). When a person says one thing yet does another, trust is compromised. Without the confidence that a person's words can be relied upon and can accurately predict future actions, trust is unlikely to develop. Trust might survive a broken promise if a plausible explanation is given along with an apology; however, a pattern of broken promises will likely provoke a serious threat to trust. A sense of fairness and fair play is an essential element of integrity, refraining from using one's authority to play favorites or to improve one's personal outcomes. In this sense, integrity speaks not only to the alignment between the principal's words and deeds but also to living according to a set of core values or principles.

Authenticity has to do with a willingness to be oneself—to truthfully represent one's beliefs and feelings, as well as owning up to one's foibles. Principals who come across as too guarded in what they are willing to reveal about themselves can be perceived as though they have something to hide or are simply playing a role and thus their motivations may be regarded with suspicion. Authenticity also involves a willingness to take responsibility for one's mistakes and avoidance of distorting the truth in order to shift blame to another. There is no passing the buck, no scapegoating, no pointing fingers at others. This means the willingness to accept responsibility not just for good things that happen, but for mistakes and negative outcomes as well. Rather than protecting his or her reputation as hoped, a principal who continually tries to cover his or her own shortcomings and mistakes by shifting blame to others will more likely earn the distrust of both teachers and superiors. Authenticity also means refraining from using one's authority to manipulate subordinates. Authentic leaders treat others as people, to be respected as persons rather than as pawns to be manipulated. In addition, authentic leaders are able to break through the barriers of role stereotyping and behave in ways that are consistent with their true self. Their basic personality is a prime motivator of behavior, not their idea of how to play some prescribed role. The perceived authenticity of the principal has been correlated to faculty trust in the principal (Hoy and Henderson 1983; Hoy and Kupersmith 1985).

8.1.4 Openness

Principals win the trust of their faculty through their willingness to extend trust, which is evident through openness with information, influence over organizational decisions, and professional discretion (Putnam 2000). Teachers see principals as trustworthy when their communication is both accurate and forthcoming (Bryk and Schneider 2002; Handford and Leithwood 2013). Principals can foster the open flow of information coming to them by being open with communication that flows from them (Bryk and Schneider 2002). When principals exchange thoughts and ideas freely with teachers, it not only enhances perceptions of trustworthiness but leads to greater openness on the part of teachers as well. Adequate explanations and timely feedback on decisions contribute to higher trust (Sapienza and Korsgaarg 1996). Some leaders withhold important information as a way to maintain power or manipulate employees (Kramer 1996; Mishra 1996). However, when principals withhold information from teachers, it evokes suspicion as teachers wonder what is being hidden and why. In schools with a greater level of trust, teachers and other staff members are more willing to disclose accurate, relevant, and complete information about problems, as well as to share their thoughts, feelings or ideas for possible solutions, making these valuable resources available for school improvement (Butler and Cantrell 1984; Mishra 1996; Zand 1997). Problems can be disclosed, diagnosed, and corrected before they are compounded.

Openness in influence comes about as leaders recognize that their teachers possess valuable professional knowledge and decentralize decision-making to harness the collective wisdom of teachers (Forsyth and Adams 2014; Hoy and Sweetland 2000, 2001). By creating decision-making structures and inviting not just teachers' involvement but influence over organizational decisions that affect them, principals can create the conditions necessary to foster mutual trust (Handford and Leithwood 2013; Mitchell et al. 2011; Tschannen-Moran 2001). This is particularly the case when the professional expertise of teachers is fundamental to the issue at hand, such as decisions related to instruction or a commitment to student learning and well-being (Bryk and Schneider 2002; Tschannen-Moran 2009). There are two primary reasons for including subordinates in decision making. The first and most common is that it can foster and strengthen teacher compliance with an initiative. The second is the belief that the involvement of teachers will result in higher quality decisions because they have valuable information and insights to share (Hoy and Tarter 2008). Teachers who reported substantial influence and autonomy in their work environments have been found to hold higher trust in their principals (Moye et al. 2005; Short and Greer 1997). Thus, an authentic professional learning community can potentially be a facilitating element of a school's student achievement (Vescio et al. 2008).

Closely related to the sharing of influence over decision-making and problem-solving is the principal's willingness to grant discretion to teachers. Discretion is rooted in a confidence in teachers' reliability and competence (which are two facets of trust) and a willingness to delegate important tasks to them. Delegating decision authority to teachers in instructional decisions that rely on teacher expertise and commitment to students not only fosters trust, it also promotes greater professionalism because discretion is at the very heart of professional practice (Bryk and Schneider 2002; Louis and Kruse 1995; Marks and Louis 1997; Tschannen-Moran 2009). Using good judgment in this context means considering the maturity and commitment of those with whom you would share information and influence, and working overtime to build capacity if it is lacking initially. Through the exercise of behaviors associated with democratic leadership, principals can achieve the goals of the organization, thus both engendering and making use of trust (Council of Chief State School Officers 2008, 2014).

A leadership style in which the principal is perceived to be approachable and open to the ideas of teachers, who is willing to accept questions and acknowledge that divergent opinions exist, and who seeks to put into practice suggestions from the faculty has been linked to greater faculty trust in the principal (Handford and Leithwood 2013; Tschannen-Moran and Gareis 2002; Tschannen-Moran and Hoy 1998). Such an open leadership style has been associated with increased motivation and commitment to shared goals as well as improved school performance (Cloke and Goldsmith 2002). A professional orientation on the part of principals has been found to engender greater trust from their teachers, to predict greater instructional capacity among a school's faculty, and to produce greater achievement among the school's students (Forsyth and Adams 2014; Tschannen-Moran 2009). Moreover, a large-scale study of principals' leadership was found to impact school performance more by strengthening teachers' professional community than by directly influencing their instructional practices (Louis et al. 2010).

8.1.5 Competence

Competence is the ability to perform a task as expected, according to appropriate standards. In schools, principals and teachers depend upon one another's competence to accomplish the teaching and learning goals of the school. When principals demonstrate the ability to get the job done, whatever that job may entail, teachers are more inclined to show trust in the principal. Teachers depend upon the principal to manage the complex tasks inherent in this role successfully in order to fulfill the similarly complex responsibilities they have in teaching young people. Leithwood et al. (2010) classify such tasks as associated with the Rational Path and the Organizational Path of school leadership, through which a principal demonstrates essential knowledge of and skills associated with "curriculum, teaching, and learning" (p. 673) and with the "structures, cultures, policies, and standard operating procedures" (p. 678) of the school. More specifically, Leithwood and his colleagues identify academic press, disciplinary climate, and protecting instructional time as key examples of classroom and school variables that may mediate student achievement. Notably, faculty trust in the principal relies heavily on the competence of principals relative to their various responsibilities as school leaders (Handford and Leithwood 2013). Therefore, trustworthy principals adopt knowledge, skills, work habits, and systems that enable them to achieve the myriad tasks necessary to operate and lead a school (Adams and Forsyth 2007; Handford and Leithwood 2013; Hoy et al. 2002).

Teachers often mention incidents in which the competence of their principal matters. In a study of three high-trust and three low-trust schools, competence was the most often mentioned element contributing to the trust or distrust of the school leader (Handford and Leithwood 2013). Skills related to competence included setting high standards, pressing for results, solving problems, resolving conflicts, working hard, and setting an example. In high-trust schools, principals are regarded with respect and even admiration. In these schools, the principals not only set a high standard, they also hold teachers accountable in ways that seem fair and reasonable to their staff.

Principals are tasked with influencing student performance by shaping the school's learning-focused mission and aligning the school's structures and culture to serve the mission (Hallinger 2005). They accomplish this by focusing on the core tasks of schooling including choosing appropriate curriculum, improving instruction, managing school context, and improving student learning (Hallinger 2003; Leithwood et al. 1999). The principal must engage with teachers regularly and effectively in order to effect change in their instructional practices (Coldren and Spillane 2007; Marks and Printy 2003; Robinson et al. 2008). Principals' leadership involves impacting practices both through faculty-wide efforts and through individualized efforts, each of which represent important means to improve instruction and, therefore, student performance (May and Supovitz 2011). Thus, competence in school leadership can take the form of teacher professional development, curriculum development, and teacher supervision (Handford and Leithwood 2013; Blase and Blase 1998). Other forms of competence in school leadership include the use of data in discussions about practice, monitoring teachers' lesson plans, and focusing a school community on its collective responsibility for educational excellence through partnerships and community development (Coldren and Spillane 2007).

The primary responsibility of principal leadership is to improve student learning outcomes by strengthening teachers' instructional practices (Brown et al. 2004; Finnigan 2010; Heck and Moriyama 2010; Robinson et al. 2008). Though research suggests the effect of principal leadership on student achievement may be indirect, it is nonetheless significant, especially in relationship to teachers' instructional performance (Cotton 2003; Leithwood et al. 2004; 2010; Hallinger et al. 1996; Hallinger and Heck 1996; Louis et al. 2010; Supovitz et al. 2010). In a meta-analysis of 27 research studies, Robinson et al. (2008) found significant links between leadership and student outcomes. They noted that leadership competence in promoting teacher learning and development was most strongly predictive of positive student outcomes, but that relationship-developing strategies were woven throughout all aspects of school leadership.

8.1.6 Reliability

The fostering and sustaining of trust also involve reliability. Reliability means following through on decisions and promises. It entails a sense of confidence that one can rest assured that another person (e.g., the principal) can be counted on to do what is expected on a regular, consistent basis. Reliability combines a sense of predictability with elements of benevolence and competence. In a situation of interdependence, when something is required from another person or group that impacts joint outcomes, partners can consistently be relied upon to supply it (Butler and Cantrell 1984; Mishra 1996). When principals demonstrate enough consistency in their behavior to inspire confidence that teachers can count on them in their time of need, teachers need not invest energy worrying whether the principal will come through in a difficult situation. Neither will they expend energy making mental provisions of how they will manage in case the principal fails to come through.

It is an accepted truism that the best predictor of future behavior is past behavior. Thus, principals who reliably act in ways that elicit trust across time and settings are more likely to earn and maintain the trust of their faculty than those who do not

(Tschannen-Moran and Gareis 2002; Bryk and Schneider 2002; Tschannen-Moran 2014b). Teachers want to be able to depend upon the actions of their principal, and teachers tend to have greater confidence in their own decision-making and actions when they feel they can predict the behavior of their principal (Handford and Leithwood 2013). Teachers may conclude that their principal means well, and even that he or she is very capable and helpful if you can get his or her attention. However, if trouble in managing the time demands of the job (e.g., being easily distracted, or lapsing in decision-making) means teachers cannot count on the principal to come through for them when needed, the teachers are unlikely to extent trust in the relationship. In a sense, the facet of reliability must be present in each of the other four facets of trust such that a principal's behaviors associated with benevolence, honesty, openness, and competence are consistent.

8.1.7 Trustworthy Leadership

Principals hold authority and responsibility for student achievement and other important educational outcomes of schooling, although their effect tends to be indirect and largely dependent upon the effectiveness of teachers. Principles work with and through teachers to pursue the educational mission of their schools; therefore, the relationship between the principals and their teachers must be one that facilitates the myriad judgments, decisions, and actions that occur within schools. Trust has been found to be associated with the qualitative nature of professional relationships and the outcomes of those relationships in terms of practice and student achievement. Interrelationships and behaviors characterized by benevolence, honestly, openness, competence, and reliability can cultivate trust between principals and teachers, and the presence of genuine trust can thereby mediate other correlates associated with student learning.

8.2 Correlates of Trust in Schools

Intuitively and empirically, trust is a powerful construct when considering influence on and through behavior in the pursuit of the educational mission of schools. Yet, trust does not operate irrespective of other important constructs. As Leithwood et al. (2010) assert, there are undoubtedly numerable mediators that must exist between leadership actions and the experiences of and outcomes for students. Here we briefly explore three such mediators, each explicitly or implicitly addressed by Leithwood and his colleagues' investigation of four Paths of Leadership. However, we contend that these three mediators, as correlates of trust, are indicative of the centrally important role that trust plays in how leadership influences student learning. Specifically, we turn our attention to the relationship of trust to academic press, collective teacher efficacy, and teacher professionalism.

8.2.1 Academic Press

Growing out of research on effective schools more than three decades ago, the construct of academic press has persistently been identified as a variable in student achievement (Leithwood et al. 2010). Murphy et al. (1982) described academic press as "the degree to which environmental forces press for student achievement on a schoolwide basis" (p. 22) and that academic press "pulls together various forces—school policies, practices, expectations, norms, and rewards—generated by both staff and students" (p. 22). The inclusion of "norms" in this definition is particularly relevant, as academic press may be leveraged by school policies and practices, but it is also dependent upon norms of behavior that exist among members of a school community. Goodard et al. (2000) explained that academic press can be characterized as a normative environment where teachers both believe that students are capable of succeeding academically and they press to help struggling students meet academic expectations. Such schools are places where teachers set high academic expectations, create a learning environment that is orderly and serious, and make an extra effort to assist students to learn. In these schools, not only do teachers and administrators have high expectations of students, but students work hard, and they respect other students who are academically motivated (Hoy and Hannum 1997; Hoy et al. 1998).

Research on academic press indicates a strong link between the construct and student achievement (Bryk et al. 1993; Goddard et al. 2000; Hoy and Hannum 1997; Hoy et al. 1998, 1990, 1991; Hoy and Tarter 1997; Alig-Mielcarek and Hoy 2005). Leithwood et al. (2010) characterized academic press as a factor in the Rational Path of School Leadership. Indeed, academic press is elemental to instructional leadership, which is a core strand of professional responsibility for educational leaders (Council of Chief State School Officers 2008, 2014). The second standard of the current school leadership standards, referred to as the instructional leadership standard (Ylimaki 2014), states that "an educational leader promotes the success of every student by advocating, nurturing, and sustaining a school culture and instructional program conducive to student learning and staff professional growth" (Council of Chief State School Officers 2008, p. 14). Core functions or roles related to instructional leadership include creating a rigorous curriculum and a motivating learning environment, which are conceptually related to the construct of academic press. The responsibility of the school leader is also to cultivate norms of behaviors among members of the school community that are conducive to student achievement. We contend that behaviors that demonstrate benevolence, honesty, openness, competence, and reliability—all facets of trust—are inherent to such a school culture.

The relationship among instructional leadership, academic press, and trust is important to explore, as Leithwood et al. (2010) contend, "enough evidence is now at hand to justify claims about significant leadership effects on students that the focus of attention for many leadership researchers has moved to include questions about how those effects occur" (p. 672). In this vein, Mitchell et al. (2015) found that instructional leadership has a significant direct effect on school academic press.

Instructional leadership was also positively correlated with academic achievement in bivariate correlations and had an indirect effect on academic achievement in a structural equation model, even when controlling for the effects of SES and school level. Although research on academic press has typically relied only on the perceptions of teachers, Mitchell et al. (2015) found a convergence in the perceptions of academic press among teachers, students and parents in a school. As in prior studies that have examined the relationship between academic press and student achievement (Bryk et al. 1993; Goddard et al., 2000; Hoy and Hannum, 1997; Hoy et al. 1998, 1990, 1991; Hoy and Tarter 1997; Alig-Mielcarek and Hoy 2005), they found academic press to be strongly correlated with and predictive of achievement aggregated to the school level. In fact, school academic press had the largest direct effect on student achievement over and above the negative effects of low SES. Strong evidence exists for the importance of creating a school culture that is characterized by academic press in order to foster student achievement.

Within the instructional leadership standard, the first function or role of the educational leader is to "nurture and sustain a culture of collaboration, trust, learning, and high expectations" (Council of Chief State School Officers 2008, p. 14). In this standard, both academic press (high expectations) and trust are alluded to, thus conceptually suggesting the important interrelationships that exist between the constructs. Indeed, our recent research into this relationship suggests that the level of academic press in a school is related to principal trustworthiness (Tschannen-Moran and Gareis 2015). When a principal is able to cultivate a learning environment that is serious in purpose (that is, focused on student achievement) and orderly, including setting expectations for the behavior of students and staff, then student achievement is likely to be higher. Such findings suggest the reciprocal influences that leadership behaviors have in the cultivation of the norms of a school that ultimately create the rich educational environment (i.e., the school culture) in which student motivation, effort, and achievement take root.

8.2.2 Collective Teacher Efficacy

Collective teacher efficacy is a motivational construct based on the shared perceptions of teachers in a school that the efforts of the faculty as a whole will have positive effects on students. These beliefs can powerfully shape group behavior and group outcomes through the goals, effort, perseverance and resilience that flow from them (Bandura 1993, 1997; Tschannen-Moran et al. 2014). Teachers are more likely to persist in efforts toward goals that they believe they can accomplish. These shared beliefs become manifest in the norms of a school and the casual conversations among teachers concerning expectations about the likelihood of success of a school faculty. Teachers' collective sense of efficacy has been linked to student achievement, even when taking into account the socioeconomic status of students (Bandura 1993; Goddard et al. 2001; Tschannen-Moran and Barr 2004).

Principals can help to cultivate and nourish strong collective efficacy beliefs through communicating confidence in the ability of teachers to promote student learning, whatever the difficulties and challenges of the particular context of the school may be. Principal leadership has been found to influence teachers' beliefs that they could make a positive difference in student performance, which in turn resulted in stronger efforts and improved outcomes (Finnigan 2010).

When a high level of trust prevails in a school, a sense of collective efficacy tends to be evident as well. This collective sense of being able to successfully fulfill the central mission of the school has been linked to teachers' trust in one another as well as to teachers' trust in students and parents (Tschannen-Moran and Goddard 2001). When a school is characterized by high trust, it is more likely that they will develop greater confidence in their collective ability to be successful at meeting their goals (Tschannen-Moran et al. 2014). A virtuous cycle in which trust, success, and collective efficacy reinforce one another can be set in motion. Thus, in a study of urban elementary schools, Tschannen-Moran (2014b) found that trust bolstered the risk taking of experimenting with new teaching practice, which was rewarded with higher student achievement, and which in turn raised the collective sense among teachers that they could make a difference even among their most disadvantaged students. In their exploration of four "paths" of school leadership that influence student learning, Leithwood et al.(2010) observed that "evidence points to considerable interaction among Paths". Within their investigation of the paths, the construct of collective teacher efficacy is posited as one of two key indicators of the Emotions Path. The other construct associated with the Emotions Path is trust. While distinct as constructs, the interrelationship between collective teacher efficacy and trust seems evident in fostering the organizational conditions critical to student achievement.

8.2.3 Teacher Professionalism

To meet the changing expectations and challenging new standards demanded by a shifting global economy and new technologies, teachers' professionalism has never been more important. Professionalism requires a commitment to the needs of clients; skillful use of assessments, and the capacity to develop individualized interventions based on the needs of clients. It also entails abiding by a set of norms, standards, and ethics established by the profession, and engaging in ongoing, disciplined, professional inquiry into the best available knowledge (Tschannen-Moran 2009). In schools where teacher professionalism is high, teachers perceived their colleagues to be committed to students—competent, cooperative, and supportive. Where professionalism is low, teachers question the professional judgment of their colleagues.

In their study of the four Emotions Paths of School Leadership that influence student achievement, Leithwood et al. (2010) do not refer explicitly to teacher professionalism; however, the construct of professional learning communities (PLCs) is included as one of two potential factors of the Organizational Path. In their review of research, Leithwood et al. state "student learning improved when teachers participated in PLCs," and leadership behaviors that facilitate the creation and effectiveness of PLCs are described as "supportive," "professional," and "protecting" (p. 680). While not synonyms of trust, the normative, interrelational, and ethical language of PLCs is suggestive of facets of trust, such as benevolence, competence, honesty, openness, and reliability.

Teachers who trust their principal are more likely to be open about both their successes and challenges in the classroom, whereas teachers who distrust their principal will be guarded and more likely to engage in self-protective behaviors that may impair the sense of professional community in a school (Tschannen-Moran 2014a). Moreover, faculty trust in principals has been linked to faculty perceptions of the professional orientation of a principal, suggesting that principals set the tone of professionalism in their buildings (Tschannen-Moran 2009). School leaders with a professional orientation do not abuse their power to enforce policies through the overuse of punishments, but neither do they abdicate their responsibility for leadership (Adams and Forsyth 2007; Hoy and Sweetland 2000). They engage in coaching and collaboration to bring underperforming teachers into alignment with professional standards, as well as to provide resources to continually extend the professional knowledge of all teachers in their building (Tschannen-Moran 2014b).

In order to support teachers in their development as professionals and as they are asked to change their fundamental beliefs and instructional techniques, they are asked to forge professional communities in their schools and disciplines. These professional communities function best when they are anchored in trust and teamwork (Putnam and Borko 1997; Seashore and Kruse 1995). A school-wide culture of trust, and especially trust in the principal, has been found to be an important precondition for the development of professional learning communities (Cranston 2011; Wahlstrom and Louis 2008). Trustworthy behavior on the part of the principal has been related to teachers' perceptions of the professionalism of their colleagues (Tschannen-Moran 2009; Tschannen-Moran and Gareis 2002). That is, where teachers felt that they could put their faith in the principal and that their principal was someone to whom they could turn for assistance with instructional matters, they rated the professionalism of their colleagues more positively. Conversely, where teachers did not trust their principals, they were also likely to regard their colleagues as not exercising professional judgment and competence. Predictably, enthusiasm for teaching was also lower when trust in the principal was lower. Thus, the relationship between faculty trust in the principal and teacher professionalism is likely one of the mechanisms at play in the indirect link between trust in the principal and student achievement.

8.2.4 Trustworthy Leadership and Correlates of Trust

Trustworthy leadership on the part of the principal has been shown to be related to three powerful aspects of school culture: academic press, collective teacher efficacy, and teacher professionalism. What's more, these three correlates are themselves strongly related to one another. Where teachers conduct themselves with a higher degree of professionalism, there is likely to be greater seriousness and celebration of the academic mission of the school and a stronger shared belief among the faculty of their capacity to make a difference. By way of contrast, where any one aspect of the school culture begins to suffer, they are all likely to decline as well. Trust, then, is an important factor associated with student achievement, as well as an important mediator of other leadership behaviors associated with student achievement.

8.3 Implications

In their exploration of school leadership influences on student achievement, Leithwood et al. (2010) provide "an initial and partial test of a new conception, metaphorical in nature, of how leadership influences student learning" (p. 673). The metaphor is of "four distinct 'Paths' along which leadership influence flows to improve student learning" (p. 673). This includes the Rational Path, Emotions Path, Organizational Path, and Family Path. The metaphor is apt, as paths simultaneously suggest both a means and intended outcome. In exploring the implications of trust as a mediating variable of school leadership and student achievement, we offer another metaphor, that of cultivation.

Metaphorically, trust may have a cultivation role in school leadership. To cultivate means to prepare and use land for raising crops. In a similar way, trust can have dual functions of both preparing a school culture for student achievement and using it as an elemental resource in the complex and continuing acts of teaching and learning. To extend the metaphor, trust may not be the seed of student achievement, but it may well be the rich soil in which the seeds of effective teaching and learning can take root and grow. The organic metaphor appeals to us, in part, because the acts of teaching and learning are inherent to human behavior and thus are grounded in human interactions.

More practically speaking, trust may not be only a factor associated with one path of school leadership, such as the Emotions Path posited by Leithwood et al. (2010). Rather, there is evidence that trust may be a mediating variable for other factors associated with student achievement, such as academic press, collective teacher efficacy, and teacher professionalism. This conceptualization is evident in the proposed revised standards for educational leadership (Council of Chief State School Officers 2014), which include a number of references to the role of leaders in cultivating trust and a culture of values, attitudes, and, importantly, behaviors that focus on student learning. The standards are clear that creating, maintaining, and sustaining such a culture (that is, cultivating such values and behaviors) is the responsibility of educational leaders. Indeed, note the repeated references to elements of leadership, school culture, and trust in two of the new standards:

> Standard 5: An educational leader promotes the success and well-being of every student by promoting the development of an inclusive school climate characterized by supportive relationships and a personalized culture of care (Council of Chief State School Officers 2014, p. 18).

This standard includes such leadership functions as the following:

- Ensures the formation of a culture defined by trust
- Ensures that each student is known, valued, and respected
- Ensures that students are enmeshed in a safe, secure, emotionally protective, and healthy environment (Council of Chief State School Officers 2014, p. 18).

Similarly, there is such language in the new Standard 6:

> Standard 6: "An educational leader promotes the success and well-being of every student by promoting professionally normed communities for teachers and other professional staff." (Council of Chief State School Officers 2014, p. 18).

Standard 6 includes leadership functions such as:

- Ensures the formation of a culture defined by trust
- Fosters and supports the growth of trust (Council of Chief State School Officers 2014, p. 18).

The principal has significant influence on the culture of a school, and the culture of a school is oftentimes reflected in the principal's values, attitudes, and behaviors. Inherent to a school culture that fosters student achievement is trust. In schools that enjoy a culture of trust, staff and students tend to have a shared focus on and expectation of student learning; teachers tend to have a shared sense that they can make a difference in students' lives; and they tend to respect one another, share expertise, and learn from one another. If schools are to reap the rewards of a trusting work environment, it is the principal's responsibility to build and sustain trusting relationships (Whitener et al. 1998).

Trustworthy leadership is cultivated over time, through repeated interactions in which behaviors associated with benevolence, honesty, openness, competence, and reliability are enacted. Indeed, by definition of the facet of reliability, trust must be maintained, once established, through repeated and consistent behavior of the school leader. The leader's own decisions and behaviors are primary means by which the norms of a school—its culture, the group's way of interacting and behaving—are cultivated and then used as a facilitating means of bringing about student well-being and achievement. In other words, trust within schools must be nurtured by school leaders not only for the inherent worth of trust but because trust plays a mediating role on other important elements of school culture and leadership that are related to student achievement (Tschannen-Moran and Gareis 2002).

Leithwood et al. (2010) argued that identifying "powerful leadership mediators" is important because school leaders "are in the business of deciding where best to focus their efforts" (p. 673). While Leithwood and his colleagues posit that trust may be one factor related to the Emotions Path of School Leadership, we would suggest that trust may in fact mediate a number of factors related to student achievement. If this is the case, then the implications for educational leadership preparation, induction and mentoring of novice school leaders, and the supervision and evaluation of educational leaders become quite important. For example, understanding and developing the dispositions and skills associated with trustworthiness in a complex, public position such as that of a school principal would be necessary for novice and experienced school leaders alike. Closely related—and perhaps even foremost—would be the need to further refine our understanding of the construct of trust and to further investigate its relationship to other factors of schools related to student achievement.

8.4 Directions for Future Research

Leithwood et al. (2010) conclude their article with a call for educational leadership research to "focus on discovering the leadership practices most likely to improve the condition or status of variables for which there is already considerable evidence of impact on student learning" (p. 698). With that focus, we briefly outline the following directions for future research on trust framed by the four Paths posited by Leithwood et al. as a "simple and compelling" conceptualization of leadership influences (p. 673):

- The Rational Path is concerned with the core enterprises of schooling, namely elements of curriculum, instruction, assessment, and student learning. Mediating variables such as academic press and disciplinary climate have been associated with the Rational Path as possible mediating variables. Trust has been shown to be associated with academic press, which raises the question of how trust might be related to other variables of the instructional enterprise, such as disciplinary climate, the articulation of a shared mission and vision for a school, formative and summative assessment practices, or remediation efforts.
- The Emotional Path includes "feelings, dispositions, and affective states" (p. 675), and Leithwood et al. identified collective teacher efficacy and trust as possible associated constructs. Collective teacher efficacy has been shown to be related to trust, but Leithwood et al. found non-significant contribution of trust to student achievement. However, if trust is associated with multiple variables, then is its role in student achievement differential or cumulative among these other variables? Also, how is trust related to other possible factors of the Emotions Path such as those alluded to in the most recently proposed educational leadership standards: sense of safety and emotional well-being of students, teacher perceptions of working conditions, the presence and pervasiveness of positive relationships within the school, and student enjoyment of student learning (Council of Chief State School Officers 2014)?
- The Organizational Path concerns structures, policies, and operating practices, for which Leithwood and his associates (Leithwood et al. 2010) identified instructional time and professional learning communities as associated variables. The relationship between professional learning communities and trust has been shown, but how is trust related to the allotment and protection of instructional time, and how is trust related to other possible organizational variables such as sufficient resources to support instruction, ability grouping practices, class size, as well as the adequacy and maintenance of the physical environment?
- The Family Path potentially includes both alterable and unalterable variables that have to do with student experiences in their domestic lives outside of school, which

Leithwood and his colleagues (Leithwood et al. 2010) cited as accounting for more than half of the variation in student achievement. Leithwood and his colleagues identified access to supportive adult influences and the presence of a computer in the home as variables. However, characterizing the Family Path in terms of variables identified in educational leadership standards may prove more meaningful, in particular, variables that may be associated with trust such as those articulated in the proposed new Standard 7—Communities of Engagement for Families:

- Promoting communities of engagement for families and other stakeholders
- Promoting understanding, appreciation, and use of the community's diverse cultural, social, and intellectual resources
- Nurturing a sense of approachability and sustaining positive relationships with families and caregivers
- Building and sustaining productive relationships with community partners in the government,
- non-profit, and private sectors
- Advocating for policies and resources for the community
- Understanding and engaging with community needs, priorities, and resources (Council of Chief State School Officers 2014).

In sum, trust would seem to play a role in each of the four paths delineated by Leithwood and his colleagues (2010). For schools to truly become the vibrant learning communities envisioned by school improvement and reform efforts, attention must be paid to issues of trust. An understanding of the conditions and processes that enable teachers and administrators to learn to trust each other and cooperate together is critical as schools are increasingly faced with the volatility of changing expectations. Schools where trust is high can help avoid rigidity and a "hunkering down" mentality that organizations often fall victim to in the midst of crisis (Daly 2009). The open communication, commitment, and professionalism that high trust environments make possible confers a strategic advantage to schools in times of change. The candor that trusting relationship fosters can allow for more effective problem solving and can provide an additional bulwark to an organization when confronting turbulent environments and new competitive forces afoot (Daly 2009; Hoy and Sweetland 2001; Mishra 1996; Tschannen-Moran 2009, 2014a; Tschannen-Moran and Hoy 2000). Thus, the challenge of cultivating high trust school environments may be one of the most important tasks facing school leaders in the times in which we live.

References

Adams, C. M., & Forsyth, P. B. (2007). Promoting a culture of parent collaboration and trust: An empirical study. *Journal of School of Public Relations, 28*, 32–56.

Alig-Mielcarek, J., & Hoy, W. K. (2005). Instructional leadership. In W. K. Hoy & C. G. Miskel (Eds.), *Educational leadership and reform* (pp. 29–54). Greenwich: Information Age Publishers.

Baier, A. C. (1994). *Moral prejudices*. Cambridge, MA: Harvard University Press.

Bandura, A. (1993). Perceived self-efficacy in cognitive development and functioning. *Educational Psychology, 28*, 117–148.

Bandura, A. (1997). *Self-efficacy: The exercise of control*. New York: Freeman.

Bigley, G. A., & Pearce, J. L. (1998). Straining for shared meaning in organization science: Problems of trust and distrust. *Academy of Management Review, 23*, 405–421.

Bird, J. J., Chuang, W., Watson, J., & Murray, L. (2009). Relationships among principal authentic leadership and teacher trust and engagement levels. *Journal of School Leadership, 19*, 153–171.

Bird, J. J., Chuang, W., Watson, J., & Murray, L. (2012). Teacher and principal perceptions of authentic leadership: Implications for trust, engagement, and intention to return. *Journal of School Leadership, 22*, 425–461.

Blase, J., & Blase, J. (1998). *Handbook of instructional leadership: How really good principals promote teaching and learning*. Thousand Oaks: Corwin.

Brown, K. M., Anfara, V. A., & Roney, K. (2004). Student achievement in high performing, suburban middle schools and low performing, urban middle schools: Plausible explanations for the differences. *Education and Urban Society, 36*, 428–456. doi:10.1177/0013124504263339.

Bryk, A. S., & Schneider, B. (2002). *Trust in schools: A core resource for school improvement*. New York: Russell Sage Foundation.

Bryk, A. S., Lee, V. E., & Holland, P. B. (1993). *Catholic schools and the common good*. Cambridge, MA: Harvard University Press.

Butler Jr., J. K., & Cantrell, R. S. (1984). A behavioral decision theory approach to modeling dyadic trust in superiors and subordinates. *Psychological Reports, 55*, 19–28.

Chugtai, A. A., & Buckley, F. (2009). Linking trust in the principal to school outcomes: The mediating role of organizational identification and work engagement. *International Journal of Educational Management, 23*, 574–589.

Cloke, K., & Goldsmith, J. (2002). *The end of management and the rise of organizational democracy*. San Francisco: Jossey-Bass.

Coldren, A. F., & Spillane, J. P. (2007). Making connections to teaching practice: The role of boundary practices in instructional leadership. *Educational Policy, 21*, 369–396.

Cotton, K. (2003). *Principals and student achievement: What the research says*. Alexandria: Association for Supervision and Curriculum Development.

Council of Chief State School Officers. (2008). *Educational leadership policy standards: ISLLC 2008*. Washington, DC: Author.

Council of Chief State School Officers. (2014). *Educational leadership policy standards: ISLLC 2014 draft for public comment*. Washington, DC: Author.

Cranston, J. (2011). Relational trust: The glue that binds a professional learning community. *Alberta Journal of Educational Research, 57*, 59–72.

Cummings, L. L., & Bromily, P. (1996). The organizational trust inventory (OTI): Development and validation. In R. Karmer & T. Tyler (Eds.), *Trust in organizations* (pp. 302–330). Thousand Oaks: Sage.

Daly, A. (2009). Rigid response in an age of accountability: The potential of leadership and trust. *Educational Administration Quarterly, 45*, 168–216.

Dasgupta, P. (1988). Trust as a commodity. In D. Gambetta (Ed.), *Trust: Making and breaking cooperative relations* (pp. 213–238). Cambridge, MA: Blackwell.

Finnigan, K. S. (2010). Principal leadership and teacher motivation under high-stakes accountability policies. *Leadership and Policy in Schools, 9*, 161–189. doi:10.1080/15700760903216174.

Forsyth, P. B., & Adams, C. M. (2014). Organizational predictability, the school principal, and achievement. In D. Van Maele, P. B. Forsyth, & M. Van Houtte (Eds.), *Trust and school life: The influence of trust on learning, teaching, leading, and bridging* (pp. 83–98). New York: Springer.

Goddard, R. D., Sweetland, S. R., & Hoy, W. K. (2000). Academic emphasis of urban elementary schools and student achievement in reading and mathematics: A multilevel analysis. *Educational Administration Quarterly, 36*, 683–702. doi:10.1177/00131610021969164.

Goddard, R. D., Tschannen-Moran, M., & Hoy, W. K. (2001). A multilevel examination of the distribution and effects of teacher trust in students and parents in urban elementary schools. *The Elementary School Journal, 102*, 3–17.

Hallinger, P. (2003). Leading educational change: Reflections on the practice of instructional and transformational leadership. *Cambridge Journal of Education, 33*, 329–351.

Hallinger, P. (2005). Instructional leadership and the school principal: A passing fancy that refuses to fade away. *Leadership and Policy in Schools, 4*, 221–239.

Hallinger, P., & Heck, R. H. (1996). Reassessing the principal's role in school effectiveness: A review of empirical research, 1980–1995. *Educational Administration Quarterly, 32*, 5–44.

Hallinger, P., Bickman, L., & Davis, K. (1996). School context, principal leadership, and student reading achievement. *The Elementary School Journal, 96*, 527–549.

Handford, V., & Leithwood, K. (2013). Why teachers trust school leaders. *Journal of Educational Administration, 51*, 194–212.

Heck, R. H., & Moriyama, K. (2010). Examining relationships among elementary schools' contexts, leadership, instructional practices, and added-year outcomes: A regression discontinuity approach. *School Effectiveness and School Improvement, 21*, 377–408. doi:10.1080/09243453.2010.500097.

Hoy, W. K., & Hannum, J. W. (1997). Middle school climate: An empirical assessment of organizational health and student achievement. *Educational Administration Quarterly, 33*, 290–311.

Hoy, W. K., & Henderson, J. E. (1983). Principal authenticity, school climate, and trust. *Alberta Journal of Educational Research, 29*, 123–130.

Hoy, W. K., & Kupersmith, W. J. (1985). The meaning and measure of faculty trust. *Educational and Psychological Research, 5*, 1–10.

Hoy, W. K., & Sweetland, S. R. (2000). Bureaucracies that work: Enabling not coercive. *Journal of School Leadership, 10*, 525–541.

Hoy, W. K., & Sweetland, S. R. (2001). Designing better schools: The meaning and nature of enabling school structure. *Educational Administration Quarterly, 37*, 296–321.

Hoy, W. K., Sweetland, S. R., & Smith, P. A. (2002). Toward an organizational model of achievement in high schools: The significance of collective efficacy. *Educational Administration Quarterly, 38*, 77–93.

Hoy, W. K., & Tarter, C. J. (1997). *The road to open and healthy schools: A handbook of change.* Thousand Oaks: Sage.

Hoy, W. K., & Tarter, C. J. (2008). *Administrators solving the problems of practice: Decision-making, concepts, cases, and consequences* (3rd ed.). Boston: Allyn & Bacon.

Hoy, W. K., Tarter, C. J., & Bliss, J. R. (1990). Organizational climate, school health, and effectiveness: A comparative analysis. *Educational Administration Quarterly, 26*, 260–279.

Hoy, W. K., Tarter, C. J., & Kottkamp, R. B. (1991). *Open schools/healthy schools.* Beverly Hills: Sage.

Hoy, W. K., Hannum, J. W., & Tschannen-Moran, M. (1998). Organizational climate and student achievement: A parsimonious and longitudinal view. *Journal of School Leadership, 8*, 336–359.

Kramer, R. M. (1996). Divergent realities and convergent disappointments in the hierarchic relation: Trust and the intuitive auditor at work. In R. Kramer & T. Tyler (Eds.), *Trust in organizations* (pp. 216–245). Thousand Oaks: Sage.

Leithwood, K., Jantzi, D., & Steinbach, R. (1999). *Changing leadership for changing times.* Philadelphia: Open University Press.

Leithwood, K., Louis, K. S., Anderson, S., & Wahlstrom, K. (2004). *Review of research: How leadership influences student learning.* New York: Wallace Foundation.

Leithwood, K., Patten, S., & Jantzi, D. (2010). Testing a conception of how school leadership influences student learning. *Educational Administration Quarterly, 46*, 671–706. doi:10.1177/0013161x10377347.

Louis, K. S., & Kruse, S. (1995). *Professionalism and community: Perspectives on reforming urban schools.* Thousand Oaks: Corwin.

Louis, K. S., Dretzkea, B., & Wahlstrom, K. (2010). How does leadership affect student achievement? Results from a national US survey. *School Effectiveness and School Improvement, 21*, 315–336.

Marks, H. M., & Louis, K. S. (1997). Does teacher empowerment affect the classroom? The implications of teacher empowerment for instructional practice and student academic performance. *Educational Evaluation and Policy Analyis, 19*, 245–275.

Marks, H. M., & Printy, S. M. (2003). Principal leadership and school performance: An integration of transformational and instructional leadership. *Educational Administration Quarterly, 39*, 370–397.

May, H., & Supovitz, J. A. (2011). The scope of principal efforts to improve instruction. *Educational Administration Quarterly, 47*, 332–352. doi:10.1177/0013161X10383411.

McAllister, D. J. (1995). Affect- and cognition-based trust as foundations for interpersonal cooperation in organizations. *Academy of Management Review, 38*, 24–59.

Mishra, A. K. (1996). Organizational responses to crisis: The centrality of trust. In R. Kramer & T. Tyler (Eds.), *Trust in organizations* (pp. 261–287). Thousand Oaks: Sage.

Mitchell, R., Ripley, J., Adams, C., & Raju, D. (2011). Trust: An essential ingredient in collaborative decision making. *Journal of School of Public Relations, 32*, 145–170.

Mitchell, R. M., Kensler, L. A., & Tschannen-Moran, M. (2015). Examining the effects of instructional leadership on school academic press and school achievement. *Journal of School Leadership, 25*, 223–251.

Moye, M. J., Henkin, A. B., & Egley, R. J. (2005). Teacher-principal relationships: Exploring linkages between empowerment and interpersonal trust. *Journal of Educational Administration, 43*, 260–277.

Murphy, J. F., Weil, M., Hallinger, P., & Mitman, A. (1982). Academic press: Translating high expectations into school practices and classroom practices. *Educational Leadership, 40*, 22–26.

Notman, R., & Henry, D. A. (2011). Building and sustaining successful school leadership in New Zealand. *Leadership and Policy in Schools, 10*, 375–394. doi:10.1080/15700763.2011.610555.

Putnam, R. D. (2000). *Bowling alone: The collapse and revival of American community*. New York: Simon and Schuster.

Putnam, R. T., & Borko, H. (1997). Teacher learning: Implications of new views of cognition. In B. J. Biddle, T. L. Good, & I. F. Goodson (Eds.), *The international handbook of teachers and teaching* (pp. 1223–1296). Dordrecht: Kluwer.

Robinson, V. M. J., Lloyd, C. A., & Rowe, K. J. (2008). The impact of leadership on student outcomes: An analysis of the differential effects of leadership types. *Educational Administration Quarterly, 44*, 635–674. doi:10.1177/0013161X08321509.

Rotter, J. B. (1967). A new scale for the measurement of interpersonal trust. *Journal of Personality, 35*, 651–665.

Rousseau, D., Sitkin, S. B., Burt, R., & Camerer, C. (1998). Not so different after all: A cross-discipline view of trust. *Academy of Management Review, 23*, 393–404.

Salfi, N. A. (2011). Successful leadership practices of head teachers for school improvement: Some evidence from Pakistan. *Journal of Educational Administration, 49*, 414–432. doi:10.1108/09578231111146489.

Sapienza, H. J., & Korsgaarg, M. A. (1996). Managing investor relations: The impact of procedural justice in establishing and sustaining investor support. *Academy of Management Journal, 39*, 544–574.

Seashore, K., & Kruse, S. D. (1995). *Professionalism and community: Perspectives on reforming urban schools*. Branchville: Broad Street.

Short, P. M., & Greer, J. T. (1997). *Leadership in empowered schools: Themes from innovative efforts*. Columbus: Merrill.

Simons, T. L. (1999). Behavioral integrity as a critical ingredient for transformational leadership. *Journal of Organizational Change Management, 12*, 89–104.

Solomon, R. C., & Flores, F. (2001). *Building trust in business, politics, relationships, and life*. New York: Oxford University Press.

Supovitz, J. A., Sirinides, P., & May, H. (2010). How principals and peers influence teaching and learning. *Educational Administration Quarterly, 46*, 31–56. doi:10.1177/1094670509353043.

Tschannen-Moran, M. (2001). Collaboration and the need for trust. *Journal of Educational Administration, 39*, 308–331.

Tschannen-Moran, M. (2003). Fostering organizational citizenship: Transformational leadership and trust. In W. K. Hoy & C. G. Miskel (Eds.), *Studies in leading and organizing schools* (pp. 157–179). Greenwich: Information Age Publishing.

Tschannen-Moran, M. (2009). Fostering teacher professionalism: The role of professional orientation and trust. *Educational Administration Quarterly, 45*, 217–247.

Tschannen-Moran, M. (2014a). The interconnectivity of trust in schools. In D. Van Maele, P. B. Forsyth, & M. Van Houtte (Eds.), *Trust and school life: The influence of trust on learning, teaching, leading, and bridging* (pp. 57–81). New York: Springer.

Tschannen-Moran, M. (2014b). *Trust matters: Leadership for successful schools* (2nd ed.). San Francisco: Jossey-Bass.

Tschannen-Moran, M., & Barr, M. (2004). Fostering student learning: The relationship between collective teacher efficacy and student achievement. *Leadership and Policy in Schools, 3*, 187–207.

Tschannen-Moran, M., & Gareis, C. R. (2002). Faculty trust in the principal: An essential ingredient in high-performing schools. *Journal of Educational Administration, 53*, 66–92.

Tschannen-Moran, M., & Garies, C. R. (2015). Faculty trust in the principal: An essential ingredient in high performing schools. *Journal of Educational Administration, 53*, 66–92.

Tschannen-Moran, M., & Goddard, R.D. (2001, April). *Collective efficacy and trust: A multilevel analysis*. In: Proceedings of the annual meeting of the American Educational Research Association, Seattle, WA.

Tschannen-Moran, M., & Hoy, W. K. (1998). Trust in schools: A conceptual and empirical analysis. *Journal of Educational Administration, 36*, 334–352.

Tschannen-Moran, M., & Hoy, W. K. (2000). A multidisciplinary analysis of the nature, meaning, and measurement of trust. *Review of Educational Research, 71*, 547–593.

Tschannen-Moran, M., Salloum, S. J., & Goddard, R. D. (2014). Context matters: The influence of collective beliefs and norms. In H. Fives & M. G. Gill (Eds.), *International handbook of research on teachers' beliefs* (pp. 246–264). New York: Routledge.

Uline, C., Miller, D., & Tschannen-Moran, M. (1998). School effectiveness: The underlying dimensions. *Educational Administration Quarterly, 34*, 462–483.

Vescio, V., Ross, D., & Adams, A. (2008). A review of research on the impact of professional learning communities on teaching practice and student learning. *Teaching and Teacher Education, 24*, 80–91.

Wahlstrom, K. L., & Louis, K. S. (2008). How teachers experience principal leadership: The roles of professional community, trust, efficacy, and shared responsibility. *Educational Administration Quarterly, 44*, 458–495.

Whitener, E. M., Brodt, S. E., Korsgaard, M. A., & Werner, J. M. (1998). Managers as initiators of trust: An exchange relationship framework for understanding managerial trustworthy behavior. *Academy of Management Review, 23*, 513–530.

Ylimaki, R. M. (Ed.). (2014). *The new instructional leadership: ISLLC standard two*. New York: Routledge/UCEA.

Zand, D. E. (1997). *The leadership triad: Knowledge, trust, and power*. New York: Oxford University Press.

Zeinabadi, H. R. (2014). Principal–teacher high-quality exchange indicators and student achievement: Testing a model. *Journal of Educational Administration, 52*, 404–420.

Chapter 9
Generation X School Leaders as Agents of Care: Leader and Teacher Perspectives from Toronto, New York City and London

Karen Edge, Katherine Descours, and Keren Frayman

Care emerged as a topic of interest within school and educational leadership research in the early 1980s. During this period, empirical and theoretical discussions often aligned to moral dimensions of leadership and the centrality of values within discussions of educational administration (Hodgkinson 1991) and schools (Beck 1994; Duke 2000; Noddings 2005). Schools were called upon to develop comprehensive focus on creating environments supporting health and happiness (Noddings 2005) and promoting their own personal growth and health (Beck 1994). Collectively, these scholars coupled schools and notions of care with, often, a focus on the role of leaders. However, from the early 2000s, research interest in care remained quiet and empirically frail. As a result, school-level and leadership care remain in their infancy and without much empirical rigor.

In the last several years, a renewed interest in leadership and care is emerging within educational leadership (Louis et al. 2016) and beyond (Gabriel 2015). This paper dovetails with this re-emerging focus and examines leadership and care within schools led by Generation X (under-40-year old) leaders in three large Global Cities. As such, the paper not only contributes to discussions of leader-teacher relationships but also marks the understanding of a new generation of leaders entering the school system in the most senior roles.

K. Edge (✉)
University College London Institute of Education, University College London, London, UK
e-mail: k.edge@ucl.ac.uk

K. Descours
New Zealand Human Rights Commission, Wellington, New Zealand

University College London Institute of Education, London, UK
e-mail: kdescours@gmail.com

K. Frayman
London Center for Leadership in Learning at the Institute of Education, UCL, London, UK
e-mail: keren.frayman@googlemail.com

Our interest in Generation X (GenX) leaders emerged in 2009, when our London-based research team observed a new, younger generation of professionals entering senior school leadership posts in several urban centers. We believe that their entry marks an important transition for education systems. First, these leaders are from Generation X, born between 1966 and 1980. GenXers bring a new set of generational propositions, expectations, and aspirations to their school leadership posts. They are widely viewed as independent and self-sufficient (Berl 2006) and heavily committed to personal and work-based friendships and social/peer networks (Zemke et al. 2000). These oft-shared traits shape GenXers' identified desire for collaboration (Smola and Sutton 2002), mobility (Duscher and Cowin 2004), diversity, and more experimental structures in organizations (Kunreuther 2003) and work/life balance (Zemke et al. 2000). Many of these characteristics are markedly different from those of their predecessors – baby boomers. Second, while there has yet to be a definitive analysis of the age of leaders participating in seminal educational leadership research studies, it has always been our assumption that, barring the current emerging evidence-base on novice leaders, much of what is known about leadership practices has been generated by and for the now retiring generation of scholars and school leaders.

GenXers appear to be markedly different from their baby-boomer predecessors in their approach to work, careers, collaboration, and work/life priorities (Edge 2014). As a result, GenX school leaders may also bring a new set of expectations, experience, and aspirations to school leadership careers. We also wonder if, and how, these identified generational patterns influence the way in which GenXers school leaders approach their work and lives. If generational assumptions hold true, then the rise of GenX school leader numbers may have important implications for leadership recruitment, development, and retention.

While we acknowledge the growing body of recent literature on novice leaders (Spillane and Lee 2013), educational leadership research has rarely been stratified to examine the possible generational influences on leadership experience and practice. As a result, there remains little research exploring the experience and aspirations of the emerging population of GenX school leaders (Stone-Johnson 2014) within and beyond education. As this new generation of leaders should have at least 25 years remaining in their careers, understanding more about their motivations and aspirations is important for policymakers, researchers, and leaders.

To address this knowledge gap, our 3-year research study engages cohorts of 20–25 GenX school leaders in each of three Global Cities (Sassen 1991)—London, New York City and Toronto (Amburn 2009). The GCL research project, funded by the Economic and Social Research Council (ESRC-UK), examines the careers, lives, leadership, and future aspirations of GenX principals and vice-principals. In 2011, we launched the study by establishing city-based advisory groups comprised of 49 academic, policy, and practice leaders. School leaders were recruited to participate in two annual interviews and optional GCL networking events. We also conducted nine school-level studies to example GenX leadership in practice.

9.1 Global City Leaders: Expressions and Expectations of Care

Our original interview and school-level analyses (Edge et al. 2013b; Wilson 2012) uncovered several emerging patterns within and across cities. Leaders reported struggling to achieve personal work/life balance, striving to support teachers' work/life balance, and outright commitment to collaboratively leading their schools. The majority of our GenX leaders consistently discussed their school-based work with what we have come to define as an "ethic of care" for the adults in their school buildings. We were surprised at the consistent emphasis leaders placed on caring for teachers. While we did not specifically ask if, or how, leaders care for their staff, almost all said they wanted to encourage teachers' work/life balance and sense of being supported. Often, leaders linked their motivation for caring for teachers as strategies to enhance teachers' happiness and confidence within and beyond the school. Leaders report also wanting to improve teacher performance in the classroom and decisions to remain in the profession.

Throughout our study, leaders consistently discuss the value they place on nurturing teachers, capacity-building, and talent-spotting (Edge et al. 2013c). Leaders also explain their aspirations for work/life balance, their awareness of teachers' need for the same, and their belief that leaders need to care for their colleagues professionally and personally (Edge et al. 2013d). However, at the same time, many GenX leaders across the three cities shared how they had not, and still do not, have good role models for their own work/life balance. While they were caring for others, they were not caring for themselves (Edge 2014).

This paper explores how nine leaders and 54 teachers across nine school-level studies respond, formally and informally, to the question: *Is it the leader's role to care for his or her staff?* Our analysis dovetails with the emerging and expanding interest in teacher (Bubb and Earley 2004; Day 2008; Day and Kington 2008) and leader wellbeing and work/life balance (Carr 1994; Devos et al. 2007; Sackney et al. 2000) and leader care in schools (Louis et al. 2016) and beyond (Gabriel 2015). More specifically, while the school-based studies did not link leader actions to measures of teacher and student attainment and learning, we intend to explore how leader's believe they express care and how teachers have come to expect and anticipate care from their leaders and its influence. Leaders' acts of caring to the emotional lives of teachers can influence school culture, teacher commitment, teacher collective efficacy and commitment which, in turn, influences improved student learning (Leithwood et al. 2010; Sun and Leithwood 2015b). The paper encapsulates our initial contribution to the growing discussion of how leaders influence teachers.

The paper begins with an introduction to the GCL study and a light touch review of the research literature informing the overall study design and conceptualization including Global Cities, generations, Generations at Work, and GenX. To situate our discussion of leadership and care, we provide a brief summary of research linked to the leaders' influence on teachers and students. More specifically, we highlight evidence on the influence and importance of leader care for employees. Next, we describe our overall GCL research program, focusing on the strategies employed to gather and analyze the nine school-based studies. We detail our grounded theory approach (Strauss and Corbin 1994) applied to the analysis of leader and teacher transcripts and present the five dominant categories of leader carefocused actions and priorities: (1) support and understanding; (2) approachability; (3) knowledge of teachers' personal lives; (4) modeling balance between work and life; and (5) caring for teachers' personal wellbeing. The findings and discussion suggest that while all leaders discuss prioritizing their care of teachers, most enact care as a means of supporting and retaining staff and increasing work/life balance and workplace satisfaction. Similarly, teachers consistently emphasize the positive influence of leaders' understanding, approachability, and recognition of the importance of their lives beyond school. Teachers and leaders also discuss the influence of personal relationships and care on their own classroom practice and student achievement.

This paper makes three unique contributions. First, our evidence is gathered from a new generation of leaders who are recognized (Edge 2014) to be more collaborative and work/life-balance-minded. However, we are aware that their views on nurturing teachers may simply be informed by current thinking about leadership practice as well as the influence of their generational tendencies. Second, our evidence looks exclusively at leaders in urban contexts across three very different education systems. Third, while our policy/practice studies (Armstrong et al. 2013a, b; Edge et al. 2013a; Mejias et al. 2013) note significant differences in the role of leaders and the structures, supports, and levels of accountability in each system, leaders' and teachers' views remain surprisingly consistent. The generational and international comparative elements of the study create a departure point for considering how leaders are approaching their roles, the expectations their teachers hold of them, and the potential implications for education systems in the future.

In this paper, we do not disaggregate the findings by the different sites of our research or by demographic attributes of the participating principals. This is because our initial cross-city analysis did not highlight any specific differences between the cities in how leaders discuss and/or are expected to approach their role in caring for teachers. Similarly, we also do not stratify our analysis by leaders' gender, background, and years of experience.

9.2 Literature Review

We begin with a brief summary of research related to leadership and the enactment of care followed by an examination of the relationship between leadership, employee experience, wellbeing and satisfaction. We conclude with an overview of the evidence influencing the overall design and conceptualization of our work drawing from sociology, psychology, and business including: generational theory; generational differences by cohort; and, Global Cities.

Leadership and the Enactment of Care Gilligan (1982) and Noddings (1986) have anchored much of the educational discussion of caring. Subsequently, studies within and beyond education have examined relationships between leaders' roles in providing support and care for their staff (Clawson 2009; Hargreaves 1998; Sun and Leithwood 2015a; Wilson 2012) and associated positive influences on employees' and teachers' experience of and commitment to work. For example, Hargreaves (1998) prioritizes the emotions of teaching and teacher development for school leaders and highlights the centrality of teacher emotions to educational improvement and outcomes.

Emerging from an interest in commitment to caring as a means of personal growth, a group of scholars argue for the building of caring schools and communities (Duke 2000) This work, linked directly to leadership practice, is also closely related to a body of work who emphasize using values or moral reasoning to inform ethical responding to problematic situations involving ethical dilemmas (Klinker and Hackmann 2004; Zaretsky 2004).

More recently, several new contributions to and conceptualizations of leader care have emerged in corporate (Ciulla 2009; Gabriel 2015; Simola et al. 2010) and educational leadership (Louis et al. 2016) to address what has been a limited scholarly consideration at best (Gabriel 2015). Discussions posit that leaders 'will always be judge by their followers against their ability to demonstrate that they care' (Gabriel, p. 317). Within education, researchers have very recently proposed and test a robust preliminary model of caring leadership (Louis et al. 2016) that includes attentiveness, motivational displacement, situationality, mutuality, and authenticity. All of these development further point to the need to develop a deeper conceptual and empirical understand of leader enactment of care and the potential influence on teachers.

In this light, studies have also linked the importance of leader–teacher relationships to teacher retention alongside work conditions and school-level policies (Müller et al. 2009). We believe the nexus of the arrival of a newer generation of leaders who self-identify as being highly collaborative and relationally driven, with the increasing pressure on many schools and school systems to retain teachers in their roles. This creates a unique point in time where leaders' demonstrations of care may be an important factor in teachers' intention to remain in the profession. Evidence from our preliminary and very small-scale study will examine how GenX leaders and their teachers consider the role of leaders in caring for staff.

Leadership and Employee Experience, Wellbeing, and Satisfaction A growing body of corporate research explores relationships between leader behavior and priorities and employee wellbeing, "work/life benefits" (Lambert 2000), or work/life support (Baptiste 2008; Forsyth and Polzer-Debruyne 2007). However, the same studies also report that the links between work/life balance and work performance remain contested. Work-related stress has also been mitigated by strategies to promote wellbeing at work (Baptiste 2008; Nielsen and Munir 2009; Skakon et al. 2010) and leaders' demonstrations of consideration and support (Skakon et al., 2010). The evidence suggests that leaders' own personal prioritization of work/life balance has been found to positively influence employees' feelings of being supported (Baptiste 2008; Forsyth and Polzer-Debruyne 2007; Lambert 2000), job satisfaction (Baptiste 2008; Forsyth and Polzer-Debruyne 2007), and organizational loyalty (Baptiste 2008; Forsyth and Polzer-Debruyne 2007). Similarly, leader stress and poor wellbeing habits have been linked to issues with follower stress and wellbeing (Skakon et al. 2010). Much of the business research related to leadership and work conditions is tied, to some degree, to conceptions of transformational leadership, with transformational leaders described as:

> the leader moving the follower beyond immediate self-interests through idealized influence (charisma), inspiration, intellectual stimulation, or individualized consideration. It elevates the follower's level of maturity and ideals as well as concerns for achievement, self actualization, and the well-being of others, the organization, and society (Bass 1999, p. 11).

Transformational leadership has been evidenced to influence employee job satisfaction (Skakon et al. 2010), reduce employee stress levels, and increase reported levels of wellbeing (Skakon et al. 2010). Transformational leadership influences wellbeing and self-efficacy (Nielsen and Munir 2009) through perception of work characteristics and creating and supporting meaningful work (Arnold et al. 2007). Similarly, transformational leadership has been directly associated with leaders' demonstration of attention to followers' need and an ethic of care for employees (Simola et al. 2010). While the evidence remains inconclusive on many of the direct relational links between leader enactment of care related to work/life balance and support, transformational leadership provides the groundwork for a discussion of how the prioritization of employee wellbeing may be identified and interpreted in schools.

Educationally focused transformational leadership studies evidence the important of school level relationships and leaders' ability to meet individuals' emotional needs and thus increase employee satisfaction (Bass and Avolio 1994; Geijsel et al. 2003; Leithwood and Jantzi 1999). Additional evidence linking teacher job satisfaction to school and student performance (Hargreaves 1998; Yukl 2002), often focuses on principal behaviors including listening, praising, supporting, and committing to care for the needs of teachers (Evans 2001; Thompson et al. 1997; Yukl 2002). While these studies emphasize the role of leaders' tending to teachers' needs, they focus most exclusively on job-related care. In the context of our school-based analysis, we interpret care, as defined through these models, to include supporting the overall wellbeing, satisfaction, and growth of teachers.

Importantly, a more nuanced understanding of how leaders influence teachers has emerged organized along four pathways of influence: Emotions Path, Rational Path, Organizational Path, and Family Path (Leithwood et al. 2010). The emotional pathway, which includes "the feelings, dispositions, or affective states of staff members, both individually and collectively" (Leithwood et al., p. 675 provides an interesting and important backdrop for our analysis of GenX leaders and their care for teachers. More recently (Sun and Leithwood 2015b, p. 570), CTE has been described as the "level of confidence a group exudes in its capacity to organize and execute the tasks required to reach desired goals" and outline four transformational leadership practices that influence CTE: inspiring group purpose, providing individualized support, modeling, and holding high performance expectations (Sun and Leithwood 2015b). Based on our analysis of the school-based studies, leader and teacher discussions of leader care directly relate to the emotional path and most specifically to CTE. As such, in the findings section, we center our discussion of leader actions to support teachers within this model and examine leader and teacher perceptions of leaders' actions that influence their own personal and professional work. When first reviewing our school-based leader and teacher GCL evidence, all leaders' and most teachers' comments about leader care for teachers aligned very closely with those actions linked to transformational leadership practices.

Generations Generations (Edmunds and Turner 2002) are often described in one of three ways: *chronological* – bounded by age (Edmunds and Turner 2005; Pilcher 1994); *social* – bounded by shared social experiences (Edmunds and Turner 2005); or *political* – bounded by shared historical experience (Pilcher 1994). Life-course perspectives may also account for the evolution of generational attitudes over time as a result of life circumstances (Gentry et al. 2011). Similarly, the notion of active and passive generations (Gentry et al. 2011) suggests that successive generations are often passive recipients of the actions and structures of active ones. A key motivation for examining GenX leaders is the potential that as the passive generation, they may feel they are passive recipients, and perhaps inheritors, of the policy contexts and school structures they have inherited from their active generation, baby boomers. While there are variations in all patterns between and within generations, they represent a helpful boundary for research and policy consideration.

In most cities, the current school-level workforce is comprised of three main generations. The most senior generation, **baby boomers,** were named after the accelerated birth-rate "boom" following the Second World War. Boomers have been described as workaholic, quality-minded, and teamplayers interested in title-based recognition (Zemke et al. 2000). Boomers also prioritize work and self-fulfillment, at times above family (Coggshall et al. 2010). At the other end of the age spectrum are **GenerationY (GenYs)** or **millennials** (born between 1978 and 1990). GenYs are highly techno-literate as a result of the evolution of personal computers, the internet, and social networking (Espinoza et al. 2010). They often prioritize digital working and crave opportunities for learning, teamwork, and real-time constant technology-facilitated connections with peers and social network-based contacts (Espinoza et al. 2010). Growing up in more diverse and tolerant societies, GenYs are well-versed in and committed to equality. They also strive to be heard and are comfortable challenging authority (Berl 2006).

Growing up in the 1970s and 80s, **GenXers** are often named "latchkey kids" to reflect their status as the first independent generation, resulting from the en masse entering of women into the workplace. They grew up in the most rapidly evolving technological era and tend to be globally minded, techno-savvy, informal (Zemke et al. 2000), and collaborative (Smola and Sutton 2002). GenXers are less patient with their careers and less willing to wait for promotion than boomers (Hewlett et al. 2009; Smola and Sutton 2002). GenXers are also often more dissatisfied with their careers than other generations (Pham et al. 2008) and often expect immediate recognition through praise, promotion, and increase in salary (Bulman 2002).

As three generations are actively engaging in teaching and leading in most schools, the imperative for understanding the potential generational implications of the current educational workforce is mounting. There remains a rather limited body of evidence on generations at work in schools. Currently, strands of education-focused generational research relate to GenY teachers (Coggshall et al. 2011; Lovely and Buffum 2007; Moore Johnson 2004; Williamson and Meyer-Looze 2010), teacher generational mix (Moore Johnson and Kardos 2005; Rinke 2009; Strauss 2005), intergenerational communication (Hess and Jepsen 2009; Walmsley 2011), generational career patterns (Stone-Johnson 2011), generational leadership perspectives (Salajan et al. 2010), and technology use (Worley 2011; Zieglar 2007).

While there is an established and accepted research base confirming leaders' influence on school- and teacher-level actions and beliefs and, in turn, leaders' influence on student achievement (Day et al. 2009; Leithwood and Jantzi 2008; Robinson et al. 2008; Sun and Leithwood 2015b), there remains little acknowledgement of the pending demographic shift in educational leaders worldwide and the potential influence this may have on leadership styles, skills, and priorities. Even with the emerging focus on generational patterns in schools, there is little research exploring the work and lives of GenX leaders, who are quickly entering or currently holding school-level leadership positions. More specifically, as a new generation of leaders enters the top roles in schools, there is the possibility of a shift in priorities, style, and approach to both leading schools and their careers. Our evidence indicated that GenX leaders often explicitly state their desire to care for their teachers in order to support their work/life balance, professional growth and on-going commitment to remaining in the profession. The findings inspired our interest to learn more about the evidence base related to leader care and specifically wellbeing and satisfaction.

Global Cities Global Cities (Sassen 1991) are identified and celebrated as powerful international epicenters of influence (Amburn 2009; Sassen 1991). They are now also annually ranked by their economic, social, entertainment, and cultural influence (Amburn 2009). From our educational vantage point, cities often serve as central nodes of education policy and practice innovation and have catalyzed global teaching, learning, and leadership trends. For example, Chicago (Bryk et al. 1998; Hess 1991; Wohlstetter and Odden 1992), New York (Elmore and Burney 1997, 2002), London (Brighouse 2007; Hargreaves 2003), and Shanghai (Vanderklippe 2014; Wang and Lin 2005) have all developed international reputations based on their reform initiatives.

Within education research and policy discourse, city jurisdictions are not without their challenges. Urban centers are often described negatively, with urban contexts discussed in terms of challenge (Chapman 2008), disadvantage (Smyth and McCoy 2009), and difficult circumstances (Harris 2002). Not surprisingly, much academic and policy discussion centers on perceived and actual city-based challenges in addressing socioeconomic inequality and escalating improvements and opportunities for all students.

In many cities, one of the most pressing urban educational issues relates directly to teacher recruitment and retention (Allen 2005; Jacob 2007; Johnson et al. 2005). Teacher recruitment challenges are often linked to fit (Ballou 1996), geography (Boyd et al. 2005), wages (Dolton and van der Klaaw 1999), and working conditions (Hanushek et al. 2004). Retention obstacles tend to be tied to teacher education (Warshauer Freedman and Appleman 2009) and job dissatisfaction linked to student discipline, motivation, and school administration (Ingersoll 2003). These factors fuel, or are fuelled by, the cyclical challenges facing city-based educational improvement efforts: the ongoing struggle to create sustained improvement momentum while working to stabilize high volumes of staff turnover (McKinnery et al. 2007). Teacher workforce instability also creates knock-on effects higher up the career ladder. As a result, many cities may also struggle with recruiting school leaders related, but not limited, to teacher apathy about leadership roles (Gronn and Lacey 2004) and waves of scheduled or early principal retirements (Howson 2008). Not surprisingly, high levels of turnover and spiraling attrition rates often inspire upswings in policy and public discussions about the suitability of candidates for the profession, work conditions, and system-level pressures facing education professionals.

9.3 Our Overall GCL and School-Based Studies Research Strategy

9.3.1 Overall GCL Project

The Global City Leaders project was designed to understand more about the experiences, lives, and aspirations of the new generation of school leaders via a 3-year mixed qualitative methods design involving three city-based policy and practice studies and 12 GenX leader networking events, 125 individual interviews, and nine school-based studies. We began the study by developing city-based studies reflecting local, province/state, and national policy and practice (Armstrong et al. 2013a, b; Edge et al. 2013a, b, c, d) of educational policy and practice that influence leaders' roles and responsibilities. We recruited city-based cohorts of 20–25 GenX principals and vice-principals via invitation emails from our district, organizational, and advisory group contacts. To develop nuanced understandings of GenX leaders, we conducted two annual interviews with each leader. These examined career choices and experiences, professional identities, future ambitions, and possible emerging GenX leadership model(s). All 120 interviews were recorded and fully transcribed using Dedoose (an online Cloud-based encrypted qualitative analysis program) to employ a multi-staged coding process and structure (Edge et al. 2013c; Miles and Huberman 1994). Transcripts were analyzed using full-grounded theory approach

(Strauss and Corbin 1994), which resulted in, for example, an application of 25,000 codes across the 65 interviews conducted in the first year (Edge et al. 2013c). The first- and second-year findings have been reported in our research reports (Edge et al. 2013b, c, d; Johnson et al. 2005.

Our analysis of 60 first-year principal and vice-principal interviews (Edge et al. 2013b, c) identified emerging patterns and tensions in leaders' career progression, early leadership experiences, future career aspirations, and life-stage challenges related to starting or having young families (Edge et al. 2013d). While there are some specific city-based patterns, several trends remain consistent across GenX leaders in all cities including their almost unilateral commitment to and/or interest in improving work/life balance, talentspotting, capacity-building, and articulating their role in caring for teachers and students (Edge et al. 2013d).

Building on these findings, we conducted a second round of individual interviews and nine school-level studies to learn more about GenX leaders in their own settings. Our light-touch schoollevel studies examine patterns from our earlier findings in more detail including GenX approaches to school priorities, talent-spotting and recruitment, collaboration, staff-building capacity, and wellbeing and work/life balance. To capture a preliminary snapshot of GenX leadership and how leaders and teachers experienced city-based school-level processes and practices, we used a stratified list of principal participants and phases (elementary, secondary, other) to randomly select three schools per city. The school-level studies engaged at least one school leader and up to six teachers in individual interviews and, in one school, focus groups.

9.3.2 School-Based Studies: Data Sources and Collection Process

This paper draws exclusively from our nine school-based studies of GenX leadership, three each from London, New York City, and Toronto. These studies provide a small preliminary snapshot into how GenX principals were approaching leadership in their schools. The interviews explored how leaders and a small sample of teachers in each school experienced and interpreted their school's approach to the major themes arising from our GenX leader interviews. These included school priorities, collaboration, talent-spotting, building teaching capacity, and wellbeing. This paper draws on our analysis of teacher and leader responses to the suite of questions related to leader caring including: Is it the role of a leader to care for their staff? Do you feel cared for? Does care play a role in your ability to improve as a teacher? Does care play a role in improving teaching and learning? Do you feel supported?

We created a city-based list of participating principals organized by primary, middle (where appropriate), and secondary phases. We also attempted to plot schools geographically. Across all cities, all principals agreed to participate on first invitation. Principals provided formal administrative consent, after which an electronic information package with instructions and consent information was delivered for communication with all teachers in the school. Teachers were asked to directly email the research team to schedule their interviews. Where this process did not work, a non-leadership team member in the school maintained a confidential roster of participants, upholding their anonymity, from senior school leaders. The need for anonymity was reiterated at each step of the recruitment process and with each individual involved.

School visits were between half to three-quarters of a day long and involved at least two research team members. Individual interviews were 35–40 min for teachers and 45–60 min for leaders. All participants signed the appropriate consent forms before beginning the interview. While data collection was intended to be exclusively conducted via individual interview, in one school, as requested by the teaching staff, three focus groups were conducted.

9.3.3 School-Based Studies: Data analysis

Each interview and focus group was fully transcribed by a member of our team and uploaded into Dedoose. We applied a grounded theory approach for the analysis (Strauss and Corbin 1994) and adopted a three-phase coding structure from the evidence in three phases. In phase one, we grouped the transcripts by school and developed a high-level coding structure representing each of the five topics from the interview instrument: school priorities, collaboration, talent-spotting, building teaching capacity, and wellbeing. Three members of our research team each individually analyzed three leader and three teacher interviews representing a cross-section of schools and cities. This process supported the development of our preliminary list of sub-codes under each of the main headings. As the analysis proceeded, the original coding structure was altered slightly to account for newly recognized themes.

For example, our review of wellbeing-related discussions from across all transcripts generated six sub-codes representing how leaders and teachers discuss their experience of, desire for, and understanding of wellbeing in their lives within and beyond school. The refined wellbeing codes included personal understanding/seeking of wellbeing, personal satisfaction with level of work/life balance, leader role in tending to wellbeing, strategies leaders use to support wellbeing, influence of wellbeing on practice, and work/life balance role models. To refine our analysis, each individual transcript was then reanalyzed by applying the overall coding framework, with team members working in tandem to assess and reinforce their inter-rater reliability and build our ongoing collective cross-city understanding of the findings.

Phase one highlighted that all nine leaders and most of the 54 teachers consistently articulated their belief that leaders should have and take responsibility for caring for their staff. Based on this evidence, we focused our attention on comprehending more about leader and teacher understanding and expectations of teacher wellbeing. During phase two, we revisited our analysis and specifically re-examined all coded data that related to one specific wellbeing-focused research question: *Is it a leader's role to care for his or her teachers?* As such, all evidence related to leader care, leader support of wellbeing, and leader actions that facilitated teacher senses of support and wellbeing were re-examined and more finely examined.

For the specific purpose of this paper, we conducted a third phase of analysis and revisited each individual school-level study. We conducted a meta-analysis across all nine schools by examining the key themes emerging from the wellbeing data. We tabulated responses from all leaders across each city and then again across cities. We followed a similar format for teacher interview evidence. From this analysis we identified overarching patterns in leader and teacher responses. For instance, some teachers spoke about being supported by leaders who were committed to being approachable; others gave examples of leaders being understanding. In the findings section, we highlight the specific patterns in how both leaders and teachers discuss care.

We are acutely aware of the small scale of the evidence base and that it is drawn from three different cities with three very different policy and leadership contexts. We reviewed the data by city to identify any city-based patterns or differences in leader and teacher responses. While we anticipated between-city differences reflecting the vastly different policy and social contexts of the education systems, we found little between-city variation in leader or teacher interpretations or expectations. For this reason, we present our analysis in aggregate from across the nine schools. We do not differentiate by city.

9.3.4 School-Based Studies: Participating Leader and School Demographics

To adhere to our anonymity requirements, we report participating school and leader details in aggregate within each city. Leader and school characteristics are also reported using approximates to ensure anonymity. In New York City, school studies were conducted at one middle and two elementary schools in the socio-economically different areas of Brooklyn and Queens. The schools educate between 500 and 800 students each. Twenty-two teachers participated in data collection. The three leaders, one male and two female, had between 2 and 4 years of experience and were aged between 32 and 40.

In London, three female leaders participated in the study, which represented one elementary, one secondary, and one special school. Leaders had between 5 and 7 years of experience and were between the ages of 29 and 36 at the time of the interview. Schools varied in size from approximately 150–400 students and were located in different areas of London. One school was in the early phase of start-up and was significantly smaller, with fewer staff members. As a result, only 15 teachers participated in interviews in London.

In Toronto, the three state-funded participating schools were located in the inner city and in Scarborough and represented both Catholic and non-Catholic school systems. One elementary and two secondary schools were included in the sample. School size varied from approximately 700 to 1800 students. One female and two male leaders with between 6 and 9 years of experience and between the ages of 38 and 41 were interviewed. Nineteen teachers in total participated in interviews.

9.4 Findings

In one of the most poignant patterns emerging from the evidence, leaders and teachers consistently discuss a very personal interpretation of supportive leader actions most frequently associated with understanding teachers as people with lives outside of school that will, at times, influence their experiences and aspirations within the school. Consistently throughout the data, leaders and teachers discuss their own interpretation of the importance of providing individualized support. We present each of the four original themes emerging from the interviews and we use the emotional path and specifically CTE to organize the care strategies and rationale shared by leaders and teachers. These leadership actions can be described as: *leader support and understanding; leader approachability; leader knowledge of teachers' personal lives (teacher only); leader modeling of balance between work and life (teacher only)*. These themes are presented in relative order of importance measured by the frequency of comments by both teachers and leaders. Within each section, we also share leaders' and teachers' thoughts and examples in their own words. We begin by exploring leaders' views followed by the teachers' thoughts on the same theme. However, where only teachers highlight the topic, leaders' comments are by nature, absent. In the discussion, we highlight some of the differences between leader and teacher views and propose future lines of research and policy actions to support the development of knowledge and practice in the field.

9.4.1 GenX Leaders Providing Support and Understanding

Leaders most frequently discuss their efforts to demonstrate and prioritize care for their teachers as being supportive and understanding. Their commitment to explicitly caring for staff members appears inextricably linked to their desire to support and retain teachers, address issues of work/life balance, and promote workplace satisfaction. Similarly, teachers describe leaders' desire to be supportive and understanding as the most important element of their caring.

Leaders' Perspectives on Support and Understanding When examining how GenX leaders discuss their care for and understanding of their staff members, six categories emerged from our original analysis: nurturing support for each other;

focusing on wellbeing; being flexible/allowing time off; understanding individual needs; supporting new staff; and including families in school-based events. Leaders consistently articulate their belief in the relationship between caring for staff, making staff feel supported, and their overall happiness and successful students. As one Toronto principal explains:

> It's my role to look out for what is best for kids but I also look out for my staff. I think that's one thing that the majority of staff will be able to say unequivocally – that I will go to bat for them, that I will support them. So, is it my role to care about staff? Kids do come first but I do think that in order to make kids more successful you need a happy staff, or at least a staff that feels valued.

Leaders also express their concern and constructive efforts to support their teachers' work/life balance. Across all schools, leaders articulate their aspirations for their teaching staff to have healthy lives beyond school. Leaders provide examples of their rationale and actions. One leader from New York City describes:

> My teachers can't be healthy, good, strong teachers every day for our children if they don't have a work/life balance. [If] you don't have a solid work/life balance then you're not going to be able to give your all when you're here. You're not going to be able to give everything you have to the kids. You're going to get burned out.

Leaders often, frustratingly, experience teacher resistance to adopting more balanced approaches to managing their work lives. Obstacles include teachers' own perceptions of work requirements resulting from peer and external accountability-driven pressures. According to one New York-based principal: "As a leader there's only so much I can do. I can't go home with [my teachers] and force [them] to not work." Leaders recognize the influence external accountability and policy demands have on teachers' perceptions of what is required and the pressure this creates on teachers, leaders, and schools. One London leader explains the challenge of trying to assume a mediating role between policy and accountability pressures and teacher wellbeing:

> If [teachers] felt under pressure and monitored all the time, they wouldn't want to be here and that wouldn't get the best out of them. But that's not [the message] I'm getting from the Ofsted framework, which is: 'I should be monitoring them all the time and they should all be consistently doing "this".' And I should have proof that I've monitored them three times every week or whatever it is.

Teachers' Perspectives on Leaders Support and Understanding Teachers across our school-based studies articulate their belief that leaders need to be supportive and understanding. Teachers appreciate when leaders recognize their individual needs, commitments to their families, and lives beyond school. From teachers' perspectives, leaders' acknowledgement of the personal lives of teachers should extend from their ongoing family commitments to isolated emergencies. This recognition was viewed most highly of all by teachers. One teacher in New York City describes how current leaders support influences their own work and experience as an educator. More specifically, they share how the leader's own role as a parent creates understanding and support for other educators with children:

> Because he has his own life and his own children, I feel like he is considerate. I feel he is able to understand more because he has children. Even if he didn't have children, I think he would understand, too, because that's his personality. He's very easygoing. He's very nice.

Teachers express how understanding is often linked, in schools, to simply being a person and for leaders to be willing to put themselves in others' places. One Toronto teacher shares: "[Our leader] is very human in a sense that if you're not feeling well, she's very understanding. If your child has something going on she's very understanding. That's a really big thing for leaders to have – that human part." Another teacher explains how fairness and consistency relate to support:

> A leader should definitely have empathy and understand where people are coming from. They need to be fair, and be across the board, if this is the policy it's for everybody. There are no favorites. They need to understand that we have lives as well and that sometimes we need to take off to go to the doctor. Principals can be on you every day, for silly things that don't have to do with teaching. Here it's not like that, which is nice.

Teachers also discuss leaders' roles in supporting work/life balance and acknowledging that teachers have lives beyond the school gates. Teachers link this support and acknowledgement to their motivation and wellbeing. One Toronto teacher shares:

> [Our leaders] get it. They know you're busy. They know that school is not everything. They know that a happy YOU is a happy teacher. If I'm able to do the things that make me happy outside of school... that's going to make me a better teacher inside of school.
> [Our leaders] recognize that.

Teachers openly link support for work/life balance to school-level resourcing and the allocation of resources and support to ensure that teachers can have lives beyond school. One New York-based teacher shares:

> Part of [the leader's] job is to make sure that we have what we need. In [that] sense, that we have what we need to do [our job so] that not so much [work] is coming home with us so we CAN have a home life. [It is a leader's job to support making sure] your work life is your work life and it doesn't overlap or infringe on your personal life. If [the leader] has those resources, then [the leader] does have some responsibility for that.

9.4.2 GenX Leaders and Approachability

After support and understanding, approachability is most frequently discussed by leaders as being core to their care for teachers. Leaders describe their own personal approachability-focused actions as: having difficult improvement-oriented conversations; treating staff members like family/community; being present/having open-door policies; and having a positive attitude. Leaders provide examples of how they create safe spaces for staff members to interact, and to resolve conflicts by having honest conversations and taking explicit steps to develop trust among staff and between teachers and their leadership teams.

Leaders' Perspectives on Approachability Most leaders state it is their desire and responsibility for teachers to feel they are approachable for both personal and professional discussions. Leaders repeatedly link approachability to their role in supporting teachers to develop as professionals and being available for purely supportive but also challenging conversations. As one principal from New York says:

> Caring to me means not just doing whatever [teachers] want or giving them whatever they want, or being the ear to them whenever they want, but also sitting down with them and saying: 'Because I care for you, and I want to change this reputation that you have at this school, what steps are we going to take to make that happen? Who can we bring in to support you?' [It is saying:] 'I want you to be successful as a teacher and we've run into some obstacles. It's in both of our best interests – and certainly for the kids' best interests – for us to make some changes.' So 'caring for' is not always being a shoulder to cry on.

Leaders are acutely aware of the need for and challenges associated with difficult conversations. However, they rest much of their discussion of approachability on their willingness to be there for staff consistently, as one London leader describes:

> It is funny that teachers have difficulty with [hard conversations] because they do it all the time with children. [They] have difficult conversations 100 times a day. When you have to have a difficult conversation with an adult, people feel sick, worry about it, people cry. It's quite strange because they spend 10 times as much time worrying about it than if they just did it. I'm as guilty of it as everyone else. But I think raising your selfawareness about it is really important. It's not something that's solvable overnight. That's the kind of thing that leads to people feeling fulfilled at work because they get feedback. People say 'thank you'. People appreciate it. Otherwise, people just hide away and it's quite difficult.

Teachers' Perspectives on Approachability Teachers echo leaders' views that leaders' approachability (16) is a key factor in demonstrating their support for teachers and enacting an ethic of care. Approachable leaders have open-door policies and take actions that make teachers feel comfortable talking to them. Teachers also state that leaders need to demonstrate that they are personable and there to support teachers when needed. One teacher describes approachability as the leader's availability for conversations and meaningful developmental discussions. Leaders also to be real people and not just business-like managers, as one London teacher describes: "[Leaders] need an approachable head and someone who is a bit more of a public face. You need someone who isn't just a business side." A New York leader adds:

> The administration here, to their credit, is very personable. I can go have a conversation and be quite frank and honest with them if I'm having a difficult time with something, or I have an idea, or I want to have a learning opportunity. All three of them are fantastic; they're willing to offer insight, they're willing provide opportunities, so that's really nice.

Support during times of difficulty is also a key element of how teachers frame a leader's approachability. Teachers suggest that leaders need to be willing to reach out and solicit approaches from teachers. One London teacher shares this experience and its influence:

> I had a particularly bad experience at a parents' evening and I was quite upset about it. The deputy head, who was my mentor at the time, actually texted me afterwards and said 'I hope

you're okay. We can talk about it. Don't worry. It's not a reflection on you.' That was really nice as well because you felt like actually someone did really care.

9.4.3 GenX Leaders' Understanding and Knowledge of Teachers' Personal Lives (Teachers Only)

While not highlighted by leaders, teachers consistently feel their leaders need to have some knowledge of their lives and experience to truly understand and support them. As one New York teacher explains:

> It's not like I expect the principal to know everything that's going on in my life. But I think he or she should be visible [and] should be interacting with the teachers and the students, so that they know more about what's going on in your classroom and maybe a little bit about what's going on in your life.

Teachers share why leaders need deep knowledge of their teachers, the strategies leaders can adopt to build that knowledge, and the potential outcomes associated with understanding the people in the school. As one Toronto teacher explains:

> [Leaders] have to get to know your staff. You have to get to know them on a personal level. I think that's really, really important because the school CANNOT run from the office down. In order to facilitate that, [leaders] need to know what's going on in their family, [they] need [to] drop by their office [and] swing by their classroom. If they're going through personal issues, [teachers] need to know you're there to talk with. All those little things pay off in dividends later, not only for the staff but for the students in the building.

Again, teachers are aware that knowledge and personal connections are not just about good times but also difficult conversations and development. One Toronto teacher shares:

> I think some principals are very good at getting to know their staff, and able to make that personal connection, and I think that that goes a long way with people. Feeling that they are cared about, that the principal takes an interest in me and what my life is about. I think also that caring about people sometimes means tough love as well.

9.4.4 GenX Leaders Modeling of Balance Between Work and Life: Serving as Appropriate Role Models (Teachers Only)

Teachers discuss the importance of developing and maintaining a healthy work/life balance. Teachers highlight the important role that their school leaders play in supporting and modelling a healthy balance for staff. Often, a leader's modelling of work/life balance or related behaviors seems to be much more influential than simple statements or encouragement by leaders. One Toronto teacher explains:

> Seeing that [leaders] don't work ridiculous hours makes you think: 'actually it's okay to go home early occasionally or some days'. It's not looked down on if you leave at 4. I know at some schools, some people think: 'Well why are you leaving, it's not okay.' I try once a week to leave around 4 o'clock. I [can] actually do something productive that evening and not be tired. I've seen that they don't work crazy hours. It's reassuring.

A London teacher also echoes the importance of leaders modelling work/life balance:

> The senior leadership team – they're here at 8; they leave [at] 5, 5.30, maybe 6. They lead by example. My mentor will make sure that I'm not working too much at my weekends just by asking: 'I hope you're not doing too much? We don't want you to be doing that much. If you're not managing to do all your work in the given time then we need to think about how we can achieve that.'

In a rare and powerful statement of support for a leadership team that is actively modeling work/life balance, one London leader from a different school shares:

> I get the impression that [our] leadership seemed to have nailed it in terms of work/life balance. They always leave in great time, clearly 'cause they're organized and they're on top of everything. Maybe they're taking work home with them – I don't know. But it's a very nice attitude they have towards telling all of us that we should leave, too. We're all working hard. They're [saying]: 'You really should go home, you shouldn't be here, go, go, go.' You're encouraged not to be here after work. But because of the kind of teachers who we are, I suppose we want to stay and get everything done, so we're usually kicked out. There's a group of us teachers who get kicked out of school every day [at] quarter [to] six when the cleaners lock up. We're not work[ing] so hard that we have no life.
>
> They've got that side of it right.

9.5 Discussion and Conclusions

The core purpose of our Global City Leaders research program is to add evidentiary flesh to the bones of the increasingly accepted strand of sociology: Generations at Work. This research establishes patterns in how members of different generations approach, design, and balance their work and personal lives. As little research has been conducted related to generational work and schools, we also seek to explore if, and how, generational theory holds true within schools and school city systems. Our intention has always been to understand more about GenerationX leaders' career, lives, leadership and aspirations in the hope that this knowledge will support leaders and policy makers in providing the support and challenge required to recruit, develop and retain leadership talent. In this paper, we draw from nine school-level studies across London, New York City and Toronto to explore a very narrow strand of evidence to examine more specifically how GenX leaders and their teachers conceptualize and articulate *leaders' role in caring for their teachers?*

Within and cross school and city analysis consistently highlighted how GenX leaders across all three cities explicitly discuss their sense of responsibility for caring for their teachers both professionally and personally. Leader and teacher discussions consistently extend beyond a typical best-practice-inspired discussion of leadership roles to a notion of care much more rooted in their own current lived experiences and challenges. Our analysis identified an interesting pattern: leaders' and teachers' discussion related to leader care for their staff and how care is enacted fit neatly into the aforementioned Emotional Path of influence (Leithwood et al. 2010). We found a high level of agreement between leaders and teachers across London, New York City, and Toronto in terms of how leaders are and should be actively demonstrating care for teachers. More specifically, teachers and leaders interpret leader care almost exclusively in the context of TCE with a particular focus on providing individualized support via support and understanding and approachability. Teachers solely focus on a third theme within individualized support: leader knowledge and understanding of teachers' personal lives. Finally, teachers also identify a second, separate, element of TCE as important: leaders being a good role model. Interestingly, teachers almost exclusively focus on leaders as role models of work/life balance which provides an interesting twist on more work-related conceptions of role modelling.

Across the three cities, leaders articulate their belief that tending to their teachers' feelings and dispositions is an important element of their work. Leaders describe the motivations behind their carebased intentions and actions supporting teacher well being, happiness at work, sense of safety and commitment to the school. Leaders comments almost always seem poised within discussions of wanting teachers to teach well and develop but also remain in the profession. However, within Toronto, discussions of teacher retention were muted due to climate of relative consistency which, in recent history, ensures a relatively stable teacher numbers. Leader views echo wider research findings linking leader behavior and prioritization of work/life balance to job satisfaction, support and organizational loyalty (Baptiste 2008; Forsyth and Polzer-Debruyne 2007; Lambert 2000). Similarly, leader enactment of transformational leadership focused on building CTE positively influences employee satisfaction, reduced stress levels, improved wellbeing (Skakon et al. 2010) and collective efficacy (Nielsen and Munir 2009).

Teachers echo leader sentiments on the first two elements of TCE and added a third individualized support strategy that was not discussed by leaders: leader knowledge and understanding of teacher personal lives. Teachers express their desire for individualized relationships with their school leaders and a recognition that, as people, they have busy and demanding lives beyond the school gates as well. This priority was did not overshadow their commitment to their schools and teaching but marked an explicit statement of the importance of leader recognition of teacher wellbeing and work/life balance beyond the school. Teachers often hinted at an underlying desire to feel trusted enough by leaders to make independent decisions about the balance between their teaching, school and family when the need occurred. Again, the strength of leader-teacher relationships appears to be an important factor in teacher satisfaction and intention to remain (Müller et al. 2009).

In discussing wellbeing more generally, teachers articulate their experience with leaders working to support them and encouraging them to support each other. Teachers express a clear sense of the influence of leader commitment to teachers collectively influences their practice and general wellbeing. Teachers describe how a positive school environment is fostered through collaboration and supported by the school leaders. One teacher explains the influence of leader care on collaboration: "There's a massive emphasis on working together, and we're all moving towards the same goals and targets, and there's no point in working against each other." Another teacher describes how teachers are inspired to support each other: "Everyone kind of pulls together and everyone works hard. It doesn't mean we're plucking off at 3:00 or 4:00. You've got to be prepared for the hours but I think everyone's wellbeing is looked after by each other…" Perhaps this is not surprising given the GenX prioritization of workplace relationships and collaboration and the high value GenX, more widely places on work-based relationships and relationships with organizational peers.

Teachers also exclusively discuss the need for leaders to be good work/life balance role models. Teachers consistently suggest their leaders care for teacher wellbeing however, many also comment that leaders also need to role model taking care of themselves. Leaders did not highlight role modelling self-care or work/life balance as part of their caring for teachers. This may be related to GenX leaders lack of their own work/life balance role models (Edge 2014). This may also speak to GenXers' interest in blending work and life and their own stated struggles to find work/life balance. Almost all leaders in the overall study struggle to find balance between their jobs and lives (Edge 2014). Some leaders also share how they are lacking work/life role models – other school leaders who are successful in their leadership roles and have lives that makes them happy beyond work. As GenXers are known for the central place of work/life balance, or at least the quest for work/life balance in their lives (Edge 2014), it is perhaps not surprising that our participating leaders have taken clear and deliberate steps to encourage teacher work/life balance, even if they continue to struggle with their own.As many GenX principals also explicitly state they have not worked with or observed principals who serve as roles models for their own healthy work/life balance (Edge 2014), teacher desire for leaders to be role models may reflect these underlying tensions.

9.5.1 GenX Leadership: Mediating the Influence of City-Based Structures and Systems

Our GCL city-based policy studies (Armstrong et al. 2013a, b; Edge et al. 2013a, b, c, d; Mejias et al. 2013) illustrate that leaders in each city work in radically different policy and practice contexts. For example, London leaders retain greater responsibility for staffing, finance, and school outcomes than leaders in Toronto. The overall structures of the education systems are also vastly different. Toronto and New York City have strong districts and layers of administrative support for school leaders when compared to London, where many schools work beyond structural support from local authorities, often in relative isolation. Finally, the high-stakes nature of accountability varies across the three cities, with London schools inspected by an external body (Ofsted) and publically ranked according to student test scores. New York leaders work within a similar but slightly less pressurized climate. Ontario has less frequent and less high-stakes student testing and a more continuous improvement-oriented system. Each of these structural configurations creates different pressures on the role of school leader; we anticipated that there would be a notable difference in how leaders discuss care and their overall role in working for and with teachers.

Perhaps the most surprising element of our school-based findings is that, even within radically different contextual environments that create vastly different leadership pressures and legal relationships between leaders and teachers, leaders and teachers did not differ across contexts in their belief in leaders' duty, ability, and commitment to care for teachers. The prioritization of people, support, being human, and striving for balance between work and life remains central. We are acutely aware of the small size of the sample; however, our early findings may in fact reinforce the importance of the role of school leaders in buffering their schools and staff members from external factors. This contributes to a growing body of literature examining comparative approaches (Baptiste 2008) and studies (Skakon et al. 2010) examining school leadership in different contexts.

If our study had simply been conducted in one city, we would not have been able to identify cross-jurisdictional patterns and differences, and this could have radically influenced our ability to understand the role and experience of leaders. Similarly, our findings highlight the importance of understanding how leaders in different jurisdictions need to work in order to support, buffer, and retain their teachers. While there is a consistent message that leaders need to be supportive and approachable, we believe there may be other actions that leaders can take to support teachers, and these will be different in different cities. For example, do the nuances of leader approachability look different in a context where leaders hire, compensate with performance-based-pay, and fire teachers (i.e. London) versus those where most human-resource-related functions are held centrally by districts and school boards? We will continue to explore these issues in our larger GCL analysis.

One of the reasons for considering leader care the generational and international implications of the pathways relates to the need to consider the wider school-level social considerations that influence a leader's ability and willingness to care for their teachers. Similarly, we provide preliminary evidence from a small set of participants, showing that the actual context within which schools operate may not influence their perception of the role of leaders in caring for staff members. This, in turn, clearly points to the different challenges leaders face in mediating external environmental challenges in caring for teacher.

9.5.2 Future Research and Policy Implications

While there are pockets of change, the accountability and standards movement shows little hope of slowing down, and leaders in our three cities report increasing workload pressures in their GCL interviews. For leaders, the volume of reporting, testing, and inspection differs according to the overarching structure of the education system. Based on our evidence, work/life-related issues will continue to be important and may even become one of the bigger concerns facing leaders directly over the coming years. As the emerging generation of leaders is predisposed to seeking work/life balance, the inherent tensions may become more apparent. GenXers have been widely observed leaving jobs and professions that do not allow them to achieve their sought-after balance between work and life. For this reason alone, additional research and, in turn, policy considerations of the implications of workload and work/life balance on leadership recruitment, enactment, and retention will become even more important in Global Cities and beyond.

This is potentially very worrying to those policy and practice leaders working to recruit and retain city-based school leaders. There is a growing need for research and development strategies to address the structural conditions of leaders' work that challenge work/life balance and their own ability to articulate and act on their work/life-balance goals. More importantly, these preliminary findings from our school-based studies suggest that selection, training, and development for this next generation of leaders should include and focus on nurturing the knowledge, skills, understandings, and attributes that leaders need to address work/life balance for leaders and teachers. GenXers and their GenY colleagues will only become more committed to perusing balance as they get older. Teachers in our study clearly state how leaders can support their work/life balance needs, and we believe there is an urgent need to build on this evidence base and create innovative strategies for leaders to assist their teachers while maintaining all current school-level objectives. Our findings perhaps indicate the urgent and important need for policymakers and researchers to reinvigorate their interest and advocacy in support not only of workload, but of work/life balance, research, and development.

9.6 Limitations

The overall Global City Leaders study is conducting preliminary research on a previously unexplored area of research. As such, we are working with a relatively small number of GenX leaders in each city to create a preliminary evidence base upon which to conduct future, more large-scale research. There is equally little research on the school-level perspectives of the overall leadership and organization of schools by GenX leaders. Our nine school-level studies are intended to make a small, early contribution to buttress our self-reported leader data with teacher views on the leadership and the lives of schools and teachers. The propositions set forth, specifically around the prominence of desires for leaders to know and care for people beyond school as well as the needs for leaders themselves to serve as work/life role models will be tested in future research by our team and others.

Our team had previously attributed the rise in leader discussions of work/life balance, collaboration, and the importance of school-based relationships (Ballou 1996; Boyd et al. 2005) to three potentially influential factors: (1) GenX leaders' expression of generationally attributed work-related characteristics (Edge 2014); (2) GenX leaders own life course issues with work/life given their caring roles for children and/or parents at home; and (3) a growing chorus of policy, practice, and union leaders highlighting the challenges associated with current school-level professional workloads and workplace conditions. The convergence of these issues creates an interesting opportunity to gather evidence and reflect on the notion of leadership and care within a small number of schools in three very different policy and practice contexts. However, we are also aware of the challenge it creates in establishing the source and influence of this generation's preoccupation with care.

The characteristics of GenXers in the workplace (Edge 2014) align closely with current research and thinking about great leadership and the knowledge, skills, and ability required to improve student outcomes and nurture school-level collaboration, diversity, and innovation (Leithwood and Jantzi 2008; Robinson et al. 2008). However, disaggregating what GenX leaders have learnt and applied from leadership theory from their generational predispositions creates evidentiary and analytical challenges. There remains a question related to if GenX leaders' leadership actions are driven by their own generational predispositions or current evidence on what constitutes instructionally meaningful leadership.

Our Global City Leaders project, including the evidence presented here, focuses on understanding more about the emerging generation of leaders and their approach to their careers, leaderships and lives. We do not explicitly set up our findings to juxtapose GenX and boomer leaders for several reasons including the complexity of the task required to conduct and international, cross generational study. Second, we believe much of the current educational leadership research cannon has been influenced by the experience of older, and consequently, more experienced leaders thus negating the influence that generation, specially a younger generation may have on leadership careers, leadership and aspirations.

Acknowledgements The authors wish to thank the ESRC (RES-061-25-0532) for their funding of the Young Global City Leaders project. We would also like to thank our Advisory Group members, participants and research team colleagues Dr. Paul Armstrong, Helen Green, and Kerrie Kennedy for their contributions to the project. Finally, the authors would like to thank the Editors and reviewers for their thoughtful and detailed comments.

References

Allen, M. B. (2005). *Eight questions on teacher recruitment and retention: What does the research say?* Denver: Education Commission of the States.

Amburn, B. (2009). The 2008 global cities index. *Foreign Policy, 169*, 68–76. Available online: http://foreignpolicy.com/2009/10/06/the-2008-global-cities-index

Armstrong, P., Edge, K., & Batlle, N. (2013a). *School leader responsibilities and accountabilities in London, New York and Toronto*. London: Institute of Education, University of London.

Armstrong, P., Edge, K., & Batlle, N. (2013b). *School leadership policy landscape: London, UK*. London: Institute of Education, University of London.

Arnold, K., Turner, N., Barling, J., Kelloway, K., & McKee, M. (2007). Transformational leadership and psychological well-being: The mediating role of meaningful work. *Journal of Occupational Health Psychology, 12*, 193–203.

Ballou, D. (1996). Do public schools hire the best applicants? *Quarterly Journal of Economics, 111*, 97–133.

Baptiste, N. R. (2008). Tightening the link between employee wellbeing at work and performance: A new dimension for HRM. *Management Decision, 46*, 284–309.

Bass, B. (1999). Two decades of research and development in transformational leadership. *European Journal of Work and Organizational Psychology, 8*, 9–32.

Bass, B. M., & Avolio, B. J. (1994). Transformational leadership and organizational culture. *International Journal of Public Administration, 17*, 541–554.

Beck, L. J. (1994). *Reclaiming educational administration as a caring profession*. New York: Teachers College Press.

Berl, P. (2006). Crossing the generational divide: Supporting generational differences at work. *Exchange: The Early Childhood Leaders' Magazine, 168*, 73–78.

Boyd, D., Lankford, H., Loeb, S., & Wyckoff, J. (2005). The draw of home: How teachers' preferences for proximity disadvantage urban schools. *Journal of Policy Analysis and Management, 24*, 113–123.

Brighouse, T. (2007). The London challenge – A personal view. In T. Brighouse & L. Fullick (Eds.), *Education in a global city: Essays from London* (pp. 71–94). London: Institute of Education.

Bryk, A., Sebring, P. B., Kerbow, D., Rollow, S., & Easton, J. Q. (1998). *Charting Chicago school reform: Democratic localism as a lever for change*. Boulder: Westview.

Bubb, S., & Earley, P. (2004). *Managing teacher workload: Work-life balance and wellbeing*. London: Sage.

Bulman, R. (2002). Teachers in the hood: Hollywood's middle-class fantasy. *The Urban Review, 34*, 251–276.

Carr, A. (1994). Anxiety and depression among school principals. Warning: Principalship can be hazardous to your health. *Journal of Educational Administration, 32*, 18–34.

Chapman, C. (2008). Towards a framework for school-to-school networking in challenging circumstances. *Educational Research, 50*, 403–420.

Ciulla, J. B. (2009). Leadership and the ethics of care. *Journal of Business Ethics, 88*, 3–4.

Clawson, J. G. (2009). *Level three leadership: Getting below the surface* (4th ed.). Upper Saddle River: Pearson-Prentice Hall.

Coggshall, J. G., Ott, A., Behrstock, E., & Lasagna, M. (2010). *Retaining teacher talent: The view from generation Y*. New York: Learning Point Associations and Public Agenda.

Coggshall, J., Behrstock-Sherratt, E., & Drill, K. (2011). *Workplaces that support high-performing teaching and learning: Insights from generation Y teachers*. Washington, DC: American Federation of Teachers and American Institutes of Research.

Day, C. (2008). Committed for life? Variations in teachers' work, lives and effectiveness. *Journal of Educational Change, 9*, 243–260.

Day, C., & Kington, A. (2008). Identity, well-being and effectiveness: The emotional contexts of teaching. *Pedagogy, Culture & Society, 16*, 7–23.

Day, C., Sammons, P., Hopkins, D., Harris, A., Leithwood, K., Gu, Q., Brown, E., Ahtaridou, E., & Kington, A. (2009). *The impact of school leadership on pupil outcomes*. (Research report RR108). London: Department of Children, Schools and Families.

Devos, G., Bouckenooghe, D., Engels, N., Hotton, G., & Aelterman, A. (2007). An assessment of well-being of principals in Flemish primary schools. *Journal of Educational Administration, 45*, 33–61.

Dolton, P., & van der Klaaw, W. (1999). The turnover of teachers: A competing risks explanation. *The Review of Economics and Statistics, 81*, 543–552.

Duke, D. (2000). *Caring safe schools for all children*. Boston: Allyn and Bacon.

Duscher, J., & Cowin, L. (2004). Multigenerational nurses in the workplace. *Journal of Nursing Administration, 34*, 493–501.

Edge, K. (2014). A review of the empirical generations at work research: Implications for school leaders and future research. *School Leadership and Management, 2*, 136–155.

Edge, K., Armstrong, P., & Batlle, N. (2013a). *School leadership policy landscape: Toronto, Ontario*. London: Institute of Education, University of London.

Edge, K., Amstrong, P., Descours, K., Dapper, E., Horton, J., & Batlle, N. (2013b). *Young global city leaders interviews: Emerging patterns from London*. London: Institute of Education, University of London.

Edge, K., Armstrong, P., Descours, K., Dapper, E., & Batlle, N. (2013c). *Global city leaders study: Research strategies*. London: Institute of Education, University of London.

Edge, K., Armstrong, P., Descours, K., Mejias, S., & Batlle, N. (2013d). *Young global city leaders interviews: Emerging patterns from New York*. London: Institute of Education, University of London.

Edmunds, J., & Turner, B. S. (2002). *Generations, culture and society*. Buckingham: Open University Press.

Edmunds, J., & Turner, B. S. (2005). Global generations: Social change in the twentieth century. *British Journal of Sociology, 56*, 559–577.

Elmore, R., & Burney, D. (1997). *Investing in teacher learning: Staff development and instructional improvement in community school district #2, New York City*. New York: Consortium for Policy Research in Education (CPRE), Teachers College, Columbia University.

Elmore, R., & Burney, D. (2002). *Continuous improvement in community district #2*. New York: Inter-American Development Bank.

Espinoza, C., Ukleja, M., & Rusch, C. (2010). *Managing millennials: Discover the core competencies for managing today's workforce*. Hoboken: Wiley.

Evans, L. (2001). Delving deeper into morale, job satisfaction and motivation among education professionals: Re-examining the leadership dimension. *Educational Management & Administration, 29*, 291–306.

Forsyth, S., & Polzer-Debruyne, A. (2007). The organisational pay-offs for perceived work–life balance support. *Asia Pacific Journal of Human Resources, 45*, 113–123.

Gabriel, Y. (2015). The caring leader – What followers expect of their leaders and why? *Leadership, 11*(3), 316–334.

Geijsel, F., Sleegers, P., Leithwood, K., & Jantzi, D. (2003). Transformational leadership effects on teachers' commitment and effort toward school reform. *Journal of Educational Administration, 41*, 228–256.

Gentry, W. A., Griggs, T. L., Deal, J. J., Mondore, S. P., & Cox, B. D. (2011). A comparison of generational differences in endorsement of leadership practices with actual leadership skill level. *Consulting Psychology Journal: Practice and Research, 63*, 39–49.

Gilligan, C. (1982). *In a different voice: Psychological theory and a women's development*. Cambridge, MA: Harvard University Press.

Gronn, P., & Lacey, K. (2004). Positioning oneself for leadership: Feelings of vulnerability among aspirant principals. *School Leadership and Management, 24*, 405–424.

Hanushek, E., Kain, J., & Rivkin, S. (2004). Why public schools lose teachers. *Journal of Human Resources, 34*, 326–354.

Hargreaves, A. (1998). The emotional practice of teaching. *Teaching and Teacher Education, 14*, 835–854.

Hargreaves, D. (2003). *Leadership for transformation within the London challenge*. In: Annual lecture at the London Leadership Centre, Institute of Education, London, UK.

Harris, A. (2002). Effective leadership in schools facing challenging circumstances. *School Leadership and Management, 22*, 15–27.

Hess Jr., G. A. (1991). *School restructuring, Chicago style*. Thousand Oaks: Corwin.

Hess, N., & Jepsen, D. (2009). Career stage and generational differences in psychological contracts. *Career Development International, 14*, 261–283.

Hewlett, S. A., Sherbin, L., & Sumberg, K. (2009). How Gen Y and boomers will reshape your agenda. *Harvard Business Review, 87*, 71–76.

Hodgkinson, C. (1991). *Educational leadership: The moral art*. Albany: SUNY Press.

Howson, J. (2008). *The state of the labour market for senior staff in schools in England and Wales*. Oxford: Education Data Surveys.

Ingersoll, R. (2003). *Is there really a teacher shortage?*(Document R-03-4). Seattle: University of Washington, Center for the Study of Teaching and Policy.

Jacob, B. (2007). The challenges of staffing urban schools with effective teachers. *The Future of Children, 17*, 129–154.

Johnson, S., Berg, J., & Donaldson, M. (2005). Who stays in teaching and why: A review of the literature on teacher retention. In *The project on the next generation of teachers*. Boston: Harvard Graduate School of Education.

Klinker, J. F., & Hackmann, D. G. (2004). An analysis of principals' ethical decision making using rest's four component model of moral behavior. *Journal of School Leadership, 14*, 434–455.

Kunreuther, F. (2003). The changing of the guard: What generational differences tell us about social change organizations. *Nonprofit and Voluntary Sector Quarterly, 32*, 450–457.

Lambert, S. J. (2000). Added benefits: The link between work-life benefits and organizational citizenship behavior. *Academy of Management Journal, 43*, 801–815.

Spillane J.P, & Lee L. (2013). Novice school principals' sense of ultimate responsibility problems of practice in transitioning to the principal's office. *Educational Administration Quarterly, 50*, 431–465.

Leithwood, K., & Jantzi, D. (1999). The relative effects of principal and teacher sources of leadership on student engagement with school. *Educational Administration Quarterly, 35*, 679–706.

Leithwood, K., & Jantzi, D. (2008). Linking leadership to student learning: The contributions of leader efficacy. *Educational Administration Quarterly, 44*, 496–528.

Leithwood, K., Patten, S., & Jantzi, D. (2010). Testing a conception of how leadership influences student learning. *Educational Administration Quarterly, 46*, 671–706.

Louis, K. S., Murphy, J., & Smylie, M. (2016). Caring leadership in schools: Findings from exploratory analyses. *Educational Administration Quarterly, 52*, 1–39.

Lovely, S., & Buffum, A. (2007). *Generations at school: Building an age-friendly learning community*. London: Sage.

McKinney, S., Berry, R., Dickerson, D., & Campbell-Whately, G. (2007). Addressing urban high-poverty school teacher attrition by addressing urban high-poverty school teacher retention: Why effective teachers persevere. *Educational Research and Review, 3*, 1–9.

Mejias, S., Edge, K., Armstrong, P., & Batlle, N. (2013). *School leadership policy landscape: New York City, USA*. London: Institute of Education, University of London.

Miles, M., & Huberman, A. (1994). *Qualitative data analysis: An expanded sourcebook*. Thousand Oaks: Sage.

Moore Johnson, S. (2004). *Finders and keepers: Helping new teachers survive and thrive in our schools*. San Francisco: Jossey-Bass.

Moore Johnson, S., & Kardos, S. (2005). Bridging the generation gap. *Educational Leadership, 62*, 8–14.

Müller, K., Alliata, R., & Benninghoff, F. (2009). Attracting and retaining teachers: a question of motivation. *Educational Management Administration & Leadership, 37*, 574–599.

Nielsen, K., & Munir, F. (2009). How do transformational leaders influence followers' affective well-being? Exploring the mediating role of self-efficacy. *Work and Stress, 23*, 313–329.

Noddings, N. (1986). *Caring: A feminine approach to ethics and moral education*. Berkeley: University of California Press.
Noddings, N. (2005). *The challenge to care in schools*. New York: Teachers College Press.
Pham, V., Miyake, L., Case, J., & Gil S. (2008). *The Gen Y perceptions study*. Available at: www.spectrumknowledge.com/img/Gen_Y_Perception_Study_CREW_Final.pdf
Pilcher, J. (1994). Mannheim's sociology of generations: An undervalued legacy. *British Journal of Sociology, 45*, 449–481.
Rinke, C. (2009). Exploring the generation gap in urban schools: Generational perspectives in professional learning communities. *Education and Urban Society, 42*, 3–24.
Robinson, V., Lloyd, C., & Rowe, K. (2008). The impact of leadership on student outcomes: An analysis of the differential effects of leadership types. *Educational Administration Quarterly, 44*, 635–674.
Sackney, L., Noonan, B., & Miller, C. M. (2000). Leadership for educator wellness: An exploratory study. *International Journal of Leadership in Education, 3*, 41–56.
Salajan, F., Schonwetter, D., & Cleghorn, B. (2010). Student and faculty inter-generational digital divide. *Computers & Education, 55*, 1393–1403.
Sassen, S. (1991). *The global city: New York, London, Tokyo*. Princeton: Princeton University Press.
Simola, S. K., Barling, J., & Turner, N. (2010). Transformational leadership and leader moral orientation: contrasting an ethic of justice and an ethic of care. *The Leadership Quarterly, 21*, 179–188.
Skakon, J., Nielsen, K., Borg, V., & Guzman, J. (2010). Are leaders' well-being, behaviours and style associated with the affective well-being of their employees? A systematic review of three decades of research. *Work and Stress, 24*, 107–139.
Smola, K., & Sutton, C. (2002). Generational differences: Revisiting generational work values for the new millennium. *Journal of Organizational Behavior, 23*, 363–382.
Smyth, E., & McCoy, S. (2009). *Investing in education: Combating educational disadvantage*. Dublin: Economic and Social Research Institute (ESRI).
Stone-Johnson, C. (2011). Talkin' bout my generation: Boomers, Xers and educational change. *Journal of Educational Change, 12*, 221–239.
Stone-Johnson, C. (2014). Not cut out to be an administrator: Generations, change and the career transition from teacher to principal. *Education and Urban Society, 46*, 606–625.
Strauss, W. (2005). Talking about their generations: Making sense of a school environment made up of Gen-Xers and Millennials. *The School Administrator, 62*, 10–14.
Strauss, A., & Corbin, J. (1994). Grounded theory methodology. In N. K. Denzin & Y. S. Lincoln (Eds.), *Handbook of qualitative research* (pp. 273–285). Thousand Oaks: Sage.
Sun, J., & Leithwood, K. (2015a). Direction-setting school leadership practices: A meta-analytical review of evidence about their influence. *School Effectiveness and School Improvement, 26*, 499–523.
Sun, J., & Leithwood, K. (2015b). Leadership effects on student learning mediated by teacher emotions. *Societies, 5*, 566–582.
Thompson, D., McNamara, J., & Hoyle, J. (1997). Job satisfaction in educational organizations: A synthesis of research findings. *Educational Administration Quarterly, 33*, 7–37.
Vanderklippe, N. (2014, April 4). What Shanghai can teach us about teaching math. *The Globe and Mail*. Retrieved from http://cached.newslookup.com/cached.php?ref_id=123&siteid=2115&id=5514060&t=1396633245
Walmsely, A. (2011). Closing the communication gap. *Educational Horizons, 90*, 25–26.
Wang, J., & Lin, E. (2005). Comparative studies on US and Chinese mathematics learning and the implications for standards-based mathematics teaching reform. *Educational Researcher, 34*, 3–13.
Warshauer Freedman, S., & Appleman, D. (2009). In it for the long haul: How teacher education can contribute to teacher retention in high-poverty. *Urban Schools Journal of Teacher Education, 60*, 323–337.

Williamson, R., & Meyer-Looze, C. (2010). *Working with Gen Y teachers: Dealing with a changing teacher workforce*. Pittsburgh: Education Partnerships Inc. Available online: http://www.eric.ed.gov/PDFS/ED538402.pdf

Wilson, S. (2012). Caring leadership applied in the classroom to embrace the needs of students. *Journal of College Teaching & Learning (TLC), 10*, 23–28.

Wohlstetter, P., & Odden, A. (1992). Rethinking school-based management policy and research. *Educational Administration Quarterly, 28*, 529–549.

Worley, K. (2011). Educating college students of the net generation. *Adult Learning, 22*, 31–39.

Yukl, G. (2002). *Leadership in organizations*. Upper Saddle River: Prentice Hall.

Zaretsky, L. (2004). Advocacy and administration: from conflict to collaboration. *Journal of Educational Administration, 42*, 270–286.

Zemke, R., Raines, C., & Filipczak, B. (2000). *Generations at work: Managing the clash of veterans, boomers, xers, and nexters in your workplace*. New York: AMA Publications.

Zieglar, S. (2007). The (mis)education of generation M. *Learning, Media and Technology, 32*, 69–81.

Part IV
The Organizational Path

Introduction

The four chapters in this part explore conditions or variables on the Organizational Path. Chapter 10 explores factors that moderate principals work. Chapter 11 is a comprehensive review of professional communities, which identifies the barriers and constraints that hinder or prevent the growth of professional community. Chapter 12 modes the effects of principal professional orientation towards leadership, professional teacher behavior, and school academic optimism on student learning outcome. The last chapter presents findings from a mixed methods study that examined how principals' learning-centered leadership in mainland China influence the professional learning of their teachers as mediated by teacher trust and teacher agency.

Variables on the Organizational Path include features of schools that structure the relationships and interactions among organizational members including, for example, cultures, policies, and standard operating procedures. The variables comprising the organizational path can act as supports that create the necessary conditions for other path variables but if absent can act as barriers or challenges that can indirectly influence student learning and outcomes. Some of the organizational path variables explored over the past few decades that have been determined to influence student learning outcomes include, but are not limited to, academic optimism, safe and orderly schools, instructional time, professional community and school collaborative structures.

This part introduction illustrates and summarizes the nature and effects on students of three organizational conditions that are conducive to student learning: safe and orderly schools, instructional time, and school collaborative structures.

Safe and Orderly Environment (SOE)

This conceptualization was a move away from traditional views of indiscipline rooted in classroom alone. Combined efforts from classroom, schools as well as parents and community, a social-ecological model, are needed to enhance school safety and reduce bullying (e.g., Astor et al. 2010; Borum et al. 2010; Swearer, Espelage). Providing an inclusive environment and inclusive instruction consistent with diverse learning styles and foster students' self-efficacy has become undoubtedly necessary for successful for all. Thus we use the S*afe, Orderly and Inclusive environment* (SOIE) to capture both orderly features of disciplinary climate and the necessity for inclusive environment.

A more holistic approach to school safety and orderliness relies on a coordination of school and community services, efficient provision of mental health services for those students who need it, threat assessment rather than violence survey, emphasis on prevention vs. suspension (on safe school vs. school violence), and increasing the use of restorative justice practices in progressive discipline vs. retributive practices (Cornell and Mayer 2010; Mayer and Furlong 2010; Swearer et al. 2010). Among all their restorative justice practices in progressive discipline, school leaders need to ensure an orderly classroom environment conducive to teaching and learning and improve interpersonal relationship between students and teachers as ultimate goal (Willms and Ma 2004). In order to reinforce such an environment, school policies need to be supported by state policies and legislations that permit principals and teachers to engender a positive disciplinary environment (Ma and Crocker 2007). Distributed leadership is found to be effective in fostering a whole community approach to develop the SOIE in schools. (Anderson et al. 2009; Leithwood et al. 2004).

Organization of Planning and Instructional Time (OPIT)

Instructional time in formal classroom settings accounts for a large portion of public investment in student learning and is a? central component of effective schooling (OECD 2013). Across OECD countries, the country average of learning time in regular school lessons is positive, but weakly, related to country average performance, while learning time in out-of-school-time lessons and individual study is negatively related to performance. The total amount of "time actually devoted to instruction" has moderate effects on student learning (e.g., Bellei 2009). Total instructional time matters less than how the time is spent, on which subjects time is spent, and the strength of the curriculum (OECD 2013). Time on task is an important contributor to achievement. The content of the curriculum in which students spend time studying, "opportunity to learn", has quite strong effects on learning (Törnroos 2005; Wang 1998).

There is little direct evidence about leadership practices for optimizing instructional time in schools except the practice of "buffering". Buffering protects the efforts of teachers from the many distractions they face from both inside and outside of schools, and helps teachers devote their time to their classroom instructional (e.g., DiPaola and Tschannen-Moran 2005). Regardless of how time is used for learning, principals are responsible for creating the conditions for the most effective use of teacher and student time for effective student learning. But time is not the only factor for student learning in terms of actual time allotted for students and teachers but time also influences principals' work. The study of principals' time has existed for a number of decades but has received less attention. This body of research is a product of school effectiveness and improvement research (Grissom et al. 2013; Horng et al. 2010; Kmetz and Willower 1982; Martin and Willower 1981). However, a few studies have explored the variable time and its influence on principals work in relation to terms of influence on student learning and outcomes (Leithwood and Azah 2015, Pollock et al. 2015). Pollock, Wang and Hauseman, in Chap. 10, approaches the use of principals' time by considering how factors such as administrative duties and responsibilities, jurisdictional policies, external influences and partnership and challenges and possibilities act as antecedents to what leaders do. They determined that principals' choices about what conditions or variables to work towards are not only subject to factors that exist within the beyond schools but these factors moderate the way that principals carry out their work and can limit their choices along the remaining three paths (rationale, emotional, and family paths).

Collaborative Cultures and Structures

We use *Collaborative Cultures and Structures* to capture key elements of teachers' instructional knowledge and experience sharing and knowledge creation, collaboration, reflection, being open, using student data to inform the discussion in professional learning communities (PLCs), common assessment and monitoring of student academic progress, shared decision-making on instructional strategies and intervention, and collective professional learning, as reflected in the studies examining effective working environment, school conditions, organizational learning, effective school, shared decision-making and professional learning communities. Our review (Sun et al. 2016) of data use research reveals that teachers felt the opportunity to work with their colleagues and discuss specific teaching strategies, share strategies and ideas they were finding successful within their classrooms, and share best practices supported by formative assessment data, and what works for others was an integral part of the process leading to increased academic scores (e.g., Fischer 2011; Henry 2011). This feature is especially prominent in schools making Adequate Yearly Progress (AYP) (Hill 2010). Generally speaking, various constructs such as collaborative school culture /School Climate/Org. Learning taken as a whole were found to be malleable to transformational school leadership (weighted mean effect size, $r = .44$) (Leithwood and Sun 2012).

Closely related to cultural constructs of this kind is the more recent notion of professional learning community (PLC). Eight features of effective PLCs majority of leading scholars in this area often argued for are: shared values and vision; collective responsibility for pupils' learning; collaboration focused on learning; individual and collective professional learning; reflective professional enquiry; openness, networks and partnerships; inclusive membership; mutual trust, respect and support (e.g., Bolam et al. 2005; Stoll et al. 2006). The majority of studies on PLCs have not found a significant positive association between PLCs and student learning. Lomos and her associates' meta-analysis (Lomos et al. 2011) reported a small but significant positive relationship (summary effect r = .12) between PLCs and student achievement. As well, professional school culture has positive correlation (.30) with teacher perceived effectiveness in specialized programs for students with disabilities (Kristoff 2003). The moderate to small association between school collaborative teaching culture and student learning is understandable as school learning culture does not contribute to student learning directly. Our meta-analysis of twenty studies that examined the impacts of transformational school leaders on various elements that touch upon *Collaborative Cultures and Structures* indicated a close-to-large impact (r = .37–.80, with an average weighted mean r = .48) (Leithwood and Sun 2012).

Based on the thorough review of more than 100 studies related to this topic, we identified the following things principals can do to promote *Collaborative Cultures and Structures*:

- Setting access goals for all users and communicating clear expectations for that data use
- Fostering data-driven knowledge construction and sharing instructional practices
- Creating a purpose for data-driven decision making through emphasizing improvements in student achievement and a vision of best practices for students
- Requesting teachers to develop professional goals related to student achievement goals directly oriented around the school learning plan
- Making collaboration a necessity through scheduled meeting times for collaboration
- Developing instructional strategies based on data
- Developing, scoring, and analyzing assessments
- Developing leadership teams for assessment and data analysis
- Establishing a structure and making time for PLCs
- Converting traditional meetings into professional development followed up by instructional support
- Communicating to teachers how students were doing using data
- Developing team norms/values/collective commitments to guide collaboration
- Creating teams pursuing specific and measurable performance goals
- Providing time for teacher collaboration built in to the school day, not as an "add-on"
- Teams focusing on key questions/LEARNING

- Having the products of teacher collaboration made explicit
- Trying not to increase costs
- Trying not to have teacher collaboration significantly impact instructional time
- Asking teachers to present quick and dirty working strategies that could be used the next day at each meeting
- Making grade-level planning a routine, and
- Putting a data system in place in schools.

In addition, we found a very typical process that teachers reported valuable, which principals can encourage in schools to foster teachers' *Collaborative Cultures and Structures*. This process includes series of teachers' collective actions of looking at both summative state-standardized test scores or benchmark tests and formative and summative classroom assessments collectively, reviewing student work, evaluating present levels of performance in the course, setting aside time for reflection and discussion, developing common assessment tools, identifying students who did not get concepts, developing interventions, writing goals to support the overall goals of the school, and developing strategies collaboratively (Sun et al. 2016).

References

Anderson, S., Moore, S., & Sun, J.-P. (2009). Positioning the principals in patterns of school leadership distribution. In K. Leithwood, B. Mascall, & T. Strauss (Eds.), *Distributed leadership according to the evidence* (pp. 111–136). New York: Routledge.

Astor, R. A., Guerra, N., & Van Acker, R. (2010). How can we improve school safety research? *Educational Researcher, 39*(1), 69–78.

Bellei, C. (2009). Does lengthening the school day increase students' academic achievement? Results from a natural experiment in Chile. *Economics of Education Review, 28*, 629–640.

Bolam, R., McMahon, A., Stoll, L., Thomas, S., & Wallace, M., with Greenwood, A., Hawkey, K., Ingram, M., Atkinson, A., & Smith, M. (2005). *Creating and sustaining effective professional learning communities*. (Research report 637). Bristol: Department of Education and Skills.

Borum, R., Cornell, D. G., Modzeleski, W., & Jimerson, S. R. (2010). What can be done about school shootings? A review of the evidence. *Educational Researcher, 39*(1), 27–37.

Cornell, D. G., & Mayer, M. J. (2010). Do school order and safety matter? *Educational Researcher, 39*, 7–15.

DiPaola, M. F., & Tschannen-Moran, M. (2005). Bridging or buffering? The impact of schools' adaptive strategies on student achievement. *Journal of Educational Administration, 43*, 60–71.

Fischer, B. E. (2011). *Using data to increase student achievement: A case study of success in a sanctioned school*. D.Ed., University of Minnesota. Available from ProQuest dissertations and theses. (873812798).

Grissom, J. A., Loeb, S., & Master, B. (2013). Effective instructional time use for school leaders: Longitudinal evidence from observations of principals. *Educational Researcher, 42*(8), 433–444.

Henry, S. S. (2011). *Principals' use of assessment data to drive student academic achievement*. Ed.D., California State University, Fullerton. Available from ProQuest dissertations and theses. (912193587).

Hill, K. L. (2010). Predictive indicators of high performing schools: A study of evaluative inquiry and the effective use of achievement test data. (Ph.D., University of Minnesota). *ProQuest Dissertations and Theses*. (610058860)

Hill, N. E., Tyson, D. F., & Bromell, L. (2009). Parental involvement in middle school: Developmentally appropriate strategies across SES and ethnicity. In N. E. Hill & R. K. Chao (Eds.), *Families, schools, and the adolescent: Connecting research, policy, and practice* (pp. 53–72). New York: Teachers College Press.

Horng, E. L., Klasik, D., & Loeb, S. (2010). Principal's time use and school effectiveness. *American Journal of Education, 116*(4), 491–523.

Leithwood, K., & Sun, J. (2012). The nature and effects of transformational school leadership: A meta-analytic review of unpublished research. *Educational Administration Quarterly, 48*, 387–423.

Kmetz, J. T., & Willower, D. J. (1982). Elementary school principals' work behavior. *Educational Administration Quarterly, 18*(4), 62–78.

Kristoff B. L. (2003). Transformational leadership, professional school culture, and perceived effectiveness in specialized programs for students with disabilities. *Dissertation Abstracts International 64* (04), A. (AAI3088477)

Leithwood, K., Seashore Louis, K., Anderson, S., & Wahlstrom, K. (2004). *How leadership influences student learning: A review of research for the Learning from Leadership Project*. Retrieved from: http://www.wallacefoundation.org/knowledge-center/Documents/How-Leadership-Influences-Student-Learning.pdf

Lomos, C., Hofman, R., & Bosker, R. (2011). Professional communities and student achievement: A meta analysis. *School Effectiveness and School Improvement, 22*(2), 121–148.

Ma, X., & Crocker, R. (2007). Provincial effects on reading achievement. *Alberta Journal of Educational Research, 53*, 87–109.

Martin, W. J., & Willower, D. J. (1981). The managerial behavior of high school principals. *Educational `Administration Quarterly, 17*(1), 69–90.

Mayer, M. J., & Furlong, M. J. (2010). How safe are our schools? *Educational Researcher, 39*(1), 7–15.

OECD. (2013). *PISA 2012 results: What makes schools successful? Resources, policies and practices* (Executive summary, Vol. IV, pp. 17–25). Paris: Author. doi.10.1787/9789264201156-en.

Pollock, K., Wang, F., & Hauseman, D. C. (2015). Complexity and volume: An Inquiry into factors that drive principals' work. *Societies, 5*(2), 537–565.

Stoll, L., Bolam, R., McMahon, A., Wallace, M., & Thomas, S. (2006). Professional learning communities: A review of the literature. *Journal of Educational Change, 7*, 221–258.

Sun, J., Przybylski, R. M., & Johnson, B. (2016). A review of research on teachers' use of student data: From the perspective of school leadership. *Educational Assessment, Evaluation and Accountability, 28*. doi:10.1007/s11092-016-9238-9.

Swearer, S. M., Espelage, D. L., Vaillancourt, T., & Hymel, S. (2010). What can be done about school bullying? Linking research to educational practice. *Educational Researcher, 39*(1), 38–47.

Törnroos, J. (2005). Mathematics textbooks, opportunity to learn and student achievement. *Studies in Educational Evaluation, 31*(4), 315–327.

Wang, J. (1998). Opportunity to learn: The impacts and policy implications. *Educational evaluation and policy analysis, 20*(3), 137–156.

Willms, J. D., & Ma, X. (2004). School disciplinary climate: Characteristics and effects on eighth grade achievement [Electronic version]. *Alberta Journal of Educational Research, 50*(2), 1–27.

Chapter 10
Complexity and Volume: An Inquiry into Factors That Drive Principals' Work

Katina Pollock, Fei Wang, and David Cameron Hauseman

> *Increased workload is the biggest change in the work of principals.*
> —Canadian Association of Principals (2014, p. 22).

The past three decades have seen a growing interest in principals' work (Horng et al. 2010; Kmetz and Willower 1982; Lee and Hallinger 2012; Martin and Willower 1981; Martinko and Gardner 1990). Specifically, there has been a growing emphasis on the work of principals in relation to improving student achievement (Hendriks and Sheerens 2013; Lomos et al. 2011; Louis et al. 2010; Robinson et al. 2008). In an effort to learn more about what principals can do to improve student achievement, the field of educational leadership has considered principals' behaviours and practices in relation to: recruiting and motivating quality teachers (Harris et al. 2010; Jacob and Lefgren 2005), articulating a school vision (Leithwood 2012; Leithwood and Riehl 2003), effective allocation of resources (Bickmore 2011; Louis et al. 2010), and supporting instructional learning (Brewer 1993; Eberts and Stone 1998; Horng et al. 2010; Knapp et al. 2006; Leithwood et al. 2004).

Investigating leadership effects on student performance has a long history within the school effectiveness and improvement movement (Hallinger et al. 2013). Over the past few decades, scholars have attempted to find both direct (Witziers et al. 2003) and indirect (Day et al. 2009; Leithwood and Jantzi 2008; Mulford 2003; Silins and Mulford 2004) effects of school leadership on student outcomes. Most current empirical studies are premised on the notion that the influence of school

---

K. Pollock (✉)
Western University, London, ON, Canada
e-mail: kpolloc7@uwo.ca

F. Wang
University of British Columbia, Vancouver, BC, USA
e-mail: fei.wang@ubc.ca

D.C. Hauseman
University of Western Ontario, London, ON, Canada
e-mail: chausema@uwo.ca

leadership on student outcomes is indirect; principals "directly operate on school organisational and instructional conditions, which in turn influence student achievements" (Hendriks and Sheerens 2013, p. 374). Hendriks and Sheerens' (2013) matching of core leadership behaviors to educational effectiveness factors is one way to consider how principals indirectly affect student outcomes.

While the majority of articles in this special issue address some component of Leithwood, Patten and Jantzi's (2010) four paths used by leaders to indirectly improve student learning, this article takes a different approach by considering what variables influence school leaders' work. Specifically, we consider the variables in Leithwood, Patten and Jantzi (2010) "organizational path," and how some of these variables influence principals' work (and therefore indirectly influence their ability to impact student achievement). Briefly, the organizational path consists of variables that can constitute principals' working conditions such as structures, culture, policies and standard operation procedures (Leithwood, Patten and Jantzi, 2010). The variables examined in this study affect what principals do along the paths, which can be considered antecedents to what leaders do. These variables can fall into the following categories: administrative duties and responsibilities, jurisdictional policies, external influences and partnerships, and challenges and possibilities. Our inquiry is in a preliminary stage, and we are therefore not able to make causal linkages using the data presented here; rather, the data is meant to raise questions and considerations for further inquiry into the phenomenon of school leadership effects and the role played by principals' work as a moderator of principals' functions and behaviours.

This study takes a broad approach to understanding what contemporary principals do. Among other things, it acknowledges the wide-ranging, diverse, and complex nature of principals' work. Most importantly, it adopts the concept of "work" to explore principals' worlds. "Work," for this article, is understood as labour or effort expended to achieve a particular set of goals (Merriam-Webster n.d.). This study includes employment-related paid and unpaid work (Drago 2007). The labour included in this study may be expended both within and outside position-related roles enacted by principals, and includes efforts that are both paid and unpaid. It is difficult in this day and age to erect clear boundaries around work efforts, just as it is to define organizational boundaries (Ryan 1996). Work can take place on and off the school site, and it can occur before or after the official opening and closing of the school day. Work also comprises particular experiential components such as physical, mental, and emotional aspects (Applebaum 1992; Gamst 1995); this is certainly the case for principals who are deeply engaged in emotional labour (Leithwood and Beatty 2007) in addition to their cognitive and observable activities. In line with studies that look at work engagement (Bakker et al. 2006; Mauno et al. 2006), this study employs a lens that acknowledges the behavioural, cognitive, *and* emotional elements of work.

10.1 Factors That Influence Principals' Work

There are a number of moderating factors that can influence a principal's workload. Some of these factors can be categorised as follows: instructional leadership, administrative/management responsibilities, partnerships, policies, and external influences.

10.1.1 Instructional Leadership

Not surprisingly, instructional leadership had a variety of meanings (Hallinger 2011). In Ontario, the Education Act does not make any specific reference to instructional leadership being part of the principals' official role (Revised Statues of Ontario 1990). However, as part of Ontario's Leadership Strategy (OLS), the Ontario Leadership Framework (OLF) does suggest that education leaders, such as curriculum leaders, principals, and supervisory officers, are to

> ...embed direct involvement in instruction in their daily work through teamwork with all staff focused on improved school and classroom practices...[and] help to create inclusive and instructionally effective learning environments that increase the likelihood that all students will be successful learners" (Institute for Education Leadership n.d., p. 7).

For the purposes of this article, we view instructional leadership as leadership of curriculum where school principals are: "developing, supervising, evaluating, and are accountable for instructional programs; hiring, supervising, evaluating, and providing professional development opportunities for school staff; supporting student advancement; and evaluating student performance and progress" (Pollock and Hauseman 2015, n.p.).

10.1.2 Administrative/Management Responsibilities

Like running any organization that has a physical site, principals are also responsible for a number of administrative or managerial responsibilities. For this article, we focus on four specific responsibilities: budgeting, personnel, building maintenance, and occupational, health and safety compliance.

Budgeting Schools have always had budgets and leaders of schools have always had some kind of interaction with these budgets, from merely knowing what the fiscal amount is and where the funds are going to site-based management with full discretion on how to spend the annual budget. However, it appears that with the onset of reform efforts and school improvement initiatives, "budgeting" has become more complex than previously experienced. In 2013, the Organization for Economic Co-operation and Development (OECD) Teaching and Learning International

Survey (TALIS) report ranked "inadequate school budget and resources" as the top barrier to principal effectiveness; in Alberta, Canada it was ranked second (OECD 2013). In Ontario, a recent study indicated that nearly one third of the 70 principals interviewed required additional professional learning to manage the school's budget or deal with other financial aspects of the position (Pollock and Hauseman 2015).

Personnel Managing personnel should be a component of instructional leadership functions, where principals develop people or redesign the organization (Horng and Loeb 2010). While this most definitely can be the case, there is a pragmatic element to working with people that requires principals to be knowledgeable about labour contracts and possess skills such as conflict resolution, the ability to supervise multiple employee groups, and to address grievances (Norton 2015).

Building Maintenance Maintaining a school site is not an easy task, and it is rarely discussed outside of the school finance literature. Principals working in older schools are faced with difficult decisions about allocation of resources, must self-educate on what needs to be prioritized, and must oversee any renovations and/or repairs (Preiss 2014). However, it is not just older buildings that require principals' time and attention; new school development projects can be just as taxing on a school principal's time. New school buildings require an effective maintenance plan that includes meeting warranty deadlines and constant revisiting as the building ages (Chan 2000).

Occupational Health and Safety Principals play a pivotal role in creating a healthy school community. Principals can do this by limiting occupational health and safety hazards and by promoting a positive and inclusive climate (Canadian Association of Principals 2014; Riley 2014). However, their work intensification can have a significant impact on their own occupational health and safety. Recognizing principals' occupational health and safety is imperative in creating a culture of wellness in schools. Studies show that principals who are exposed to long work hours are more likely to have unhealthy life styles (e.g., in regards to weight gain, smoking, and/or alcohol consumption) (Kemeny 2002; Shields 2000; Vezina 2002). Such unhealthy lifestyle habits can eventually undermine the overall health of school communities, and even affect teaching and learning in schools.

10.1.3 Partnerships

A "partnership," for this article, is understood as a relationship with an outside organization or group (as opposed to relationships with individual parents or families). Many advocate that partnerships can be a way to support student achievement (Hands 2010), and can be considered a part of instructional leadership. Even though partnerships can indirectly support student achievement, we have separated this category from instructional leadership, as it does not facilitate principals' direct involvement in curriculum instruction in their daily work. Schools are being encouraged to engage in outside partnerships for all sorts of reasons: to generate revenue, such as by renting out building space after school hours (Clandfield 2010); to foster closer connections to services that the school cannot effectively provide, such as supplemental educational services (Koyama 2011); or as a way of engaging ethnic, racial, and religious communities with the school and with student learning (Auerbach 2010; Rogers et al. 2012). Effective partnerships require trusting relationships, a central purpose, and leadership, to name but a few components (Best and Holmes 2010). For many principals, engaging in partnerships at the school level requires engaging in partnership-building and maintenance tasks that can at times take them away from direct school functions.

10.1.4 Policies

Reform movements and accountability initiatives over the past 10 years or so have utilized policies as tools to initiate and support educational change. However, the way we understand "policy," and its implications is complex, and "it would appear that everyone has an individually constructed concept of policy" (Pollock 2006, p. 35). However, for this article, we understand "policy" as a way to change practice through official, formal legislation, mandates, government initiatives, and board regulations. Policies act to regulate, constrain, and/or monitor actions and outcomes. In Ontario, principals' work is not only influenced by the Ontario Education Act 1990, but according to the Ontario College of Teachers, principals are also expected to have a working knowledge of at least 17 different provincial and federal legislations (Ontario College of Teachers 2009). In addition to the formal legislation, principals are subject to provincial ministry initiatives and strategies, such as: the Aboriginal Education Strategy; the Equity and Inclusive Education Strategy; the Parents in Partnership: Parent Engagement Policy; the First Nations, Metis, and Inuit (FNMI) Policy Framework; Growing Success: Assessment, Evaluation, and Reporting in Ontario Schools; the Ontario curriculum; and the Ontario Leadership Strategy.

What we know from recent studies in Canada and Ontario is that policies are playing a more significant role in principals' work than in the past. We know generally that many school principals feel that their role is constrained by the number of initiatives imposed on a school (Blakesley 2012; Fink 2010; Smith 2009). Not only do principals in Ontario feel constrained by formal policy initiatives, but multiple policy initiatives within short time periods have also influenced how they do their work (Pinto 2015). The Organization for Economic Co-operation and Development (OECD) Teaching and Learning International Survey (TALIS) report ranked "government regulation and policy" as third on its list of barriers to principal effectiveness (OECD 2013).

10.1.5 Other External Influences

In addition to the aforementioned partnerships with organizations and groups outside of schools, current Canadian literature suggests other external influences can have an impact on principals' work. Some examples of external influences captured here include: technology, changing student demographics, district school board initiatives, and labour issues.

Technology Advances in information and communication technology have made principals' work more complicated (Pollock and Hauseman 2015). From a positive perspective, information and communication technology can provide principals with additional channels through which they can reach students, parents, and the wider community (Hauseman and Pollock 2014; Fullan 2014; Sheninger 2014). However, the downside to these technologies is that they require principals to expend significant time and energy learning how to use them. Some principals have had to engage in steep learning curves to operate devices such as smart phones and utilize different forms of social media (Brockmeier et al. 2005; Leithwood and Azah 2014). Work-life boundaries can become blurred as some principals are expected to complete tasks or respond to emails in an unrealistic timeframe. Approximately, 49% of principals reported that technological changes the way people communicate. This is challenging because principals feel they are always "on call" (Pollock and Hauseman 2015). The amount of emailing has increased to a level that principals indicated there were "too many memos and emails from the district which increase[d]workload and distract[ed] principals" (Leithwood and Azah 2014). Lastly, an unforeseen consequence of advances in information and communication technology is the increased prevalence of cyberbullying (Canadian Association of Principals 2014). Principals have reported having to spend enormous amounts of time managing "discipline-related problems emerging from tech-facilitated bullying and gossip" (Canadian Association of Principals 2014, p. 41). Cyberbullying has become such an issue that the Canadian Association of Principals concluded: "the fallout from social media use in the school community places a significant burden on administrator's time" (2014, p. 41).

Changing Student Demographics Changing student demographics influence principals' work in three ways. First, the student population influences the size, location, type of school, number of special classrooms, and make-up of the student population and the educational services required to support individualized needs, special programs, and discipline. Declining student enrolment also influences principals' workload. Similar to most developed countries, Canada is experiencing a demographic shift towards an aging population (OECD 2013). A declining student population means there are currently fewer students enrolled in formal schooling. In addition to following the regulations for possible school closure that require extensive consultations with many stakeholders, principals indicated that declining student enrolment could also mean impending layoffs. Staff members are often extremely concerned about job security in these situations, and employment uncertainty can be a barrier to building and sustaining a healthy and positive school environment (Pollock and Hauseman 2015).

Lastly, changing student demographics also includes principals' growing awareness of increased student diversity. Student diversity can include differences based on race, ethnicity, religion, sexual orientation, socio-economic status, cultural heritage, or ability, for example (Ryan 2011). When 70 Ontario principals were asked how they understood student diversity, they tended to respond in terms of race, ethnicity, religion, socio-economic status, student mental health, and different learning styles/abilities (Pollock and Hauseman 2015). This is not surprising, as Canada is a country of immigrants, and has one of the highest per capita immigration rates in the world (Kelley and Trebilcock 2010). Currently, slightly more than 20% of Canada's population was born outside of the country, and a number of different ethnic groups call Canada home (Statistics Canada 2011). As the student population becomes more diverse, principals spend more time fostering relationships with external cultural, religious, and ethnic organizations (Alberta Teachers' Association 2009) and local community organizations (Flessa et al. 2010).

District School Board Demands Schools do not exist in a vacuum; they are part of a larger system that includes school boards/districts, and larger political jurisdictions. Since the development of schooling systems, school principals have often been thought of as "middle managers"—the "overseer[s] of buses, boilers and books" (Whyte 1956, p. 4)—within a hierarchy steeped in bureaucratic processes. From this perspective, principals carry out a number of functions, such as buffering teachers from "outside distractions" (Hendriks and Sheerens 2013). Pressures brought on by external demands can impede principals from focusing on the instructional aspect of their work. Schools have always been accountable in one way or another (Darling-Hammond 1989; Elmore 2005; Firestone and Shipps 2007; Pollock and Winton 2015; Stone et al. 1989) and there are multiple accountability approaches. The current dominant accountability approach in Canada is performance-based accountability (PBA) (Ben Jaafar and Earl 2008). Different approaches to accountability have generated multiple initiatives that directly affect the function of principals and their work. Principals in the Canadian Association of Principals study report that "accountability mandates from the provincial governments and school districts translated to 'reams of paperwork' and 'countless hours filling out reports'" (2014, p. 37). Administrators believe that these accountability measures "force us to report results in a manner that takes away from kids" (p. 37).

Labour Issues Throughout the history of education in Canada, labour relations in the educational sector have been relatively stable, with the occasional periodic dispute. Over the years, provincial government turnovers, legislative changes, and new educational policies have had and continue to have a dramatic impact on work relationships between teachers and school principals. In Ontario and British Columbia, principals are not part of teachers' union but rather are considered part of 'management'. The removal of Ontario principals from the teachers protective labour association has changed the nature of labour relations so that the way principals interact with other educators and staff has also changed (Murakami and Pollock 2014; Pollock and

Hauseman 2015; Wallace 2010). Sixteen percent of Ontario Principals recently identified contracts "that prevent staff from being flexible and willing to support students" as having a negative effect on their workload (Leithwood and Azah 2014, p. 20). The Canadian Association of Principals has also documented that principals in British Columbia "devote far more of their time to warding off and adjudicating labour-management disputes than is the case in other provinces. This deprives them of time that could be used to focus on improving instruction" (2014, p. 83).

10.2 Methodology

Data gathered for this study comes from Ontario, Canada. In Canada, the federal role in schooling is limited; public education falls under provincial jurisdiction (Murakami et al. 2014). In Ontario, 72 district school boards are spread across the following four types of publicly funded school systems:

- English;
- French;
- English-Catholic; and
- French-Catholic.

Data gathered for this study comes primarily from members of a jurisdictional association representing English-language principals and vice-principals in the province. No Catholic or French speaking district school boards were included in this study. A mixed method research design was employed to gather data for this study (Creswell 2009). Data collection methods included focus groups with practicing principals and a large-scale online survey. Each of these methods is described in detail below.

10.2.1 Focus Groups

The focus groups were conducted with principals primarily to gain feedback while developing the online survey. A total of three focus group sessions were conducted with eight principals as part of the survey development process. A diverse sample of participants representing different career stages, genders and locations (rural, urban, suburban) were involved in the focus group sessions. Each focus group session consisted of two distinct parts. During the first hour, participating principals were asked to discuss the nature of their work. In the second part of the focus group sessions principals piloted the survey questions, offering feedback on the survey's overall design, formatting of questions, and content.

10.2.2 Online Survey

The online survey was designed to best represent the broad range of tasks, responsibilities, behaviours, and practices expected of principals in contemporary times, and it was revised a number of times to achieve this goal. Much of the literature cited earlier, and recent changes to jurisdictional education policy (e.g., regulations surrounding equity and inclusion in schools and school-based hiring practices) were captured in the survey questions. After the initial draft of the online survey was reviewed by the study funder, the second stage of survey development involved piloting a revised version of the tool with current school principals during focus groups, which were described in detail above. The final stage of survey development involved incorporating valuable feedback offered by focus group participants into the tool. The final online survey contained 60 questions and asked principals about their work in the following 12 areas:

- how they spend their time;
- duties and responsibilities;
- accountability and external influences;
- challenges and possibilities;
- well-being and job satisfaction;
- work and life balance;
- supports;
- the Ontario Leadership Framework;
- professional development;
- school-level partnerships;
- personal information; and
- school details.

In addition to collecting data on the 12 areas mentioned above, the survey offered principals the opportunity to qualify their responses by providing additional comments when answering certain questions, or/and when they had completed the survey. Only three open-ended survey questions received the number of responses necessary to conduct meaningful quantitative analysis. The analysis involves counts and percentages of the patterns and themes as identified from the comments. Those questions inquired about school-level partnerships with external programs or agencies (1240 unique responses), accountability (854 unique responses), and coping mechanisms (250 unique responses). The "Additional Comments" section at the end of the survey received 788 unique responses. Qualitative data has been woven throughout the article to reinforce findings.

Examples of the questions utilized to measure each of the 12 areas of principals' work explored in the survey can be found in Table 10.1. These are used to highlight antecedents and moderating factors influencing principals and their work.

Table 10.1 Examples of survey items

Area of inquiry	Example of survey question
How principals spend their time	On average, how many hours do you work per week?
Duties and responsibilities	Below are some school-based social programs, please check those that have an impact on your work as a principal
Accountability and external influences	Please rank in order the stakeholders you feel most to least accountable to:
Challenges and possibilities	To what extent does each of the following statements characterize you and your relationship with your school superintendent?
Well-being and job satisfaction	To what extent do you agree or disagree with the following statements about you and your work?
	(a) my school is a good place to work;
	(b) I have a choice in deciding what I do at work;
	(c) I never seem to have enough time to get my work done;
	(d) I can decide when to take a break during my working day;
	(e) I feel pressured to work long hours;
	(f) I can make my own decisions about how I do my work;
	(g) The pace of my work is too fast;
	(h) I know how to get my job done;
	(i) I have the appropriate resources to do my job; and
	(j) My job makes a difference in the school community
Work and life balance	Do you feel you have an appropriate balance between your work and your life outside of work?
Supports	How much support do you receive from the following organizations?
The Ontario leadership framework	Does your current work as a principal reflect the direction of the Ontario Leadership Framework?
Professional development	Within the past 2 years, please rank the top three skills you have needed to develop in order to navigate the changing educational agenda (increased parental involvement, economy focused education, new systems of accountability, *etc.*)?
School-level partnerships	Approximately how many community groups and/or community organizations (*i.e.*, churches, charities, local businesses) are you currently involved in within your school community?
Personal information	What is the highest level of formal education you have completed?
School details	What is the current school enrollment?

10.2.3 Online Survey Sample

The sample consisted of members of the jurisdictional association representing principals and vice-principals in Ontario at the time the survey was online. The sample is made up of principals employed in the English-language school boards at the time the survey was online. The research team was provided with a list of e-mail addresses for all 2701 members of the jurisdictional principals' association, who, at the time of the survey, were designated as principals working in Ontario. Utilizing SurveyMonkey software, each of these principals was sent an individualized URL that led to the online survey. These links were active for 26 days. Despite having direct access to the respondents, a number of additional strategies were employed to encourage principals to share their opinions and make their voices heard using the survey. The research team sent weekly e-mail reminders to principals who had yet to complete the survey. Further, website updates and tweets were also employed to encourage participation. These strategies help explain why the survey was able to achieve such a high response rate (52.68%). The response rate is based on 1423 completed surveys available for analysis after accounting for missing data and eliminating ineligible respondents.

Characteristics of the Sample The sample of principals who participated in the online survey was diverse in some ways, and less diverse in others. For example, 62.8% of the principals who responded to the online survey self-identified as female, while the remaining 36.2% of participants self-identified as male. A total of 77.3% of principals worked in elementary school contexts, while 16.4% were secondary principals, and 2.9% were principals of both elementary and secondary schools. The average number of years of experience as a principal for the total sample is 7.6 years. Respondents' average school size was 493 students, and school sizes ranged from 25 to approximately 2200 students. When asked about the highest level of formal education they had completed, 54.3% reported having a Master's degree in addition to their undergraduate degrees. This is compared to 41.6% of the sample who hold bachelor's degrees as their highest level of formal education. An additional 2.4% of principals in this sample indicated that they have earned a professional degree (*i.e.*, LLB, JD), while only 1.3% have completed a doctorate or other terminal degree.

As mentioned earlier, the principals who participated in this study were less diverse in other areas. For instance, the vast majority of principals (91.4%) self-identified as heterosexual. A total of 3.4% of principals who responded to the online survey self-identified as gay or lesbian, with smaller numbers of participants self-identifying as bisexual and transgendered (both under 1% of the sample). It is worth mentioning that an additional 2.7% of participating principals indicated that they would prefer to not disclose this information. Ethnicity is another area where the sample lacks diversity, with 92.5% of the entire sample self-identifying as Caucasian. A further 1.6% of the sample self-identified as black, with 1.3% self-identifying as South Asian. While these percentages are representative of the Ontario principal workforce, they do not represent the Ontario general population where approximately 25% are from visible minoritized groups (Statistics Canada 2011), or Ontario's student population (Pollock et al. 2014).

10.2.4 Data Analysis

The data analysis focuses on areas that influence principals' work, such as jurisdictional policies, administrative duties and responsibilities, external influences, partnerships, and challenges and possibilities. These variables speak more to the "organizational path" than the other pathways as identified in Leithwood, Anderson,

Mascall and Strauss' book chapter (2010). The analysis of these organizational variables supplements, if not precedes, Leithwood and colleagues' study by looking into the antecedents and moderators that have significant impact on school principals' work. In the present study factor analysis was used to investigate variable relationships for the aforementioned complex areas (e.g., jurisdictional policies, administrative duties and responsibilities, external influences, partnerships, and challenges and possibilities). Such analysis is designed to identify similar patterns of responses in the multiple observed variables. The factor analysis also investigates concepts that are not easily measured directly by reducing a large number of variables into a few interpretable underlying and potent factors. Variables that significantly explain the overall variance of the factors are used in the multiple regression analysis, which is employed to understand, among the organizational variables, which ones have a significant impact on principals' work.

Principal components analysis with varimax rotation and Kaiser Normalization were conducted to obtain conceptually similar and significant clusters of issues on how principals spend their time, their responses to jurisdictional policies, external influences, and challenges and possibilities. These two procedures produce results designed to cluster individual variables into single factors. Eigenvalues are employed when making decisions about the number of factors that will be extracted as part of the factor analysis process. In this case, Eigenvalues, equal to or greater than 1.00 were extracted.

Additional descriptive statistics and correlation analysis were also conducted to supplement the factor analysis. The descriptive statistics were presented in percentages to provide a summary of a particular area in the data. Correlation analysis was used to explore relationships among variables that might have predictive abilities across factors.

10.3 Results

The changing work structure has a significant impact on principals as well as on their school performance. Principals are experiencing increased expectations at work both in terms of the number of tasks they are expected to undertake and the duration of time they are required to complete those tasks; they have many tasks to perform and less time to carry them out. The research findings report on factors that contribute to principals' work intensification, and how such factors influence principals' leadership practices. Each of the following four areas consisted of factors that moderate principals' work:

- administrative duties and responsibilities;
- jurisdictional policies;
- external influences and partnerships; and
- challenges and possibilities

Antecedents on principals' work for these four areas will be discussed in the remainder of this article.

10.3.1 Administrative Duties and Responsibilities

Our research indicates that principals spend approximately 59 h per week at work, 14 h a week more than other Canadian occupational managers (Association of Professional Executives of the Public Service of Canada 2013). Most of the principals who responded to this survey indicated that they are hardworking by nature, but that workload demands are making the position increasingly challenging. For instance, in qualitative responses reported in the "Additional Comments" section, one principal mentioned, "I am not afraid of hard work or long hours because of my personal work ethic but I do feel resentful that I am chained to the job." Another principal stated, "I love my job. I love what I do. I just cannot do it."

As the volume of principals' work increases, their administrative duties and responsibilities are becoming more complicated as well. Fifteen variables related to principals' administrative duties and responsibilities utilized in the survey are listed in Table 10.2.[1] Analysis of the 15 variables (orthogonal rotation) yielded four factors,[2] accounting for 29.9%, 10.2%, 8.6%, and 7.3% of the total variance respectively, a total of 55.9% of the total variance explained. The factor loadings are presented in Table 10.2. To enhance the interpretability of the factors, only variables with factor loads as follows were selected for inclusion in their respective factors: >0.51 (factor one), >0.57 (factor two), >0.57 (factor three), and >0.82 (factor four). The factors are named, respectively, *administrative management, instructional leadership, interactions with students and parents,* and *professional development.* These factors indicate that principals spend their time each week mostly on these four areas.

Specifically, with regard to administrative management, principals reported spending more time on budget (factor loading = 0.71) and personnel (factor loading = 0.68). Budget and personnel are more correlated to administrative management than occupational health and safety, building maintenance, internal school management, and district school board office committees. The analysis also brought attention to principals' occupational health and safety, which has a significant correlation to the administrative management factor with a loading of 0.66. Among the items of the second factor, classroom walk-throughs are highly correlated to instructional leadership (factor loading = 0.82). On average, principals spend 12.7% of their day in classrooms. The analysis also revealed that principals spend a significant amount of time interacting with students and parents. Such interaction focuses particularly on student discipline (factor loading = 0.81) on which principals spend an average of 7.6 h per week; 52.7% of principals confirm that is the amount of time they should spend on student discipline. Principals' professional development (PD) is another important factor in terms of how principals spend their time. In order to navigate the current educational climate, principals felt that it was important to

---

[1] Boldface shows loadings for each factor and underlines indicate cross loadings. This also applies to other tables on factor analysis results

[2] The item "community" has cross loadings on factor 1 and 2 and is deleted in order to enhance the quality of variables for final factor analysis

Table 10.2 How principals spend their time

Variables	Administrative management Factor 1	Instructional leadership Factor 2	Interaction with students & parents Factor 3	Professional development Factor 4
Student discipline	−0.117	−0.043	**0.806**	0.031
Student-related activities	0.103	0.189	**0.599**	0.182
Student transportation	0.207	0.186	0.441	−0.089
Working with parents	0.355	0.217	**0.574**	0.087
DSB office committees	**0.519**	−0.257	0.095	0.497
Principals' PD	0.002	0.191	0.108	**0.822**
Curriculum & instructionalleadership	0.232	**0.573**	−0.025	0.517
Budget	**0.710**	0.204	0.180	0.115
Personnel	**0.686**	0.019	0.150	0.117
Internal school management	**0.610**	0.092	−0.088	0.089
Walking hallways, playground, lunchroom	0.131	**0.611**	0.296	−0.034
Classroom walk-throughs	0.139	**0.819**	0.150	0.174
Building maintenance	**0.631**	0.497	0.181	0.043
Occupational health & safety	**0.683**	0.230	0.155	−0.159

develop their skills in the area of emotional intelligence, communication skills, and knowledge of teaching and learning. Seventy-four percent of school principals expressed their desire for more time and opportunities to engage in professional development. Based on principals' estimate, Table 10.3 presents an overview of how they spend their time on each of the activities at their work. In average, principals spent approximately 7.6 h per week on student discipline and 7.5 h per week on internal school management. These two activities take up a significant amount of principals' time among all their work activities.

10.3.2 Policies

Recent jurisdictional policy changes are another factor having an impact on principals' work. Recent policy changes that have influenced principals' work, listed in descending order, with the most impactful at the top, can be found in Table 10.4. In particular, policies such as Regulation 274/12 (a policy amending school-level hiring practices), Growing Success (a policy governing assessment, evaluation, and reporting in Ontario Schools) and Bill 212 (the jurisdictional Safe Schools Act) are having a large impact on principals' work.

Table 10.3 Time spent on each activity

Variables	Number of hours spent per week
Student discipline	7.6
Student-related activities	5.2
Student transportation	1.2
Working with parents	5.6
DSB office committees	5.4
Principals' PD	2
Curriculum & instructional leadership	5
Budget	1.8
Personnel	5.6
Internal school management	7.5
Walking hallways, playground, lunchroom	5.8
Classroom walk-throughs	3.1
Building maintenance	1.8
Occupational health & safety	1.5

Table 10.4 Provincial policies that influence principals' work

Policies	None	A lot	N/A
Regulation 274/12 – Hiring Practice	0.7%	79.6%	1.0%
Growing success	0.1%	77.4%	0.3%
Safe school act – Bill 21	0.2%	69.1%	0.4%
Bill 13 – Anti-bullying	0.3%	65.7%	0.3%
Bill 115 – Putting students first act	1.0%	65.4%	0.1%
Full day kindergarten – Full day early learning statute amendment act	11.6%	50.5%	18.6%
Information and communication technologies in Ed management	4.0%	48.3%	1.7%
Equity and inclusive education strategy	1.2%	43.1%	1.2%
Occupational health and safety act	3.3%	34.8%	Nil
Parents in partnership: Parent engagement policy	3.1%	24.0%	0.3%
Fluctuating enrolment/school closures	27.3%	23.4%	10.9%
Aboriginal education strategy/FNMI policy framework	29.8%	6.8%	4.3%
Urban priority high schools initiative	39.6%	2.2%	49.2%

Additional analysis also indicated that provincial policies are influencing principals' work. With a factor loading of 0.787, provincial mandates were found to significantly affect the work of principals (See Table 10.5).

Correlation analysis suggests that school principals who indicated that Regulation 274/12 had an impact on their work also showed that they spend more hours each week performing administrative management duties ($r = 0.091$), in areas such as budgeting, personnel, occupational health and safety, building maintenance, internal school management, and district school board office committees. For instance, one principal indicated: "Reg. 274 reduces the principal's ability to hire the best

Table 10.5 Provincial policies and principals' work

Policies	Safe schools Factor 1	Enrolment & technology Factor 2	Aboriginal & early childhood education Factor 3	Hiring & school improvement Factor 4
Aboriginal education strategy	0.345	−0.008	**−0.539**	−0.055
Bill 115	**0.581**	−0.020	−0.141	0.288
Bill 13 – Anti-bullying	**0.768**	−0.027	−0.044	0.020
Equity & inclusive education strategy	**0.654**	0.063	−0.033	−0.115
Fluctuating enrolment/school closures	−0.017	**0.603**	−0.408	−0.140
Full day kindergarten	0.144	−0.035	**0.763**	0.007
Growing success	0.349	0.363	0.029	0.288
Information & communication technologies	0.053	**0.758**	0.060	0.096
Occupational health & safety act	**0.488**	0.329	0.038	−0.104
Parents in partnership	**0.477**	0.379	0.310	−0.172
Regulation 274/12	0.130	0.271	0.042	**0.631**
Safe schools act	**0.608**	0.090	0.055	0.085
Urban priority high schools initiative	0.122	0.216	−0.031	**−0.672**

candidate, plus it has resulted in countless hours of work for Human Resources and Administrators." Another principal used the "Additional Comments" section of the survey to state: "the implementation of Reg. 274 has made this work extremely stressful and difficult, as I have not been able to choose the best person for my school and community." Regulation 274/12 seems particularly problematic for principals as it represents both a loss of autonomy and can have a negative impact on the teaching and learning occurring at the school-level.

The Growing Success policy is also having an impact on principals' work. Correlation analysis suggests that principals who rated high on the Growing Success tend to spend more time on both administrative management ($r = 0.058$) and instructional leadership ($r = 0.064$). The impact of Bill 212 (the jurisdictional safe schools act) also prompts principals to spend more time interacting with students and parents ($r = 0.118$). Although the correlation between the impact of these policies and principals' work is relatively small, it does imply that a single jurisdictional policy can increase principals' workload and shift the focus of their daily practice. Take Regulation 274/12 as an example; the comments by principals quoted above reveal that Regulation 274/12 represents a loss of autonomy, forces principals to hire perceived to be lower quality teaching staff, and diverts principals' attention away from

Table 10.6 Principals' perceptions of the impact of provincial policies on their work

Variables	None	A little	Some	A lot	N/A
Aboriginal education strategy	29.8%	39.7%	18.8%	6.8%	4.3%
Bill 115	1.0%	5.3%	27.1%	65.4%	0.1%
Bill 13 – Anti-bullying	0.3%	3.9%	29.1%	65.7%	0.3%
Equity & inclusive education strategy	1.2%	10.5%	44.3%	43.1%	1.2%
Fluctuating enrolment/school closures	27.3%	19.3%	18.0%	23.4%	10.9%
Full day kindergarten	11.6%	5.2%	13.2%	50.5%	18.6%
Growing success	0.1%	2.2%	19.2%	77.4%	0.3%
Information & communication technologies	4.0%	11.5%	34.0%	48.3%	1.7%
Occupational health & safety act	3.3%	18.2%	43.1%	34.8%	Nil
Parents in partnership	3.1%	25.1%	46.5%	24.0%	0.3%
Regulation 274/12	0.7%	4.0%	13.9%	79.6%	1.0%
Safe schools act	0.2%	4.2%	24.8%	69.1%	0.4%
Urban priority high schools initiative	39.6%	4.9%	2.4%	2.2%	49.2%

instructional leadership (Pollock et al. 2014). These are all unintended consequences of a policy decision in which principals had little voice, and which may ultimately impact student learning. Percentages from principals' ratings regarding each provincial policy are displayed in Table 10.6. The results reveal principals' perceptions of each provincial policy and its impact on their work.

10.3.3 External Influences and Partnerships

In addition to policy impact from district school boards and the Ministry of Education, external organizations and partnerships also exert various influences on principals' work and their work environment. The ways in which external influences and partnerships moderate the work of school principals will be discussed in the following subsections.

External Influences A factor analysis on the influence of external organizations on principals' work yields three factors: system organizations, school-community connection, and unions (see Table 10.7),[3] these three factors account for 36.0%, 18.7%, and 10.3% of the total variance (65.0%), respectively.

The results show that within the educational system, the Literacy and Numeracy Secretariat (LNS) has the greatest correlations with the system organizations. The LNS was established in 2004 to work with schools and district school boards across Ontario to build capacity and implement strategies to improve reading, writing, and math skills. Though the LNS was only mentioned by two principals in the "Additional Comments" section, these two principals indicated that the LNS provides a positive

---

[3] The item School Council is not included in the analysis as its influence originates within the school.

Table 10.7 External influences

Organizations	System organizations Factor 1	School-community connection Factor 2	Unions Factor 3
District school board	**0.565**	−0.397	0.227
Ministry of education	**0.659**	−0.299	0.367
Ontario college of teachers	**0.733**	0.191	0.306
Education quality and accountability office	**0.715**	−0.073	0.275
Literacy and Numeracy Secretariat (LNS)	**0.819**	0.095	−0.003
Ministry of labour	<u>0.554</u>	0.049	<u>0.521</u>
Teachers' unions	0.190	0.018	**0.875**
Other unions (e.g., CUPE)	0.161	0.103	**0.861**
Church/Faith Organization	0.121	**0.788**	0.007
Professional associations (e.g., OPC)	**0.706**	0.254	0.028
Community organizations (e.g., youth employment)	0.159	**0.862**	0.075
Other	−0.114	**0.722**	0.067

Note: To enhance the interpretability of the factors, only variables with factor loads as follows were selected for inclusion in their respective factors: >0.56 (factor one), >0.72 (factor two) and >0.86 (factor three).

influence on principals' ability to be instructional leaders. For example, one principal stated: "Instructionally, I have found the conferences and monographs, *etc.* from LNS to be very helpful in my work as a curriculum leader." The LNS's influence on principals' work is also reflected in the policy titled *Growing Success*. Second to the LNS's influence on principals' work is that of the Ontario College of Teachers, the regulatory body for the teaching profession in Ontario.

Data analysis indicated that the Ministry of Labour has cross loadings on both system organizations and unions. In simpler terms, this finding implies that the Ministry of Labour, and in turn, occupational health and safety concerns, play a unique role in moderating principals' work by impacting the way principals interact with other system organizations and unions. The additional comments provided by principals who participated in the survey offer further evidence to highlight the power the Ministry of Labour wields over principals in Ontario's school system. For instance, typical comments related to this issue focused on how the attention principals pay to Ministry of Labour requirements takes time away from their roles as instructional leaders. One principal mentioned: "the amount of health and safety legislations and requirements that have nothing to do with education need to be reduced or given to other staff to oversee." Another principal stated: "Occupational Health and Safety, Ministry of Labour…coupled with the downloading of work have all contributed to a very fast paced job." These comments typify principals' views of how attention paid to occupational health and safety requirements takes time away from their roles as instructional leaders.

Partnerships Principals in Ontario are expected to build relationships with community organizations and agencies connected to the students and communities the school serves. Approximately 75.8% of school principals in our sample were involved in between one and five partnerships at the school level. These findings indicate community organizations—such as faith-based organizations or youth employment agencies—have an influence on what principals do. In the "Additional Comments" section of the survey, principals indicated that school-community connections add more tasks and activities to their workload and diminish time available for high-priority tasks, such as those related to instruction. For example, one principal wrote that partnerships "add significantly to my workload and take away time that could be spent on instructional leadership and interacting with students and staff." Similarly, another principal stated that various partnerships "all significantly add to my workload, but all of these are very important." Notably, unions also play an important role in principals' work, particularly the provincial teachers' unions that does not include principals. This separation of principals and teachers into two different professional groups creates conflict, and was evident in recent labour strife between the provincial teachers' union and the Ontario government. Data analysis shows that approximately 31.7% of school principals feel that unions not at all or only somewhat respect them.

10.3.4 Challenges and Possibilities

Principals identified a number of challenges and possibilities associated with their work. Analysis revealed two main areas: work with teachers, and interactions with the school community and social environment. Some of these challenges can turn into possibilities; for example, with the development of high levels of trust between teachers and principals, some of their work can have a positive indirect effect on student achievement. Challenges related to student mental health and special education appear to be particularly complex in nature. Although our presentation of findings focuses mainly on challenges, they imply that such challenges can also be possibilities for principals if they are able to cope with and mitigate some of these challenges appropriately.

Teachers Teachers present principals with some of the greatest challenges and possibilities found in their work. A factor analysis yielded the following four teacher-related factors eliciting an impact on principals and their work: principal-teacher interaction (24.5%), teacher readiness and resistance (18.0%), induction and turnover (9.2%), and teacher professional development and growth (8.5%).

These factors account for 60.2% of the total variance explained, and are represented in Table 10.8.

Challenges related to student mental health and special education appear to be particularly complex in nature. Being open to discussing classroom issues with teachers speaks to principals practicing the instructional leadership aspects of their

Table 10.8 Possibilities and challenges: Teachers

Principal-teacher teacher readiness induction & teacher PD				
Items	Interaction Factor 1	& resistance Factor 2	Turnover Factor 3	& growth Factor 4
Discuss classroom issues with teachers	**0.781**	0.016	−0.023	−0.112
Open to hearing different perspectives	**0.761**	−0.042	0.009	0.095
Let teachers know the expectations	**0.757**	0.029	0.015	−0.133
Care about teachers' personal welfare	**0.608**	−0.231	0.051	0.179
Lack of teacher knowledge and skills	0.065	**0.621**	0.055	0.377
Lack of time for teacher planning and PD	0.059	0.122	−0.002	**0.851**
Lack of time to evaluate teachers	−0.095	0.164	0.311	**0.693**
Difficult recruiting and hiring the right teachers	0.025	0.238	**0.720**	0.151
Teacher turnover	0.048	0.012	**0.807**	0.065
Difficulty terminating under-performing teachers from the school	−0.062	**0.532**	0.464	0.043
Teacher and staff apathy and resistance to change	−0.150	**0.792**	0.146	0.123
Lack of trust between teachers and parents/guardians	−0.047	**0.786**	0.066	0.011

role, while a willingness to hear different perspectives requires trust between principals and teachers. Both of the variables described above demonstrate possibilities available in contemporary work, particularly around building capacity: the benefits of building relationships with teachers and carving out time to be instructional leaders. However, these possibilities, which are built on positive relationships between principals and teachers, may be undermined by lack of trust between principals and teachers (factor loading = 0.786), and resistance from teachers and staff (factor loading = 0.792). These dual threats pose the greatest challenges to principals in their work. Further, principals also face challenges from teacher induction and turnover, which can change the composition in teacher quality, and eventually have a disruptive effect on school performance. A lack of time for teacher professional development (factor loading = 0.851) and growth through teacher evaluation (factor loading = 0.693) are additional teacher-related challenges that impact principals' work.

School Community and Environment The myriad of challenges and possibilities encountered by principals in their work stems not only from teachers, but also from students, parents, the school community, and the larger political context (see Table 10.9).

After preparing the data for analysis using an orthogonal rotation of the variables, the 12 variables listed in the left-hand column of Table 10.9 clustered around the three factors at the top of the table. The three factors—school community (32.6%), political environment (14.9%), and student mental health and discipline (9.5%)—account for 57.0% of the total variance explained. The analysis indicates that negative stereotypes about the school community (factor loading = 0.812), racial or ethnic tensions at the school-level (factor loading = 0.796), and social problems with the community (factor loading = 0.744) are the most important elements associated with school community. Thus, the school community is having an impact on principals' work. Within the larger political context, pressure to constantly adopt new programs (factor loading = 0.783), and a lack of recognition for principals (factor loading = 0.709) also significantly affect principals' work. The cross loadings of "lack of special education support/resources" on factor 2 and 3 merit attention. It reveals that the political environment may affect the adequacy of support and resources that are needed for special education. It also suggests that issues concerning students' mental health and discipline can be aggravated or alleviated, dependent on the availability and adequacy of special education support and resources. Notably, mental health issues among students/parents (factor loading = 0.804), and student discipline (factor loading = 0.750) were identified as important factors that impact principals' work. For instance, in the "Additional Comments" section, principals mentioned: "the significant increase in initiatives from the Ministry and Board in the past five years has greatly impacted our ability to manage our schools." Another principal put it more bluntly, stating simply: "the pressures increase yearly." Principals also play a pivotal role in creating an environment that supports healthy choices and safe schools. A perceived lack of special education support/resources has cross loadings, or a large effect, on both the political environment and mental health and discipline. Perhaps this challenge is best explained by the following comment provided by one of the participating principals:

> …mental health of students and parents is a huge issue that impacts not only on my time, but my own emotions and wellbeing. I did not receive psychiatric training, but often feel as if I should have, given the amount of time I spend with adults with severe mental health issues.

This finding and the quote above demonstrate that special education and student mental health and discipline issues have a strong and interrelated influence on the work principals do on a daily basis.

10.4 Discussion

Scholars have put a great deal of effort into determining how school leadership influences student performance. Many of these efforts have focused on developing direct or indirect-effects models to determine promising leadership practices (Bossert et al. 1982; Hendriks and Sheerens 2013; Hallinger et al. 2013; Mulford 2003; Silins and Mulford 2004). These inquires continue today (Leithwood, Patten and Jantzi, 2010), and are generating some promising practices for principals. Our findings, however, suggest that other factors not mentioned in the models, such as student mental health and discipline, political environment, system organizations, school–community connections, unions, and administrative management, to name a few, also need to be considered. Including these factors may help to extend the model to its antecedents and present a comprehensive picture of principals' work.

Table 10.9 Possibilities and challenges: School community and environment

Items	School community Factor 1	Political environment Factor 2	Student mental health & discipline Factor 3
Pressure to constantly adopt new programs	0.071	**0.783**	0.097
Provincial mandates (SE, ELL, *etc.*)	0.031	**0.787**	0.171
Lack of recognition for principals	0.152	**0.709**	0.024
Lack of special education support/resources	−0.070	0.455	0.426
Union issues	0.113	**0.534**	0.116
Student discipline (bullying, aggressive behaviour, *etc.*)	0.176	0.121	**0.750**
Mental health issues among students/parents	0.157	0.093	**0.804**
Parents/guardians apathetic or irresponsible about their children	0.315	0.188	**0.648**
Lack of support from the school's community	**0.581**	0.207	0.327
Social problems in the school's community (poverty, gangs, drugs, *etc.*)	**0.744**	0.043	0.347
Racial or ethnic tensions in the school's community	**0.796**	0.108	−0.012
Negative stereotypes about this school's community	**0.812**	0.036	0.136

They demonstrate that while principals do engage in many of the practices associated with instructional leadership, there are other factors that influence their work and compel them to engage in other practices as well. The increasing number of tasks required of principals complicates their work. More than this though, these tasks take time that principals often do not have. Many refer to this phenomenon as work intensification (Allan et al. 1999).

Current models imply that the groups of practices included within them are predominantly the only practices that principals engage in to fulfill their role. These models also give the impression that principals' work occurs in isolation. This is not the case. Our findings indicate a number of factors—some connected to instructional leadership and others not—interact to complicate principals' work. For example, multiple policies influence principals' work. Our data indicates that Regulation 274/12 and Bill 212 play a large role in what principals do in Ontario. These policies also influence principals' ability to engage in practices thought to directly/indirectly influence student outcomes. However, each policy does so in very different ways. For example, many Ontario principals believe that Regulation 274/12, which deals with hiring practices, influences their work because it is perceived to reduce principals decision-making when hiring teachers; it prevents them from hiring teachers they believe are the best fit for their school context. Ultimately, not having the best teachers will have an impact on student learning.

Our data also indicated that two other policies influence principals' focus on student learning: The Growing Success initiative and the Safe Schools Act. The Growing Success (2010) policy focuses on assessment, reporting processes for Ontario schools. This policy does support principals' work in relation to instructional leadership by providing a framework for assessment and including a formalized reporting process. However, some procedures required for data management can take away from other more relevant tasks that have a more direct impact on student outcomes. Bill 212, the Safe Schools Act, also influences principals' work. While this policy appropriately prompts principals to spend more time interacting with students and parents (which is also not necessarily a negative outcome), it also requires principals to devote considerably more time to paper work. This paper pushing, in turn, takes time away from engaging in instructional leadership practices.

Principals do not work in a vacuum; the work they do is always connected to a variety of practices and contexts. This was clear when we considered external influences such as system organizations, school–community connections and teacher unions. Since schools became part of school districts they have always had some connection to system organizations. However, it is the level of interaction with existing system organizations and the increase in interactions with additional system organizations that can also influence the work of school principals. For example, we have argued elsewhere that Ontario is experiencing a move to more centralized control of public education (Galway et al. 2013; Murakami and Pollock 2014; Sattler 2012). Our findings demonstrate that the Literacy and Numeracy Secretariat (LNS), for example, which is part of the Ministry of Education, has a significant impact on system organizations. In one sense, this is not surprising since the LNS is meant to support principals and schools in improving students outcomes and principals' instructional leadership endeavors. However, it is yet another initiative that demands more time from principals.

In addition to Ontario's traditional system organizations (district school boards and the ministry of education), other organizations impact schools such as the Educational Quality and Accountability Office (EQAO), the Ontario College of Teachers (OCT) and the Ministry of Labour. Of these organizations, our analysis determined that Ministry of Labour Policies, laws, and programs influence principals' work most significantly. As indicated in the findings, the Ministry of labour plays a unique role in moderating principals' work by influencing the way principals interact with other system organizations and teacher unions. The Ministry of Labour's mandate is not to promote student success but to "advance safe, fair and harmonious workplace practices" (Ontario Ministry of Labour n.d., n.p.). It does this by requiring that principals attend to occupational health and safety, employment rights and responsibilities, and labour relations. Ontario principals have a duty to abide by regulations that serve the employees in the school building rather than student learning. The repercussions of not fulfilling these duties can be severe for principals, and therefore, they tend to prioritize some of these tasks over other practices that may have a stronger connection to instructional leadership and student outcomes.

School–community connection and unions also influence principals' work. As mentioned earlier, Canada (and Ontario) caters to an increasingly diverse student population. Approximately, 76% of school principals are involved in between one and five partnerships at the school level. Successful partnerships occur when there is a (a) clear goal established; (b) relationships built on trust; (c) way to communicate and share information; (d) process for decision-making; (e) ongoing connections; and (f) key stakeholders involved (Finn-Stevenson 2014; Thomas et al. 2010). All of these necessary partnership components require principal involvement, and this involvement translates into additional formal and informal meetings, and additional communications and tasks specific to the partnership—all requiring additional time. While the outcome may indirectly influence student outcomes, there is only so much time that individuals have during a day, week or month, and so principals have to prioritize their work tasks. Our analysis of possibilities and challenges also indicates that even though principals are involved in multiple partnerships within their schools, they do so at times when there is lack of support from the school's community and in situations that are less than ideal, such as when school communities are facing social issues such as poverty, gangs and drug use, racial or ethnic tensions—all issues that add to the complexity of school principals' work.

Ontario principals face other challenges that interfere with efforts to improve student learning. One of these involves union issues. Ontario has a highly unionized teacher workforce. Principals are not part of teacher unions. Our findings indicate tensions between unions (both teacher and other) and principals. Many principals indicated that they did not feel respected by the unions with which they dealt. As in any highly unionized work place, managers (principals in this case) have to figure out ways to work with others. Our findings suggest that teachers presented principals with some of the greatest challenges in their work. This is not surprising, given that the largest labour group principals work with are teachers. Instructional leadership involves working with teachers and so it is not a surprise that principal–teacher interaction ranked the highest of all four factors when it came to who presented principals with some of the greatest challenges.

Principals also have to deal increasingly with mental health issues. Recent studies have identified that student mental health is an emerging concern that needs to be addressed (Canadian Association of Principals 2014; Leithwood and Azah 2014; Pollock et al. 2014). Issues connected to student mental health and well-being are also influencing principals' work. As our findings indicate, student mental health is often not a single factor, but is connected to student discipline and dealing with parents. When principals utilize their time to engage in activities such as finding community resources, securing referrals or mediating transitioning plans for students, they will not be engaged in instructional leadership tasks, activities or behaviors.

Our analysis demonstrates how various factors and antecedents interact to complicate principals' work. Further exploration of direct/indirect models need to take into consideration factors that moderate principals' work. Many parts of our analysis are not surprising to both practitioners and researchers; the more important question is to ask why? What is happening? Our data indicate that principals are experiencing two things: loss of autonomy and work intensification. Because of a more centralized schooling system and subsequent changes in how work is to be carried out, principals are becoming more like atypical middle managers with reduced power and decision-making. Evidence to support this includes a reduced voice in hiring teachers, increased influences outside the school site, and extensive policy driven action and practices, to name a few.

Principals are experiencing work intensification. In addition to some of the factors reported here that influence principals' work, we know that principals are working long hours. This work is also intensifying at a rapid pace (Leithwood and Azah 2014; Pollock et al. 2014). Ontario principals spend approximately 59 h/week at work (Pollock et al. 2014), 8 h/week more than Canadian occupational managers (Statistics Canada n.d.) and public sector professional executives, who work on average 51 h/week (Association of Professional Executives of the Public Service of Canada 2013). Yet, 87% of principals indicated they never seem to have enough time to do their work, while more than 72% of participating principals felt pressured to work long hours and only 38% felt they had the resources necessary to do their job properly. The trend toward work intensification is not isolated to Canada. In a 2013 survey by the National Association for Head Teachers in the UK, 78.9% of school leaders reported that their workload had increased compared to a year ago. Also, the 2013 Teaching and Learning International Survey shows that participating countries consistently ranked high workload, inadequate resources, and government regulations as the top three barriers to principal effectiveness. Not only is principals' work intense, requiring multiple task and activities, it is complex as many of these factors are interconnected.

10.5 Conclusions

Many studies of educational leadership focus on how educational leadership affects student achievement and school performance, and whether such an effect is direct (Witziers et al. 2003) or indirect (Mulford 2003; Silins and Mulford 2004). A common understanding among scholars is that educational leadership plays a pivotal role in improving student achievement. Leadership approaches, such as transformational leadership (Leithwood and Jantzi 2000) and instructional leadership (Marks and Printy 2003), are often identified as particularly important. Given the increasing complexity of principals' work and increasingly diverse student populations in schools, many factors interact to have an impact on school leaders and their work. In addition to looking into how leadership affects student achievement and school performance, it is also important to investigate what factors influence principals' choices of leadership approaches and practices. We argue that principals' choices of leadership approaches and practices are subject to factors that exist within and beyond schools. Such factors moderate the way that principals carry out their work and limit their choices in exercising their professional autonomy. Our study provides empirical evidence on factors that should be taken into account in leadership roles and practices. Sensitivity to these factors will help to enhance the effects of school principals' work, which ideally will lead to better student achievement and school performance.

References

Alberta Teachers' Association (ATA). (2009). *Leadership for learning: The experience of administrators in Alberta schools.* Retrieved from https://www.teachers.ab.ca/SiteCollectionDocuments/ATA/Publications/Research/PD-86-14%20Leadership%20for%20Learning.pdf

Allan, C., O'Donnell, M., & Peetz, D. (1999). More tasks, less secure, working harder: Three dimensions of labour utilisation. *Journal of Industrial Relations., 41*, 519–535.

Applebaum, P. D. (1992). *The concept of work: Ancient, medieval and modern.* Albany: SUNY Press.

Association of Professional Executives of the Public Service of Canada. (2013). *APEX 2012 executive work and health survey.* Available online: http://www.apex.gc.ca/uploads/key%20priorities/health/2012%20health%20survey%20results%20-%20eng.pdf

Auerbach, S. (2010). Beyond coffee with the principal: Toward leadership for authentic school-family partnerships. *Journal of School Leadership, 20*, 728–757.

Bakker, A. B., van Emmerik, H., & Euwema, M. C. (2006). Crossover of burnout and engagement in work teams. *Work and Occupations, 33*, 464–489.

Ben Jaafar, S., & Earl, L. (2008). Comparing performance-based accountability models: A Canadian example. *Canadian Journal of Education, 31*, 697–728.

Best, A., & Holmes, B. (2010). Systems thinking, knowledge and action: Towards better models and methods. *Evidence and Policy, 6*, 145–159.

Bickmore, K. (2011). Policies and programming for safer schools: Are anti-bullying approaches impeding education for peacebuilding? *Educational Policy, 24*, 648–687.

Blakesley, S. (2012). Juggling educational ends: Non-Indigenous Yukon principals and the policy challenges that they face. *International Journal of Education Policy and Leadership, 7*, 1–14.

Bossert, S. T., Dwyer, D. C., Rowan, B., & Lee, G. V. (1982). The instructional management role of the principal. *Educational Administration Quarterly, 18*, 34–64.

Brewer, D. (1993). Principals and student outcomes: Evidence from U.S. high schools. *Economics of Education Review, 12*, 281–292.

Brockmeier, L. T., Sermon, J. M., & Hope, W. C. (2005). Principals' relationship with computer technology. *NAASP Bulletin, 89*, 45–57.

Canadian Association of Principals. (2014). *The future of the principalship in Canada: A national research study.* Retrieved from http://www.teachers.ab.ca/SiteCollectionDocuments/ATA/Publications/Research/The%20Future%20of%20the%20Principalship%20in%20Canada.pdf

Chan, T. C. (2000). Beyond the status quo: Creating a school maintenance program. *Principal Leadership, 3*, 64–67.

Clandfield, D. (2010). The school as a community hub: A public alternative to the neoliberal threat to Ontario schools. *Our Schools Our Selves, 19*, 5–74.

Creswell, J. W. (2009). *Research design: Qualitative, quantitative, and mixed method approaches* (3rd ed.). Los Angeles: Sage.

Darling-Hammond, L. (1989). Accountability for professional practice. *Teachers College Record, 91*, 59–80.

Day, C., Sammons, P., Hopkins, D, Harris, A., Leithwood, K, Gu, Q., Brown, E., Ahtaridou, E., & Kington, A. (2009). *The impact of school leadership on pupil outcomes (Research report RR108).* Nottingham: National College for School Leadership: (NCSL).

Drago, R. (2007). *Striking a balance: Work, family, life*. Boston: Dollars and Sense.
Eberts, R. W., & Stone, J. A. (1998). Student achievement in public schools: Do principals make a difference? *Economics of Education Review, 7*, 291–299.
Elmore, R. (2005). Accountable leadership. *The Educational Forum, 69*, 134–142.
Fink, D. (2010). *The succession challenge building and sustaining leadership capacity through succession management*. New York: Sage.
Finn-Stevenson, M. (2014). Family, school, and community partnerships: Practical strategies for afterschool programs. *New Directions for Youth Development, 144*, 89–103.
Firestone, W. A., & Shipps, D. (2007). How do leaders interpret conflicting accountabilities to improve student learning? In W. A. Firestone & C. Riehl (Eds.), *A new agenda for research in educational leadership* (pp. 81–100). New York: Teachers College Press.
Flessa, J., Gallagher-Mackay, K., & Parker, D. C. (2010). Good, steady progress: Success stories from Ontario elementary schools in challenging circumstances. *Canadian Journal of Educational Administration and Policy, 100*, 1–38.
Fullan, M. (2014). *The principal: Three keys to maximizing impact*. San Francisco: Jossey-Bass.
Galway, G., Sheppard, B., Weins, J., & Brown, J. (2013). The impact of centralization on local school governance in Canada. *Canadian Journal of Educational Administration and Policy, 145*, 1–34.
Gamst, F. C. (1995). *Meanings of work: Considerations for the 21st century*. New York: SUNY Press.
Hallinger, P. (2011). A review of three decades of doctoral studies using the principal instructional management rating scale: A lens on methodological progress in educational leadership. *Educational Administration Quarterly, 47*, 271–306.
Hallinger, P., Wang, W., & Chen, C. (2013). Assessing the measurement properties of the principal instructional management rating scale: A meta-analysis of reliability studies. *Educational Administration Quarterly, 49*, 272–309.
Hands, C. (2010). Why collaborate? The differing reasons for secondary school educators' establishment of school-community partnerships. *School Effectiveness and School Improvement, 21*, 189–207.
Harris, D. N., Rutledge, S. A., Ingle, W. K., & Thompson, C. C. (2010). Mix and match: What principals look for when hiring teachers and implications for teacher quality policies. *Education Finance and Policy, 5*, 228–246.
Hauseman, D.C., & Pollock, K. (2014, November). *Principals' work with ICT: A doubled-edged sword*. Presented at the University Council for Educational Administration (UCEA) conference, Washington, DC.
Hendriks, M., & Sheerens, J. (2013). School leadership effects revisited: A review of empirical studies guided by indirect-effects models. *School Leadership and management, 33*, 373–395.
Horng, E. L., & Loeb, S. (2010). New thinking about instructional leadership. *Phi Delta Kappan, 92*, 66.
Horng, E. L., Klasik, D., & Loeb, S. (2010). Principal's time use and school effectiveness. *American Journal of Education, 116*, 491–523.
Institute for Education Leadership. (n.d.). *Putting Ontario's leadership framework into action: A guide for school and system leaders*. Retrieved from http://live.iel.immix.ca/storage/2/1284580690/FrameworkAction.pdf
Jacob, B.A., & Lefgren, L. (2005). *Principals as agents: Subjective performance measurement in education (RWP05–040)*. Retrieved from http://www.nber.org/papers/w11463.pdf
Kelley, N., & Trebilcock, M. J. (2010). *The making of the mosaic: A history of Canadian immigration policy*. Toronto: University of Toronto Press.
Kemeny, A. (2002). Déterminés à réussir – un portrait des bourreaux de travail au Canada. *Statistique Canada, 64*, 2–8.
Kmetz, J. T., & Willower, D. J. (1982). Elementary school principals' work behavior. *Educational Administration Quarterly, 18*, 62–78.

Knapp, M.S., Copland, M.A., Plecki, M.L., & Portin, B.S. (2006). *Leading, learning, and leadership support*. Available online: https://depts.washington.edu/ctpmail/PDFs/Synthesis-Oct16.pdf

Koyama, J. (2011). Principals, power, and policy: Enacting supplemental educational services. *Anthropology and Education Quarterly, 42*, 20–36.

Lee, M., & Hallinger, P. (2012). National contexts influencing principals' time use and allocation: Economic development, societal culture and educational system. *School Effectiveness and School Improvement, 23*, 461–482.

Leithwood, K. (2012). *The Ontario leadership framework 2012: A discussion of research foundations*. Retrieved from http://iel.immix.ca/storage/6/1345688978/Final_Research_Report_-_EN.pdf

Leithwood, K., & Azah, V.N. (2014). *Elementary principals' and vice-principals' workload studies: Final report*. Retrieved from http://www.edu.gov.on.ca/eng/policyfunding/memos/nov2014/ExecutiveSummaryOct7_EN.pdf

Leithwood, K., & Beatty, B. (2007). *Leading with teacher emotions in mind*. Thousand Oaks: Corwin.

Leithwood, K.A., & Riehl, C. (2003). What we know about successful school leadership. A report by Division A of AERA National College for School Leadership.

Leithwood, K., & Jantzi, D. (2000). The effects of transformational leadership on organizational conditions and student engagement with school. *Journal of Educational Administration, 38*, 112–129.

Leithwood, K., & Jantzi, D. (2008). Linking leadership to student learning: The contributions of leader efficacy. *Educational Administration Quarterly, 44*, 496–528.

Leithwood, K., Louis, K.S., Anderson, S., & Wahlstrom, K. (2004). *How leadership influences student learning: A review of research for the Learning from Leadership Project*. Retrieved from http://www.wallacefoundation.org/knowledge-center/school-leadership/key-research/Documents/How-Leadership-influences-Student-Learning.pdf

Leithwood, K., Anderson, S., Mascall, B., & Strauss, T. (2010). School leaders' influences on student learning: The four paths. In T. Bush, L. Bell, & D. Middlewood (Eds.), *The principles of educational leadership and management* (pp. 13–30). London: Sage.

Leithwood, K., Patten, S., & Jantzi, D. (2010). Testing a conception of how school leadership influences student learning. *Educational Administration Quarterly, 46*, 671–706.

Lomos, C., Hofman, R. H., & Bosker, R. J. (2011). Professional communities and student achievement—A meta-analysis. *School Effectiveness and School Improvement, 22*, 121–148.

Louis, K., Dretzke, B., & Wahlstrom, K. (2010). How does leadership affect student achievement: Results from a national US survey. *School Effectiveness and School Improvement, 21*, 315–336.

Marks, H. M., & Printy, S. M. (2003). Principals leadership and school performance: An integration of transformational and instructional leadership. *Educational Administration Quarterly, 39*, 370–397.

Martin, W. J., & Willower, D. J. (1981). The managerial behavior of high school principals. *Educational Administration Quarterly, 17*, 69–90.

Martinko, M. J., & Gardner, W. L. (1990). Structured observation of managerial work: A replication and synthesis. *Journal of Management Studies, 27*, 329–357.

Mauno, S., Kinnunen, U., & Ruokolainen, M. (2006). Exploring work- and organization-based resources as moderators between work-family conflict, well-being, and job attitudes. *Work and Stress, 20*, 210–233.

Merriam-Webster. (n.d.). *Work*. Retrieved from http://www.merriam-webster.com/dictionary/work

Mulford, B. (2003). *School leaders: Changing roles and impact on teacher and school effectiveness*. Retrieved from http://www.oecd.org/edu/school/2635399.pdf

Murakami, E., & Pollock, K. (2014). Editorial introduction. *Comparative and International Education, 43*, Article 1.

Murakami, E., Torenson, M., & Pollock, K. (2014). Expectations for the preparation of school principals in three jurisdictions: Sweden, Ontario, and Texas. *Comparative and International Education, 43*, Article 7.

Norton, M. S. (2015). *The principal as human resources leader: A guide to exemplary practices for personnel administration.* New York: Routledge.

OECD. (2013). Education at a glance 2013: OECD indicators. Paris: Author. Retrieved from http://www.oecd-ilibrary.org/education/education-at-a-glance-2013_eag-2013-en

Ontario College of Teachers. (2009). Ontario College of Teachers Principals Qualification Program 2009. Retrieved from https://www.oct.ca/-/media/PDF/Principals%20Qualification%20Program%202009/principals_qualification_program_e.pdf

Ontario Ministry of Labour. (n.d.). About the Ministry. Available online at http://www.labour.gov.on.ca/english/about/index.php (Accessed 22 September 2014).

Pinto, L. E. (2015). Fear and loathing in neoliberalism: School Administrator responses to policy layers. *Journal of Educational Administration and History, 46*, 140–154.

Pollock, K. (2006). Policy as outcome: Inequities generated from unintended policy outcomes. *Comparative and International Education/Éducation Comparée et Internationale, 35*, 35–47.

Pollock, K., & Hauseman, D. C. (2015). School leadership in Canada. In H. Ärlestig, C. Day, & O. Johannson (Eds.), *Cross country histories of school leadership research: Focus and findings* (pp. 202–232). Dordrecht: Springer.

Pollock, K., & Winton, S. (2015). Juggling multiple accountability systems: How three principals manage these tensions. *Educational Assessment, Evaluation and Accountability*, published online. doi:10.1007/s11092-015-9224-7.

Pollock, K., Wang, F., & Hauseman, D.C. (2014). *The changing nature of principals' work: Final report.* Retrieved from http://www.edu.uwo.ca/faculty_profiles/cpels/pollock_katina/OPC-Principals-Work-Report.pdf

Preiss, B. (2014, October 15) *State school principals face impossible choices on building maintenance. The Victoria Age.* Retrieved from http://www.theage.com.au/victoria/state-school-principals-face-impossible-choices-on-building-maintenance-20141015-116k7x.html

Revised Statues of Ontario. (1990). Education Act, c.E.2.

Riley, P. (2014). *Australian principal occupational health, safety and wellbeing survey: 2011–2014 data.* Retrieved from http://www.principalhealth.org/au/2011-14_Exec%20Summary_Final.pdf

Robinson, V., Lloyd, C., & Rowe, K. (2008). The impact of leadership on student outcomes: An analysis of the differential effects of leadership types. *Educational Administration Quarterly, 44*, 635–674.

Rogers, J., Freeton, R., & Terriquez, V. (2012). Enlisting collective help: Urban principals' encouragement of parent participation in school decision-making. In S. Auerbach (Ed.), *School leadership for authentic family and community partnerships: Research perspectives for transforming practice* (pp. 55–77). New York: Routledge.

Ryan, J. (1996). The new institutionalism in a postmodern world: De-differentiation and the study of institutions. In R. Crowson, W. L. Boyd, & H. Mawhinney (Eds.), *The politics of education and the new institutionalism: Reinventing the American school* (pp. 189–2020). London: Falmer.

Ryan, J. (2011). Administrative approaches to diversity: Imposing and sharing meaning. In J. MacBeath & T. Townsend (Eds.), *International handbook on leadership for learning* (pp. 1125–1142). Dordrecht: Springer.

Sattler, P. (2012). Education governance reform in Ontario: Neoliberalism in context. *Canadian Journal of Educational Administration and Policy, 128*, 1–28.

Sheninger, E. (2014). *Digital leadership: Changing paradigms for changing times.* Thousand Oaks: Corwin.

Shields, M. (2000). Les longues heures de travail et la santé. *Statistique Canada, 12*, 53–62.

Silins, H., & Mulford, B. (2004). Schools as learning organisations—Effects on teacher leadership and student outcomes. *School Effectiveness and School Improvement, 15*, 443–466.

Smith, A. J. (2009). Generative leadership: Profile of effective 21st century secondary school principals (Order, NR49647). Available from ProQuest Dissertations & Theses Global. (304) 833–957.

Statistics Canada. (2011). Immigration and ethnocultural diversity in Canada. Retrieved from http://www12.statcan.gc.ca/nhs-enm/2011/as-sa/99-010-x/99-010-x2011001-eng.pdf

Statistics Canada. (n.d.). Table 282–0026: Labour force survey estimates (LFS). by actual hours worked, class of worker, National Occupational Classification for Statistics (NOC-S) and sex. Retrieved from http://www5.statcan.gc.ca/cansim/a05?lang=eng&id=2820026&pattern=2820026&searchTypeByValue=1&p2=35

Stone, B., Jabbra, J. G., & Dwivedi, O. P. (Eds.). (1989). *Public service accountability: A comparative perspective*. Hartford: Kumarian.

Thomas, M., Rowe, F., & Harris, N. (2010). Understanding the factors that characterise school-community partnerships. *Health Education, 110*, 427–444.

Vezina, M. (2002). *Évolutions des conditions de travail et santé psychique*. Toulouse: Octares.

Wallace, J. (2010). Facing reality: Including the emotional in school leadership programmes. *Journal of Educational Administration, 48*, 595–610.

Whyte, W. (1956). *The organization man*. New York: Simon & Shuster.

Witziers, B., Bosker, R. J., & Kruger, M. L. (2003). Educational leadership and student achievement: The elusive search for association. *Educational Administration Quarterly, 39*, 398–425.

Chapter 11
Creating Communities of Professionalism: Addressing Cultural and Structural Barriers

Joseph Murphy

Over the last quarter century a good deal of attention has been given to the topic of professional learning communities. During that time, some parts of the community storyline have been fleshed out quite thoroughly while others remain thinly developed. For example, we have learned a good deal about the pillars that support professional communities. Specifically, we see that scholars have drawn on four interrelated bodies of research. One is the emergence of the importance of "social capital," an idea generally attributed to James Coleman. A second is the theory of "learning organizations" initially developed by Senge. A third is the growing scholarship on "teams" in productive organizations. The last is the development of the concept of "communities of practice," a framework forged by Lave and Wenger in the 1990s.

Over this time, scholars have also forged logic models that explain how professional communities function. The collective logic model features six norms: shared vision, collaboration, trust, shared leadership, ownership, and shared responsibility. It is these elements that define professional learning culture and foster teacher learning and teacher professional capital (see especially Kruse et al. 1995; Louis and Marks 1998; Printy 2008; Stoll et al. 2006; Vescio et al. 2008; Visscher and Witziers 2004). Thus professional community promotes both learning, i.e. intellectual capital (e.g. deeper content knowledge, enriched pedagogical skills) (Borko 2004; Levine and Marcus 2010; Printy 2008) and professional cultural capital (e.g. commitment) (Darling-Hammond et al. 2002; McLaughlin and Talbert 2001; Saunders et al. 2009). The capital accumulating in both of these areas is of two types, that accruing to individuals (i.e. human capital) and that accruing to the group (i.e. social capital). Both are important. However, it is the focus on social capital development that distinguishes teacher communities from many other reforms. Increased capital, in turn, leads to changes in the ways teachers undertake work with students (Curry

---

J. Murphy (✉)
Vanderbilt University's Peabody College, 210B Payne Hall, Box 414, 230 Appleton Place, 37023-5721 Nashville, TN, USA
e-mail: joseph.f.murphy@Vanderbilt.Edu

© Springer International Publishing AG 2017
K. Leithwood et al. (eds.), *How School Leaders Contribute to Student Success*, Studies in Educational Leadership 23, DOI 10.1007/978-3-319-50980-8_11

2008; Horn 2010; Vescio et al. 2008). Improved instruction and classroom climate, in turn, lead to better learning outcomes for students (Bryk et al. 2010; Hattie 2009; Mitchell and Sackney 2006; Vescio et al. 2008).

At the same time, gaps in the research on communities of professional practice remain. A critical need is to carefully examine cultural and structural barriers that make the infusion of professional culture so difficult. A second need is to document how schools, especially school leaders, can surmount cultural and structural problems. It is these issues on which we focus in this integrative review.

11.1 Methodology

In this section, we outline the architecture and design for this review on making professional communities a possibility using scaffolding provided by Hallinger (2012a, b, 2014). The goal of the review was twofold. We sought to understand challenges that inhibit the growth of professional community. We also wanted to form an empirical understanding of the ways in which educators could meet these challenges. In both cases, we wished to grow this knowledge in the complexity of schooling and the rapids of continuous school improvement. Around these two goals, the focus is on substantive and conceptual strands of implementation. We do not address methodological issues. Research questions mirror the two goals of the review. The framework for the review is a mixture of research on change and implementation, school improvement, and community.

The goals and conceptual scaffolding required examination of theoretical analyses and research across broad swaths of the literature. On a targeted front, we pulled and examined all abstracts from 1990 to 2013 under the headings of professional learning communities, teacher learning communities, communities of instructional practice, communities of inquiry, professional learning communities, and communities of commitment. We included legacy reviews and current scholarly reviews, all empirical studies, and strong interpretative and theoretical analyses that were derivative of empirical research work.

At the same time, it was clear to us based on previous work that the answers sought would not be uncovered solely through targeted procedures (Murphy and Torre 2014). We, therefore, read extensively across the broad area of school improvement. Here we searched for evidence, both confirming and disconfirming, that was ribboned through empirically anchored work. For example, findings were reinforced or found anew in studies of school change, school improvement, program implementation, school culture, and so forth. In this part of the work, we lacked the structure employed with the targeted approach discussed above. We simply read everything we could until we began to reach saturation, when fresh insights on constraints and supports became less and less discernible (see Glaser and Strauss 1967). Consistent with guidance from foundational texts in qualitative methods (Miles and Huberman 1994), we were especially on the lookout for non-confirming evidence.

In summary, we followed a broad approach to sourcing the review, what Hallinger (2012a) refers to as "an exhaustive review" in his categorization scheme. We did not include dissertations, non-refereed articles, conference presentations (with a few exceptions for foundational work), or textbooks. On the other hand, we sorted in all refereed journal articles. Because we employed a pattern of cascading references from originally consumed articles, we extended the hourglass beyond our original 1990–2013 guideline.

We employed the following procedure to extract data, one that mirrors the creation of grounded theory (Glaser and Strauss 1967; Strauss and Corbin 1998). The work is best described as "inductive thematic analysis" (Hayes 2000, p. 178). After six months of new reading, and based on our earlier research in this area, we created a conceptual map scaffolded on the goals of the review. Our framework became refined at the detail level as we continued reading. Using coded segments of the map, we coded each piece of work read, usually at the paragraph or sentence level. Everything that had been read was then recopied. Each code was then cut and placed on a separate data sheet, with the name and date of the article, page number, and code. These were then sorted by code. This then, along with our binder of conceptual and theoretical memos, was our "data." Consistent with inductive synthetic work, "making sense" of the data were completed by reading and rereading codes until we formed categories within codes, what grounded theorists refer to as open coding. This process both exposed what the research had to tell us and allowed us to continually test the vitality of our emerging research narrative. The synthesis from this work follows.

11.2 Barriers

11.2.1 Structural Challenges

Over the last 50 years, scholars have documented how "the structure of the organization directs and defines the flow and pattern of human interactions in the organization" (Johnson 1998, p. 13), how the beliefs and values of educators are shaped by the structures in which they work (Smylie and Brownlee-Conyers 1992; Useem et al. 1997). Structures reflect values and principles that thus exercise considerable pull on the possibility of communities of practice developing in schools (McLaughlin and Talbert 2001; Stoll et al. 2006).

Unfortunately, the prevailing structure of schooling hinders the formation of teacher professional community (Bidwell and Yasumoto 1999; Donaldson 2001; Jackson 2000). Researchers conclude that the institutional nature of schooling creates a framework that encourages isolation, autonomy, and privatization while damping down cooperation and undercutting professional community norms (Harris 2004; Murphy 2006; Scribner et al. 1999).

Five aspects of structure merit analysis. First, existing organizational arrangements benefit some members of the school, actors who often challenge or fail to support the creation of alternative structures that threaten their advantaged positions (Chrispeels and Martin 2002; Crowther et al. 2002). For example, McLaughlin and Talbert (2001, p. 127) do an excellent job of exploring this reality in the context of high school departments, exposing how "informal career systems and seniority structures leave communities of practice on the margins of secondary education."

In addition, the current organizational system is the only one that most educators have known. It is difficult to move to the unknown even when one can glimpse its contours. In addition, even if the change process is set in motion, there are strong inclinations to regress to the familiar. As Lieberman and Miller (1999, p. 126) remind us, "new behaviors are difficult to acquire, and in the end it is easier to return to old habits than to embrace new ones"; needed changes are often "abandoned in favor of more familiar and more satisfying routines" (Little 1987, p. 493).

Third, existing structures are not especially malleable (Donaldson 2001; Murphy 1991). The "forces of organizational persistence" (Smylie and Hart 1999, p. 421) and "institutional precedent" (Smylie 1992, p. 55) are quite robust (McLaughlin and Talbert 2001). Hierarchy has a well-developed root structure and enjoys a good deal of legitimacy (Murphy 1991, 2015). Schools also have mastered the ritual of change (Meyer and Rowan 1975) and the ability to absorb new ideas and initiatives in ways that leave existing organizational structures largely unchanged (Cohen 1988; Elmore 1987; Weick 1976). The reality in many schools of limited financial resources exacerbates structural obstacles standing in the way of the formation of professional communities (Drago-Severson 2004).

Fourth, structures influence the use of time in schools and generally in ways that make shared work a mere footnote in the teacher workday (Cosner 2011; Desimone 2002; Scribner et al. 1999). The traditional school "offers few opportunities to interact with colleagues outside of abbreviated interchanges. Extended periods of adult-to-adult interaction in the workplace are irregular, episodic, and rare" (Grossman et al. 2001, p. 987). Shortage of time, in turn, acts to calcify the already inflexible institutional backbone of schooling (Firestone and Martinez 2007; Foster and St. Hilaire 2003). Indeed, there is a general sense in research that time is the "biggest obstacle" (Doyle 2000, p. 38), the most significant "barrier" (Blegen and Kennedy 2000, p. 5; LeBlanc and Shelton 1997, p. 44), and "the most pervasive problem" (Wasley 1991, p. 137) in forging professional community.

Fifth, while some currents buoy the idea of professional culture, stronger currents support the movement to centralization and to the hardening of the hierarchical forms of schooling (Murphy 2013b). Especially problematic for the development of community are the following ideas embedded in hierarchical structures introduced above: the idea of a single leader (Moller and Katzenmeyer 1996); traditional relational dynamics featuring a boss and subordinates (Conley 1989); the idea that the leader is "synonymous with boss" (Moller and Katzenmeyer 1996, p. 4); and the metaphor of leader as supervisor (Murphy 2005; Myers 1970). Also problematic here are two elements featured in these structures: time schedules (Conley 1991; Coyle 1997) and systems for dividing up work responsibilities (Harris 2003; Pellicer and Anderson 1995; Printy 2004; York-Barr and Duke 2004). Both of these strands promote segmentation and separation (Katzenmeyer and Moller 2001).

11.2.2 Cultural Challenges

We also learn that the cultural seedbed of schooling is often toxic to the growth of learning communities (Grossman et al. 2001; Saunders et al. 2009; Smylie 1996). More specifically, there are powerful professional norms and values that push and pull teachers in directions at odds with the concept of collaborative professional work (Lortie 1975; Rosenholtz 1989; Young 2006). While scholars use different terms to describe these values and norms (e.g. autonomy, civility, conflict avoidance, privacy, non-interference, and so forth), there is consensus that they exert negative influence over the growth of teacher professional communities (Levine and Marcus 2010; McLaughlin and Talbert 2001; Pounder 1999). The result of these cultural norms is that teachers spend very little time attending to the work of their colleagues (Curry 2008) nor do they express any great desire to do so (Griffin 1995; Visscher and Witziers 2004). We explore these unproductive cultural norms below.

A core perspective that is deeply entwined in the cultural tapestry of schools is what can best be labeled the norm of legitimacy. Research confirms that what "counts" as authentic activity is what happens inside in classrooms (Goldstein 2004; Little 1982). For both the public and teachers themselves, teaching is defined almost exclusively by time spent inside classrooms working with students (Little 1988; Saunders et al. 2009). Time spent away from the classroom is viewed as lacking legitimacy (Smylie and Brownlee-Conyers 1992).

A second cultural norm is the divide between teaching and administration (Murphy et al. 1987; Rallis 1990). A key aspect of this deeply embedded norm is the belief that the job of teachers is to teach and the task of administrators is to lead (Goldstein 2004; MacBeath 2009). A second aspect is that teachers are expected to implement designs developed by higher ups in the bureaucracy (Boles and Troen 1996; Teitel 1996; Wasley 1991). Teachers are to follow (Moller and Katzenmeyer 1996; Murphy 2005). This role separation is heavily reinforced by the common structures of schooling we explained above.

Related to the above principle is the norm of the managerial imperative, what Keedy (1999, p. 787) refers to as the "norm of the authority and power of administrators." This viewpoint has a deep root structure, one that consistently chokes out perspectives on professional communities (Bryk et al. 2010). At the heart of this standard is the belief that schooling outside of classrooms is the rightful domain of formal school leaders. Given this culture, teachers are "reluctant to challenge traditional patterns of principals' authority" (Smylie 1992, p. 55). Understandings have been forged over time between administrators and teachers (Murphy et al. 1987; Murphy 2013b; Sizer 1984). Both groups often show reluctance to overturn such negotiated arrangements, especially when doing so would damage established patterns of power and autonomy (Harris 2003; Smylie 1992). Cast in starker terms, the argument holds that teachers are powerless to influence activities beyond the classroom (Troen and Boles 1994), that principals are resistant to actions that would change this dynamic (Bishop et al. Bishop et al. 1997; Brown and Sheppard 1999; Goldstein 2004), and that efforts on the part of teachers to challenge the norm would produce unpleasant repercussions (Clift et al. 1992), including micropolitical dynamics that threaten patterns of power and status (Chrispeels and Martin 2002; Cochran-Smith and Lytle 1999; Visscher and Witziers 2004).

Scholars have also provided considerable information on the norm of autonomy at the heart of the teaching profession (Grossman et al. 2001; Levine and Marcus 2007; Smylie and Hart 1999). As noted above, most teachers work alone, disconnected from their peers (Ancess 2003; Stigler and Hiebert 1999). They "value autonomy more than the chance to influence others' work" (Levine and Marcus 2007, p. 128). They see this freedom from external review as a right of the job (Murphy 2013b; Uline and Berkowitz 2000). They equate professionalism with autonomy (Murphy 2013a). And they practice the art of non-interference in the instructional affairs of their colleagues in the school (Teitel 1996; Wilson 1993). This powerful norm undermines the development of productive relationships that form the center of gravity of communities of practice.

Tightly linked to cultural values about autonomy is the norm of privacy (Feiman-Nemser and Floden 1986; Grossman et al. 2001; Levine and Marcus 2007) – what Griffin (1995) calls "the privacy of practice"(p. 40). As Uline and Berkowitz (2000) document, the interaction rules in a culture of privacy mirror those found in highly autonomous climates and "include never interfering in another teacher's classroom affairs, and always being self-reliant with one's own" (p. 418). The standard of professional privacy is construed "as freedom from scrutiny and the right of each teacher to make independent judgments about classroom practice" (Little 1988, p. 94). While Little (1990) acknowledges that providing help to colleagues is acceptable within tight parameters, in a culture of non-interference and non-judgmentalness teachers are primarily expected to address problems alone (Feiman-Nemser and Floden 1986; Moller and Eggen 2005; Useem et al. 1997). As was the case with the previous norms, the norm of privacy undercuts collaboration, sharing, and responsibility for colleagues which help define communities of professionalism (Siu 2008).

Researchers have also documented that the teacher culture in general and the culture of schools in particular are characterized by egalitarian norms (York-Barr and Duke 2004). The egalitarian ethic of teaching –"the fact that all teachers hold equal position and rank separated by number of years of experience and college credit earned" (Wasley 1991, p. 166) "rather than function, skill, advanced knowledge, role, or responsibility" (Lieberman et al. 1988, p. 151) – holds that all teachers are equal (Katzenmeyer and Moller 2001). Professional communities on the other hand clash with this norm (Friedkin and Slater 1994; McLaughlin and Talbert 2001; Pounder 1999). Without some renorming of the profession, practice communities will be hard pressed to grow.

The norm of civility also often hinders the development of a culture of professional collaboration. As Griffin (1995) reminds us, "schools are nonconfrontative social organizations, at least in terms of how teachers interact with one another" (p. 44). There is strong pressure for cordiality and getting along with others (Conley 1991; Hart 1990; Levine and Marcus 2007; Lortie 1975). The avoidance of conflict and hurt feelings trumps productive exchanges (Chrispeels and Martin 2002; Grossman et al. 2001). Peer critique is considered to be unprofessional and requests for assistance are seen as signs of incompetence (Dannetta 2002). Linked to this are well-ingrained modes of interaction among teachers, such as contrived collegiality and "induced collaboration" (Little 1990, p. 509), actions that promote the appearance of cooperation while maintaining deeply ingrained norms of autonomy, privacy, and egalitarianism. Threaded through all these norms are the values of conservatism and aversion to risk taking (Lortie 1975; Rosenholtz 1989), values that privilege the status quo in the face of learning and change that anchor professional communities.

11.3 Support For Creating Professional Learning Communities

To date, we have examined how the concept of communities of professional practice can founder. Practitioners, developers, researchers, and policy makers require a firm understanding of these dynamics. Equally important, however, they require an operational manual and a well stocked toolbox to create conditions that nurture the formation and growth of teacher communities (Clift et al. 1992; Darling-Hammond et al. 1995). Leithwood et al. (1999, p. 215) capture this as follows: "The principal challenge facing those designing schools as learning organizations is to determine the organizational conditions that foster individual and collective learning and to build these conditions into the school." Fullan and Ballew (2002, p. 14) outlines the assignment thus: "the obligation is to remove barriers to sharing, create mechanisms for sharing, and reward those who do share." Research that deals with the values of communities of practice is readily available. Knowledge directly addressing the creation of professional communities (as opposed to understanding its qualities) is less well-developed, however (Blanc et al. 2010).

Scholars have forged a variety of overlapping frameworks to array the factors and conditions that support the formation of professional communities of practice. Stoll et al. (2006, p. 23) employ four categories: focussing on learning processes; making the best of human and social resources; managing structural resources; and interacting with and drawing on external agents. Mullen and Hutinger (2008, p. 280) also describe four sets of actions: manage resources, provide support and direction, exert appropriate pressure to achieve goals, and mediate group dynamics. Printy (2008, p. 211) discusses three functions: communicate vision, support teachers, and buffer teachers from outside influences. Saunders et al. (2009, p. 1028) highlight the centrality of time, administrative support, and structures. This is consistent with our suggestion that the traditional "functions" of principals (e.g. coordinating, monitoring) can be employed to foster collaborative work (Murphy et al. 1987). More parsimonious frames have been provided by Kruse et al. (1995, p. 34): structural conditions and characteristics of human resources; by Hurd (cited in Morrissey 2000, p. 6): structural conditions and collegial relationships; and by McDougall, Saunders and Goldenberg (2007, p. 54): settings and processes. Taking a slightly different approach, Scribner et al. (1999) describe administrative, moral, and political support directed in the service of forming professional culture. Below we build on this scholarship to examine supports for communities of professional practice. In the process, we add new sub-elements to the overall architecture and contextualize and add nuance to the collective body of evidence.

11.3.1 Creating Structures and Time

As discussed above, structures shape what unfolds in schools, heavily determining what can and what cannot be accomplished. Structures or "conditions" (Stein and Coburn 2008, p. 585) allow values and norms to flourish, or cause them to wither (Brooks et al. 2004; Cochran-Smith and Lytle 1999; Kruse et al. 1995). Our focus at this point in the analysis is on the positive side of the chronicle, that is, how practices and forums in schools can help collaborative communities grow. We begin by reviewing what is known about creating supportive collaborative structures.

A recurring theme across our research over time is that structural change does not predict organizational performance, student learning in the case of schools (Murphy 1991, 2013a). Research also helps us see that simply giving teachers a platform to converse will not ensure the growth of valued professional norms and human and social capital (Levine and Marcus 2007; Newmann et al. 2001). At the core then, structure is about "interactive settings" (Cosner 2009, p. 255) and "interaction patterns" (p. 273). It is about opportunities for forging relationships, for establishing patterns of networks, and for nurturing professional exchange through new avenues of communication (Cochran-Smith and Lytle 1999; May and Supovitz 2011; Spillane et al. 2001; Stoll et al. 2006). In short, it is about promoting professional collaboration (Ancess 2003; Cosner 2009; Morrissey 2000; Newmann et al. 1989; Stein and Coburn 2008).

Research exposes ways to work "structurally" to establish and grow professional community. On the issue of forums, there is near unanimous agreement that schools must re-purpose existing space and current time configurations (Cosner 2009; Rossmiller 1992; Stein and Coburn 2008). For example, community-building work is conspicuous by its absence from many faculty meetings. These settings, and many others, can be re-shaped to deepen collaboration. Concomitantly, as we explore below, there is general agreement that new forums will need to be created. A variety of community-building structures are needed, not simply reliance on meetings (Leithwood et al. 2006b; McLaughlin and Talbert 2001).

Investigators also advance the idea that both formal and informal opportunities for crafting community need to be captured, with an eye open especially for the informal opportunities that often lay fallow (Cosner 2009; McLaughlin and Talbert 2001). Joining together teachers who in informal ways already demonstrate working connections, beliefs, and relationships can be an important aspect of the community-building plan (Penuel et al. 2009; Useem et al. 1997).

Creating structures that promote both horizontal and vertical networks and exchanges is a wise strategy position (Johnson and Asera 1999). Here scholars point to collaborative structures that stimulate cross-grade and cross-departmental linkages, what Cosner (2009, pp. 268–269) calls "new interaction patterns." Also underscored here are forums that allow teachers from various teams to collaborate (Kruse et al. 1995; Stein and Coburn 2008), by "structuring communities with overlapping boundaries and multimembership" (Printy 2008, p. 217).

As we described above, the handmaiden to structure is time. Without time, the establishment of collaborative forums becomes nearly impossible (Cochran-Smith and Lytle 1999; Darling-Hammond and McLaughlin 1995; Eilers and Camacho 2007; Morrissey 2000; Wenger and Snyder 2000). Alternatively, research on professional teacher community reveals that in schools where community flourishes time is made available for shared work and collaborative learning (Huberman et al. 2011; Youngs 2007). A similar conclusion is evident in studies of effective schools and productive leadership (Blase and Blase 2004; Drago-Severson 2004).

Studies have also uncovered clues about how space and time can be employed in the service of community development. One strategy to enhance exchange is to bring members of current or proposed collaboratives into close physical proximity (Bulkley and Hicks 2005; Leithwood et al. 1997; Supovitz 2008). Research informs us that proximity can aid in overcoming the dysfunctional norms such as privatization that we explored above (Ancess 2003; Gray et al. 1999; Kruse et al. 1995). Another approach is to take maximum advantage of formal teacher leadership positions in school (e.g. data coach), to have them structure and lead forums in which small groups of teachers can interact (Cosner 2009; Murphy 2005). Relatedly, collaboration can be fostered by threading shared leadership throughout the school (Leithwood et al. 2006a; Silins and Mulford 2004; Smylie 1996). Lastly, schools moving to foster communities of professional practice can establish what Saunders et al. (2009, p. 1011) call "predictable, consistent settings"; what Blase and Blase (2004, p. 68) refer to as "teacher collaborative structures"; and what Ermeling (2010, p. 387) describes as "dedicated and protected times where teachers meet on a regular basis to get important work done." As suggested above, these can be new arrangements or re-purposed existing settings. Whatever the designs, these predictable, patterned forums are the most efficacious method of enhancing community development among teachers (Pounder 1999).

Investigators also provide information on specific forums in play in schools working toward the goal of creating more robust collaboration (Penuel et al. 2009, 2010). Re-purposed staff and departmental meetings find a home here (Cosner 2009; Mitchell and Castle 2005; Spillane et al. 2001). So too do re-packaged schedules that allow for late start or early dismissal on selected days (Cosner 2009; King 2001). Creating blocks of time for teachers to observe in the classrooms of colleagues is a special category of collaboration (Blase and Blase 2004; Harris 2003). Ad hoc groups such as book study teams, inquiry groups, and action research teams are found in some community-anchored schools (Cosner 2009; King 2001; Newmann et al. 2001). So too are structures and time for teachers to collaborate around school governance and planning (Leithwood et al. 2006b; McLaughlin and Talbert 2001). Induction and mentoring programs can provide forums to stimulate collaboration and learning (Cosner 2009; Kruse et al. 1995; Youngs 2007). So also can the use of cooperative teaching arrangements (Johnson and Asera 1999). The most widely used strategy is the creation of a master schedule that creates common planning time for groups of teachers, usually by grade level, subject area, or teaching team (Cosner 2009).

In addition, a crosscutting analysis of the research on teacher communities uncovers some of the essential ingredients of these collaborative forums. We discover that these gatherings for work and learning should: occur frequently, for a reasonable block of time, and across the full year (Felner et al. 2007; Raywid 1995); be intensive (Murphy 2005); focus on student learning and instructional matters (Johnson and Asera 1999); maximize interdependency (Cosner 2009; Kruse et al. 1995); privilege evidence; and feature specific tasks that structure time usage (Center for Teaching Quality 2007; Penuel et al. 2009).

11.3.2 Supporting Learning

Time and working structures are important and necessary. But they provide insufficient fuel to communities of practice (Ancess 2003; Ermeling 2010; Wenger 2000; Wenger and Snyder 2000). Professional communities achieve valued outcomes by nurturing the development of professional capital and by promoting teacher learning. Research across school improvement studies confirms that leaving this to unfold by chance is ill advised. What is required is "learning to learn," the development of the knowledge and the mastery of skills that make teacher growth possible. Supovitz (2002, p. 1618) refers to this as "continuous capacity building" and Cochran-Smith and Lytle (1999, p. 294) describe it as "inquiry as stance." We examine the "learning" in the "learning to learn" paradigm for professional communities below.

For most teachers, working with students is a nearly all-consuming activity. Consequently, they generally spend very little time working with other adults. Not surprisingly, therefore, developing "managerial skills in dealing with people" (Ainscow and Southworth 1996, p. 234) appears to be a critical ingredient in helping teachers work productively in learning communities (Adams 2010; Borko 2004). Or, as Little (1987) reports, "the specific skills and perspectives of working with a colleague are critical" (p. 512) for teacher communities to develop. The centrality of forging relationships is essential to the work of practice communities (Ancess 2003; Cochran-Smith and Lytle 1999; Cosner 2009); so too is the formation of relationship-building capabilities (Bryk et al. 2010; Lynch and Strodl 1991).

Researchers have uncovered a variety of interpersonal capacities that promote productive working relationships with peers (Brooks et al. 2004). They find that professional development should assist teachers in developing proficiencies around a number of interpersonal skills (Crow and Pounder 2000). For example, Katzenmeyer and Moller (2001) conclude that growth should begin with personal knowledge. Professional development in this area builds from the assumption that focussing "on increasing their own self awareness, identity formation, and interpretive capacity" (Zimpher 1988, p. 57) is critical. It is this wisdom that allows teachers to discover the values, behaviors, dispositions, and professional concerns that underlie personal performance and to understand their colleagues, especially those whose experiences and viewpoints do not mirror their own (Katzenmeyer and Moller 2001).

A bundle of competencies that promote productive working relations surface in the research as candidates for inclusion in the advancement of professional learning communities. For example, researchers conclude that "skills that will make teachers sensitive to seeing others' points of view" (Katzenmeyer and Moller 2001, p. 67) and "sensitive to others' needs" (LeBlanc and Shelton 1997, p. 38) are important. Also, because educators often "report that they became more influential through using good listening techniques with peers" (Katzenmeyer and Moller 2001, p. 93), gaining proficiency in the area of listening skills is important. In a similar view, because friction sometimes surfaces in professional interactions teachers in communities are advantaged when they possess well-developed facilitation skills (Cochran-Smith and Lytle 1999; Murphy 2005; Zimpher 1988). In its broadest form, facilitation means "knowing how to help a group take primary responsibility for solving its problems and mitigat[ing] factors that hinder the group's ability to be effective" (Killion 1996, p. 72). More specifically, it includes the cardinal ability to establish trust and to navigate through problems (Kilcher 1992). There is also agreement that community is strengthened when teachers develop consulting skills (Manthei 1992) and proficiency in conferencing with colleagues (Murphy 2005; Zimpher 1988). The "principles and skills of advising" (Little 1985, p. 34) are also key ingredients helping establish a productive climate for collaborative work. So too are influencing skills (Hart 1995; Katzenmeyer and Moller 2001).

In addition, the development of community is enriched when a variety of skills for attacking joint work endeavors and a set of group process skills for understanding and managing the "group dynamics" that accompany collaborative work are provided (Ancess 2000; Kilcher 1992). Most essential here is the broad array of communication skills needed to interact with colleagues (Ancess 2003; LeBlanc and Shelton 1997). Indeed, the conclusion that inquiry communities "benefit from ongoing learning and practice in effective communication" (Killion 1996, p. 72) is clearly illuminated in the research. Problem-solving and decision-making skills are also found to be quite important. As Killion (1996) reports, "knowing various decision-making methods, selecting the most appropriate method for a particular situation, and having a repertoire of strategies for helping others reach a decision with the chosen methods are [also] critical skills" (p. 74). Communities are also advantaged when teachers have well-developed skills in conflict management (Hart 1995; Murphy 2005) and conflict resolution (Fay 1992). Although it is underemphasized in the process-focussed teacher community research, promoting learning also necessitates deep knowledge in content or discipline areas (Cochran-Smith and Lytle 1999; Eilers and Camacho 2007; Leithwood et al. 2004; McLaughlin and Talbert 2001). Part of the content knowledge includes critical skills such as evidence-based teaching and establishing markers of success (Cosner 2011; Levine and Marcus 2007). That is, as Kruse et al. (1995, p. 38) nicely put it, "Professional community is based on an intellectual and practical grasp of the knowledge base and skills underlying the field." In addition, in order "to help teachers engage thorny issues of teaching and learning [...] and critique each other's practice" (Levine and

Marcus 2007, p. 135) deep grounding in one's subject discipline is necessary (Timperley 2005; York-Barr and Duke 2004). Indeed, this may be the most essential learning required for teacher communities to reach their potential (McLaughlin and Talbert 2001).

11.4 The Critical Role of the Principal

Although we possess less knowledge than we might desire, we have accumulated some understandings about principals and communities of professional practice over the last 20 years. Investigators inform us, for example, that community-building work unfolds within three domains: preemptive prevention, removal of existing barriers, and/or the construction of an infrastructure to support the development of professional communities. We also understand that the principal has a cardinal position in this work, a conclusion uncovered in nearly every study of teacher communities of professional practice (Cosner 2011; Louis et al. 2010; Stoll et al. 2006). Research also reveals that there are significant differences in the nature of leadership in schools with robust communities and those with weak communities (Mangin 2007; Youngs and King 2002). That is, "principals can construct their role to either support or inhibit the strength and quality of teacher community" (McLaughlin and Talbert 2001, p. 101). With increasing frequency, research confirms that it is the principal who acts as the catalyst to bring important supports to life (Bryk et al. 2010; Mitchell and Sackney 2006). Without effective leadership, resources, time, and structures have almost no hope of emerging to support collaborative work (Cosner 2009; Hayes et al. 2004). We also know that leadership and professional community are interdependent, having an iterative relationship (McLaughlin and Talbert 2001; Murphy 2005). Perhaps most importantly, there is a growing knowledge base which suggests that of all the ways that principals have at their disposal to influence student learning, developing, and supporting collaborative communities of professional practice is one of the most powerful (Murphy and Torre 2014; Supovitz et al. 2010).

For many leaders supporting communities of practice requires a difficult transformation of their own understanding of leadership and their own leadership practice (Goldstein 2004). "The implications for school principals are considerable" (Crowther et al. 2002, p. 64), and this repositioning presents a real challenge for principals (Brown and Sheppard 1999; Murphy 2005). As we explained in detail above, communities of practice are in some essential ways "at odds with the dominant conceptions of the principalship that have been in place in most educational systems for decades" (Crowther et al. 2002, p. 6). New metaphors for leaders emerge as well (Beck and Murphy 1993; Sergiovanni 1991a, b) – metaphors that reflect the role of the principal not in terms of one's fit in the organizational structure but in terms of membership in a community of leaders (Beck and Murphy 1993; Scribner et al. 1999).

More specifically, our review concludes that school leaders have core responsibilities here. They need to build the infrastructure to make professional communities operate. They also need to hold at bay the natural entropy associated with reform. They must help keep communities viable and vibrant. They need to layer in multiple, integrated supports.

One of the main conclusions that has emerged from the research in this area over the last two decades is that it is nearly impossible, to create learning communities from which formal leaders are absent (Louis et al. 2010; Printy 2008). As we discussed above, the principals must be part of communities, not simply distant overseers (Barnett and McCormick 2004; Halverson et al. 2007; Scribner et al. 1999). Principals should model values and principles of community (Gurr et al. 2006; Young 2006). Deep engagement permits school leaders to undertake an assortment of supportive tasks, both symbolic and substantive, such as modeling appropriate behavior, being highly visible, monitoring progress, demonstrating consideration, and so forth (Drago-Severson 2004; Louis 2007; Mitchell and Sackney 2006). Being part of the community tapestry enhances legitimacy of the principal and permits more effective use of the person-centered leadership practices that are much needed in collaborative work (Adams 2010; Leithwood et al. 2006a; Printy 2008).

Scholars confirm that a keystone role for leaders is to ensure that communities of practice are clear, understood, and actionable. Also, values, principles, and expectations need to be bolstered by "enabling policies" (Lieberman and Miller 1999, p. 28). Little (1987) concurs, arguing that "at its strongest – most durable, most rigorously connected to problems of student learning, most commanding of teachers' energies, talents, and loyalties – cooperative work is a matter of school policy" (p. 512) and that "high levels of joint action are more likely to persist" (p. 508) when a supportive policy structure is in place (Bishop et al. 1997).

Research on reform, implementation, change, and school improvement, document the need for sufficient resources. Nowhere is this conclusion more compelling than in the area communities of learning (Grossman et al. 2001; Mitchell and Sackney 2006; Mullen and Hutinger 2008; Wenger 2000). Resources, in addition to time, that surface in the scholarship on professional community include materials, such as "teachers' guides, activity sheets, and commercially prepared videos" (Burch and Spillane 2003, p. 530). Protocols that direct collaborative work into productive channels is a type of material often highlighted in the research on productive communities of practice (Cosner 2011; Saunders et al. 2009). These activities help generate shared language, maintain focus, teach group process skills, and reinforce professional values, while damping down dysfunctional behavior and entropy often observed in work teams (Cosner 2011; Ermeling 2010; Young 2006).

Access to external expertise to help teachers work more effectively together is also underscored in the research (King 2001; McLaughlin and Talbert 2001; Saunders et al. 2009). Such assistance can assume the form of content experts (Murphy 2005), models of best practice (Curry 2008; Levine and Marcus 2007), appropriate research (Vescio et al. 2008), and facilitation (Borko 2004; Saunders et al. 2009). Commitments such as these often require principals to secure new resources or reallocate existing ones to purchase materials, expertise, and time

(Ancess 2003; Cosner 2009, 2011). In collaborative communities, all of these resources are employed to deepen professional norms and teacher learning (Silins and Mulford 2004; Wenger and Snyder 2000).

For communities of practice to function effectively, principals need to become central figures in communication systems, employing both formal and informal procedures (Brooks et al. 2004; Cosner 2011; Walker and Slear 2011). When this happens, understanding is deepened, questions can be answered, and misconceptions are addressed before they can become dysfunctional (Cosner 2011; Kochanek 2005; Saunders et al. 2009).

Additional "managing communities" responsibilities for leaders can be culled from the research. Not surprisingly given its importance in the general literature on effective leadership (Murphy 2015), the principal plays an essential role in ensuring that explicit understandings of the rationale for, workings of, and outcomes expected from teacher communities are established (Printy 2008; Quint 2006). Investigators also find that principals with well-functioning professional communities are adept at buffering teachers from external pressures that can cripple progress (King 2001; Rossmiller 1992). They filter demands that are not aligned with community work (Cosner 2011; Robinson 2007) and reshape others so that they fit (Printy 2008).

The necessity for ongoing monitoring of processes and outputs of collaborative work is routinely seen in the research as well (Dinham et al. 1995; Quint 2006; Stoll et al. 2006). Participation in community meetings, review of group documents, and comparative benchmarking are often featured in the monitoring portfolio (Heller and Firestone 1995; MacBeath 2005; Mullen and Hutinger 2008). Monitoring which keeps "leaders in touch with teacher's ongoing thinking and development" (Levine and Marcus 2007, p. 134) leads directly to another responsibility, that of ensuring that collaborative work teams receive useful feedback. A school culture that honors shared engagement (Ancess 2003; Cochran-Smith and Lytle 1999; Harrison and Lembeck 1996) is yet another research-anchored instrument in the managing collaboration toolbox. So, too, is a system of incentives and rewards that motivates teachers to honor mutually of vision, work, and accountability. Currently, the picture that emerges from the research is one in which there are few external incentives for community work (Murphy 2005). In fact, there are numerous disincentives (Little 1988) to change to mutual work at the heart of teacher communities. In many schools, there is limited acknowledgment for the work and few rewards for the additional effort community-based endeavors require (Crowther et al. 2002). While "rewarding teachers who are willing to move beyond their classrooms to lead is a complicated issue" (Moller and Katzenmeyer 1996, p. 13), in the end schools "must provide incentives and rewards for teachers who take the lead in tackling tasks and solving problems" (Boles and Troen 1996, p. 60). Principals, in turn, need to identify and employ strategies to acknowledge teachers in ways teachers value (Harrison and Lembeck 1996; Smylie et al. 2002). Studies consistently find that the responsibility for showcasing and providing recognition for quality work rests squarely with the principal (Drago-Severson 2004; Mulford and Silins 2003).

11.5 Conclusion

The profession has placed a stake in the ground about the need to build powerful culture in schools. Culture in conjunction with academic process, it is argued, will produce the higher levels of academic and social learning that is so much in demand. Particularly heartening is the accumulation of evidence that a focus on culture has the potential to reach students in peril, creating belonging and engagement where too little exists today.

At the heart of all the new work on culture is the concept of community – community of pastoral care for students, community of engagement for parents, and community of professionalism for teachers (Murphy and Torre 2014). Of the three, the body of scholarly knowledge is deepest in the domain of teacher community. In particular, we saw that considerable information has been layered around professional learning communities. Understanding of the forces fueling teacher professional communities and of the logic model that exposes the DNA of community has grown considerably.

But much work is still needed in linking these powerful norms empirically to mediating factors and organizational outcomes. Equally important, understanding of how to bring teacher community to life is underdeveloped. Actions rest too heavily at times on the platform of structural fallacy. Insufficient study has been undertaken to analyze the growth of the norms that define teacher learning communities. Change is a difficult enough challenge in general. When new ideas run against deepseated ways of doing schooling (i.e. culture) and collide with the sturdy structures of the existing educational system, change is all the more arduous. And no reform is being asked to overhaul the structure and culture of schooling more than communities of professional practice.

In this paper, we reviewed the research about the organizational barriers that get in the way of communities of practice taking root and flourishing in schools. Without a deep understanding of and maps of the schooling landscape, the outcome of community-building work is unlikely to be positive. The possibility of dysfunctional communities was raised. We closed our analysis with research insights about effective strategies to employ in support of community development.

References

Adams, C. (2010). Social determinants of student trust in high poverty elementary schools. In W. K. Hoy & M. DiPaola (Eds.), *Analyzing school contexts: Influences of principals and teachers in the service of students* (pp. 255–280). Charlotte: Information Age.

Ainscow, M., & Southworth, G. (1996). School improvement: a study of the roles of leaders and external consultants. *School Effectiveness and School Improvement, 7*(3), 229–251.

Ancess, J. (2000). The reciprocal influence of teacher learning, teaching practice, school restructuring, and student learning outcomes. *Teachers College Record, 102*(3), 590–619.

Ancess, J. (2003). *Beating the odds: High schools as communities of commitment*. New York: Teachers College Press.

Barnett, K., & McCormick, J. (2004). Leadership and individual principal-teacher relationships in schools. *Educational Administration Quarterly, 40*(3), 406–434.
Beck, L., & Murphy, J. (1993). *Understanding the principalship: Metaphorical themes 1920s1990s.* New York: Teachers College Press.
Bidwell, C. E., & Yasumoto, J. Y. (1999). The collegial focus: Teaching fields, collegial relationships, and instructional practice in American high schools. *Sociology of Education, 72*(4), 234–256.
Bishop, H. L., Tinley, A., & Berman, B. T. (1997). A contemporary leadership model to promote teacher leadership. *Action in Teacher Education, 19*(3), 77–81.
Blanc, S., Christman, J. B., Liu, R., Mitchell, C., Travers, E., & Bulkley, K. E. (2010). Learning to learn from data: Benchmarks and instructional communities. *Peabody Journal of Education, 85*(2), 205–225.
Blase, J., & Blase, J. (2004). *Handbook of instructional leadership: How really good principals promote teaching and learning.* Thousand Oaks: Corwin.
Blegen, M. B., & Kennedy, C. (2000). Principals and teachers, leading together. *NASSP Bulletin, 84*(616), 1–6.
Boles, K., & Troen, V. (1996). Teacher leaders and power: Achieving school reform from the classroom. In G. Moller & M. Katzenmeyer (Eds.), *Every teacher as a leader: Realizing the potential of teacher leadership* (pp. 41–62). San Francisco: Jossey-Bass.
Borko, H. (2004). Professional development and teacher learning: Mapping the terrain. *Educational Researcher, 33*(8), 3–15.
Brooks, J. S., Scribner, J. P., & Eferakorho, J. (2004). Teacher leadership in the context of whole school reform. *Journal of School Leadership, 14*(3), 242–265.
Brown, J., & Sheppard, B. (1999, April). *Leadership, organizational learning, and classroom change.* Paper presented at the annual meeting of the American Educational Research Association, Montreal, QC, Canada.
Bryk, A. S., Sebring, P. B., Allensworth, E., Luppescu, S., & Easton, J. (2010). *Organizing schools for improvement: Lessons from Chicago.* Chicago: University of Chicago Press.
Bulkley, K. E., & Hicks, J. (2005). Managing community: Professional community in charter schools operated by educational management organizations. *Educational Administration Quarterly, 41*(2), 306–348.
Burch, P., & Spillane, J. P. (2003). Elementary school leadership strategies and subject matter: Reforming mathematics and literacy instruction. *Elementary School Journal, 5*, 519–535.
Center for Teaching Quality. (2007). *Teaching and learning conditions improve high school reform efforts.* Chapel Hill: Author.
Chrispeels, J. H., & Martin, K. J. (2002). Four school leadership teams define their roles within organizational and political structures to improve student learning. *School Effectiveness and School Improvement, 13*(3), 327–365.
Clift, R., Johnson, M., Holland, P., & Veal, M. L. (1992). Developing the potential for collaborative school leadership. *American Educational Research Journal, 29*(4), 877–908.
Cochran-Smith, M., & Lytle, S. (1999). Relationship of knowledge and practice: Teacher learning in communities. In A. Iran-Nejad & C. D. Pearson (Eds.), *Review of research in education* (pp. 249–306). Washington, DC: American Educational Research Association.
Cohen, D. K. (1988). *Teaching practice: Plus ça change* (Issue paper 88-3). East Lansing: Michigan State University, The National Center for Research on Teacher Education.
Conley, S. C. (1989, March). *Who's on first? School reform, teacher participation, and the decision-making process.* Paper presented at the annual meeting of the American Educational Research Association, San Francisco, CA.
Conley, S. (1991). Review of research on teacher participation in school decision making. *Review of Research in Education, 17*(17), 225–266.
Cosner, S. (2009). Building organizational capacity through trust. *Educational Administration Quarterly, 45*(2), 248–291.

Cosner, S. (2011). Supporting the initiation and early development of evidence-based grade-level collaboration in urban elementary schools: Key roles and strategies of principals and literacy coordinators. *Urban Education, 46*(4), 786–827.

Coyle, M. (1997). Teacher leadership vs school management: Flatten the hierarchies. *Teacher Leadership, 70*(5), 236–239.

Crow, G. M., & Pounder, D. G. (2000). Interdisciplinary teacher teams: Context, design, and process. *Educational Administration Quarterly, 36*(2), 216–254.

Crowther, F., Kaagan, S. S., Ferguson, M., & Hann, L. (2002). *Developing teacher leaders: How teacher leadership enhances school success*. Thousand Oaks: Corwin.

Curry, M. (2008). Critical friends groups: The possibilities and limitations embedded in teacher professional communities aimed at instructional improvement and school reform. *Teachers College Record, 110*(4), 733–774.

Dannetta, V. (2002). What factors influence a teacher's commitment to student learning? *Leadership and Policy in Schools, 1*, 144–171.

Darling-Hammond, L., & McLaughlin, M. W. (1995). Policies that support professional development in an era of reform. *Phi Delta Kappan, 76*(8), 597–604.

Darling-Hammond, L., Bullmaster, M. L., & Cobb, V. L. (1995). Rethinking teacher leadership through professional development schools. *Elementary School Journal, 96*, 87–107.

Darling-Hammond, L., Ancess, J., & Ort, S. (2002). Reinventing high school: Outcomes of the coalition campus schools project. *American Educational Research Journal, 39*(3), 639–673.

Desimone, L. (2002). How can comprehensive school reform models be successfully implemented? *Review of Educational Research, 72*(3), 433–479.

Dinham, S., Cairney, T., Craigie, D., & Wilson, S. (1995). School climate and leadership: Research into three secondary schools. *Journal of Educational Administration, 33*(4), 36–58.

Donaldson, G. A. (2001). *Cultivating leadership in schools: connecting people, purpose, and practice*. New York: Teachers College Press.

Doyle, M. (2000, April). *Making meaning of teacher leadership in the implementation of a standards-based mathematics curriculum*. Paper presented at the annual meeting of the American Educational Research Association, New Orleans, LA.

Drago-Severson, E. (2004). *Helping teachers learn: Principal leadership for adult growth and development*. Thousand Oaks: Corwin.

Eilers, A.M., & Camacho, A. (2007). School culture change in the making: Leadership factors that matter. *Urban Education, 42*(6), 616–637.

Elmore, R. F. (1987). Reform and the culture of authority in schools. *Educational Administration Quarterly, 23*(4), 60–78.

Ermeling, B. A. (2010). Tracing the effects of teacher inquiry on classroom practice. *Teaching and Teacher Education, 26*(3), 377–388.

Fay, C. (1992). Empowerment through leadership: In the teachers' voice. In C. Livingston (Ed.), *Teachers as leaders: Evolving roles* (pp. 57–90). Washington, DC: National Education Association.

Feiman-Nemser, S., & Floden, R. F. (1986). The cultures of teaching. In C. W. Wittrock (Ed.), *Handbook of research on teaching* (3rd ed., pp. 505–526). New York: Macmillan.

Felner, R., Seitsinger, A., Brand, S., Burns, A., & Bolton, N. (2007). Creating small learning communities: Lessons from the project on high-performing learning communities about 'what works' in creating productive, developmentally enhancing, learning contexts. *Educational Psychologist, 42*(4), 209–221.

Firestone, W. A., & Martinez, M. C. (2007). Districts, teacher leaders, and distributed leadership: changing instructional practice. *Leadership and Policy in Schools, 6*, 3–35.

Foster, R., & St. Hilaire, B. (2003). Leadership for school improvement: Principals' and teachers perspectives. *International Electronic Journal for Leadership in Learning, 7*(3), 1–18.

Friedkin, N. E., & Slater, M. R. (1994). School leadership and performance: A social network approach. *Sociology of Education, 67*(2), 139–157.

Fullan, M., & Ballew, A. C. (2002). *Leading in a culture of change*. San Francisco: Jossey-Bass.

Glaser, B. G., & Strauss, A. L. (1967). *The discovery of grounded theory: Strategies for qualitative research*. New Brunswick: Aldine Transaction.

Goldstein, J. (2004). Making sense of distributed leadership: The case of peer assistance and review. *Educational Evaluation and Policy Analyis, 26*(2), 173–197.

Gray, J., Hopkins, D., Reynolds, D., Wilcox, B., Farrell, S., & Jesson, D. (1999). *Improving schools: Performance and potential*. Philadelphia: Open University Press.

Griffin, G. A. (1995). Influences of shared decision making on school and classroom activity: Conversations with five teachers. *Elementary School Journal, 96*, 29–45.

Grossman, P., Wineburg, S., & Woolworth, S. (2001). Toward a theory of teacher community. *Teachers College Record, 103*(6), 942–1012.

Gurr, D., Drysdale, L., & Mulford, B. (2006). Models of successful principal leadership. *School Leadership and Management, 26*(4), 371–395.

Hallinger, P. (2012a). A conceptual framework for systematic reviews of research in educational leadership and management. *Journal of Educational Administration, 51*, 26–149.

Hallinger, P. (2012b). *Reviewing reviews of research in educational leadership: A proposed conceptual framework and empirical assessment*. Hong Kong: Asia Pacific Centre for Leadership and Change, Hong Kong Institute of Education.

Hallinger, P. (2014). Reviewing reviews of research in educational leadership: An empirical assessment. *Educational Administration Quarterly, 5*(4), 539–576.

Halverson, R., Grigg, J., Prichett, R., & Thomas, C. (2007). The new instructional leadership: Creating data-driven instructional systems in school. *Journal of School Leadership, 17*(2), 159–194.

Harris, A. (2003). Teacher leadership as distributed leadership: Heresy, fantasy or possibility? *School Leadership and Management, 2*(3), 313–324.

Harris, A. (2004). Distributed leadership and school improvement. *Educational Management Administration and Leadership, 32*, 11–24.

Harrison, J. W., & Lembeck, E. (1996). Emergent teacher leaders. In G. Moller & M. Katzenmeyer (Eds.), *Every teacher as a leader: Realizing the potential of teacher leadership* (pp. 101–116). San Francisco: Jossey-Bass.

Hart, A. W. (1990). Impacts of the school social unit on teacher authority during work redesign. *American Educational Research Journal, 27*(3), 503–532.

Hart, A. W. (1995). Reconceiving school leadership: emergent view. *Elementary School Journal, 96*, 9–28.

Hattie, J. (2009). *Visible learning: A synthesis of over 800 meta-analyses relating to achievement*. New York: Routledge.

Hayes, N. (2000). *Psychological research*. Buckingham: Open University Press.

Hayes, D., Christie, P., Mills, M., & Lingard, B. (2004). Productive leaders and productive leadership: Schools as learning organisations. *Journal of Educational Administration, 42*(5), 520–538.

Heller, M. F., & Firestone, W. A. (1995). Who's in charge here? Sources of leadership for change in eight schools. *Elementary School Journal, 96*, 65–86.

Horn, I. S. (2010). Teaching replays, teaching rehearsals, and re-visions of practice: Learning from colleagues in a mathematics teacher community. *Teachers College Record, 112*, 225–259.

Huberman, M., Parrish, T., Hannan, S., Arellanes, M., & Shambaugh, L. (2011). *Turnaround schools in California: Who are they and what strategies do they use?* San Francisco: WestEd.

Jackson, D. S. (2000). The school improvement journey: Perspectives on leadership. *School Leadership and Management, 20*, 61–78.

Johnson, B. L. (1998). Organizing for collaboration: a reconsideration of some basic organizing principles. In D. G. Pounder (Ed.), *Restructuring schools for collaboration: Promises and pitfalls* (pp. 9–25). Albany: State University of New York Press.

Johnson Jr., J. F., & Asera, R. (1999). *Hope for urban education: A study of nine high-performing, high-poverty, urban elementary schools*. Washington, DC: US Department of Education, Planning and Evaluation Services.

Katzenmeyer, M., & Moller, G. (2001). *Awakening the sleeping giant: Helping teachers develop as leaders*. Newbury Park: Corwin.

Keedy, J. L. (1999). Examining teacher instructional leadership within the small group dynamics of collegial groups. *Teaching and Teacher Education, 15*(7), 785–799.

Kilcher, A. (1992). Becoming a change facilitator: The first-year experience of five teacher leaders. In C. Livingston (Ed.), *Teachers as leaders: Evolving roles* (pp. 91–113). Washington, DC: National Education Association.

Killion, J. P. (1996). Moving beyond the school: teacher leaders in the district office. In G. Moller & M. Katzenmeyer (Eds.), *Every teacher as a leader: Realizing the potential of teacher leadership* (pp. 63–84). San Francisco: Jossey-Bass.

King, M. (2001). Professional development to promote schoolwide inquiry. *Teaching and Teacher Education, 18*(3), 243–257.

Kochanek, J. R. (2005). *Building trust for better schools: Research-based practices*. Thousand Oaks: Corwin.

Kruse, S., Louis, K. S., & Bryk, A. (1995). An emerging framework for analyzing school-based professional community. In K. S. Louis & S. Kruse (Eds.), *Professionalism and community: Perspectives on reforming urban schools* (pp. 23–44). Thousand Oaks: Corwin.

LeBlanc, P. R., & Shelton, M. M. (1997). Teacher leadership: The needs of teachers. *Action in Teacher Education, 19*(3), 32–48.

Leithwood, K., Jantzi, D., Ryan, S., & Steinbach, R. (1997, April). *Distributed leadership in secondary schools*. Paper presented at the annual meeting of the American Educational Research Association, Chicago, IL.

Leithwood, K., Jantzi, D., & Steinbach, R. (1999). *Changing leadership for changing times*. Philadelphia: Open University Press.

Leithwood, K., Louis, K., Anderson, S., & Wahlstrom, K. (2004). *How leadership influences student learning*. New York: Wallace Foundation.

Leithwood, K., Day, C., Sammons, P., Harris, A., & Hopkins, D. (2006a). *Successful school leadership. What it is and how it influences pupil learning*. London: Department of Education and Skills.

Leithwood, K., Jantzi, D., & McElheron-Hopkins, C. (2006b). The development and testing of a school improvement model. *School Effectiveness and School Improvement, 17*(4), 441–464.

Levine, T. H., & Marcus, A. S. (2007). Closing the achievement gap through teacher collaboration: Facilitating multiple trajectories of teacher learning. *Journal of Advanced Academics, 19*, 116–138.

Levine, T. H., & Marcus, A. S. (2010). How the structure and focus of teachers' collaborative activities facilitate and constrain teacher learning. *Teaching and Teacher Education, 26*(3), 389–398.

Lieberman, A., & Miller, L. (1999). *Teachers – Transforming their world and their work*. New York: Teachers College Press.

Lieberman, A., Saxl, E. R., & Miles, M. B. (1988). Teacher leadership: Ideology and practice. In A. Lieberman (Ed.), *Building a professional culture in schools* (pp. 148–166). New York: Teachers College Press.

Little, J. W. (1982). Norms of collegiality and experimentation: Workplace conditions of school success. *American Educational Research Journal, 19*(3), 325–340.

Little, J. W. (1985). Contested ground: the basis of teacher leadership in two restructuring high schools. *Elementary School Journal, 96*(2), 47–63.

Little, J. W. (1987). Teachers as colleagues. In V. Richardson-Koehler (Ed.), *Educators' handbook: A research perspective* (pp. 491–518). White Plains: Longman.

Little, J.W. (1988). Assessing the prospects for teacher leadership. In A. Lieberman (Ed.), *Building a professional culture in schools* (pp. 78–105). New York: Teachers College Press.

Little, J. W. (1990). The perspective of privacy: Autonomy and initiative in teachers' professional relations. *Teachers College Record, 91*(4), 509–536.

Lortie, D. C. (1975). *Schoolteacher: A sociological study*. Chicago: University of Chicago Press.

Louis, K. (2007). Trust and improvement in schools. *Journal of Educational Change, 8*, 1–24.
Louis, K., & Marks, H. (1998). Does professional community affect the classroom? Teachers' work and student experiences in restructuring schools. *American Journal of Education, 106*(4), 532–575.
Louis, K. S., Dretzke, B., & Wahlstrom, K. (2010). How does leadership affect student achievement? Results from a national US survey. *School Effectiveness and School Improvement, 21*(3), 315–336.
Lynch, M., & Strodl, P. (1991, February). *Teacher leadership: Preliminary development of a questionnaire*. Paper presented at the annual conference of the Eastern Educational Research Association, Boston.
McDougall, D., Saunders, W. M., & Goldenberg, C. (2007). Inside the black box of school reform: Explaining the how and why of change at getting results schools. *International Journal of Disability, Development and Education, 54*, 51–89.
McLaughlin, M. W., & Talbert, J. E. (2001). *Professional communities and the work of high school teaching*. Chicago: University of Chicago Press.
MacBeath, J. (2005). Leadership as distributed: a matter of practice. *School Leadership and Management, 25*(4), 349–366.
MacBeath, J. (2009). Distributed leadership: Paradigms, policy, and paradox. In K. Leithwood, B. Mascall, & T. Strauss (Eds.), *Distributed leadership according to the evidence* (pp. 41–57). London: Routledge.
Mangin, M. M. (2007). Facilitating elementary principals' support for instructional teacher leadership. *Educational Administration Quarterly, 43*(3), 319–357.
Manthei, J. (1992, April). *The mentor teacher as leader: The motives, characteristics and needs of seventy-three experienced teachers who seek a new leadership role*. Paper presented at the annual meeting of the American Educational Research Association, San Francisco, CA, (ERIC Document Reproduction Service No ED 346042).
May, H., & Supovitz, J. A. (2011). The scope of principal efforts to improve instruction. *Educational Administration Quarterly, 47*(2), 332–352.
Meyer, J.W., & Rowan, B. (1975, April). *Notes on the structure of educational organizations: Revised version*. Paper presented at the annual meeting of the American Sociological Association, San Francisco, CA.
Miles, M. B., & Huberman, A. M. (1994). *Qualitative data analysis* (2nd ed.). Thousand Oaks: Sage.
Mitchell, C., & Castle, J. B. (2005). The instructional role of elementary school principals. *Canadian Journal of Education/Revue Canadienne de l'education, 28*(3), 409–433.
Mitchell, C., & Sackney, L. (2006). Building schools, building people: The school principal's role in leading a learning community. *Journal of School Leadership, 16*(5), 627–640.
Moller, J., & Eggen, A. B. (2005). Team leadership in upper secondary education. *School Leadership and Management, 25*(4), 331–347.
Moller, G., & Katzenmeyer, M. (1996). The promise of teacher leadership. In G. Moller & M. Katzenmeyer (Eds.), *Every teacher as a leader: Realizing the potential of teacher leadership* (pp. 1–18). San Francisco: Jossey-Bass.
Morrissey, M. S. (2000). *Professional learning communities: An ongoing exploration*. Austin: Southwest Educational Development Laboratory.
Mulford, B., & Silins, H. (2003). Leadership for organisational learning and improved student outcomes – What do we know? *Cambridge Journal of Education, 33*(2), 175–195.
Mullen, C. A., & Hutinger, J. L. (2008). The principal's role in fostering collaborative learning communities through faculty study group development. *Theory Into Practice, 47*(4), 276–285.
Murphy, J. (1991). *Restructuring schools: Capturing and assessing the phenomena*. New York: Teachers College Press.
Murphy, J. (2005). *Connecting teacher leadership and school improvement*. Thousand Oaks: Corwin.

Murphy, J. (2006). *Preparing school leaders: An agenda for research and action*. Lanham: Rowman and Littlefield.

Murphy, J. (2013a). *The architecture of school improvement: Lessons learned*. Thousand Oaks: Corwin.

Murphy, J. (2013b). The architecture of school improvement. *Journal of Educational Administration, 51*(3), 252–263.

Murphy, J. (2015). Forces shaping schooling and school leadership. *Journal of School Leadership, 25*(6), 1064–1087.

Murphy, J., & Torre, D. (2014). *Creating productive cultures in schools: For students, teachers, and parents*. Thousand Oaks: Corwin.

Murphy, J., Hallinger, P., Lotto, L. S., & Miller, S. K. (1987). Barriers to implementing the instructional leadership role. *Canadian Administrator, 27*(3), 1–9.

Myers, M. S. (1970). *Every employee a manager: More meaningful work through job enrichment*. New York: McGraw-Hill.

Newmann, F. M., Rutter, R. A., & Smith, M. S. (1989). Organizational factors that affect school sense of efficacy, community, and expectations. *Sociology of Education, 62*(4), 221–238.

Newmann, F. M., Smith, B., Allensworth, E., & Bryk, A. S. (2001). Instructional program coherence: What it is and why it should guide school improvement policy. *Educational Evaluation and Policy Analyis, 23*(4), 297–321.

Pellicer, L. O., & Anderson, L. W. (1995). *A handbook for teacher leaders*. Thousand Oaks: Corwin.

Penuel, W., Riel, M., Krause, A., & Frank, K. (2009). Analyzing teachers' professional interactions in a school as social capital: A social network approach. *Teachers College Record, 111*, 124–163.

Penuel, W., Riel, M., Joshi, A., Pearlman, L., Kim, C. M., & Frank, K. A. (2010). The alignment of the informal and formal organizational supports for reform: Implications for improving teaching in schools. *Educational Administration Quarterly, 46*, 57–95.

Pounder, D. G. (1999). Teacher teams: Exploring job characteristics and work-related outcomes of work group enhancement. *Educational Administration Quarterly, 35*(3), 317–348.

Printy, S. M. (2004). The professional impact of communities of practice. *UCEA Review, 46*, 20–23.

Printy, S. M. (2008). Leadership for teacher learning: A community of practice perspective. *Educational Administration Quarterly, 44*(2), 187–226.

Quint, J. (2006). *Meeting five critical challenges of high school reform: Lessons from research on three reform models*. New York: Manpower Demonstration Research Corporation.

Rallis, S. F. (1990). Professional teachers and restructured schools: Leadership challenges. In B. Mitchell & L.L. Cunningham (Eds.), *Educational leadership in changing contexts of families, communities, and schools*, 89th yearbook of the National Society for the Study of Education, Part II (pp. 184–209). Chicago: National Society for the Study of Education.

Raywid, M. (1995). Professional community and its yield at Metro Academy. In K. S. Louis & S. Kruse (Eds.), *Professionalism and community: Perspectives on reforming urban schools* (pp. 43–75). Thousand Oaks: Corwin.

Robinson, V. M. J. (2007). *School leadership and student outcomes: Identifying what works and why*. Sydney: Australian Council for Educational Leaders.

Rosenholtz, S. J. (1989). *Teachers' workplace: The social organization of school*. White Plains: Longman.

Rossmiller, R. A. (1992). The secondary school principal and teachers' quality of work life. *Educational Management Administration and Leadership, 20*(3), 132–146.

Saunders, W. M., Goldenberg, C. N., & Gallimore, R. (2009). Increasing achievement by focusing grade-level teams on improving classroom learning: A prospective, quasi-experimental study of title I schools. *American Educational Research Journal, 46*(4), 1006–1033.

Scribner, J. P., Cockrell, K. S., Cockrell, D. H., & Valentine, J. W. (1999). Creating professional communities in schools through organizational learning: An evaluation of a school improvement process. *Educational Administration Quarterly, 35*, 130–160.

Sergiovanni, T. J. (1991a). The dark side of professionalism in educational administration. *Phi Delta Kappan, 72*(7), 521–526.

Sergiovanni, T. J. (1991b). *The principalship: A reflective practice perspective* (2nd ed.). Boston: Allyn and Bacon.

Silins, H., & Mulford, B. (2004). Schools as learning organisations: Effects on teacher leadership and student outcomes. *School Effectiveness and School Improvement, 3*(4), 443–466.

Siu, W. (2008). Complexity theory and school reform. *NASSP Bulletin, 92*(2), 154–164.

Sizer, T. R. (1984). *Horace's Compromise: The dilemma of the American high school*. Boston: Houghton Mifflin.

Smylie, M. A. (1992). Teacher participation in school decision making: Assessing willingness to participate. *Educational Evaluation and Policy Analyis, 14*, 53–67.

Smylie, M. A. (1996). Research on teacher leadership: Assessing the state of the art. In B. J. Biddle, T. L. Good, & I. F. Goodson (Eds.), *International handbook of teachers and teaching* (pp. 521–592). Boston: Kluwer Academic.

Smylie, M. A., & Brownlee-Conyers, J. (1992). Teacher leaders and their principals: Exploring the development of new working relationships. *Educational Administration Quarterly, 28*(2), 150–184.

Smylie, M. A., & Hart, A. W. (1999). School leadership for teacher learning: A human and social capital development perspective. In J. Murphy & K. S. Louis (Eds.), *Handbook of research on educational administration* (2nd ed., pp. 421–441). San Francisco: Jossey-Bass.

Smylie, M. A., Conley, S., & Marks, H. M. (2002). Exploring new approaches to teacher leadership for school improvement. In J. Murphy (Ed.), *The educational leadership challenge: Redefining leadership for the 21st century* (pp. 162–188). Chicago: University of Chicago Press.

Spillane, J. P., Diamond, J. B., Walker, L. J., Halverson, R., & Jita, L. (2001). Urban school leadership for elementary science instruction: Identifying and activating resources in an undervalued school subject. *Journal of Research in Science Teaching, 38*(8), 918–940.

Stein, M. K., & Coburn, C. E. (2008). Architectures for learning: A comparative analysis of two urban school districts. *American Journal of Education, 114*(4), 583–626.

Stigler, J. W., & Hiebert, J. (1999). *The teaching gap: Best ideas from the world's teachers for improving education in the classroom*. New York: Free Press.

Stoll, L., Bolam, R., McMahon, A., Wallace, M., & Thomas, S. (2006). Professional learning communities: A review of the literature. *Journal of Educational Change, 7*(4), 221–258.

Strauss, A. L., & Corbin, J. M. (1998). *Basics of qualitative research: Techniques and procedures for developing grounded theory*. Thousand Oaks: Sage.

Supovitz, J. (2002). Developing communities of instructional practice. *Teachers College Record, 104*(8), 1591–1626.

Supovitz, J. (2008). Instructional influence in American high schools. In M. M. Mangin & S. R. Stoelinga (Eds.), *Effective teacher leadership: Using research to inform and reform* (pp. 144–162). New York: Teachers College Press.

Supovitz, J., Sirinides, P., & May, H. (2010). How principals and peers influence teaching and learning. *Educational Administration Quarterly, 46*, 31–56.

Teitel, L. (1996). Finding common ground: Teacher leaders and principals. In G. Moller & M. Katzenmeyer (Eds.), *Every teacher as a leader: Realizing the potential of teacher leadership* (pp. 139–154). San Francisco: Jossey-Bass.

Timperley, H. (2005). Distributed leadership: Developing theory from practice. *Journal of Curriculum Studies, 37*(4), 395–420.

Troen, V., & Boles, K. (1994). Two teachers examine the power of teacher leadership. In D. R. Walling (Ed.), *Teachers as leaders: Perspectives on the professional development of teachers* (pp. 275–286). Bloomington: Phi Delta Kappa.

Uline, C. L., & Berkowitz, J. M. (2000). Transforming school culture through teaching teams. *Journal of School Leadership, 10*, 416–444.

Useem, E. L., Christman, J. B., Gold, E., & Simon, E. (1997). Reforming alone: Barriers to organizational learning in urban school change initiatives. *Journal of Education for Students Placed at Risk, 2*, 55–78.

Vescio, V., Ross, D., & Adams, A. (2008). A review of research on the impact of professional learning communities on teaching practice and student learning. *Teaching and Teacher Education, 24*, 80–91.

Visscher, A. J., & Witziers, B. (2004). Subject departments as professional communities? *British Educational Research Journal, 30*(6), 785–800.

Walker, J., & Slear, S. (2011). The impact of principal leadership behaviors on the efficacy of new and experienced middle school teachers. *NASSP Bulletin, 95*, 46–64.

Wasley, P. A. (1991). *Teachers who lead: The rhetoric of reform and realities of practice.* New York: Teachers College Press.

Weick, K. E. (1976). Educational organizations as loosely coupled systems. *Administrative Science Quarterly, 21*(2), 1–19.

Wenger, E. (2000). Communities of practice and social learning systems. *Organization, 7*(2), 225–246.

Wenger, E., & Snyder, W. (2000). Communities of practice: The organizational frontier. *Harvard Business Review, 78*, 139–146.

Wilson, M. (1993). The search for teacher leaders. *Educational Leadership, 50*(6), 24–27.

York-Barr, J., & Duke, K. (2004). What do we know about teacher leadership? Findings from two decades of scholarship. *Review of Educational Research, 74*(3), 255–316.

Young, V. (2006). Teachers' use of data: Loose coupling, agenda setting, and team norms. *American Journal of Education, 112*(4), 521–548.

Youngs, P. (2007). How elementary principals' beliefs and actions influence new teachers' experiences. *Educational Administration Quarterly, 43*, 101–137.

Youngs, P., & King, M. B. (2002). Principal leadership for professional development to build school capacity. *Educational Administration Quarterly, 38*(5), 643–670.

Zimpher, N. L. (1988). A design for the professional development of teacher leaders. *Journal of Teacher Education, 39*, 53–60.

Further Reading

Buckner, K. G., & McDowelle, J. O. (2000). Developing teacher leaders: Providing encouragement, opportunities, and support. *NASSP Bulletin, 84*(616), 35–41.

Murphy, J., & Torre, D. (in press). Vision: essential scaffolding. *Educational Management, Administration and Leadership.*

Spillane, J. P., Hallett, T., & Diamond, J. B. (2003). Forms of capital and the construction of leadership: Instructional leadership in urban elementary schools. *Sociology of Education, 76*, 1–17.

Chapter 12
Effects of Principal Professional Orientation Towards Leadership, Professional Teacher Behavior, and School Academic Optimism on School Reading Achievement

Roxanne Mitchell and John Tarter

Academic optimism is an emerging concept in the literature on effective schools (Bevel and Mitchell 2012; Hoy and Miskel 2013; Hoy et al. 2006; Kirby and DiPaola 2011; McGuigan and Hoy 2006; Mitchell and Tarter 2016; Smith and Hoy 2007; Wagner and DiPaola 2011; Wu et al. 2013). The driving idea behind this perspective is that collective efficacy, faculty trust in students and parents, and academic emphasis combine into a unitary element of school culture predicting achievement. The research linking antecedent variables to academic optimism and achievement has been promising; Kirby and DiPaola (2009) found connections from community engagement to academic optimism and then hence to achievement. Wu et al. (2013) and Mitchell and Tarter (2016) found a connection between enabling school structure and academic optimism. Hoy and Miskel (2013) suggested a need for further investigations into both the antecedents and correlates of academic optimism. The purpose of this paper is to analyze elements in the school that could likely support the development and be correlated with academic optimism and together can effect achievement.

12.1 Conceptual Framework

School Academic Optimism (SAO) is not dispositional optimism or a belief that things will get better. Rather, it is a construct that brings together three powerful streams of research from empirical studies on efficacy, trust, and climate in a combination that argues the school is not simply a pawn of SES. The school can make contributions to student success independently of the SES of the school and the

---

R. Mitchell (✉) • J. Tarter
Educational Leadership, Policy and Technology Studies, The College of Education, University of Alabama, Box 870302 301 Graves Hall, Tuscaloosa, AL 35487, USA
e-mail: rmmitchell@ua.edu; ctarter@ua.edu

prior achievement of students (Hoy et al. 2006; McGuigan and Hoy 2006). This line of research stems from Bandura's (1997) work on collective efficacy, Seligman's (2003) work on positive psychology, and decades of work by Hoy and colleagues on school climate and culture. Noting that over the past three decades empirical studies had demonstrated consistently that collective efficacy, faculty trust in clients and academic emphasis were predictive of achievement individually (Goddard 2001; Goddard and Goddard 2001; Goddard et al. 2000). Hoy et al. (2006) posited that these variables would come together to create a culture of optimism that would over power the negative effects of socio-economic status and other demographic variables on achievement. Several studies have confirmed that these three variables do indeed come together to create the general latent construct that they referred to as SAO and that SAO is predictive of student achievement (Bevel and Mitchell 2012; Hoy et al. 2006; Kirby and DiPaola 2009, 2011; McGuigan and Hoy 2006; Mitchell et al. 2016; Smith and Hoy 2007; Wagner and DiPaola 2011; Wu et al. 2013)

The essence of the concept is that three school properties; collective efficacy, faculty trust in clients, and academic emphasis work together to foster a culture of school success. Collective efficacy research grew out of the research on individual teacher efficacy (Goddard 2001; Goddard and Goddard 2001; Goddard et al. 2000). It is a cognitive dimension of the faculty that describes the faculty's belief that they can collectively have a positive impact on student outcomes. Unlike individual teacher efficacy it is a school property. Teachers in schools with a high sense of collective efficacy will persist in the face of obstacles in striving to meet student needs and instructional goals. Faculty trust in students and parents grew out of research on trust in schools (Hoy and Tschannen-Moran 1999). It is an affective dimension that refers to the faculty's beliefs that they can trust and collaborate with students and parents to bring about positive results for students. Teachers who believe they can trust students and parents will be more inclined to include them in matters that are related to instruction and learning (Tschannen-Moran 2001). Of the three types of faculty trust (faculty trust in the principal, faculty trust in colleagues, and faculty trust in students and parents), it is the factor most closely associated with student achievement. Academic emphasis refers to the school's emphasis on achieving high standards and the expectation that all students can succeed (Hoy and Tarter 1997; Hoy et al. 1991, 1998). It is the behavioral dimension of a culture of academic optimism. In schools with high academic emphasis teachers and administrators believe that students are capable of learning, they press students to achieve academically, they persist in helping struggling students, and they reward academic accomplishments. Hoy and Tarter found academic emphasis to be the primary contributor to the health of the school.

Earlier research has given some demonstration to the notion that organizational properties of the school will contribute to the quality of the school (Mitchell and Tarter 2011; Tarter and Hoy 2004). Extending that research to look for antecedents and correlates of academic optimism prompts an exploration into the facilitating quality of the structure of the school, the professional behavior of teachers, and the socioeconomic status of the students. The theory anticipating positive relationships of these concepts to academic optimism arises from a theory of congruence, that is, the greater the degree of mutual support among elements of a system, the more effective the system (Dean et al. 2013; Hoy and Miskel 2013).

Enabling School Structure (ESS) is the conceptual description of the school's rules, regulations, and decision-making properties (Hoy and Sweetland 2000). Schools are seen to have rules in the formal organization that hinder or facilitate the work of the teachers. Enabling structure emphatically does not argue for more or less bureaucratic intensity; instead, it makes a case for functional and dysfunctional bureaucratic arrangements. A functional bureaucratic arrangement would be one where rules and regulations are flexible and the authority structure is perceived as being collaborative. In such a structure, teachers' opinions are valued particularly in areas that involve instruction. A dysfunctional bureaucratic arrangement is one where rules are strictly adhered to, the authority structure is autocratic, and teachers are made to feel as though their input is not valued. Only three studies have explored the effects of ESS on AO. One study explored this relationship in elementary schools in the U.S. (McGuigan and Hoy 2006), one study examined this relationship in elementary schools in Taiwan (Wu et al. 2013), and one study was conducted in elementary and middle schools in the U.S. (Mitchell et al. 2016). While the study of this relationship is in its infancy, the results are promising, all three studies found that ESS had a significant effect on SAO which in turn had a significant effect on measures of school achievement. To our knowledge only one study to date has explored the relationship between ESS and professional teacher behavior (PTB) but no study has explored the relationship between SAO and PTB. Other research findings report that ESS is correlated with faculty trust in the principal, decreased truth spinning, decreased role conflict (Hoy and Sweetland 2001), and increased parent trust in the principal and the school (Adams and Forsyth 2007), and Mitchell and Tarter (2011) Tarter and Hoy (2004) found ESS to be predictive of teachers' overall perception of quality and school effectiveness.

Professional Orientation Verses Bureaucratic Orientation Tschannen-Moran (Tschannnen-Moran 2009) argued that while the structure of the school can be conceptualized as a school property, it results from the principal's orientation towards leadership. She further argued that the Enabling School Structure Scale actually measures teachers' perceptions regarding the principal's orientation towards leadership. A principal's orientation towards leadership is seen as existing on a continuum and points to the principal's leadership style and behavior. At the extremes a principal can either have a professional orientation or a bureaucratic orientation towards leadership. She posited that enabling school structures are created because of the principal's professional orientation towards leadership. Principals who have a professional orientation towards leadership tend to move away from reliance upon bureaucratic structures such as authority, rules, regulations, policies, procedures, and job specialization towards a more professional leadership orientation grounded in trust that relies on building relationships with teachers and promotes professional teacher behavior. Teachers are viewed as colleagues who are capable of meeting the needs of students. The role then of the principal is to support teachers' efforts. In contrast, when a principal has a bureaucratic orientation towards leadership this will result in reliance upon establishing an "authoritarian culture of control with constrained communication, micromanagement, a proliferation of rules, and a rigid response to external threats (p. 221)". Inherent in a bureaucratic orientation towards leadership is a lack of trust towards teachers. Teachers are not viewed as professionals or as colleagues. They require strict management in order to bring about positive results for students. This fits well within Hoy and Sweetland's (2000) conceptualization regarding structure being either enabling or hindering. Principals with a professional orientation towards leadership establish enabling structures whereas principals with a bureaucratic orientation are more prone to establish hindering structures. In a study of 80 middles schools in a Mid-Atlantic state in the U.S.A. Tschannen-Moran found that principal professional orientation toward leadership was positively correlated with and predictive of teacher professional behavior. Principal professional orientation was also correlated with faculty trust in the principal, faculty trust in colleagues, and faculty trust in clients.

Professional Teacher Behavior (PTB) is the teachers' seriousness about their work as well as their commitment to students and each other. Professional teacher behavior is a composite of teacher behaviors captured by two climate measures (the Organizational Description Questionnaire—OCDQ and the Organizational Health Inventory—OHI). Two metaphors for school climate are the health of school and the openness of the school. The health of the school captures the positive relationships within the school and the openness in the school captures the personality of the school on a continuum from open to closed (Goddard et al. 2000). The OCDQ was designed to measure the openness of the school and the OHI was designed to capture the health of the school. A second order factor analysis by Hoy and Sabo (1998) of both measures produced four factors, one of which was a factor that captured teacher relationships with each other that included four dimensions: teacher commitment, teacher collegiality, teacher affiliation, and teacher disengagement. They named this factor teacher professionalism and defined it as teacher behavior characterized by commitment to students, respect for the competence of colleagues, warm friendly interactions, and engagement in the teaching task. Teacher commitment refers to teachers' seriousness about their work, affiliation refers to teachers' enthusiasm for their work and whether they like one another, collegiality refers to whether teachers treat each other as professional colleagues and their willingness to collaborate with each other. Teacher disengagement was a negative factor which referred to teachers' involvement or lack thereof with the teaching task and with one another. Teachers who are engaged in professional behavior show respect for the competence of their colleagues, they are collaborative and supportive, they demonstrate autonomous judgment, they are enthusiastic about their work, and they are committed to the success of their students. Openness in teacher-teacher relationships is one of the indicators of the health of the school (Hoy and Sabo 1998). Not surprisingly, Hoy et al. (2002) found both collegial leadership of the principal and faculty trust in colleagues to be correlated with professional teacher behavior. Moreover, Hoy and Sabo (1998) found professional teacher behavior to be significantly correlated with math, reading and writing achievement in a study that included 87 middle schools. Hoy and Sweetland (2001) using the same sample of schools later found that teacher professionalism was significantly correlated with teacher empowerment.

Socioeconomic Status (SES) describes the relative placement of the school in a range of economic levels. The common measure used is the percentage of students within the school who participate in the free or reduced lunch program. This measure is not without criticism (Sirin 2005). However, due to the lack of availability of other reliable measures, much of the research on schools has used this measure to quantify the schools' SES level.

12.2 Theoretical Rationale and Hypotheses

Because enabling school structure represents a type of leadership characterized by the principals' professional orientation towards leadership that is grounded in establishing trusting relationships with teachers we would expect that enabling school structure is related to both school academic optimism and professional teacher behavior. In fact, we would argue that ESS sets the stage for the development of both SAO and PTB. Prior studies have shown a connection between SAO and achievement and between PTB and achievement (Bevel and Mitchell 2012; Hoy et al. 2002, 2006; Kirby and DiPaola 2009, 2011; McGuigan and Hoy 2006; Mitchell et al. 2016; Smith and Hoy 2007; Wagner and DiPaola 2011; Wu et al. 2013). Therefore, we expect that both SAO and PTB will be directly related to a measure of reading achievement aggregated to the school. However, no study to our knowledge has explored the relationship between SAO and PTB. We also anticipate that because teacher behavior is intrinsic to optimism, we would expect a strong relationship between PTB and SAO. The theory anticipates that a significant correlation between professional teacher behavior (PTB) and academic optimism should be expected. Academic Optimism and Organizational Climate Index are composite constructs (Hoy et al. 2002, 2006), and their respective subtests have been found to be associated with trust, efficacy, effectiveness, and teacher initiated action over the years (Bandura 1997; Hoy et al. 1991; Hoy and Miskel 2013; Tarter and Hoy 2004).

While there is individual teacher optimism within a classroom, academic optimism is the property of the organizational school. It seems unlikely that academic optimism could come about in schools whose formal structure got in the way of developing efficacy, trust, and behavioral expectations, which is to say that the more enabling the structure, the greater will be the optimism. Finally, there was an assumption that SES would be related to optimism. In the original work on academic optimism (Hoy et al. 2006), SES has a modest direct correlation to optimism even though academic optimism made its own independent contribution to academic achievement. One would expect that among schools with paltry resources, forging academic optimism would be challenging. Because the variables that make up academic optimism have been shown to decline in middle school and high school, we included school level as one of the control variables in our analysis (Mitchell et al. 2016). Given the preceding sense of relationships between the variables and optimism, it was hypothesized that:

> H1: Enabling School Structure will be correlated with and predictive of school academic optimism and professional teacher behavior, and these variables together will explain a significant portion of the variance in a measure of school achievement while controlling for school level and SES.

12.3 Methodology

12.3.1 Data Sources

The school was the unit of analysis. In the Spring Semester of 2014 seventy-seven schools in the northwestern region of a southern state in the U.S. were invited to participate in this study. The schools represented a convenience sample. Schools were selected based on convenience of access by a group of student researchers. The schools represented rural, urban, and suburban areas and were limited to those that had 15 or more faculty members. Of the 77 schools invited to participate, 60 schools agreed to participate in the study for a 78% response rate. For the purpose of this study, the sample had to be limited to 54 schools because six of the schools that participated did not give the achievement tests used in this study. The sample included 45 elementary schools and nine middle schools.

12.3.2 Data Collection

Survey instruments were randomly assigned to 1665 teachers who had gathered for regularly scheduled faculty meetings at their individual schools. All teachers present at the faculty meetings participated in the data collection. One of the student researchers attended the faculty meeting and personally handed out the written surveys, explained the procedures and the purpose of the study, answered questions, and collected the surveys prior to leaving. Protocols of anonymity, confidentiality, and voluntary participation were scrupulously followed, guided by University Institutional Review Board procedures as well as formal IRB protections in many of the districts that participated in the study.

12.3.3 Instruments

Enabling School Structure (Professional Orientation Towards Leadership), (Hoy and Sweetland 2001) was measured using a 12 item Likert type scale with a response set that ranges from "never" coded as 1 to "always" coded as 5. Sample items include "The administrative hierarchy of this school enables teachers to do their job", "In this school the authority of the principal is used to undermine teachers" (item reverse scored), and "Administrative rules in this school are guides to solutions rather than rigid procedures". The reported reliability of this scale is 0.96 (Hoy and Sweetland 2001).

School Academic Optimism was measured using the 30-item Likert type *School Academic Optimism Scale* (Hoy et al. 2006) which includes three subscales (*Collective Teacher Efficacy, Academic Emphasis, Faculty Trust in Clients*). Sample items include "Teachers in this school are able to get through to the most difficult students", "Teachers in this school trust their students", and "The school sets high standards for performance". The reported reliability of the scales that make up the SAO scale range from 0.91 to 0.98 (Hoy et al. 2006; McGuigan and Hoy 2006; Smith and Hoy 2007).

Professional Teacher Behavior was measured using the professional teacher behavior subscale of the Organizational Climate Index (Hoy and Sabo 1998). It is a 7-item, Likert type scale that includes such items as "Teachers help and support each other" and "Teachers respect the professional competence of their colleagues". The reported reliability of this scale is 0.94 (Tschannnen-Moran 2009).

SES was measured using the percentage of students on free and reduced lunch. The percentage was subtracted from 1.0 so as to result in higher values being greater levels of SES, which is the common understanding of the term.

School level was dummy coded with 1 for elementary schools and 0 for middle schools. There were 45 elementary schools (consisting of grades K-5) and nine middle schools (consisting of grades 6–8).

Achievement was measured using aggregated reading scores representing the percentage of students who passed the Alabama Reading and Math Test (ARMT) per school for the 2012 school year.

12.3.4 Analytic Technique

The unit of analysis was the school, thus individual teacher scores were aggregated to the school level. Achievement scores and information regarding the percent free and reduced lunch were only available as school means, which prevented us from performing hierarchical linear modeling. *Enabling school structure*, the observed variables that make up *School Academic Optimism* (*Collective Efficacy, Faculty*

Trust in Clients and *Academic Emphasis*) and *Professional Teacher Behavior* were conceived of as school properties. In order to justify aggregation to the school our first level of analysis involved calculation of the Intraclass Correlations for these variables (ICC). We calculated both the ICC-1 and the ICC-2. ICC-1 represents the variance attributed to group membership and ICC-2 represents within group agreement between teachers in the sample. We calculated both ICCs using a Random Effects ANOVA. We also calculated the reliabilities of the scales in our sample.

To answer our hypothesis that stated that "enabling school structure will be correlated with and predictive of school academic optimism and professional teacher behavior, and those variables together will explain a significant portion of the variance in a measure of school achievement while controlling for school level and SES", we chose to use a combination of correlational analysis and structural equation modeling (SEM). Correlational analysis allowed us to test the relationships of the variables in the study. We calculated the bivariate correlations for all of our variables and a measure of reading achievement aggregated to the school. Finally, we conducted a path analysis using IBM SPSS AMOS Graphics 19 to test the effects of our predictor variables on our school reading achievement variable while controlling for the effects of SES and school level. The choice of SEM provided an appropriate way to test the effects of our observed predictor variable (ESS) on two mediating variables (SAO and PTB) and to test the direct effects of our mediating and control variables on a measure of school achievement. According to Schumacker and Lomax (2010), "the use of simple bivariate correlations is not sufficient for examining a sophisticated theoretical model...the use of structural equation modeling permits complex phenomena to be statistically modeled and tested (p. 7)". We saw no need to reconfirm that SAO is a unitary latent variable made up of collective efficacy, faculty trust in clients, and academic emphasis because this has already been demonstrated in multiple studies (Bevel and Mitchell 2012; Hoy et al. 2006; Kirby and DiPaola 2009, 2011; McGuigan and Hoy 2006; Mitchell et al. 2016; Smith and Hoy 2007; Wagner and DiPaola 2011; Wu et al. 2013)

12.4 Results

12.4.1 Intraclass Correlations

Our preliminary analysis which included calculating the ICCs for our variables was as follows: Five Random Effects ANOVAs using SPSS 22 to estimate the extent to which our observed variables (*Enabling School Structure, Professional Teacher Behavior, Faculty Trust in Clients, Collective Efficacy* and *Academic Emphasis*) varied within and between schools were calculated. The ICC-1s confirmed the nested nature of our variables. The F-tests of significance indicated that as expected the proportion of variance between schools in *Enabling School Structure* (27%), *Professional Teacher Behavior* (17%), *Academic Emphasis* (25%), *Faculty Trust in*

Clients (30%), and *Collective Efficacy* (34%) were statistically significant. Significant ICC-2's that were above the .60 threshold recommended by Cohen et al. (2001), for all but one of our variables indicated strong within group agreement; *Enabling School Structure* (ICC-2 = 0.87, $p < 0.01$), *Professional Teacher Behavior* (ICC-2 = 0.41, $p < 0.01$), *Academic Emphasis* (ICC-2 = 0.63, $p < 0.01$), *Faculty Trust in Clients* (ICC-2 = 0.70, $p < 0.01$), and *Collective Efficacy* (ICC-2 = 0.74, $p < 0.01$). These results indicated a significant variance in teacher perception attributed to differences between schools that justified our aggregation of these variables to the school as well as strong within group agreement for all but one of our variables.

12.4.2 Scale Reliabilities

We also calculated the Cronbach's Alpha reliabilities of the scales used in our study. All scale reliabilities were greater than 0.70; ESS (0.92), PTB (0.91) and the scales making up the latent variable SAO (CE = 0.91, FTC = 0.92, AE = 0.87). See Table 12.1 for a depiction of these results.

12.4.3 Bivariate Correlations

Our hypothesis stated that ESS would be correlated with SAO and PTB, thus we explored the bivariate correlations of the variables in our study. ESS was positively correlated with both PTB ($r = 0.32$, $p < 0.05$) and SAO ($r = 0.29$, $p < 0.05$). SAO and SES were positively correlated with Reading achievement ($r = 0.51$, $p < 0.01$) and ($r = 0.47$, $p < 0.01$) respectively. PTB and SAO were positively correlated with each other ($r = 0.36$, $p < 0.01$). SES was correlated with SAO ($r = 0.48$, $p < 0.01$). Finally, school level was not correlated with any of the variables in our study. However, due to its known relationship with the observed variables that make up SAO we left this in our structural model (Forsyth et al. 2011; Mitchell et al. 2016). See Table 12.2 for a depiction of the correlational analysis.

12.4.4 Structural Equation Model

Finally, we used IBM SPSS AMOS Graphics 19 to create our structural equation model. Our model consisted of one exogenous predictor variable, ESS, that was hypothesized to have a direct effect on two endogenous mediating predictor variables (SAO and PTB), and two exogenous control variables, SES and School Level. Our two endogenous mediating variables were hypothesized to have direct effects on school reading achievement. Hypothesis 1 which stated that Enabling School

Table 12.1 Intraclass correlation coefficients for observed variables & scale reliabilities

Variable	ICC-1	ICC-2	F Ratio	Reliability
ESS	.27	.87	2.59**	.92
PTB	.17	.41	1.68**	.91
AE	.25	.63	2.65**	.87
CE	.30	.70	3.92**	.91
FTC	.34	.74	3.29**	.92

**Significant at .01 level

Table 12.2 Bivariate correlations

	PTB	SAO	SES	Level	Reading
ESS	0.318*	0.288*	0.078	0.139	0.236
PTB	1	0.358**	−0.088	−0.216	0.117
SAO	–	1	0.480**	−0.149	0.504**
SES	–	–	1	0.238	0.465**
Level	–	–	–	1	0.140
Reading	–	–	–	–	1

$N = 54$, *$p < .05$, **$p < .10$

Structure would be correlated with and predictive of school academic optimism and professional teacher behavior, and these variables together would explain a significant portion of the variance in a measure of school achievement while controlling for school level and SES was partially supported. ESS had a significant direct effect on PTB ($\lambda = 0.35$, $p < 0.01$) and SAO ($\lambda = 0.28$, $p < 0.01$). While school level was not significantly correlated with any of the variables in our study in the bivariate correlational analysis, it had a significant negative effect on both of our endogenous predictor variables; PTB ($\lambda = -0.26$, $p < 0.05$) and SAO ($\lambda = -0.30$, $p < 0.01$). SAO had a significant direct effect on reading achievement ($\lambda = 0.38$, $p < 0.01$). However, PTB did not have a significant effect on reading achievement as we anticipated. SES had a significant effect on both SAO ($\lambda = 51$, $p < 0.01$) and reading achievement ($\lambda = 0.29$, $p < 0.05$). Together SAO and SES explained 33% of the variance in reading achievement with SAO making the greatest contribution to the explanation.

12.4.5 Goodness-of-Fit

To test the goodness of fit, we used the chi-square test of model fit. According to Schumacker and Lomax (2010) the chi-square test of model fit is the best statistical test of significance to test the theoretical model. Our model had good model fit, as evidenced by a non-significant chi-square of (13.09, $p = 0.11$).

12.4.6 Power Analysis

To test the power of our model we used G*Power 3.1. Schumacker and Lomax (2010) recommended after assessing the goodness-of-fit that it is important to calculate the power of the model to reject the null hypothesis. They recommended the use of G*Power 3.1 as a reliable source for testing the power of the model. Based on an NCP of 19.15 and 8 degrees of freedom there was a 99% chance that we would correctly reject the null hypothesis. See Fig. 12.1 for our final structural equation model with all significant paths remaining.

This study tested the effects of the principal's professional orientation towards leadership/enabling school structure (ESS) on two mediating variables; school academic optimism (SAO) and professional teacher behavior (PTB) on the outcome variable school reading achievement (RA). Data were drawn from a sample of 54 schools (including 45 elementary schools and nine middle schools); the school was the unit of analysis. Data analysis supported a path to RA in which a structural variable, ESS was the immediate antecedent of SAO and PTB. Two control variables, school level and SES were included in the model. SES had a significant effect on SAO but not on PTB. School level had a negative effect on both PTB and SAO suggesting that both variables were higher in elementary school and declined in middle school. SES paired with SAO in predicting RA. As expected, SAO had a greater effect on RA than SES. The significance of the findings lies in the confirmation of SAO as an important influence on RA and in demonstrating the importance of ESS in establishing a context in which AO and PTB can flourish.

12.5 Discussion

Academic optimism is an emerging and promising construct that needs more research. There are variables that intervene in the relationship of optimism to dependent variables other than academic achievement, and those relationships should be subject to theory building and testing. The study of correlates of optimism is in large part a study of antecedents and correlates of the construct.

Moderate correlations of optimism to enabling school structure (a type of leadership that describes the principals' professional orientation towards leadership) and professional teacher behavior were anticipated. Enabling structures are characterized by two-way communication and the creation of procedures that nurture the work of teachers (Hoy and Sweetland 2000). In the analysis at hand, the fact that enabling school structures were predictive of optimism ($\lambda = 0.28, p < 0.01$) confirms other findings (McGuigan and Hoy 2006; Mitchell et al. 2016; Wu et al. 2013), and leads us to argue that a professional orientation towards leadership is a necessary condition for the formation of optimism. The varied nature of teacher work and the range of skills necessary preclude autocratic rule (Hattie 2009). Enabling school structure describes behaviors of the principal that are supportive and allow sufficient

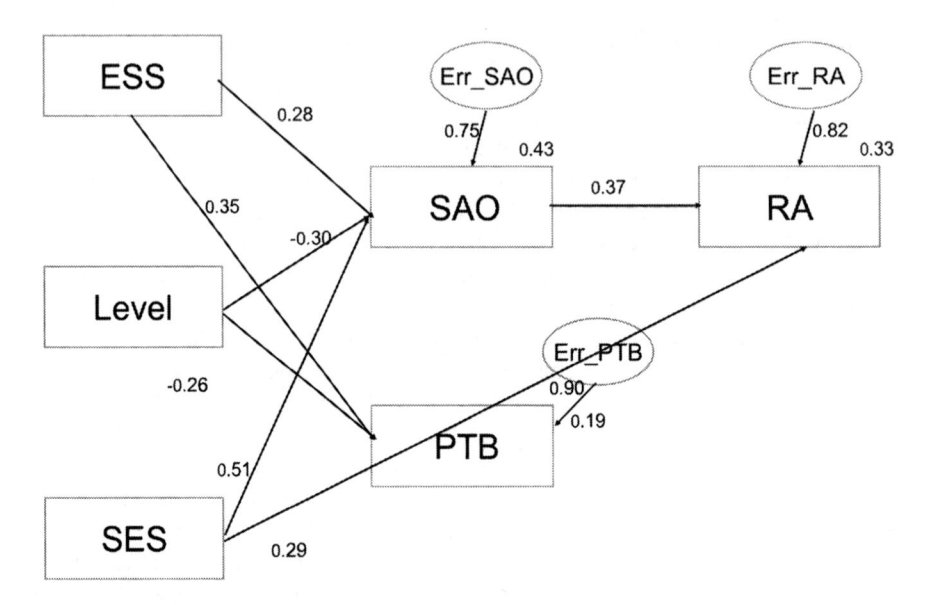

Fig. 12.1 Final Model: ESS, SAO PTB and RA with significant paths

coordination and collaboration for the teachers to contribute to the success of the organization (Hoy et al. 2002). Henry Mintzberg's (1983) general sense that teachers are professional in that they have substantial control over how they teach and what actually gets taught provides a theoretical lens. The key part of the school organization is the teaching staff whose work can be enhanced by actions that support the activities of teachers. Thus, the principal who provides the organizational context for professional work will likely find the school more successful in its professional obligations. Hattie (2009) characterizes these activities as "creating a conversation" between teachers and administrators about establishing mutual goals for the school and building useful feedback mechanisms to assess progress toward the goals. Marks and Printy (2003) provide some empirical support for this analysis in describing instructional leaders whose influence is found in the organizing of shared instructional responsibilities. That is, the administrator creates a context for success through, in part, the building of a working community. Such a school would stand in contrast to centralized authority and control of lower performing schools (Hattie 2009).

We also anticipated that enabling structure would pave the way for professional teacher behavior. This study confirmed this assumption. Enabling structure was predictive of professional teacher behavior ($\lambda = 0.35$, $p < 0.01$) suggesting that when leaders adopt a professional orientation towards leadership they establish norms that free up teachers to engage in behaviors that are collegial, that involve collective deliberation, inquiry and professionalism (Tschannnen-Moran 2009). A close reading of the organizational literature gives the impression that these findings are obvious. However, they are only obvious after they have been demonstrated (Gage

1991). The continuing research should look to what specific behaviors will these enabling and professionally oriented leaders exercise. Unlike findings by Hoy and Sabo (1998) our study did not support the connection between professional teacher behavior and achievement.

The correlation of professional teacher behavior to school academic optimism ($r = 0.36$, $p < 0.01$) suggests that both optimism and professional teacher behavior may require the development of professional norms of practice. Hattie (2009) supports professional development that specifies classroom strategies, provides video/audio feedback, microteaching, and practice is the most effective vehicle for professional development. Researchers interested in examining the gap in the literature implied by the professional teacher behavior/academic optimism relationship might consider exploring the kinds of professional development in the school and the means of choosing that professional development that foster this relationship.

The fact that academic optimism contributed more to the explanation of reading achievement than SES is provocative and lends support to a growing body of research that has had similar findings (Bevel and Mitchell 2012; Hoy and Miskel 2013; Hoy et al. 2006; Kirby and DiPaola 2011; McGuigan and Hoy 2006; Mitchell et al. 2016; Smith and Hoy 2007; Wagner and DiPaola 2011; Wu et al. 2013). This study suggests that the composite variable academic optimism could be an important school condition populated on the Organizational Path (Leithwood et al. 2010) predicting student achievements. The implications for administrators, point to the powerful influence of setting the stage for the formation of a culture of optimism that can outweigh the deleterious effects of poverty on achievement. This influence is likely to be more significant in middle school and beyond where both optimism and professional teacher behavior seem to lag.

Finally, the intent of the investigation reported here was to test some important school elements in their relationship to academic optimism and then to plan research to fill in gaps in the literature that would increase our understanding of how to build optimism. More research is needed that explores specific strategies used by professionally oriented leaders to establish a culture that supports academic optimism and professional teacher behavior, and in so doing has the potential to influence achievement above and beyond the effects of demographic variables such as poverty. These findings have important implications for principals. We agree with Tschannen-Moran (2009) in that the professional orientation of the principal and the ability of the principal to establish enabling structures are necessary to foster a culture of professionalism and optimism among teachers that allows teachers the freedom and discretion to address student needs.

12.6 Materials and Methods

Data for this manuscript were collected from schools in a Southern State in the USA. Data are not available due to Institutional Review Board restrictions related to confidentiality. Data were collected by a cohort of six doctoral students under the supervision of the authors of this manuscript at regularly scheduled faculty meetings from 1665 teachers in 54 schools. Individual teacher data were aggregated to the school. Information regarding the percent of students on the free and reduced lunch program per school were collected from the State Department of Education website. Please contact the corresponding author for additional information.

References

Adams, C. M., & Forsyth, P. B. (2007). Promoting a culture of trust: An empirical study. *Journal of School Public Relations, 28*, 32–56.
Bandura, A. (1997). *Self-efficacy: The exercise of control.* New York: W. H. Freeman.
Bevel, R. K., & Mitchell, R. M. (2012). The effects of academic optimism on elementary reading achievement. *Journal of Educational Administration, 50*, 773–787.
Cohen, A., Doveh, E., & Erick, U. (2001). *Trust in schools: A core resource for improvement.* New York: Sage.
Dean, S., Vaux, N., & Tarter, C. J. (2013, November). *Collegial leadership, teacher professionalism, faculty trust: Predicting teacher academic optimism in elementary schools.* Presented at the annual meeting of the University Council of Educational Administration, Indianapolis, IN.
Forsyth, P. B., Adams, C., & Hoy, W. K. (2011). *Collective trust: Why schools can't do without it.* New York: Teachers College Press.
Gage, N. L. (1991). The obviousness of social and educational research results. *Educational Researcher, 20*, 10–16.
Goddard, R. D. (2001). Collective efficacy: A neglected construct in the study of schools and student achievement. *Journal of Educational Psychology, 93*, 467–476.
Goddard, R. D., & Goddard, Y. L. (2001). A multilevel analysis of the relationship between teacher and collective efficacy in urban schools. *Teaching and Teacher Education, 17*, 807–818.
Goddard, R. D., Sweetland, R., & Hoy, W. K. (2000). Academic emphasis of urban elementary schools and students achievement in reading and mathematics: A multi-level analysis. *Educational Administration Quarterly, 36*, 583–702.
Hattie, J. (2009). *Visible learning.* New York: Routledge.
Hoy, W. K., & Miskel, G. G. (2013). *Educational administration* (9th ed.). New York: McGraw Hill.
Hoy, W. K., & Sabo, D. J. (1998). *Quality middle schools.* Thousand Oaks: Corwin.
Hoy, W. K., & Sweetland, S. R. (2000). School bureaucracies that work: Enabling, not coercive. *Journal of School Leadership, 10*, 524–541.
Hoy, W. K., & Sweetland, S. R. (2001). Designing better schools: The meaning and measure of enabling school structures. *Educational Administration Quarterly, 37*, 296–321.
Hoy, W. K., & Tarter, C. J. (1997). *The road to open and healthy schools: A handbook for change (Elementary and secondary school edition).* Thousand Oaks: Corwin.
Hoy, W. K., & Tschannen-Moran, M. (1999). The five faces of trust: An empirical confirmation in urban elementary schools. *Journal of School Leadership, 9*, 184–208.
Hoy, W. K., Tarter, C. J., & Kottkamp, R. B. (1991). *Open schools/healthy schools.* Beverly Hills: Sage.
Hoy, W. K., Hannum, J., & Tschannen-Moran, M. (1998). Organizational climate and student achievement: A parsimonious and longitudinal view. *Journal of School Leadership, 8*, 336–359.
Hoy, W. K., Smith, P. A., & Sweetland, S. R. (2002). The development of the organizational climate index for high schools: Its measure and relationship to faculty trust. *High School Journal, 86*, 38–49.

Hoy, W. K., Tarter, C. J., & Woolfolk Hoy, A. (2006). Academic optimism of schools: A force for student achievement. *American Educational Research Journal, 43*, 425–446.

Kirby, M. M., & DiPaola, M. (2009). Academic optimism and achievement: A path model. In W. K. Hoy & M. DiPaola (Eds.), *Studies in school improvement* (pp. 77–94). Greenwich: Information Age.

Kirby, M. M., & DiPaola, M. F. (2011). Academic optimism and community engagement in urban schools. *Journal of Educational Administration, 49*, 542–562.

Leithwood, K., Patten, S., & Jantzi, D. (2010). Testing a conception of how school leadership influences student learning. *Educational Administration Quarterly, 46*, 671–706.

Marks, H. M., & Printy, S. M. (2003). Principal leadership and school performance: An integration of transformational and instructional leadership. *Educational Administration Quarterly, 39*, 370–397.

McGuigan, L., & Hoy, W. K. (2006). Principal leadership: Creating a culture academic optimism to improve achievement for all students. *Leadership and Policy in Schools, 5*, 203–229.

Mintzberg, H. (1983). *Power in an around organizations*. Englewood Cliffs: Prentice-Hall.

Mitchell, R. M., & Tarter, C. J. (2011). A systems approach to effectiveness in Catholic elementary schools: A replication and extension. *Journal of School Leadership, 2*, 789–818.

Mitchell, R., & Tarter, C. (2016). A path analysis of the effects of principal professional orientation towards leadership, professional teacher behavior, and school academic optimism on school reading achievement. *Societies, 6*(1), 5. MDPI AG. Retrieved from http://dx.doi.org/10.3390/soc6010005

Mitchell, R. M., Mendiola, B.J., Schumacker, R.E., & Lowery, J.A. (2016). Creating a school context of success for all students: The role of enabling school structure & academic optimism in an urban elementary and middle school setting. *Journal of Educational Administration 54*, published online.

Schumacker, R. E., & Lomax, R. G. (2010). *A beginner's guide to structural equation modeling* (3rd ed.). New York: Routledge.

Seligman, M. E. (2003). *Authentic happiness: Using new positive psychology to realize your potential for lasting fulfillment*. Washington, DC: Free Press.

Sirin, S. R. (2005). Socioeconomic status and academic achievement: A meta-analytic review of research. *Review of Educational Research, 75*, 417–453.

Smith, P. A., & Hoy, W. K. (2007). Academic optimism and student achievement in urban elementary schools. *Journal of Educational Administration, 45*, 556–568.

Tarter, C. J., & Hoy, W. K. (2004). A systems approach to quality in elementary schools: A theoretical and empirical analysis. *Journal of Educational Administration, 42*, 539–554.

Tschannen-Moran, M. (2001). Collaboration and the need for trust. *Journal of Educational Administration, 39*, 306–331.

Tschannnen-Moran, M. (2009). Fostering teacher professionalism in schools: The role of leadership orientation and trust. *Educational Administration Quarterly, 45*, 217–247.

Wagner, C. A., & DiPaola, M. F. (2011). Academic optimism of high school teachers: Its relationship to organizational citizenship behaviors and student achievement. *Journal of School Leadership, 21*, 893–926.

Wu, J. H., Hoy, W. K., & Tarter, C. J. (2013). Enabling school structure, collective responsibility and a culture of academic optimism: Toward a robust model of school performance in Taiwan. *Journal of Educational Administration, 51*, 176–193.

Chapter 13
Leading Teacher Learning in China: A Mixed Methods Study of Successful School Leadership

Shengnan Liu and Philip Hallinger

How do school leaders contribute to school improvement? This question, stated in various forms, has occupied the attention of scholars for the past 60 years (Grobman and Hynes 1956; Hallinger and Heck 1998; Leithwood et al. 2010; Robinson 2006). During this period, the field of educational leadership and management made considerable progress in identifying "paths" through which school leaders influence student learning (e.g., Hallinger 2011; Hallinger and Heck 1998; Leithwood et al. 2010). For example, in 1998 Hallinger and Heck concluded, "More recently, researchers have… sought to understand not only if principals have effects on school outcomes, but more particularly the paths through which such effects are achieved" (p. 187). By understanding the nature of these "strategic paths," scholars are able to point towards practical avenues of action of potential interest to both practitioners and policymakers.

The reorientation of scholarship towards exploring the linkages between leadership and student learning has yielded new directions for research and practice. One path that has emerged in recent years as a high value target is the path that links school-level leadership and teacher professional learning (Barth 1990; Hallinger et al. 2014; Knapp et al. 2010; Li et al. 2016; Saphier et al. 2006; Vanblaere and Devos 2016). For example, Robinson (2006) emphasized leadership behaviors such as supporting, organizing, coaching, and modeling teacher participation in professional learning.

S. Liu
Faculty of Education, East China Normal University, Shanghai Shi, China
e-mail: liushengnan2013@163.com

P. Hallinger (✉)
College of Public Health Sciences, Chulalongkorn University,
244 Phayathai Rd, Bangkok 10110, Thailand

Faculty of Education, University of Johannesburg, Johannesburg, South Africa
e-mail: hallinger@gmail.com

The relatively new global focus on *leadership and teacher learning* also has relevance for educational research, policy, and practice in mainland China. Major curriculum reforms adopted since the turn of the twenty-first century have mandated new system-wide goals that require China's teachers to experiment with new methods of teaching and learning (Dello-Iacovo 2009; Ding 2010; Qian and Walker 2013). Consequently, we have observed a new interest in how school leaders create conditions that support productive learning among *both* teachers and students in China's schools (Cravens 2008; Qian and Walker 2013; Tang et al. 2014; Walker et al. 2012; Walker and Qian 2015; Wang 2016; Zhang and Pang 2016).

In this chapter, we present findings from a mixed-methods study aimed at understanding how principals in mainland China influence the professional learning of their teachers. The study addressed two main research questions:

1. What is the relationship between learning-centered leadership, teacher trust, teacher agency, and teacher professional learning in Chinese schools?
2. How do successful principals influence teacher learning in China?

In the first stage of the study, we analyzed survey data collected from 1259 teachers in 38 primary and secondary schools in three Chinese provinces. These analyses addressed the first research question. In the second stage, we conducted qualitative case studies of two principals rated highly by their teachers during the quantitative phase of the research. Our findings extend prior research on leadership and learning conducted in both Western (e.g., Leithwood and Jantzi 2006; Sleegers et al. 2014; Thoonen et al. 2012; Vanblaere and Devos 2016; Wahlstrom and Louis 2008; Youngs and King 2002) and East Asian societies (Chen et al. 2016; Hallinger and Lu 2014; Li et al. 2016; Qian and Walker 2013; Qian et al. 2016; Wang 2016; Zhang and Pang 2016).

13.1 Theoretical Perspective

The lineage of learning-centered leadership can be traced back to earlier conceptions of instructional leadership and transformational leadership (Cravens 2008; Hallinger 2011; Hallinger and Murphy 1986; Leithwood et al. 2010). Whereas instructional leadership emphasizes the role school leaders play in fostering student learning, transformational leadership gave priority to the means by which leaders built broader capacity for learning and change in schools (Hallinger 2011; Leithwood et al. 2010). Thus, a distinctive feature of learning-centered leadership is capacity building to promote the learning of all members of the school community (Barth 1990; Leithwood et al. 2010; Saphier et al. 2006).

In the study, we defined learning-centered leadership as "a process whereby school leaders engage in intentional efforts to guide, direct, support, and participate in teacher learning with the goal of increasing their professional knowledge, and ultimately promote student learning and school effectiveness" (Cravens 2008; Knapp et al. 2010; Saphier et al. 2006). We examined four dimensions of learning-

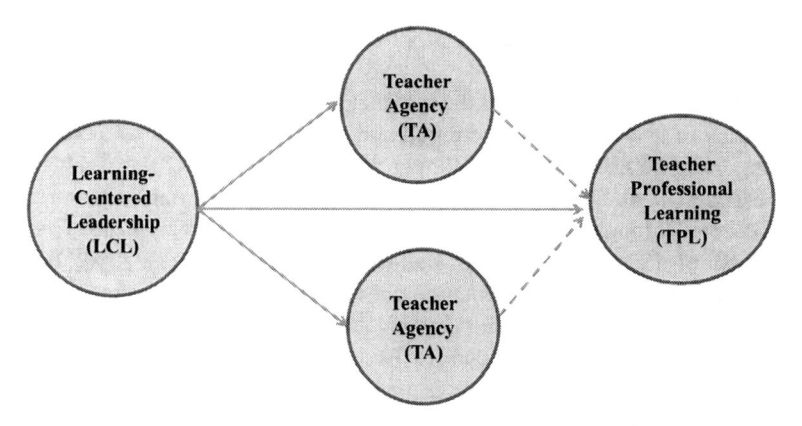

Fig. 13.1 Hypothesized model of leadership and teacher learning in Chinese schools

centered leadership. These included building a vision of learning, managing the learning program, providing learning support, and modeling. Support for each of these dimensions can be found in the literature on leadership and learning (e.g., Barth 1990; Bryk and Schneider 2002; Day 2009; Frost 2006; Hallinger 2011; Hallinger and Heck 2002; Knapp et al. 2010; Leithwood et al. 2010; Li et al. 2016; Printy et al. 2009; Robinson et al. 2008).

The conceptual model that guided the study proposes that learning-centered leadership has both direct and indirect effects on teacher learning (see Fig. 13.1). More specifically, we propose that teacher trust and agency represent "internal paths" through which principals influence the professional learning of teachers. If the model were supported empirically, it would mean that some leadership practices (e.g., setting goals, providing feedback, modeling) contribute directly to the professional learning of teachers, while other practices "create conditions" that motivate and support the professional learning of teachers (e.g., supporting collaboration, delegating authority to middle-level, and teacher leaders). As suggested above, this research is part of a broader global effort aimed at understanding the means by which leaders contribute to school improvement.

In the study, we conceptualized teacher professional learning as a form of "workplace learning" as opposed to "pre-service teacher preparation." The workplace learning of teachers often takes place in "formal settings" such as professional development workshops, teaching research groups, and mentoring programs (Timperley 2011). However, teachers also learn through informal interactions that occur during the course of peer teaching, collaborative planning, shared assessment, and informal mentoring (Lai et al. 2016; Little 2012). Whether intended or not, the culture of the school shapes teacher attitudes towards the need for learning, the value of collegial exchange, and the costs and benefits of experimentation with new methods (Barth 1990; Lai et al. 2016; Little 2012; Rosenholtz 1989; Saphier et al. 2006). Fundamental issues for both system- and school-level leaders concern how to motivate and support teachers, not only to engage in continued learning, but to do so with both enthusiasm and the intent to put new knowledge into practice (Barth

1990; in de Wal et al. 2014; Lai et al. 2016; Li et al. 2016; Saphier et al. 2006; Thoonen et al. 2012).

A growing literature highlights the role that principals, middle-level, and teacher leaders play in fostering teacher learning and school improvement (Cravens 2008; Goldring et al. 2009; Heck and Hallinger 2014; Knapp et al. 2010; Saphier et al. 2006; Sleegers et al. 2014; Vanblaere and Devos 2016). Learning-centered leadership is enacted through practices that support both teacher development and student learning (Barth 1990; Cravens 2008; Hallinger 2011; Saphier et al. 2006). It should noted, however, that this role orientation does not describe the traditional role practice of principals in either China (Cravens 2008; Walker et al. 2012; Walker and Qian 2015) or in many other countries (Lee and Hallinger 2012). China's school principals have generally focused more time and attention on managerial and political roles than on instructional leadership (Bush et al. 1998; Cravens 2008; Lee and Hallinger 2012; Tang et al. 2014; Walker et al. 2012; Walker and Qian 2015). Thus, the study sought to offer insight into how successful leaders foster productive learning cultures in Chinese schools.

Scholars have proposed trust as a condition that enables the efforts of school leaders to gain faculty cooperation for efforts to improve their schools (e.g., Bryk and Schneider 2002; Sleegers et al. 2014). Studies have documented the positive impact of teacher trust on teacher motivation (Li et al. 2016; Thomsen et al. 2015; Thoonen et al. 2012), willingness to engage in professional learning (Darling-Hammond and Richardson 2009; Hallinger and Lu 2014; Li et al. 2016; Tschannen-Moran 2009; Vanblaere and Devos 2016), school improvement (Bryk and Schneider 2002; Leithwood and Jantzi 2006), and readiness for change (Leithwood and Jantzi 2006). In this study we defined trust as teachers' willingness to be open with and rely on the competence, integrity, and good will of leaders and other faculty members.

A key task in any school improvement process lies in transferring "ownership" of change from leaders to teachers. Recognition of this imperative has highlighted the role of "teacher agency" (Barth 1990; Frost 2006; Saphier et al. 2006; Shen 2015). Teacher agency has cognitive, emotional, and behavioral dimensions reflected in attitudes of self-efficacy, optimism, and constructive engagement (Frost 2006; Shen 2015). Lai et al. (2016) proposed that teacher agency bears a direct relationship to professional learning. However, Hökkä (2012) found that a strong sense of agency does not promote school development if the social context does not provide opportunities for teacher collaboration. This highlights the importance of what Rosenholtz (1989) referred to as "workplace norms" in shaping teacher attitudes towards collaboration and learning. Frost (2006) concluded that human agency provides a "bridge" between the actions of school leaders and teacher learning.

13.2 Method

This study employed a sequential exploratory research design (Creswell 2012) to explore learning-centered leadership in rural Chinese schools. This mixed methods research design followed three main stages: collection and analysis of qualitative data in selected schools, quantitative analysis of survey data, and interpretation (Creswell 2012). Although case studies were collected in a variety of schools, the qualitative portion of this chapter focuses on leadership and teacher learning in two urban schools.

School Sample: Quantitative The study was conducted in three provinces in mainland China, which represent different levels of educational development: Shanghai, Ningxia, and Haining. Data collection occurred between May and October, 2015, during the latter stages of the study. After obtaining the permission of principals and teachers, surveys were distributed in faculty meetings in 38 public schools; these consisted of both primary and secondary schools.

Participation in the study was voluntary, and the main sample is best described as a purposeful convenience sample. The sample was purposeful in the sense that the selection of schools incorporated several key variables including region and school level. The characteristics of the teacher sample were generally representative of the population of China's teachers in terms of gender, rank, and experience (see Ding 2010; Liu et al. 2016b).

School Sample: Qualitative Consistent with a sequential exploratory research design, the qualitative portion of the study took place before and then concurrently with the quantitative data collection. The qualitative phase of the study took place over a period of 3 years, starting in late 2012. Our goal for this portion of the study was to identify and then examine, in depth, school leaders working in a variety of different school contexts.

In this chapter, we focus on two "successful learning-centered leaders" working in urban schools. This characterization is supported by teacher ratings of their principals on four main constructs; this is reflected in Fig. 13.1 and Table 13.1, where the teacher ratings of principals from Wu Tong and Yang Ming Schools are compared with the full set of principals participating in our study.

As indicated in Fig. 13.2, the mean scores of the two principals appeared substantially higher than the grand mean of all principals on the four main constructs. Notably, these differences also carried over to dimensions of learning-centered leadership (see Table 13.1). In order to verify this perceived difference, we conducted independent samples t-tests on the main variable of interest, learning-centered leadership. The t-tests (not tabled) revealed that the ratings of the selected principals were significantly higher than the full sample of principals in terms of learning-centered leadership ($p<0.001$). This result provided the rationale for referring to these principals as "successful learning-centered leaders" and focusing on understanding their patterns of practice in the qualitative portion of the study.

Table 13.1 Comparison of teacher perceptions of the case study and full sample of principals

	Mean	SD	Min	Max
Wu Tong School				
Learning-centered leadership	4.38	0.31	3.84	5.00
Builds a learning vision	4.43	0.39	3.33	5.00
Provides learning support	4.52	0.33	3.75	5.00
Manages learning program	4.34	0.40	3.50	5.00
Modeling	4.35	0.47	3.75	5.00
Teacher trust	4.50	0.44	3.12	5.00
Teacher agency	4.30	0.38	3.38	5.00
Teacher professional learning	4.36	0.33	3.80	5.00
Yang Ming School				
Learning-centered leadership	4.86	0.49	3.04	5.00
Builds a learning vision	4.86	0.66	2.00	5.00
Provides learning support	4.88	0.38	3.75	5.00
Manages learning program	4.75	0.57	3.00	5.00
Modeling	4.89	0.46	3.20	5.00
Teacher trust	4.88	0.37	4.00	5.00
Teacher agency	4.86	0.28	3.92	5.00
Teacher professional learning	4.89	0.31	3.76	5.00
All principals				
Learning-centered leadership	4.04	0.61	1.84	5.00
Builds a learning vision	4.04	0.68	1.00	5.00
Provides learning support	4.14	0.60	1.38	5.00
Manages learning program	4.00	0.67	1.50	5.00
Modeling	4.06	0.70	1.00	5.00
Teacher trust	4.25	0.59	1.88	5.00
Teacher agency	4.04	0.56	1.42	5.00
Teacher professional learning	4.06	0.56	1.80	5.00

Variables and Measures We began with English language forms of several different instruments designed to measure our variables. In order to apply them in China, we used a sequence of translation and content validation procedures aimed at ensuring accuracy of translation, succinctness of expression, ease of understanding, and cultural adequacy (see Liu et al. 2016a).

In operationalizing our measurement scales, we borrowed and/or adapted items from instruments developed by various international scholars. Our measurement instrument consisted of 91 items distributed over the four main variables. Although the four main constructs were each comprised of several dimensions, in this chapter our quantitative analysis is limited to the composite variables (i.e., Leadership, Trust, Agency, Teacher Learning). All four scales employed a five-point Likert-type scale whereby a higher score signifies a stronger presence of the construct.

Data Collection The questionnaire was submitted to 1700 teachers from whom we obtained 1259 valid questionnaires representing a response rate of almost 80%.

```
5.00
4.50
4.00
3.50
3.00                                                    ▨ Yang Ming School Principal
2.50                                                    ▨ WuTong School Principal
                                                        ■ Mean of All Principals
2.00
1.50
1.00
      Leadership    Teacher Trust   Teacher Agency   Teacher Learning
```

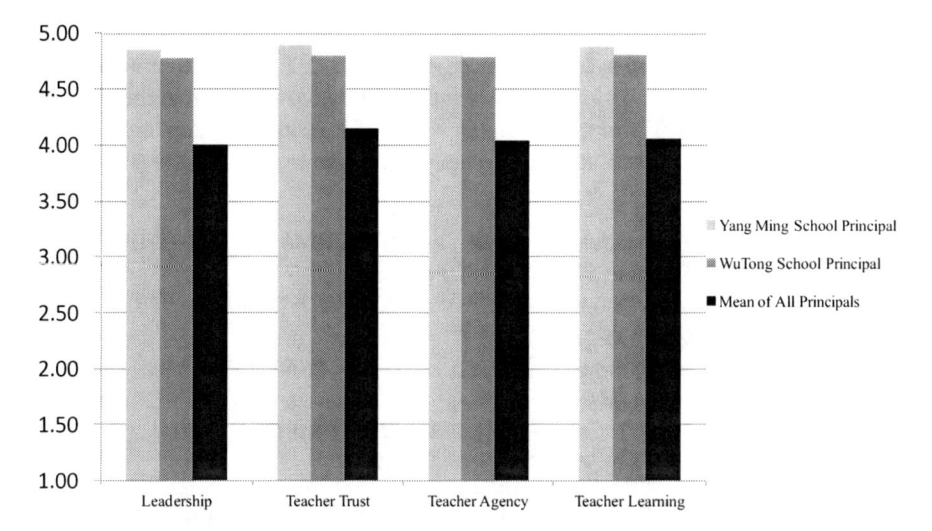

Fig. 13.2 Comparison of mean teacher ratings of selected principals on the four constructs

Demographic information was collected on gender, teaching experience, school level, professional rank, location, and education background. Although the sample characteristics varied from school to school (e.g., rural vs. urban), the overall teacher sample was broadly similar to the national teacher population (Ding 2010).

Qualitative data were collected during quarterly, 1-week visits to the schools between 2013 and 2015. During each visit, in-depth interviews were conducted with the school's principal and a variety of teachers; these semi-structured interviews were conducted on a one-to-one basis with nearly all the middle-level leaders and teachers at each school.

Qualitative data were collected using three methods. First, we conducted in-depth interviews with school leaders and a sample of teachers from each of the schools. Formal interviews were recorded and transcribed. Second, on-site observations were conducted several times in each of the schools over a 3-year period. Observations were conducted during staff meetings, teacher "research group" activities, lesson competitions, joint lesson planning sessions, teacher mentoring (*Shi Tu Dai Jiao*), and model lessons given using different pedagogies (*Tong Ke Yi Gou*). Finally we analyzed a range of documents including memos, activity schedules, workshop programs, school news, and teaching materials.

Data Analysis As noted at the outset of this section, data analysis proceeded in two stages. These are described below.

Quantitative Data Analysis We assessed the measurement model implied in Fig. 13.1 through a three-step process. First, we calculated Cronbach's alpha coefficients to evaluate the internal consistency of the main variables and subscales (Hair et al. 2013). The alpha coefficients exceeded the minimum desired level of 0.70 for all of the measured variables.

In the second step we used confirmatory factor analysis (CFA) to estimate factor loadings for subscales and average variance extracted (AVE) for the four main variables. Analysis of the second-order factor model further confirmed that the average variance extracted (AVE) for the four main variables exceeded the standard of 0.50. Moreover, the data-to-model fit was excellent for all four main variables (Hair et al. 2013).

- Learning-Centered Leadership (χ^2/df = 3.074; RMSEA = 0.041[< 0.08], CFI = 0.963[> 0.90], and SRMR = 0.029 [< .08]);
- Teacher Trust (χ^2/df = 3.030; RMSEA = 0.040 [< 0.08], CFI = 0.976 [> 0.90], and SRMR = 0.024 [< .08]);
- Teacher Agency (χ^2/df = 3.631; RMSEA = 0.046 [< 0.08], CFI = 0.949 [> 0.90], and SRMR = 0.038 [< 0.08]);
- Teacher Professional Learning (χ^2/df = 3.606; RMSEA = 0.045 [< 0.08], CFI = 0.945[> 0.90], and SRMR = 0.041[< 0.08]).

Finally, we tested data fit for the full model. All of the model-fit indices were deemed acceptable (i.e., χ^2/df = 2.428; RMSEA = 0.034 [< 0.08], CFI = 0.927 [>0.90], and SRMR = 0.038 [<0.08]). Thus, we concluded that the measurement model met desired standards of reliability and validity.

We employed structural equation modeling (SEM) with Mplus Version 7.0 (Muthén and Muthén 1998–2012) to analyze the structural parameters within the measurement model. An advantage of SEM over earlier multi-step procedures used for mediation analysis lies in its ability to measure relationships among mediating constructs in a single analytical model (Hayes 2009). Mplus enables examination of the significance of indirect effects of multiple mediators (Preacher and Hayes 2008). It should be noted that in this chapter we limit the depth of description of the quantitative results in order to retain space for the case study analyses. More thorough analyses can be found in other papers (e.g., Liu et al. 2016a; Hallinger et al. 2016).

Qualitative Data Analysis The qualitative data were first analyzed and compiled into case studies of the selected schools. Then data collected from the schools were synthesized to surface cross-school trends. In this chapter we have limited data presentation to the case study briefs.

13.3 Does Principal Leadership Influence Teacher Professional Learning?

Quantitative analyses sought to determine whether our conceptual model of leadership and learning provided a valid description of these dynamics in the Chinese context. SEM enables researchers to determine which "paths" between variables in a proposed model are significant and which ones are not. The partial mediation model proposed in Fig. 13.1 yielded an acceptable fit to the data on our stated

```
                                    x2/df = 2.439 ; CFI=.926 ;
                              GFI=.830 ; SRMR= .039 ;RMSEA=.034.
```

                         Teacher Trust
         .728***   (TT)   .132***

                              .582***
    Learning-centered   Teacher Professional
       Leadership   .411***   Learning
          (LCL)   (TPL)

         .344***   .408***
                        Teacher Agency
                             (TA)

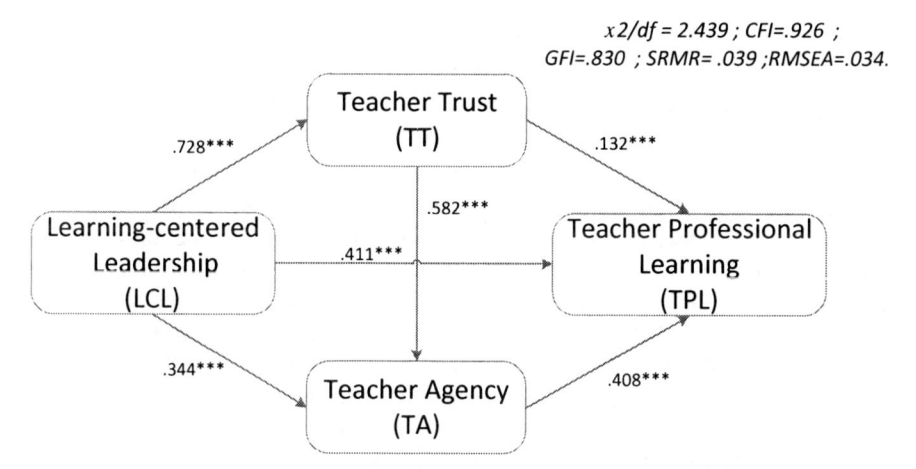

Fig. 13.3 Structural equation mode of principal leadership and teacher learning

parameters, and a significantly better fit than the full mediation model. The chi-square for the change with 3 degrees of freedom was 181.437 (p<0.01).

The standardized parameter estimates shown in Fig. 13.3 provide indications of significance and effect sizes associated with the partial mediation model. These data support several conclusions. Learning-Centered Leadership had moderate direct effects on Teacher Professional Learning (β = 0.411, p<.001), Teacher Trust (β = .728, p<.001), and Teacher Agency (β = 0.344, p<.001). Teacher Agency had a moderate direct effect on Teacher Professional Learning (β = 0.408, p<.001). The direct effects of Teacher Trust on Teacher Professional Learning, however, were somewhat smaller (β = 0.132, p<.001). Thus, our analysis indicated that a portion of leadership effects on teacher learning did operate through trust and agency.

Affirmation of the partial mediated model leads to two practical conclusions. First, it points towards productive learning-centered leadership practices that principals can employ to directly support the workplace learning of their teachers (see Liu et al. 2016a for more detail). Second, the partial mediation model highlights two paths (i.e., Teacher Trust and Agency) that can serve as "intermediate targets" for principal action (see Liu et al. 2016b for more detail). Simply stated, the model suggests that principals who foster teacher trust and agency can gain greater teacher engagement in professional learning.

13.4 How Do Successful Principals Influence Teacher Learning in China?

Although the quantitative analysis offered a broad picture of the relationship of leadership and teacher learning, it offered fewer insights into how these dynamics play out in the working lives of Chinese principals and teachers. In this section, we present case studies of two principals who demonstrated successful learning-centered leadership in the Chinese context.

Wu Tong Primary School Wu Tong Primary School is situated in Shanghai, the leading economic city of mainland China. Wu Tong Primary School was considered a model school in the early 1990s. However, as its neighborhood began to decline towards the turn of the millennium, so did student performance. Consequently, many of the better teachers abandoned the school, and a cycle of continuing deterioration in school quality set in. This was the situation when Ms. Zhou became the principal of Wu Tong Primary School in 2010. Over the years, the school's reputation had suffered, and Principal Zhou faced a school that was searching for a new beginning. In 2012, the Shanghai municipal government launched the New High Quality School Project (NHQS). The purpose of the NHQS was to improve schools with weak student performance. Wu Tong Primary School was selected in the first batch of schools to participate in the NHQS project.

Consistent with the main trend of China's post-2000 education reforms, a fundamental goal of NHQS was to motivate schools to move away from a test-taking orientation and towards more holistic approaches to education. After 5 years of effort, Wu Tong Primary School moved from the bottom quartile to a rank of 7th out of 25 primary schools in the district. As a result, Principal Zhou was encouraged by the Shanghai Education Authority to establish a "distinguished principal's workshop" to help principals working in other low-performing schools. This formally recognized her success in building a learning community in her school and strengthening student performance.

We can see a broad pattern of learning-centered leadership in the graph presented in Fig. 13.4. Principal Zhou was rated highly across all four dimensions of learning-centered leadership. Moreover, her scores on all four dimensions were substantially higher than those of the full group of 38 principals who participated in this study. We will continue the case study by examining each of these four leadership dimensions, drawing upon our qualitative data.

Builds a Learning Vision Upon joining the NHQS project, Ms. Zhou proposed a new vision for the school:

> When we entered the NHQS project, it was the right time to propose a new school vision. Like the proverb says: 'strike while the iron is hot.' Our vision was to become a school with academic excellence for students, superb teaching, where all students have opportunities to reach their personal best within five years. (Principal Zhou, May 8, 2015)

The concept behind this vision was to create a learning community in the school, a culture in which learning was valued for everyone. More specifically, to achieve the vision Principal Zhou believed it would be essential to stimulate the learning and development of her teachers. Therefore, she encouraged teachers to attend to their own professional learning both as a means of improving teaching quality and instilling students with the desire to reach their potential. This vision provided a basis for focusing school resources on specific areas, guiding teacher activities, and evaluating school effectiveness (Hallinger and Heck 2002). It made teachers feel that there

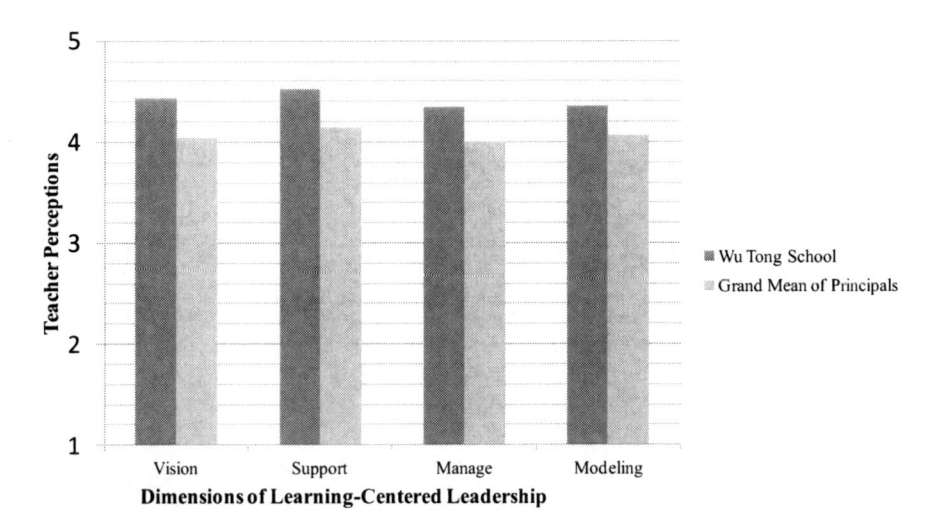

Fig. 13.4 Comparison of Wu Tong School principal with all principals on dimensions of learning-centred leadership

was a collective effort aimed at something meaningful. As observed by one of her teachers: "Our principal not only proposed a vision for change, but also means to achieve it. The vision gave us a common focus and a foundation for building trust both among teachers and with the school's leadership" (Teacher Liu, May 22, 2015). A second teacher stated:

> The morale at our school had been low for years. It is no exaggeration to say that the New High Quality School Project was like a lifesaver for our school at that time. It was a great motivation to the teachers. In our eyes, it was an opportunity to stop the decline that we all could see and move towards a more positive future. Our new vision and the project in general created a stronger sense of collective responsibility to work hard for the development of our school. (Teacher Ren, May 8, 2015)

For many teachers, it is easy to take a vision as a slogan or as a fuzzy image of the future. Therefore, in order to realize her vision, Principal Zhou proposed a series of medium- and long-term goals and strategies. One teacher recalled: "Principal Zhou emphasized the importance of breaking the vision into manageable goals. This made our teachers feel that the vision was achievable. It was our collective effort in daily life that was necessary to make it happen" (Teacher Ou, May 8, 2015). In seeking to motivate her staff, Ms. Zhou appealed to both personal and professional concerns; these encompassed factors associated with both transformational (e.g., capacity development and intrinsic motivation) and transactional leadership (e.g., higher qualifications and reward). She articulated her approach quite clearly:

> I often told my teachers that the New High Quality School Project would have two important outcomes. First, it would contribute to the development of our school, and second to their own professional and career development as teachers. By learning and gaining new skills through the project they would become more proficient and able to achieve greater

impact on students. This would also enable them to get higher economic reward and social prestige. (Principal Zhou, 13 May, 2015)

Provides Learning Support To make schools more productive learning places for teachers, Principal Zhou advocated reducing bureaucracy and decentralizing decision-making. She also made an effort to create a norm to "appreciate education" for all learners. This was aimed at encouraging teachers to take initiative and responsibility for their own learning (i.e., agency). In terms of practical actions, Principal Zhou provided teachers with access to learning resources and timely feedback on their efforts to use new skills in their classrooms. Teachers interpreted Principal Zhou's efforts as strong expressions of support and consideration: "Our principal protects teachers' learning time by minimizing bureaucratic routines. As the facilitator of teacher learning, [Principal Zhou] provides time and resources that we need to learn" (Teacher Ou, May 8, 2015). Another teacher stated: "Bureaucratic routines which take up teachers' time are very common in schools. But our principal emphasizes the need for having a relaxed environment and favorable conditions for teacher and student learning" (Teacher Tian, May 22, 2015). A third commented:

> When I look back, I can say that our school's culture has changed during these past years. We feel no sense of distance with the principal or Teaching Research Group leaders. We use their first names and feel that we are co-workers. Everybody in our schools is polite and respectful. Principal Zhou's door is open to all teachers. We feel like a kind of 'extended-family' atmosphere in our school. (Teacher Ren, June 5, 2015)

These remarks suggest less social distance and hierarchy at Wu Tong School than is typical in many Chinese schools (Tang et al. 2014; Walker et al. 2012). Principal Zhou's efforts in terms of building a learning community were constructed as a result of having an informal and harmonious relationship with her teachers. She encouraged a working style that deemphasized social hierarchy among the teachers as well as with the school's administrators. Teachers indicated that her leadership style made a difference in their efforts to learn and develop, and also contributed to the vibrancy at Wu Tong School. One of the younger teachers recalled the following incident:

> Two years ago, Principal Zhou observed my class and left a note for me which I kept to this day. She said, 'I appreciated your teaching style today with your class. In my eyes, you have great potential as a teacher. I believe that you will have great professional influence in our city in the next few years if you continue to work hard.' (Teacher Ren, May 28, 2015)

Notably, Principal Zhou's efforts to support educators were not limited to the younger teachers. As in many other societies, Chinese principals face the challenge of motivating mid- and late-career teachers. One of the senior teachers at Wu Tong Primary School described how Principal Zhou's efforts to build a learning community impacted her motivation and commitment:

> Our principal designed a career development plan for teachers in different stages in our careers. Although I will retire in five years, Principal Zhou still regarded me highly and gave me respect. For example, last year, I was named a 'Senior Teacher' with responsibilities to coach less-experienced colleagues. Being given this title and responsibility made me feel obliged to renew my own thinking so I could effectively guide the younger teachers.

This was a responsibility and opportunity that I never had before. (Teacher Ou, June 5, 2015)

The examples above suggest that Principal Zhou used her vision of "appreciating education" to enact a strategy that strengthened teachers' motivation as both educators and learners. Notably, by meeting the different needs of different teachers, she promoted trust and agency. This created an environment in which teachers felt it was both safe and valued to engage in experimentation, reflection, and risk taking. In the principal's own words:

> To feel the experience of success is very important for all teachers, especially those who may have felt less successful in the past. We have tried to offer many different opportunities for teachers to develop, for example by distributing professional literature, encouraging collaboration, showing model lessons, and launching many kinds of teaching skills competition in our school. Every semester, nearly all teachers will participate in these collegial contests. These competitions not only urge them to learn new things, but promote sharing of successful experience that strengthens their self-belief and their teaching practice. (Principal Zhou, May 22, 2015)

Manages the Learning Program Principal Zhou acknowledged a need to offer more assertive leadership when she arrived at Wu Tong due to the school's unimpressive performance in the recent past. Thus, for example, she initiated the "appreciate education" vision without significant teacher input. However, she also realized that making the vision come to life in her school would require a transfer of ownership of the vision from herself to the teachers:

> We must encourage teachers and provide them with emotional support. But that is not enough. We also need to make them believe that devoting time to their own learning will really benefit their teaching and help students. So we try to help them form the habit of learning. (Principal Zhou, May 22, 2015)

In Principal Zhou's eyes, a key to successful achievement of the vision was empowering teachers and giving them ownership of their collective efforts in terms of school development. So although she used her authority to propose the new vision, Principal Zhou also sought to involve teachers in determining how to make the vision come to life in the school. This combination of "top-down" and "bottom-up" strategies built trust and yielded a new level of teacher engagement in the school:

> Different from other schools, all the teacher-learning projects in our school are designed from the 'bottom up' by first-line teachers. At the end of the semester, our Teaching Research Group leader will conduct a needs analysis and submit learning plans. Then, school leaders check them. I feel that we are given voice and choice in our professional learning. (Teacher Ren, May 22, 2015)

> Nearly all of our learning activities in our school are organized by Teaching Research Groups. We have the right to decide what to learn, how to learn, and when to learn. So all of us have a responsibility for managing our learning as teachers. Our leaders the role of supporters and supervisors. They are very accessible to teachers. (Teacher Ou, June 5, 2015)

In order to make the learning activities more effective, Principal Zhou proposed many strategies: "Guidance from master teachers is important for the growth of beginning teachers. In order to motivate master teachers, we relate the senior teachers' professional promotion to the professional development of younger teachers" (Principal Zhou, May 22, 2015). A teacher stated: "The content of school-based training is quite rich. For example, teaching skills, educational technology, educational philosophy, and up-to-date pedagogical theories. In fact, for most of teachers, they would like to engage in professional learning, if it is well organized" (Teacher Ou, June 5, 2015).

Modeling In a paper where we analyzed the effects of learning-centered leadership in terms of the four dimensions, we were surprised to find that modeling was not a significant practice employed by our sample of Chinese principals (Liu et al. 2016a). However, as suggested in Fig. 13.4 and Table 13.1, Principal Zhou was a "positive outlier" on this dimension of learning-centered leadership. This suggests that teachers perceived her as employing modeling in her leadership practice more frequently than is typical among Chinese school leaders. This feature of her leadership also came through quite vividly in the interviews. If leaders convey their priorities through their actions, then Principal Zhou's were unmistakably focused on the quality of teaching and learning:

> She is a workaholic in my eyes. She is the first to arrive and the last one to leave school every day. As a special-class teacher in chemistry herself, Principal Zhou often observes classes and gives us feedback. We often joke that if Principal Zhou is not in the classroom, she must be on the way to the classroom. (Teacher Ren, May 22, 2015)

Modeling is inspirational, as it articulates and reinforces the core values of a leader. Principal Zhou's passion for learning and commitment to personal professional development were conveyed to other leaders as well as to her teachers: "I have been the assistant principal for three years and I have seen the tremendous changes in our school. Principal Zhou is dynamic, enterprising, open to change and supportive of others who are trying to change" (Teacher Zhao, June 5, 2015). A second teacher commented: "Our principal often participates in our formal or informal discussion of teaching problems. As a special-grade teacher, she is often seen by staff as a source of instructional advice" (Teacher Ren, May 22, 2015).

The portrait of Principal Zhou as a learning-centered leader reprises themes that abound in the broader literature on instructional (Hallinger and Murphy 1986), transformational (Leithwood and Jantzi 2006), and shared (Heck and Hallinger 2014) leadership. Moreover, her clarity of values and vision, resourcefulness, knowledge of teaching and learning, delegation of responsibilities for instructional leadership, and focus on creating conditions that support teacher learning (e.g., trust and agency) distinguish her leadership practice from that of the broader set of principals in our sample.

Yang Ming School Yang Ming Middle School was established in 1865 in the Southern city of Guangzhou. The school was recognized by the Ministry of Education as a model school during the current era of Chinese curriculum reform.

Yang Ming School has 250 teachers, 80% of whom hold Master degrees. It is a well-resourced school, both in terms of facilities and human resources.

The school has long adhered to a philosophy of "elite education." Its students generally score very well on National College Entrance Exam, and over 95% of graduates enter "key universities" in China. Students at Yang Ming have won many awards in regional, national, and international science and technology competitions. Yang Ming School attaches great importance to meeting the needs of students with different interests and helping them reach their potential. Thus, Yang Ming has a very diverse curriculum.

The current principal at Yang Ming, Mr. Dou, has worked as a teacher, Vice Principal and Principal at the school for 25 years. "It is no exaggeration to say that I have contributed all my youth and strength to the school and witnessed the development of school. This is the first, but also the last school in which I have worked" (Principal Dou, Sept 5, 2014). Principal Dou was rated highly across all four dimensions of learning centered leadership, and scored consistently higher than the grand mean of principals participating in the study (see Fig. 13.5).

One of the notable innovations implemented in recent years at Yang Ming School was the flipped classroom.[1] This reform, initiated by front-line teachers, required significant change in teaching and learning practices supported by sustained professional learning. We will use this reform as a focus for our discussion of leadership and teacher learning at Yang Ming School.

Builds a Learning Vision As suggested above, the Yang Ming's school vision was characterized by values of excellence, innovation, and diversity. Qualitative data suggested that teachers and administrators were guided by a vibrant, shared vision of learning for students as well as teachers. In the principal's view, Yang Ming School's vision is a source of inspiration for teachers:

> Our school vision is stable and does not change with fads. When I entered the school twenty years ago, our principal proposed that our goal was to cultivate the elites. Many years have passed, but our school vision is like the power of the spirit moving from generation to generation. Though it is rarely mentioned explicitly, the spirit of excellence has been infused into our faith and our practice as leaders and teachers. (Principal Dou, Sept 5, 2014)

> The connection between an inspirational vision and the daily practice of school staff was reinforced in the responses of teachers during our interviews. As one of the famous key schools in our province, we are proud of our students. All of our teachers strive to make excellence a habit… Our vision [of excellence, innovation, and diversity] is not just a slogan; instead it is embedded in the day-to-day actions of teachers. (Teacher Cai, January 5, 2015)

But what is "excellence"? In a society where learning is often dominated by exam results, Yang Ming School took a broader view of "learning":

---

[1] The flipped classroom is a pedagogical model in which the typical lecture and homework elements of a course are reversed. Short video lectures are viewed by students at home before the class session, while in-class time is devoted to exercises, projects, or discussions. (https://net.educause.edu/ir/library/pdf/eli7081.pdf).

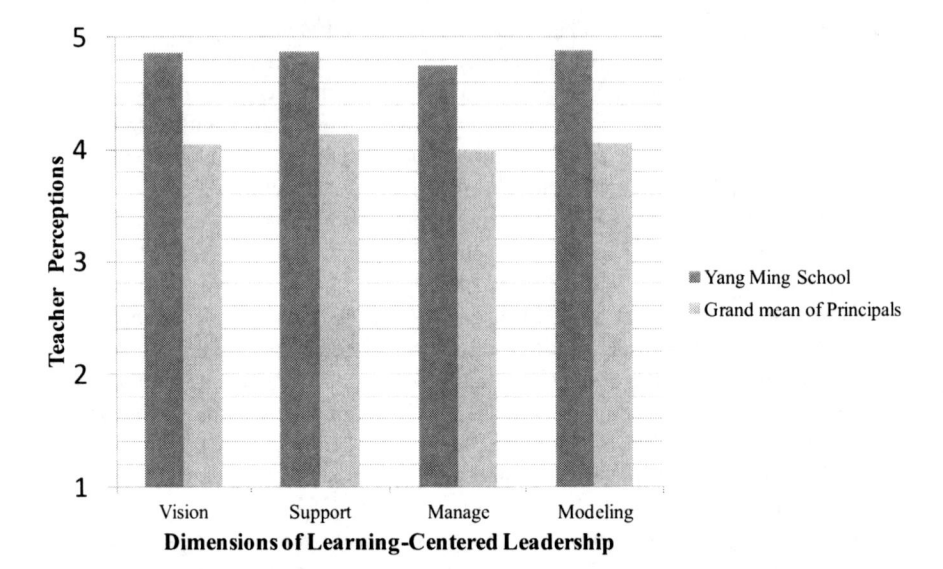

Fig. 13.5 Comparison of Yang Ming School principal with all principals on dimensions of learning-centred leadership.

> The vision in our school does not just refer to 'academic focus,' but also the future development of our students. Our school seeks to cultivate future world leaders, scholars, and entrepreneurs. This vision gives us a kind of moral power compared with schools that only focus on examination results. For example, our main motivation in adopting the flipped classroom was to develop students' higher-order thinking. As teachers we have the responsibility to try different things that challenge our students and then to see what works. (Teacher Yang, Sept 4, 2014)

> Our principal always says that we should take a long-term view of student development. The purposes of the flipped classroom are to promote individualized instruction among our teachers and autonomous learning among our students. These are consistent with our focus on the cultivation of diverse talents among both students and teachers. (Teacher Cai, January 5, 2015)

When examining the Yang Ming School's historical record, one can conclude that it has reached and maintained a level of sustained high performance because of which its vision has become embedded in the practice of leaders and teachers. In this context, the principal's role appears to include articulating and reinforcing prevailing values, rather than introducing new ones. We observed that the principal, although widely respected among his staff, led from the background rather than front and center. With this in mind, we found that teachers were less concerned with "who" to follow than with how to achieve the school's vision of excellence, innovation, and diversity.

Provides Learning Support Disparities in reputation, financial resources, teaching facilities, and student resources are readily observed between "key schools" and "ordinary schools" in China. As a key school, Yang Ming School is associated with higher-quality teaching staff, better facilities, more government investment, and higher-achieving students from more advantaged families. Teachers at Yang Ming School are, therefore, able to access rich learning resources to meet their professional needs. However, the availability of resources does not mean they are always used to bring about productive learning and change; this should be where leadership "makes a difference" (Frost 2006; Hallinger 2011; Knapp et al. 2010; Saphier et al. 2006).

Teachers were consistent in emphasizing the importance of dual forms of "support for our learning": tangible support and "invisible support." Examples of tangible support we observed included resources such as flexible time, funds for coursework, expert guidance, and local universities with up-to-date programs and facilities. Teachers noted their appreciation for these resources and their principal's capacity to organize them efficiently:

> Our principal has often emphasized that although the college entrance examination is important, it is *not the only important thing for our students*. Most of them will apply for entrance into foreign universities or sit for the independent entrance exams for famous universities in China. So we look at preparation of their broader qualifications as the core education provided by our school. So, our principal provides the resources we need to meet these needs and always encourages us to try something new in our classrooms. (Teacher Yang, Sept 4, 2014)

However, the effective use of tangible resources only appeared to come into full bloom when combined with "invisible" forms of support such as encouragement, feedback, and personalized assistance. "Invisible support" was a means of "activating" the potential of tangible resources. We observed that this type of support increased teachers' trust, sense of agency, and collective efficacy.

> Our school has rich learning resources. As long as your request is reasonable, school leaders will find a way to satisfy your need. However, in my mind, the biggest support we get from our school leaders is their understanding, encouragement, and open mind [about our ideas]. As sources of moral support, we value them the most. (Teacher Lin, Sept 5, 2014)

> We felt heavy pressure when our teaching reforms did not achieve the desired result at first. Not only teachers, but also students were not used to the flipped classroom. Their test scores actually dropped during that period. I even considered disbanding our learning group at that time. However, our principal always comforted and supported me. He reminded all of us that 'it is very normal to have setbacks during the period of change. If you keep your faith and persist, you will overcome; don't despair.' This gave us the strength to continue until we achieved success. (Teacher Yang, January 5, 2015)

> I always insist that young people should not stick to old ideas and must have the courage to innovate. It does not matter if you succeed right away, but you should always try your best and follow what you believe in. (Principal Dou, Sept 5, 2014)

While these observations and assertions may appear "obvious," it should be noted that they are not typical in the Chinese context. In China, leaders, teachers, and students are highly sensitive to "keeping face." As teachers and as learners, staff behaviour is easily influenced by fear of failure or embarrassment. At a "key school" like Yang Ming the pressure for high performance can easily push leaders and teachers into taking the safe road. Thus, we suggest that leaders play a potentially crucial role in this context by ensuring that tangible resources are used widely and creating a safe environment for teacher learning. The latter is enacted both through the provision of moral support and by creating norms that support risk-taking and innovation (Barth 1990; Saphier et al. 2006).

Manages the Learning Program As noted above, the flipped classroom initiative was instituted by front-line teachers, not by the principal or higher education authorities. Although its aims were highly consistent with China's top-down curriculum reforms, it was a voluntary endeavour. As such, there were no strict rules or regulations in place to ensure implementation or compliance. One teacher recalled:

> I was the first person to initiate the flipped classroom learning. As a self-organized learning group, we never relied on negative management, such as roll call, supervision, and outcome assessment to determine our approach. We just wanted to create conditions so teachers would want to participate, to enjoy working together, and to benefit from it. (Teacher Yang, January 4, 2015)

> Our learning group was launched from bottom to top. I have been part of the flipped classroom initiative for three years. Since we work together informally, we don't have the typical institutional restrictions or material rewards to motivate us to become engaged or to learn. Even so, learning with like-minded colleagues has been a wonderful experience for me. I think that for most of us, common interests and harmonious relationships have fuelled our work together. (Teacher Cai, January 5, 2015)

> The reason that I have continued to work with the flipped classroom group is that we all benefit as teachers from learning together. Activities are effectively organized by the head of our group; time isn't wasted. We get timely guidance and effective feedback that has helped us in learning new practical skills. (Teacher Lin, January 5, 2015)

These excerpts suggest that positive, process-oriented management led by teacher leaders has contributed to trust, agency, and ultimately to an environment of productive teacher learning. Through timely, direct, and personalized feedback, teachers have benefitted from professional learning activities such as workshops and team meetings (Hwang et al. 2003). As an ordinary teacher, Teacher Yang led the flipped classroom group in Yang Ming School. Moreover, as a teacher engaged in implementing the innovation himself, he had a clearer idea of what teachers needed and what worked than did the principal. Thus, while the principal emerged as an important source of support, he led from the background and allowed a senior teacher to assume center stage for the flipped classroom initiative. This became a good example of distributed instructional leadership in the school.

Modeling As discussed earlier, the results of the broader quantitative analysis revealed only a limited use of modeling among principals in this study. Nonetheless, as indicated in the graph presented in Fig. 13.5, Principal Dou was rated highly on this dimension of learning-centered leadership. Modeling is grounded in the values of the leader (Barth 1990; Hallinger 2011; Leithwood and Jantzi 2006). This was evident with respect to Prinicpal Dou:

> I often emphasize to our teachers that we should be 'educators' first, instead of 'the principal or teacher.' If our identity is to be an educator, we will treat teaching as our career instead of as a job. This is what can give us meaning in our work. (Principal Dou, Sept 5, 2014)

Teachers were quite consistent in highlighting how Principal Dou's educational values, passion, and work orientation carried over into the attitudes of teachers:

> Principal Zhou is a special-class principal in Guangdong province. Two years ago he was recognized as a 'National Model Worker.' We all respect him very much. He has often said that people should never be too old to learn and we can see that in his own life and work as a teacher and principal. (Teacher Lin, January 5, 2015)

At the same time, it is the reality in China that principals have many administrative affairs to handle, and spend a considerable portion of their time outside of the school (Tang et al. 2014; Walker and Qian 2015; Zhang and Pang 2016). This shapes the role that principals play as "learning leaders," especially in schools as large as Yang Ming. Therefore, teacher leaders hold a unique position in the professional support to ordinary teachers:

> A principal with excellent morals and teaching skills is important. However, as an ordinary teacher, I actually have relatively few opportunities to interact with our principal directly. In fact, my own more active involvement in professional learning came about not because of our principal, but from Teacher Yang's passion and engagement. (Teacher Li, January 5, 2015)

With this in mind, we observed that "leader modeling" was not limited to the role played by Principal Dou. With Principal Dou's explicit support, there was no limitation on the roles that teachers could assume (e.g., head of a department, teaching team, or teaching research group) at Yang Ming. Perhaps more significant, however, was the support Principal Dou provided to ordinary teachers such as Teacher Yang in heading informal initiatives. The significance of this emerged in interviews where teachers discussed how they were touched by Teacher Yang's passion as for learning:

> Teacher Yang is an able man in our eyes. He is one of the few people I know who is committed to education. He has great passion about teaching reform. To be frank, I was quite skeptical about the flipped classroom at first. But Teacher Yang's enthusiasm strongly influenced me to participate in and to persist even until now. He has set a good example for all of us. (Teacher Liu, August 27, 2014)

Based on the above-mentioned excerpts, we speculate that high power distance in social relations combine with a hierarchical administrative system to shape and even limit the role that Chinese principals play in "directly" influencing the professional learning of teachers (Hwang et al. 2003; Qian et al. 2016; Wang 2016). Nonetheless, as observed in the broader literature, principals retain an important role by reinforcing key values and delegating authority, implicitly or explicitly, to others (Qian et al. 2016; Walker et al. 2012; Zhang and Pang 2016). It may be that in the Chinese context teacher leaders have the potential to be even more influential than principals in shaping the norms and practices that contribute to collegial exchange and learning (Qian et al. 2016; Wang 2016). Thus, the effect of modeling may be more clearly evidenced in the role of teacher leaders than principals.

13.5 Discussion

In this chapter we presented results from a mixed-methods study of principal leadership and teacher learning in China. As discussed earlier, concepts such as "learning-centered" and "instructional" leadership are still relatively new in the Chinese education context. With this in mind, the current study was undertaken to validate a model of leadership for teacher learning, as well as to surface distinctive practices that distinguish this role in mainland China. In this final section, we highlight the limitations of the study, situate our findings in a broader context, and suggest implications for research and practice.

Limitations of the Study We wish to highlight three main limitations of this study. First, the study was conducted in only three provinces of China. Although our school sample varied on several relevant criteria, China is a huge country with great variations in the conditions of schooling. Therefore, we acknowledge that our findings may not represent the practices of educational leadership throughout China.

Second, the current study did *not* include measures of student learning. Therefore, although learning-centered leadership was associated with teacher engagement in professional learning, we cannot confirm that these effects carry over to student learning. Thus, the current study does not "close the circle" when it comes to research on leadership, teacher learning, and student achievement.

Finally, we note that the current study employed cross-sectional research. "Snapshot" studies of school processes (e.g., leadership and teacher learning) that actually unfold over a period of time can neither fully capture nor confirm the "causal nature of relationships" among constructs (Hallinger and Heck 1998; Heck and Hallinger 2014). Therefore, although we refer to the "effects" of leadership on teacher learning, we are actually limited to describing the strength of association in these relationships.

Interpretation and Implications of the Findings Quantitative analysis supported our conceptual model of leadership and teacher learning (see Figs. 13.1 and 13.2) for this set of schools in China. More specifically, we found that teacher trust and agency partially mediated the positive effects of learning-centered leadership on teacher professional learning. This finding suggests that leadership and learning processes in China were broadly similar to descriptions published in the Western literature (e.g., Leithwood and Jantzi 2006; Sleegers et al. 2014; Thoonen et al. 2012; Wahlstrom and Louis 2008; Youngs and King 2002). Since scholars believe that societal context influences the exercise of leadership, our proposed model, based largely on prior Western research, could not have been taken for granted (Hallinger and Leithwood 1996; Walker and Dimmock 2002).

In addition, the results of our mixed-methods analysis support Belchetz and Leithwood's (2007) assertion that a broadly similar set of effective school leadership practices are enacted in distinctive ways across different school contexts. In this study, for example, we noted that the Chinese socio-cultural context is characterized by much larger power distance (i.e., hierarchical relations) than is typically observed in the USA, Canada, UK, Netherlands, or Australia, where the bulk of published research in educational administration has been conducted (Walker and Dimmock 2002). The question about whether teacher trust and agency would be as influential in shaping teacher engagement in professional learning in China – where order-giving and order-taking based on status, rank, and seniority are "the norm" – was an open one (Tang et al. 2014; Walker et al. 2012). Nonetheless, as indicated, the quantitative analysis highlighted teacher trust and agency as relevant "strategic targets" for Chinese principals interested in fostering teacher learning and productive change in their schools. These broad trends were elaborated in the qualitative case studies, which described practices of two successful principals on the dimensions of learning-centered leadership (e.g., vision, modeling). The case studies elaborated how different patterns of leadership practice can shape teacher attitudes (i.e., trust and agency) and behavior (i.e., professional learning). The principals in both case studies engaged their role as "learning leaders" with passion, energy, focus, and activity. This carried over into teachers' attitudes towards engaging in workplace learning, and indeed towards teachers' collaborating for change in their schools.

Notably, although both principals were rated as "strong learning-centered leaders," their leadership styles were refined to meet the needs of their particular school contexts. For example, Principal Zhou entered Wu Tong School at a time when there was a clear need for a revitalization – if not turnaround – in school performance. Principal Zhou employed a principal-directed approach to reform. This was reflected in her use of clearly defined goals, as well as visible active leadership of reforms that engaged teachers in learning. In contrast, Principal Dou had assumed the principalship of a school with a continuing history of success and a strong positive learning culture. Though perceived by teachers as a highly supportive leader, he worked in the background, delegating responsibility for leading reform activities to other leaders. Prior to Zhou's tenure as principal, the school already possessed a shared vision and a strong learning culture with norms that supported teacher trust, agency, and learning. Zhou therefore saw his role as working with the existing strengths to foster the shared vision of excellence, innovation, and diversity.

Variations in the contexts of the two schools in the study may explain some of the differences in the learning-centered leadership strategies employed by the two "successful principals." Indeed, the contrast in their learning-centered leadership styles reprises findings reported by scholars in the USA (e.g., Hallinger and Heck 2011; Hallinger and Murphy 1986) and the UK (e.g., Day 2009); these studies found that principals adapted their leadership styles to the needs of the schools in a strikingly similar fashion. Leadership during the "turnaround" phase emphasized clear measurable goals that provided a common direction for staff and fostered coherence in program development. After schools had achieved success, leaders relied on a shared vision embedded in the culture of the school and distributed leadership to provide meaning, synergy, and direction for school development (see also Hallinger and Heck 2002). Although we only presented two cases in this chapter, they suggest a similar kind of variation in leadership style among these successful leaders.

A second broad finding of interest that emerged from the case studies concerned the means by which the two principals responded to the socio-cultural environment that prevails in China. More specifically, we observed that these principals found ways to enhance and reap the benefits of trust and teacher agency, even in a hierarchical environment where leaders and teachers were accustomed to giving and receiving orders. Both principals worked actively to overcome the potentially negative effects of this norm on teacher satisfaction and commitment. They found ways to navigate the prevailing culture even as they sought to manage the introduction of programs (e.g., flipped classroom) that embraced countervailing values (Walker and Hallinger 2007). This was evident, for example, in the use of modeling as a leadership practice by the principals. In analyses reported elsewhere (Liu et al. 2016a), we found that modeling was not verified as a significant leadership practice employed among the full set of 38 principals. Although modeling was still potentially significant in the Chinese context, it took on a different character; social norms and a strongly hierarchical bureaucratic education system created distance between principals and teachers. This appeared to reduce the frequency and strength of modeling among the principals as a group. Nonetheless, our case studies highlight the fact that modeling could still represent an influential practice in terms of stimulating teacher learning if the principal was both intentional in articulating his/her values and delegated authority to middle-level and teacher leaders.

In sum, the results suggest that the conceptual model proposed in this chapter can be employed by scholars to guide future research on learning-centered leadership in China (see also Chen et al. 2016; Qian et al. 2016; Wang 2016; Zhang and Pang 2016). The study presented in this chapter not only offers a clear definition of learning-centered leadership for the Chinese context, but also initial support for its efficacy in supporting at least one "high value path" that shapes school improvement. Moreover, our initial validation of the scales used in this study offers scholars in China robust tools for future research in China.

In terms of practical implications, the conceptual model and operational constructs described in this chapter could serve as heuristics for China's policymakers and practitioners as they continue to develop a model of "learning-centered leadership with Chinese characteristics." As noted, learning-centered leadership has both a short history in China and an uncertain relationship with the traditional role of the school principal. Our findings could, for example, shape the direction and content of principal preparation and professional development. Thus, we hope that the findings presented in this chapter will stimulate discussion and cause practitioners to reflect on the role that they can play in furthering teacher learning and school improvement.

References

Barth, R. S. (1990). *Improving schools from within.* San Francisco: Jossey-Bass.
Belchetz, D., & Leithwood, K. (2007). Successful leadership: Does context matter and if so, how? In C. Day & K. Leithwood (Eds.), *Successful principal leadership in times of change: An international perspective.* Dordrecht: Springer.
Bryk, A., & Schneider, B. (2002). *Trust in schools: A core resource for improvement.* New York: Russell Sage Foundation.
Bush, T., Coleman, M., & Xiaohong, S. (1998). Managing secondary schools in China. *Compare, 28*, 183–195.
Chen, P., Lee, C. D., Lin, H., & Zhang, C. X. (2016). Factors that develop effective professional learning communities in Taiwan. *Asia Pacific Journal of Education, 36*, 248–265.
Cravens, X. C. (2008). *The cross-cultural fit of the learning-centered leadership framework and assessment for Chinese principals.* Unpublished doctoral dissertation, Vanderbilt University, Nashville.
Creswell, J. W. (2012). *Qualitative inquiry and research design: Choosing among five approaches.* Thousand Oaks: Sage.
Darling-Hammond, L., & Richardson, N. (2009). Teacher learning: What matters. *Educational Leadership, 66*, 46–53.
Day, C. (2009). Capacity building through layered leadership: Sustaining the turnaround. In A. Harris (Ed.), *Distributed leadership* (pp. 121–137). Dordrecht: Springer.
Dello-Iacovo, B. (2009). Curriculum reform and 'quality education' in China: An overview. *International Journal of Educational Development, 29*, 241–249.
Ding, G. (2010). *National survey and policy analysis for teacher professional development in primary and secondary schools.* Shanghai: East China Normal University Press.
Frost, D. (2006). The concept of 'agency' in leadership for learning. *Leading & Managing, 12*, 19–28.
Goldring, E., Huff, J., Spillane, J. P., & Barnes, C. (2009). Measuring the learning-centered leadership expertise of school principals. *Leadership and Policy in Schools, 8*, 197–228.
Grobman, H., & Hynes, V. (1956). What makes a good principal? *NASSP Bulletin, 40*(223), 5–16.
Hair, J. F., Ringle, C. M., Hult, G. T. M., & Sarstedt, M. (2013). *A primer on partial least squares structural equation modeling (PLS-SEM).* Thousand Oaks: SAGE.
Hallinger, P. (2011). Leadership for learning: Lessons from 40 years of empirical research. *Journal of Educational Administration, 49*, 125–142.
Hallinger, P., & Heck, R. H. (1998). Exploring the principal's contribution to school effectiveness: 1980-1995. *School Effectiveness and School Improvement, 9*, 157–191.
Hallinger, P., & Heck, R. H. (2002). What do you call people with visions? The role of vision, mission and goals in school leadership and improvement. In K. Leithwood & P. Hallinger (Eds.), ` international handbook of educational leadership and administration* (pp. 9–40). Dordrecht: Springer.
Hallinger, P., & Heck, R. H. (2011). Exploring the journey of school improvement: Classifying and analyzing patterns of change in school improvement processes and learning outcomes. *School Effectiveness and School Improvement, 22*, 1–27.
Hallinger, P., & Leithwood, K. (1996). Culture and leadership in educational administration. *Journal of Educational Administration, 34*, 98–116.
Hallinger, P., & Lu, J. F. (2014). Modeling the effects of principal leadership and school capacity on teacher professional learning in Hong Kong primary schools. *School Leadership and Management, 35*, 481–501.
Hallinger, P., & Liu, S. (2016). Learning-centered leadership and teacher learning in urban and rural schools in China: Meeting the dual challenges of equity and effectiveness. *International Journal of Educational Development, 51*, 163–173
Hallinger, P., & Murphy, J. (1986). The social context of effective schools. *American Journal of Education, 94*, 328–355.

Hallinger, P., Lee, M. S., & Ko, J. (2014). Exploring the impact of school principals on teacher professional communities in Hong Kong. *Leadership and Policy in Schools, 13*, 229–259.

Hayes, A. F. (2009). Beyond Baron and Kenny: Statistical mediation analysis in the new millennium. *Communication Monographs, 76*, 408–420.

Heck, R. H., & Hallinger, P. (2014). Modeling the effects of school leadership on teaching and learning over time. *Journal of Educational Administration, 52*(5), 653–681.

Hökkä, P. (2012). *Teacher educators amid conflicting demands: Tensions between individual and organizational development*. Unpublished doctoral dissertation, University of Jyväskylä, Jyväskylä.

Hwang, A., Francesco, A. M., & Kessler, E. (2003). The relationship between individualism-collectivism, face, and feedback and learning processes in Hong Kong, Singapore, and the United States. *Journal of Cross-Cultural Psychology, 34*, 72–91.

in de Wal, J. J., den Brok, P. J., Hooijer, J. G., Martens, R. L., & van den Beemt, A. (2014). Teachers' engagement in professional learning: Exploring motivational profiles. *Learning and Individual Differences, 36*, 27–36.

Knapp, M. S., Copland, M. A., Honig, M. I., Plecki, M. L., & Portin, B. S. (2010). *Learning-focused leadership and leadership support: Meaning and practice in urban systems*. Seattle: Center for the Study of Teaching and Policy, University of Washington.

Lai, C., Li, Z., & Gong, Y. (2016). Teacher agency and professional learning in cross-cultural teaching contexts: Accounts of Chinese teachers from international schools in Hong Kong. *Teaching and Teacher Education, 54*, 12–21.

Lee, M., & Hallinger, P. (2012). National contexts influencing principals' time use and allocation: Economic development, societal culture, and educational system. *School Effectiveness and School Improvement, 23*, 461–482.

Leithwood, K., & Jantzi, D. (2006). Transformational school leadership for large-scale reform: Effects on students, teachers, and their classroom practices. *School Effectiveness and School Improvement, 17*, 201–227.

Leithwood, K., Patten, S., & Jantzi, D. (2010). Testing a conception of how school leadership influences student learning. *Educational Administration Quarterly, 46*, 671–706.

Li, L., Hallinger, P., & Ko, J. (2016). Modeling the effects of principal leadership and school capacity on teacher professional learning in Hong Kong primary schools. *International Journal of Educational Management, 30*, 76–100.

Little, J. W. (2012). Professional community and professional development in the learning-centered school. In M. Kooy & K. van Veen (Eds.), *Teacher learning that matters: International perspectives* (pp. 22–46). London: Routledge.

Liu, S., Hallinger, P., & Feng, D. (2016a). Learning-centered leadership and teacher learning in China: Does trust matter? *Journal of Educational Administration, 54*(6), 661–682.

Liu, S., Hallinger, P., & Feng, D. (2016b). Motivating teachers to learn in China: Does leadership make a difference? *Teaching and Teacher Education*.

Muthén, L. K., & Muthén, B. O. (1998–2012). *Mplus user's guide* (7th ed.). Los Angeles: Muthén & Muthén.

Preacher, K. J., & Hayes, A. F. (2008). Asymptotic and resampling strategies for assessing and comparing indirect effects in multiple mediator models. *Behavior Research Methods, 40*, 879–891.

Printy, S. M., Marks, H. M., & Bowers, A. (2009). Integrated leadership: How principals and teachers share instructional influence. *Journal of School Leadership, 19*(5), 504–532.

Qian, H., & Walker, A. (2013). How principals promote and understand teacher development under curriculum reform in China. *Asia-Pacific Journal of Teacher Education, 41*, 304–315.

Qian, H., Walker, A., & Xiaowei, Y. (2016). Building and leading a learning culture among teachers: A case study of a Shanghai primary school. *Educational Management Administration & Leadership*. doi:10.1741143215623785.

Robinson, V. M. (2006). Putting education back into educational leadership. *Leading and Managing, 12*(1), 62–76.

Robinson, V. M. J., Lloyd, C., & Rowe, K. J. (2008). The impact of leadership on student outcomes: An analysis of the differential effects of leadership type. *Educational Administration Quarterly, 44*(5), 635–674.

Rosenholtz, S. J. (1989). *Teachers' workplace: The social organization of schools*. WhitePlains: Longman.

Saphier, J., King, M., & D'Auria, J. (2006). Three strands form strong school leadership. *Journal of Staff Development, 27*, 51–57.

Shen, X. Y. (2015). *Institutional legitimacy, teacher agency, and the development of teacher teaching expertise*. Unpublished doctoral dissertation, Beijing Normal University, Beijing.

Sleegers, P., Thoonen, E., J. Oort, F., & Peetsma, T. (2014). Changing classroom practices: The role of school-wide capacity for sustainable improvement. *Journal of Educational Administration, 52*, 617–652.

Tang, S. B., Lu, J. F., & Hallinger, P. (2014). Leading school change in China: A preliminary investigation. *International Journal of Educational Management, 28*(6), 655–675.

Thomsen, M., Karsten, S., & Oort, F. J. (2015). Social exchange in Dutch schools for vocational education and training: The role of teachers' trust in colleagues, the supervisor and higher management. *Educational Management Administration & Leadership, 43*, 755–771.

Thoonen, E. E., Sleegers, P. J., Oort, F. J., & Peetsma, T. T. (2012). Building school-wide capacity for improvement: The role of leadership, school organizational conditions, and teacher factors. *School Effectiveness and School Improvement, 23*, 441–460.

Timperley, H. (2011). *Realizing the power of professional learning*. London: McGraw-Hill Education.

Tschannen-Moran, M. (2009). Fostering teacher professionalism in schools: The role of leadership orientation and trust. *Educational Administration Quarterly, 45*, 217–247.

Vanblaere, B., & Devos, G. (2016). Relating school leadership to perceived professional learning community characteristics: A multilevel analysis. *Teaching and Teacher Education, 57*, 26–38.

Wahlstrom, K. L., & Louis, K. S. (2008). How teachers experience principal leadership: The roles of professional community, trust, efficacy, and shared responsibility. *Educational Administration Quarterly, 44*, 458–495.

Walker, A., & Dimmock, C. (2002). Moving school leadership beyond its narrow boundaries: Developing a cross-cultural approach. In K. Leithwood & P. Hallinger (Eds.), *Second international handbook of educational leadership and administration* (pp. 67–204). Dordrecht: Kluwer.

Walker, A., & Hallinger, P. (2007). Navigating culture and context: The principalship in East and Southeast Asia. In R. MacLean (Ed.), *Learning and teaching for the twenty-first century: Papers in honor of Professor Phillip Hughes*. Dordrecht: Springer.

Walker, A., & Qian, H. (2015). Review of research on school principal leadership in mainland China, 1998–2013: Continuity and change. *Journal of Educational Administration, 53*(4), 467–491.

Walker, A. D., Hu, R. K., & Qian, H. Y. (2012). Principal leadership in China: An initial review. *School Effectiveness and School Improvement, 23*, 369–399.

Wang, T. (2016). School leadership and professional learning community: Case study of two senior high schools in Northeast China. *Asia Pacific Journal of Education, 36*, 202–216.

Youngs, P., & King, M. B. (2002). Principal leadership for professional development to build school capacity. *Educational Administration Quarterly, 38*, 643–670.

Zhang, J., & Pang, N. S.-K. (2016). Investigating the development of professional learning communities: Compare schools in Shanghai and Southwest China. *Asia Pacific Journal of Education, 36*, 217–230.

Part V
The Family Path

Introduction

The two chapters in this part aim to deepen understanding about aspects of families and family/school relationships that can be influenced by leaders and that have important consequences for student success at school. Chapter 11 is a meta-analytic review of evidence about those family conditions and family-school relationships while Chap. 12 reports the results of a quasi-experimental study aimed at improving some of those conditions and relationships and the effects those efforts had on a wide array of student outcomes.

Parent involvement in their children's learning is widely acknowledged as having a positive effect on student academic success (e.g. Fan and Chen 2001; Harris et al. 2009; Hoover-Dempsey et al. 2005). Family participation is twice as predictive of students' academic success as family socioeconomic status (Bonci et al. 2011). Some of the more intensive programs designed to encourage parent participation have reported effects that are ten times greater than other relevant factors (Walberg 1981). Parents, this evidence indicates, have the greatest influence on the achievement of young people by supporting their learning in the home rather than supporting activities in school (Bonci et al. 2011).

Our initial research about the Four Paths (summarized in Chap. 1) found that the Family Path explained the largest amount of variation in student achievement. Family-related factors are of two types: unalterable and alterable. Unalterable family-related variables are those over which the school has little or no influence (e.g., parental education, parental income); whereas, alterable family variables are potentially open to influence from the school and its leadership. Our conception of the Family Path includes only the alterable family variables. For many years such variables have been referred to as "family educational culture" (e.g., Walberg 1981).

The educational culture of the home includes: parenting style, parental expectations for children's work at school, direct instructional support for school learning (e.g., parents reading with their children at home), active parent interest in the school's curriculum, and the monitoring of children's engagement with their school work (Hattie 2009). Evidence (e.g., Jeynes 2005) points to three aspects of a family's educational culture as being especially influential - parent expectations for children's success at the school and beyond (PE), Forms of Communication between parents and children (FC), and Parents' Social and Intellectual Capital related to schooling (PSIC). These features of a child's home environment directly influence much of the social and intellectual capital students need to be successful at school (Epstein et al. 2002; Henderson and Mapp 2002; Ma et al. 2013).

Parent Expectations

Parental expectations are defined as "The degree to which a student's parents [hold] high expectations of the student's promise of achieving at high levels" (Jeynes 2005, p. 246). Personally held and challenging but achievable goals (or expectations) are at the heart of most contemporary theories of human motivation (e.g. Bandura 1986). Many people, whether children or adults, either rise or fall to the level of expectations that valued others have for them; their own goals and sense of confidence about what is possible for them are, to a great extent, socially constructed. Consistent with this theory, Jeynes' (2005) meta-analysis identified "parental expectations" as having the greatest impact on student achievement among all forms of parental involvement in schools by a large margin – a significant effect size of. 58 (p. 253). Hattie (2009) reported a significant effect size of 0.58 ($r = .28$) on the impact of parent expectations on student learning.

Leithwood and Patrician (Chap. 12) argue that leaders influence such expectations when they help identify the existing expectations parents have for their children's schooling, persuade parents that their children are capable of high levels of achievement, and extend parents' views of what is possible for their children when they are successful at school. School leaders can guide parents in setting expectations around homework, organization, and grades in a way that gives students a chance to take responsibility for their own success (Hill et al. 2009).

Forms of Communication in the Home

Schools typically spend considerable effort on creating meaningful ways of communicating with parents. Efforts such as these include school newsletters, curriculum nights at school, online messaging systems and the like. While these communication efforts remain important, it is the communication between parents and their children that makes the greater contribution to students' school success. Underlying most such communication is what the literature refers to as "parenting styles". While it may seem presumptuous to view parenting styles as something schools might influence, the styles described in this literature are centrally defined by different approaches to communication between parents and their children. In his meta-analysis, Jeynes defines parenting style as "The extent to which a parent demonstrates a supportive and helpful parenting approach". He goes on to indicate that:

> In the studies included in this meta-analysis, most frequently this referred to a simultaneous ability to be loving and supportive and yet maintain an adequate level of discipline in the household. It also included styles in which the parent demonstrated such qualities as trust and being approachable. (2005, p. 246).

So creating effective parent/child communications necessarily entails clarifying with parents, in some way, the advantages of adopting a supportive yet firm approach to interacting with their children, as compared with more extreme forms of either autocratic or laissez-faire approaches. And while this is, broadly speaking, about "parenting styles", it need not be framed in that way. Supportive-yet-firm approaches to parent/child interactions are applicable with something as school-specific as monitoring homework. Parent and teacher consultation and collaboration create the climate for maximum realization of a student's potential (Epstein et al. 2002). Schools can ask their parents, for instance, what forms of communication works best for them and stay tuned for changes in the answers. Teachers' use of student achievement results to review students' academic progress with students and parents is an effective practice to enhance communication between parents and children (Sun et al. 2016).

Parents Social and Intellectual Capital Related to Schooling

Social Capital is the power and information present in parents' social relationships that can be used to leverage additional resources helpful in furthering their children's success at school. Often considered key to the building of social capital are three mechanisms[1]: trust; access to sources of information that promote the common good over individual self-interest and; norms and sanctions within a community that promote the common good over individual self-interest. Intellectual capital is the knowledge and capabilities of parents with the potential for collaborative action.

Many low income parents will differ from middle income parents in two ways that help explain differences in their children's potential for success at school (Bolivar and Chrispeels 2011). Low income parents often are unable to gain access to and benefit from the resources available in the school; they are less familiar with the "grammar of schooling", for example. In addition, they often do not have opportunities for taking forms of collective action which foster the exchange and development of collective knowledge or intellectual capital; working two or three jobs to "make ends meet" reduces the time available to interact with other parents, for example.

---

[1] Coleman (1988).

"The more people do for themselves, the larger community social capital will become, and the greater will be the dividends upon the social investment" (Ferlazzo 2011, p. 11). Parent engagement is nurtured when parents believe they should be involved in their children's education and schooling and have a positive sense of efficacy about the usefulness of their involvement (Hoover-Dempsey and Sandler 1977).

Limited qualitative data points to the crucial role of school leaders in fostering effective parental involvement generally. Strategies identified by this research include providing professional development to parents about how to assist students at home (e.g., Walker et al. 2005) and offering workshops for immigrants on the education system; teacher-led workshops on math, science and computers on the weekends; and workshops for all parents on effective discipline at home and how best to help students with their homework (Warren et al. 2009). Schools and districts embarking on parent engagement efforts targeted at improving student outcomes should build in sufficient time and opportunity for staff learning and sometimes for staffs to undergo significant shifts in their attitudes toward the parents and to build trust with them (see Chap. 12). Principles of mutual respect and trust are foundational to establishing effective partnership programs. School leaders who are successful in building productive relationships with parents:

- create a welcoming environment
- use frequent and various communication methods
- involve parents in decisions that affect their child
- make an attempt to learn about parents' strengths, skills, talents, and experiences
- provide strategies and resources for parents to support their children's learning
- initiate the process of building relationships with parents
- have teachers that believe in parents as partners in their children's learning
- provide professional development for teachers about promoting effective parental involvement in children's learning (Stelmack n.d.).

References

Bandura, A. (1986). *Social foundations of thought and action*. Englewood Cliffs: Prentice Hall.
Bolivar, J., & Chrispeels, J. (2011). Enhancing parent leadership through building social and intellectual capital. *American Educational Research Journal, 48*(1), 4–38.
Bonci, A., Mottram, E., McCoy, E., & Cole, J. (2011). *A research review: The importance of families and the home environment*. London: National Literacy Trust. Retrieved from http://www.literacytrust.org.uk/research/nlt_research/4715_a_research_review_the_importance_of_families_and_the_home_environment
Coleman, J. S. (1988). Social capital in the creation of human capital. *American Journal of Sociology, 94*, S95–S120.
Epstein, J., Sanders, M., Simon, B., Salinas, K., Jansorn, N., & Van Voorhis, F. (2002). *School, community, and community partnerships: Your handbook for action* (2nd ed.). Thousand Oaks: Corwin.

Fan, X., & Chen, M. (2001). Parent involvement and students' academic achievement: A meta-analysis. *Educational Psychology Review, 13*, 1–22.

Ferlazzo, L. (2011). Involvement or engagement? *ASCD Journal, 68*(8), 10–14.

Harris, A., Andrew-Power, K., & Goodall, J. (2009). *Do parents know they matter? Raising achievement through parental engagement*. London: Continuum.

Hattie, J. (2009). *Visible learning: A synthesis of meta-analyses relating to achievement*. New York: Routledge.

Henderson, A., & Mapp, K. L. (2002). *A new wave of evidence: The impact of school, family, and community connections on student achievement (Annual synthesis)*. Austin: National Center for Family & Community Connections with Schools.

Hill, N. E., Tyson, D. F., & Bromell, L. (2009). Parental involvement in middle school: Developmentally appropriate strategies across SES and ethnicity. In N. E. Hill & R. K. Chao (Eds.), *Families, schools, and the adolescent: Connecting research, policy, and practice* (pp. 53–72). New York: Teachers College Press.

Hoover-Dempsey, K. V., & Sandler, H. (1997). Why do parents become involved in their children's education? *Review of Educational Research, 67*(1), 3–42.

Hoover-Dempsey, K. V., Walker, J. M. T., Sandier, H. M., Whetsel, D., Green, C. L., Wilkins, A. S., & Closson, K. (2005). Why do parents become involved? Research findings and implications. *The Elementary School Journal, 106*(2), 105–130.

Jeynes, W. (2005). A meta-analysis of the relation of parent involvement to urban elementary school student academic achievement. *Urban Education, 40*(3), 237–269.

Ma, X., Shen, J., & Krenn, H. (2013). The relationships between parental involvement and adequate yearly progress among urban, suburban and rural schools. *School Effectiveness and School Improvement, 25*(4), 629–650.

Stelmack, B. (n.d.). *Parental involvement: A research brief for practitioners*. Retrieved from: http://www.curriculum.org/secretariat/files/Mar8ParentalInvolvement.pdf

Sun, J., Przybylski, R. M., & Johnson, B. (2016). A review of research on teachers' use of student data: from the perspective of school leadership. *Educational Assessment, Evaluation and Accountability, 28*(1). doi:10.1007/s11092-016-9238-9.

Walberg, H. J. (1981). Childhood traits and environmental conditions of highly eminent adults. *The Gifted Child Quarterly, 25*(3), 103–107.

Walker, J. M. T., Wilkins, A. S., Dallaire, J. R., Sandler, H. M., & Hoover-Dempsey, K. V. (2005). Parental involvement: Model revision through scale development. *The Elementary School Journal, 106*(2), 85–104.

Warren, M. R., Hong, S., Rubin, C. H., & Uy, P. S. (2009). Beyond the bake sale: A community-based relational approach to parent engagement in schools. *Teachers College Record, 111*(9), 2209–2254.

Chapter 14
Effects of Family Educational Cultures on Student Success at School: Directions for Leadership

William H. Jeynes

This chapter argues for school leaders' improvement efforts to include considerably more attention to alterable variables in the home that considerable research now demonstrates have a significant influence on student success at school. While a wide range of relevant evidence is used to make this case, I rely quite extensively on the results of my own previous meta-analytic reviews. It should also be noted that the chapter inevitably touches on changes that have occurred over the past 50 years strongly impacting the nature of the family unit. These changes provide an important backdrop to the research reviewed in this chapter because a significant amount of that research was conducted when "traditional" family structures prevailed, when taken-for-granted gender roles differed from what is currently common and when the linguistic, religious and ethnic diversity of families served by schools was much less prevalent than it is at the present time. The chapter reflects the results of research in the largely U.S. social contexts common at the time it was conducted. Readers are encouraged to adapt the results of this research to their own current social circumstances as well as their personal beliefs and values.

It is only natural that principals and education academics emphasize the role that school-based variables play in influencing student scholastic outcomes (Mann 2010; Reinking and Bradley 2008). However, the results of decades of research consistently show that family factors have more of an effect on student academic achievement than do school-based factors (Coleman et al. 1982; Kyriakides and Creemers 2008; Leithwood et al. 2010). Of the four paths of leadership that are addressed by Leithwood and his colleagues in this book and in prior articles (e.g., Leithwood et al. 2010), the family path is perhaps the most important and accounts for a good portion of the variance in achievement. Other prominent studies suggest that family factors may explain as much as 50% of the variance in student scholastic outcomes between schools (Coleman et al. 1982; Kyriakides and Creemers 2008). In contrast,

W.H. Jeynes (✉)
College of Education, California State University, Long Beach, Long Beach, CA, USA
e-mail: william.jeynes@csulb.edu

studies suggest that school factors contribute about 20% of the variance between schools (Coleman et al. 1982; Creemers and Reezigt 1996). With these results in mind, a school leader who embraces the potential of the family path could significantly increase pupil achievement (Jeynes 2006b).

Admittedly, in recent decades many principals and teachers have dismissed family effects on school outcomes because they think that they can do little to help parents contribute to the success of their children at school. (Berliner and Glass 2014; Robinson 2014). Moreover, it is only natural for educators to study largely education journals and similar publications, sociologists to study sociological ones, psychologists to read psychological publications, economists examine economic works, and so forth (Jeynes 2012b). While such a proclivity may be understandable, school leaders would benefit from a more interdisciplinary understanding of their work if they are to maximize the potential benefits for the young (Jeynes 2000; National Academy of Sciences 2005). In other words, research indicates that one path is not enough (Leithwood et al. 2010; National Academy of Sciences 2005).

When school leaders begin to focus on family variables, however,, it is important to distinguish between what are *alterable* family variables and what are unalterable. Unalterable family variables are those over which the school has no influence (e.g., parental education and parental income). *Alterable* family variables, sometimes referred to as family educational culture, are potentially open to influence from the school and its leadership. Furthermore, increasing amounts of evidence leads us to conclude that there are significantly more alterable family factors than was believed twenty-five years ago (Hattie 2009; Jeynes 2015b).

Three family factors have the most profound effects on children: (1) The extent to which parents are involved in their children's lives, (2) the degree to which children are loved (Levine 2012), and (3) parental family structure (Jeynes 2003b, 2010, 2011b; Shirakawa 2010). Quantitative research indicates that the effects of parental involvement tend to have an impact of about .60 to .75 of a grade point (Jeynes 2003a, 2005a, 2007). Parental family structure has a similar level of an impact, i.e., the scholastic difference between youth in intact families in which both the mother and father are present and children from the never married single parent family structure is usually about .60-.75 of a grade point. The impact of parental- involvement and family structure has a similar impact on children's behavior (Shirakawa 2010; Weaver and Schofield 2015). Parental love also plays a major role in helping children to succeed (Levine 2012; Stipek and Seal 2001). Parental engagement and making it a priority to keep the family together are often considered two of the major expressions of love that parents can show (Broder 1993; Hagelin 2005). Nevertheless, parental love can be demonstrated in many different ways and can be a tremendous asset and source of strength to children as they develop.

Of the three primary family factors which influence student outcomes, parental involvement has the greatest impact, is the most alterable, and is the one most open to influence by school leaders; it is the primary, although not exclusive focus of this chapter. School leaders are also able to influence the nature of parent/child relationships, as well as parents' understanding of the impact of family structure (McLanahan and Sandefur 1994; Jeynes 2011b; Wallerstein et al. 2002); these two variables will also receive some attention in the chapter.

14.1 Rediscovering the Importance of Parental Involvement

Parental involvement has become an extremely active area of research and practice in education today (Hornby 2011). To be sure, the notion of this involvement is hardly new (Harris et al. 2009; Wartman and Savage 2008). It was both practiced and encouraged in both the Old Testament and the New Testament (Jeynes 2011b; Wartman and Savage 2008). Within the American context, the Pilgrims and Puritans, as well as other early settlers, emphasized parental engagement to levels that would be difficult to fathom in contemporary minds (Hiner 1988; Jeynes 2002a; Morgan 1986). Parental involvement and support continued to have a central place in American education throughout the 1700s, 1800s, and for the first six decades of the 1900s (Cornog 1998; Gutek 2014; Jeynes 2003b). However, a series of developments in American history has helped elevate parental involvement as a very popular topic of research and practice.

Mother and father involvement was so widely practiced from the early 1600s until the early 1960s that social scientists only sparingly used the term, because parental engagement in children's lives was almost assumed (Harris et al. 2009). However, beginning in 1963 huge changes to the traditional family unit escalated. The U.S. divorce rate skyrocketed and out of wedlock births also rose precipitously (Phillips 1988; Weaver and Schofield 2015). During the 1963–1980 period that ensued, divorce rates surged for seventeen consecutive years (Phillips 1988; Weaver and Schofield 2015). Similarly, by the early 1990s out of wedlock births had swelled by seven times (U.S. Department of Health and Human Services 2012; U.S. Department of Justice 1999). Terms like "latch key children" and "deadbeat dads.", which had been almost unheard of for most of American history, were, by the 1960s and 1970s, at the forefront of discussions among family scholars (Harris et al. 2009; Weaver and Schofield 2015). Moreover, many fathers fled from their responsibilities to pay alimony and child support. Also, large numbers of mothers made it difficult for their former husbands to visit the children which encouraged fathers to reduce child support. In addition, countless children born out of wedlock were unaware of who their fathers even were (Baskerville 2007; Mincy et al. 2015; Turkat 1995). Mothers also entered the national workforce in greater numbers and higher percentages than ever before (Morrison 2005). While a portion of these women were from intact families and others from single parent households, in both cases this translated into parents spending less time with their children, on average, than had been the case in past generations (Shirakawa 2010; Weaver and Schofield 2015).

In the midst of this new social environment in which the involvement of mothers and fathers could no longer be assumed, the phrase and study of "parental involvement" gained popularity (Harris et al. 2009; Wartman and Savage 2008). Although it was far from a new practice, to be sure, it was nonetheless a needed one; it was a reminder to fathers and mothers from both intact and single-parent families. On the one hand, family members from intact families were not to assume that a stable family structure alone would guarantee high quality- and plenteous quantity- of time with their children (Wartman and Savage 2008; Weaver and Schofield 2015). On the other hand, it was an exhortation to single-parents to not let the financial and psychological challenges of being a lone parental caretakers cause them to overlook just how important loving and involved parenting really is (Wartman and Savage 2008; Weaver and Schofield 2015).

14.2 The Rise of Parental Involvement Research

As a result of the decline of the traditional family and the academic, behavioral, and psychological impact that it had, different dimensions of family research began to rise to address increasing concerns about these family-based trends (Acock and Kiecolt 1989; Allison and Furstenberg 1989). Initially, the focus was on single-parent families, particularly those that had experienced parental divorce (Cherlin 2009). One of the reasons why divorce initially received even more attention than never married families is because marriage involved a vow, "'til death do we part." The frequency with which family structure was studied was strongly related to the decline in achievement test scores that was taking place concurrent to the surge in divorce rates (Cherlin 2009; Carter and Glick 2013). Social scientists found that the exact period of time in which SAT scores plummeted for seventeen consecutive years, 1963–1980, were precisely the same years during which the divorce rate surged for 17 consecutive years (Carter and Glick 2013; Stevenson and Wolfers 2007). That very same year (1963) this decline began was also the year when juvenile -crime rates and -measures of anti-social behavior began to surge (Carter and Glick 2013; Jeynes 2002c).

As rates of never married single-parenthood also continued to surge, an increasing amount of research focused on the reasons why children flourished in intact family structures more than they did in alternative home arrangements (Wallerstein et al. 2002). Several possible explanations for the different academic and behavioral outcomes that arose for students coming from various family backgrounds were proposed. Differing levels of average parental involvement was among the foremost of these explanations (Cherlin 2009; Jeynes 2002b; Wallerstein et al. 2002). That is, even though there are many dedicated single-parents, when there is a fatherless or motherless home, raising children is, on average, simply harder (Cherlin 2009; Wallerstein et al. 2002). When there are two of the child's parents available, they can take care of their children in shifts, relieve one another when either one is tired, and jointly offer more to their children in assistance, love, and care than either of the parents could have offered individually (Cherlin 2009; Wallerstein et al. 2002).

Other reasons why family dissolution is associated with unfavorable academic and behavioral outcomes among children have been explored. Perhaps the foremost of these other factors is psychological distress (Bronfenbrenner 1979; Olds and Schwartz 2009). Research has shown that when there is an absent parent, children are more likely to become depressed, suicidal, take illegal drugs, consume large amounts of alcohol, and become sexual promiscuous (Jeynes 2001, 2015a, Carter and Glick 2013). Additional reasons for the negative impact of single parent family structures include a feeling of not being loved, a sense of betrayal by one's parents, reduced family income, and a decrease in access to parent's education-based knowledge (Carter and Glick 2013; Jeynes 2005b, 2006b).

The growing body of research on parental family structure's impact on children eventually yielded a new discipline within family studies - the study of parental involvement (Jeynes 2011b). This new research focus also caused academics to look beyond family structures because even though a dearth of parental engagement was more likely to take place in a one-parent household, it was also possible in intact families (Jeynes 2011b). This was also a significant development, because it suggested that parental involvement is more *alterable* than previously thought, at least by educators, than is family structure. Schools, for example, can offer a supplemental parenting role with their students to help avoid the potentially negative effects of single parenthood

The academic community quickly embraced the importance of parental involvement (Steinberg 2004). Countless centuries of writings and speeches and decades of research confirm that family factors, considerably more than the schools, are the primary determinants of childhood development and academic achievement (Hagelin 2005; Sax 2009; Smith et al. 2003). A home environment of love and responsibility is absolutely essential if youth are to reach their full potential (Hagelin 2005; Sax 2009). Baumrind's (Baumind 1971) evidence indicates that children develop best if they are raised in a home atmosphere that has a balance of love and structure (see also Coleman 2012; Levine 2012). When children are constantly criticized and put down, their ability to perform at their highest levels diminishes (Stipek and Seal 2001; Sax 2009). As part of the expression parental love, parents improve their children's chances of success by encouraging them to exercise self-discipline by, for example, completing their school assignments on time (Hagelin 2005; Stipek and Seal 2001).

14.3 Home-Based Components of Parental Involvement

Meta-analyses of parent involvement research now indicate that the home-based components of parental involvement are, on average, more powerful than such typical school-based activities as attending school assemblies and events, checking homework and volunteering in school (Harris et al. 2009; Jeynes 2010). The remainder of this section reviews evidence about the contribution to student success of five forms of home-based parent involvement.

Parent Expectations Jeynes (2010) and Hattie (2009) both conclude that parents' high, but reasonable, expectations are the most powerful of the home-based parent involvement components (see also Klein 2007; Winter 2006). But parents should not express high expectations in a way that that rigidly emphasizes, "You will go to Harvard, Princeton, or Oxford". Expectations should be expressed in a loving and supportive way that subtly communicates to children that they should do their best. High expectations should not be communicated to youth and adolescents in a manner that causes undo stress. As a result of growing up in the kind of an atmosphere created by such expressions of expectations, young people come to understand that people should give their best effort and aim high (Klein 2007; Winter 2006).

Parenting Style A second aspect of home-based involvement is *parental style*. Young people flourish best, on average, when they are raised in an environment that provides both love and structure. Baumrind (Baumind 1971) did much to help consolidate this notion in the minds of academics by asserting that the *authoritative* parent who combined love and structure was ideal. Research suggests that the most efficacious teachers also provide this type of balance between love and structure (Chapman and Campbell 2016; Fogarty 2007). According to meta-analytic research, *parental style* is second only to *parental expectations* as the most vital form of parental involvement (Jeynes 2005a, 2007). Sadly, the word *love* is probably the most feared four-letter word among scholars and often those in schools, as well. However, studies suggest that if schools reach out to children and families with an attitude of love, parents are much more likely to become engaged in their children's schooling (Mapp et al. 2008). Studies utilizing nationwide data sets and meta-analyses indicate that part of the reason why parents become more involved- and students excel more- in religious schools than in public schools is because they feel loved more (Jeynes 1999, 2012a). When school leaders create an atmosphere of both love and structure in their schools and encourage parents to do the same in their homes, students and their families tend to flourish.

Reading at Home A third component of home-based parental involvement is reading with one's children. Evidence suggests that the sooner parents begin to read to their children the better. Hence, it is wise for reading to begin in one's household well before the child knows the alphabet (Risley and Hart 2006). Some parents even start reading to and talking with their children at birth or even before birth (Risley and Hart 2006). Early verbal interaction and reading with children is associated with children learning to speak and read considerably earlier than children who do not have such early stimulation from their parents (Risley and Hart 2006).

Communication Evidence indicates that communication between parents and children needs to be both pretty frequent and positive for it to have its greatest impact (Chapman and Campbell 2016; Meyer 2009). To enhance parent-child communication in the home, school staffs should not only convey to parents just how important this is, but also demonstrate exemplary forms of communication with students as well as with parents (Jansen 2011); one of the chief complaints of low-SES parents is that educators speak down to them (Jeynes and Littell 2000).

In loving communication, people view others as more important than themselves (Chapman and Campbell 2016). If parents comprehend that they do not like educators speaking down to them, they will more easily fathom why children do not enjoy their parents speaking down to them.

Home-Based Parental Involvement and Student Age In the most detailed meta-analyses on parental involvement, effect sizes for overall parental involvement are smaller at the secondary school level than they are at the elementary school level by nearly 30% (Jeynes 2005a, 2007, 2016). Nevertheless, effect sizes for *home-based* and *subtle* aspects of that involvement are actually larger for secondary school students than they are for their counterparts in elementary schools. For example, healthy communication is one component of *homed-based* parental engagement. The influence of this communication between parents and their children is about 33% greater at the secondary school level than it is at the elementary school level. Also, the effect sizes for parenting styles which balance love and structure in the home, are 12–14% larger for secondary school students than for students in elementary schools. This trend does not hold for every aspect of home-based parental involvement, but it does hold overall.

Additional Thoughts on Home-Based Parental Involvement A primary explanation for why many studies have overlooked the prominence of home-based components of parent involvement is because these components often work in subtler ways than do school-based components. Moreover, school-based components of involvement (e.g., how often a parent participates in school activities and checks homework) are frequently easier to measure than those based in the home as, for example, parents' high but reasonable expectations (Mann 2010; Reinking and Bradley 2008; Wartman and Savage 2008). The generally subtler manifestation of home based vs school-based parent involvement may help explain why principals often do not rate the engagement of parents as highly as do parents themselves. (Norris 1999; Osborne and deOnis 1997).

14.4 School-Based Components of Parental Involvement

While research now points to the superior effects of home-based as compared with school-based components of parent engagement, school-based components should not be neglected. This section reviews the results of research about five such components.

Check Homework There is a considerable amount of research claiming that one of the greatest predictors of completing homework is whether parents check it over before its submission, in order to make sure it is done (Froiland et al. 2013). Assigning homework is, of course, a school-based activity. But to engage parents productively, evidence indicates that teachers should initiate the following steps (a) reserve a space on the whiteboard (or wherever the homework is typically displayed) where the homework is daily displayed, so that students can easily discern the nature of the homework; (b) communicate the contents of the assignment in a way that is easily understood by students children; (c) describe the contents of the homework in a way that can be understood by adults not present in the classroom (Froiland et al. 2013). There is a much greater likelihood that students' work will be completed if their parents understand what is expected.

Parent Participation in School Activities Whether family members attend school and especially classroom activities, is a major measure of parental intensity and commitment, particularly during a student's elementary school years. It is important to acknowledge, however, that lack of this form of engagement may not be due to lack of commitment but rather a function of the nature and extent of the challenges some parents face in their work lives (e.g., working two jobs) as well as their previous negative experiences of schools.

For parents able to attend school activities, however, the advantages of such engagement are considerable. First, each timeparents attend such an activity, they are demonstrating their support for their child in way that can easily be perceived both by the child and the teacher (Froiland et al. 2013). Second, especially when the participation is in a classroom environment, there is an opportunity for additional interaction between the parents and the teacher. Each time parents and teachers are exposed to each other it yields the potential for greater understanding of the teacher, parent, and child.

Communication with Teacher and School In order for communication to have its greatest positive impact, it must be multidimensional. Just as healthy and productive communication is key in the expression of home-based parental involvement, it is also the life-blood of bonds between the parent and teacher (Vangelisti 2004). In other words, a student can have the best teacher and parent in the world, but if they are going in entirely different and disparate directions with regard to the child, not much will be accomplished. Pilgrims and the Puritans, for example, espoused the notion of "the Holy Triad," of the church, family, and education, as vital to the success of any society (Hiner 1988). They asserted that in order to reap the full benefits of these three members of the Holy Triad, there needed to be a free flow of communication between all three components, not merely two of them. This means that such positive interactions between the parents and children will clearly add to the efficacy of schooling and childrearing.

The benefits of communication increase as more avenues of communication are activated. Puritans and Pilgrims were such enthusiastic proponents of parent-teacher communication that they advocated elementary school teachers visit the homes of each one of their students before the school year commenced to get an accurate assessment of the strengths and weaknesses of each student. The Puritan practice of having parent/teacher meetings to open the school year is especially salient, because of all the early groups of settlers, the Puritans influenced the course of American education more than any other groups (Greaves 1969). Their emphasis on parental involvement and the "holy triad" was embraced by many of the colonies and eventually a large portion of the United States (Greaves 1969; Hiner 1988; Morgan 1986)

Partnership with Teacher Meta-analyses about both parental involvement and the achievement gap, indicate that parents partnering with teachers is one of the most significant ways of raising student achievement (Jeynes 2015a). Society has changed, however, with reference to this partnership. For most of modern history, the parent was the senior partner and educators were focused on supporting and strengthening the home base and the child's potential. In contemporary times, however, it is often the parent who has been relegated to the status of junior partner and frequently succumbs to the dictates of the school and the state (Gatto 2001). What has resulted from this development is that the goals of schooling have become increasingly standardized with an emphasis on high stakes testing (Gatto 2001; Jeynes 2006a; Thomas 2005).

It is vital that the educators not dominate the partnership. When the parent is relegated to a secondary role, the promise of the partnership dissipates, because it is really not a partnership at all (Gatto 2001; Hornby and Lafaele 2011). One of the reasons partnerships are so important is because parents generally have a much wider appreciation of what they consider to be their child's development than do educators. They view school-based instruction as involving the whole child, rather than just the academic side. Parents are much more concerned than educators sometimes allowed to be about a child's character development, emotional maturity, social skills, health, and artistic orientation (Gatto 2001). Many of today's teachers work in a policy environment that is concerned primarily with academic achievement and getting along with the other students in the class. It has become increasingly difficult for educators to avoid adopting on the emphasis on high stakes testing and state academic and multicultural mandates (Bernstein 1994; Thomas 2005). An active parental role helps maintain balance in what would otherwise be a child development sequence heavily dominated by state and federal requirements and standards.

Drawing from Community Resources Parents can usually see the advantages their engagement in schooling will have for their children (Froiland et al. 2013; Hoover-Dempsey and Sandler 1997). Therefore, encouraging their involvement can be relatively easy in many cases. To other community members, whose offspring do not attend school, the rationale for participation will be less obvious. So schools need to take more definitive action to show the community that it is to their benefit to become more directly involved in education and school leaders should adopt a more proactive approach to interacting with their communities. While educators often assert that they want individual neighborhoods to be more school conscious, there may be an even greater need for schools to become more community conscious.

Administrators and teachers alike need to be humble enough to realize that many impoverished families and community leaders view schools as "takers" (Jeynes 2011a). That is, they believe school leaders are frequently asking for additional funds via bake sales, hidden fees, and candy fundraising efforts that force families to either ask their friends and neighbors to donate money or make up the fundraising shortfall themselves (Jeynes 2011a). In the eyes of many in the community, it is already enough that most of their local taxes go to support the public schools, as well as a portion of their state and federal taxes. Many people in impoverished communities believe it is "over the top" for schools to frequently hold out their hands for more funds. This type of school orientation is enough to cause countless community members to balk at the idea of involvement. School leaders will draw in more community support, if there is a sense that educators are more concerned with giving to the community than they are taking from the community.

14.5 How School Leaders Can Maximize the Positive Impact of the Family on School Achievement

1. *Help teachers take into account, in their work with students, the effects of family structure on children.* There are a variety of reasons why youngsters flourish better in intact families rather than in single-parent families. First, family dissolution through divorce, the death of a parent, or a tenuous relationship that comes to an end is often a very distressing experience for children (Cherlin 2009; Pew Research Center 2007). Second, marital break-up nearly always causes a drop in family income (Cherlin 2009; Pew Research Center 2007). Third, parental household absence also means that the children have less access to the educational assets that the parents have and are prepared to offer (Cherlin 2009; Pew Research Center 2007). Fourth, youth often question the extent to which they are loved when parental relationships collapse (Roberts 2014; Wallerstein et al. 2002). Fifth, as a result of family break-up, overall children nearly always spend less time with their two parents (Pew Research Center 2007; Wallerstein et al. 2002). Family break-up often leads to additional home transitions, which are usually challenging for children (Cherlin 2009; Wallerstein et al. 2002). For example, parental divorce is often followed by remarriage or cohabitation in which children need to adjust to a new parental figure in the household (Cherlin 2009; Jeynes 2006b). Additional family transitions, on average, are often difficult for children (Pew Research Center 2007; Wallerstein et al. 2002). Educational leaders need to appreciate the importance of going the "extra mile" to help students who come from single-parent families (Olds and Schwartz 2009).
2. *Encourage fathers to take a more active role with their children, especially their boys.* When principals and teachers use the term "parental involvement," what they often mean is "mother involvement.". A meta-analytic review of evidence about the effects of father involvement indicates that nearly half of the benefits associated with parental engagements is generated from dads (Jeynes 2015b). Boys from single-parent families are much more likely to end up in gangs than their counterparts in two-parent families (Gerdes 2012; Popenoe 2009). Generally speaking, about 90 percent of adolescents and pre-adolescents in gangs come from single-parent families (Jeynes 2011a, 2012a; Popenoe 2009). Children from families with low levels of parental engagement face similar challenges.

This trend emerges largely because many boys join gangs in search of surrogate fathers (Popenoe 2009). As David Blankenhorn (1998, p. 88) observes, "Put simply, we have too many boys with guns primarily because we have too few fathers."

The United States lags some other nations in its emphasis on drawing in fathers and American educational leaders would be wise to look at some of the best practices abroad. Great Britain's *Sure Start* program, for example, appears superior to similar initiatives in the United States such as *Head Start* (Potter and Carpenter 2008). First, Sure Start focuses more specifically on drawing in fathers into the educational process. *Sure Start* advocates that special consideration be given to non-custodial fathers. Nevertheless, these advocates also assert that fathers in two-parent families need to appreciate their salience in the family. *Sure Start* is designed to communicate to both single and two-parent fathers how they can help lift the educational outcomes of boys (Potter and Carpenter 2008).

A second way that *Sure Start* encourages father involvement is by combatting sexist stereotypes depicting males as not very nurturing. Potter and Carpenter (2008) note that fathers often reported eschewing school-parent gatherings because they felt that women stared at them in a judgmental way. *Sure Start* attempts to address these concerns by making teachers more aware of these stereotypes and the paternal perceptions of them. *Sure Start* leaders also point out that many school leaders discourage father participation by providing knitting classes and aerobics workouts, which are overwhelmingly attended by mothers, but not providing other activities that encourage fathers to come to the schools. *Sure Start* efforts have resulted in a surge in fathers coming to schools by providing weightlifting classes (Potter and Carpenter 2008).

3. *Educate school staffs and parents about the most beneficial kinds of parental involvement.* There is a substantial amount of practical information and direction that educators can provide for parents and children that can help them familiarize themselves with the full benefits of family engagement. Much of this information has been touched on in earlier sections of this chapter. For teachers to be efficacious in providing the guidance provided by this information they need to be cognizant of parental involvement research and a significant proportion of school leaders and teachers are unaware of this research (Henderson and Mapp 2002; Jeynes 2011b). With limited knowledge, they often restrict themselves to the well-known forms of school-based parent involvement missing out on the potential impact they might have by encouraging those forms of family engagement, discussed above, such as nurturing high by realistic parent expectations, helping parents develop productive forms of communication with their children in the home and learning about and using family's social capital.

Meta-analytic reviews of evidence and nationwide data sets provide have powerful sources of advice about the engagement of children of different ages. This evidence suggests that that the type of parenting most efficacious during a student's elementary school years is often not the most suitable during a student's adolescent years (Hulbert 2003; Steinberg 2004). Specifically, family activities such as checking homework, establishing household rules for when it is time for work and leisure, and attending school functions are associated with higher scholastic outcomes to a statistically significant degree among elementary school students, but have little or no relationship with these outcomes at the secondary school level (Jeynes 2005a, b, Jeynes 2007). These results are consistent with other research that indicates that the most successful parents are those that adapt to the changing dynamics in their children's lives (Berzonsky 2004; Pratt and Fiese 2004).

Younger children are often far more comfortable with direct parental participation than are adolescents (Borman and Schneider 1998; Cherlin 2008; Graber and Brooks-Gunn 1996). In contrast, adolescents may respond in a variety of ways and often feel more comfortable with less direct parental intervention (Downey and Eccles 2005; Fuller 2009). But whatever adolescents might prefer their parents to believe, parental participation does have a notable and probably, in some respects, even a remarkable relationship with teenage academic outcomes (Jeynes 2003a, Jeynes 2005a, b, Jeynes 2007). Most academics, parents, and teachers are not cognizant of this relationship and current educational policy does not reflect this reality (Henderson and Mapp 2002). Instead most educational tactics are based on overt manifestations of parental involvement that have a propensity to be more efficacious in a pupil's elementary school years rather than the subtler aspects of that involvement salient at the secondary school level.

4. *Help teachers identify sources of social capital in the home that can be a source of strength to students.* The social capital available to children in the home can give them a decided advantage in their success at school (Coleman et al. 1982; Halpern 2005). Social capital largely consists of culture, relationships, and moral foundations such as the work ethic that are a source of strength for youngsters (Coleman et al. 1982; Halpern 2005). Teachers should be helped to identify sources of such strength that could bolster their efforts to help students succeed (Halpern 2005; Snyder et al. 2011). For example, if a grandmother is a source of inspiration regarding the value of hard work and perseverance in the midst of hardship, then educators can encourage more of a connection with the grandmother. Similarly, leaders need to guide and mentor teachers regarding mobilizing parents with high levels of integrity, character, and their emphasis on the work ethic. Such mobilization consists of helping those parents realize that they can have a more positive influence on their children's school success than they commonly realize.

Teachers are at least partially responsible for the pervasive retreat of many caregivers from participation in the classrooms (Agnew and Brezina 2014; Greenlaw 2006; MacMillan 2004). Parents often feel that their presence and influence in schools is actually unwanted by educators (Agnew and Brezina 2014; Greenlaw 2006). Not only should parents' social capital be valued by schools but parents should be encouraged to share their sources of social capital with schools. Reluctant teachers should be encouraged to welcome the involvement of family members and to build on families' social capital (Agnew and Brezina 2014; Greenlaw 2006; Halpern 2005; Greenlaw 2006; MacMillan 2004).

5. *Encourage teachers to learn more about their students' family circumstances.* Almost every child will appreciate efforts by an educator to become better acquainted with his or her life. Most youth begin the school year convinced that their teachers are knowledgeable, but they also want to know that they care. There is a significant relationship between the extent to which students believe that their teachers care about them and their school performance (Jeynes 2006a). Children perform better academically when teachers love and care for the whole child rather than just focusing on academic achievement.

How can educators obtain information about their students' home lives without being obtrusive. The goal is not to force the student to share information that he or she does not desire to share at all but to make the student feel comfortable and consider the teacher to be confidant and a supporter, who will use the family and background information to enhance the student's classroom experience and help the student reach his or her potential.

There are a number of ways that educators can increase the chances that students will volunteer relevant family information. In order to "break the ice" one of the most effective ways of obtaining information from children, especially at the elementary school level, is to have them draw a picture of their family (Dunn et al. 2002; Mayne and Ritchie 2009). The teacher can ask the student to describe who each person is in the family drawing and what each family member is doing. It is absolutely amazing how much students want to share and willingly do so (Dunn et al. 2002; Mayne and Ritchie 2009). On many occasions teachers will hear about tensions in the family, intimidation among siblings, rivalries, whether the parents are good role models, etc. (Dunn et al. 2002; Mayne and Ritchie 2009).

Having the student share information about their family through art is an excellent first step with several advantages (Dunn et al. 2002; Mayne and Ritchie 2009). First, it is non-threatening, so that children can share as much or as little as they would like (Dunn et al. 2002; Mayne and Ritchie 2009). Second, it is an excellent means of determining just how much children wish to share about their family and general background. Third, it provides students who wish to talk about their family and community an opening to share without fear of judgment (Dunn et al. 2002; Mayne and Ritchie 2009).

A logical next step is to give students a couple of writing assignments. One of the assignments can involve children sharing their autobiography. This can be an excellent opportunity to understanding children's past history, as well as to teach them the meaning of words such as "autobiography" and "biography." When a child writes an "autobiography," he or she will almost always share something about family context and the quality of the relationship between family members (Feeney 2010; Mayne and Ritchie 2009). A second writing assignment that an instructor can give the children is more direct and involves writing about one's family.

Each of the five guidelines above encourages the school to learn more about, for example, the presence of parents in the home, the length of time the student spends alone in the home, the quality of the relationship the child has with the parent(s); the extent to which there is loud music or other disruptions and whether there is a quiet place to study and the availability of family assistance (Mayne and Ritchie 2009).

14.6 Concluding Thoughts

For centuries parents and educators have known that family culture has a major impact on the success of children at school. Evidence from recent research confirms what the general population has known for centuries. When parents are both motivated and mobilized to become more active in their children's education, they can make a profound difference in their children's success at school. When school leaders identify features of parenting that matter and work to develop those features with their parent communities, the impact is likely to be as significant as most improvement efforts focused on the school organization itself.

References

Acock, A. C., & Kiecolt, J. (1989). Is it family structure or socioeconomic status? Family structure during adolescence and adult adjustment. *Social Forces, 68*, 553–571.
Agnew, R., & Brezina, T. (2014). *Juvenile delinquency: Causes & control*. Oxford: Oxford University Press.
Allison, P. D., & Furstenberg, F. F. (1989). How marital dissolution affects children-variations by age and sex. *Developmental Psychology, 25*, 540–549.
Baskerville, S. (2007). *Taken into custody: The war against fathers, marriage, and the family*. Nashville: Cumberland House.
Baumind, D. (1971). Current patterns of parental authority. *Developmental Psychology, 4*, 1–103.
Berliner, D. C., & Glass, G. V. (2014). *Fifty myths and lies that threaten America's public schools: The real crisis in ducation*. New York: Teachers College Press.
Bernstein, R. (1994). *Dictatorship of virtue: Multuralism, and the battle for America's future*. New York: Knopf.
Berzonsky, M. (2004). Identity style, parental authority, and identity commitment. *Journal of Youth & Adolescence, 33*(3), 213–220.
Blankenhorn, D. (1998). Fatherlessness is to blame for poverty in single-parent families. In N. Bruno Leone (Ed.), *Inequality: Opposing viewpoints in sexual problems* (pp. 86–98). San Diego: Greenhaven.
Borman, K. M., & Schneider, B. L. (1998). *The adolescent years: Social influences and educational changes*. Chicago: University of Chicago.
Broder, M. S. (1993). *The art of staying together: A couple's guide to intimacy and respect*. New York: Hyperion.
Bronfenbrenner, U. (1979). *The ecology of human development*. Cambridge, MA: Harvard University Press.
Carter, H., & Glick, P. C. (2013). *Marriage & divorce: A social and economic study*. Cambridge, MA: Harvard University Press.
Chapman, G. D., & Campbell, R. (2016). *The five love languages of children: The secret to loving children effectively*. Chicago: Northfield.

Cherlin, A. J. (2008). *Public and private families: An introduction.* Boston: McGraw Hill.
Cherlin, A. J. (2009). *The marriage go-round: The state of marriage and the family in America today.* New York: Knopf.
Coleman, D. (2012). *The thriving family.* Dublin: Hachette.
Coleman, J., Hoffer, T., & Kilgore, S. (1982). *High school achievement: Public, Catholic, and private schools compared.* New York: Basic.
Cornog, E. (1998). *The birth of empire: DeWitt Clinton & the American experience, 1769-1828.* New York: Oxford University Press.
Creemers, B. P. M., & Reezigt, G. J. (1996). School level conditions affecting the effectiveness of instruction. *School Effectiveness and School Improvement, 7,* 197–228.
Downey, G., & Eccles, J. S. (2005). *Navigating the future: Social identity, coping, and life tasks.* New York: Russell Sage.
Dunn, J., O'Conner, T. G., & Levy, I. (2002). Out of picture: A study of family drawings by step-, single-parent, and non-step families. *International Journal of Clinical Child and Adolescent Psychology, 31*(4), 505–512.
Feeney, S. (2010). *Who am I in the lives of children?: An introduction to early childhood education.* Upper Saddle River: Merrill.
Fogarty, R. (2007). *Ten things new teachers need to succeed.* Thousand Oaks: Corwin.
Froiland, J. M., Peterson, A., & Davison, M. L. (2013). The early effects of parent involvement and parent expectation in the USA. *School Psychology International, 34*(1), 33–50.
Fuller, J. R. (2009). *Juvenile delinquency: Mainstream and crosscurrents.* Upper Saddle River: Pearson/Prentice Hall.
Gatto, J. T. (2001). *The underground history of American education.* New York: Oxford Village Press.
Gerdes, L. I. (2012). *Juvenile crime.* Detroit: Greenhaven.
Graber, J. A., & Brooks-Gunn, J. (1996). *Transitions through adolescence: Interpersonal domains and context.* Mahwah: Erlbaum.
Greaves, R. L. (1969). *The Puritan revolution and educational thought.* Philadelphia: Westminster.
Greenlaw, L. (2006). *An irresponsible age.* London: Harper Perennial.
Gutek, G. (2014). *Philosophical, ideological, and theoretical perspectives on education.* Boston: Pearson.
Hagelin, R. (2005). *Home invasion.* Nashville: Nelson.
Halpern, D. (2005). *Social capital.* Cambridge: Polity.
Harris, A., Andrew-Power, K., & Goodall, J. (2009). *Do parents know they matter?: Raising achievement through parental engagement.* London: Continuum.
Hattie, J. (2009). *Visible learning: A synthesis of meta-analyses relating to achievement.* New York: Routledge.
Henderson, A. T., & Mapp, K. L. (2002). *A new wave of evidence: The impact of school, family, and community connections on student achievement.* Austin: Southwest Educational Development Laboratory.
Hiner, N. R. (1988). *The cry of Sodom enquired into: Educational analysis in seventeenth century New England. The social history of American education.* Urbana: University of Illinois Press.
Hoover-Dempsey, K., & Sandler, H. (1997). Why do parents become involved in their children's education? *Review of Educational Research, 67,* 3–42.
Hornby, G. (2011). *Parental involvement in childhood education: Building effective school-family partnerships.* New York: Springer.
Hornby, G., & Lafaele, R. (2011). Barriers to parental involvement in education: An explanatory model. *Educational Review, 63,* 37–52.
Hulbert, A. (2003). *Raising America: Experts, parents, and a century of advice about children.* New York: Knopf.
Jansen, J. D. (2011). *We need to talk.* Northcliff: Booksorm.
Jeynes, W. (1999). The effects of religious commitment on the academic achievement of black and Hispanic children. *Urban Education, 34*(4), 458–479.

Jeynes, W. (2000). Assessing school choice: A balanced perspective. *Cambridge Journal of Education, 30*(2), 223–241.

Jeynes, W. (2001). The effects of recent parental divorce on their children's consumption of alcohol. *Journal of Youth and Adolescence, 30*(3), 305–319.

Jeynes, W. (2002a). *Divorce, family structure, and the academic success of children.* Binghamton: Taylor & Francis/Haworth.

Jeynes, W. (2002b). Examining the effects of parental absence on the academic achievement of adolescents: The challenge of controlling for family income. *Journal of Family and Economic Issues, 23*(2), 189–210.

Jeynes, W. (2002c). The relationship between the consumption of various drugs by adolescents and their academic achievement. *American Journal of Drug and Alcohol Abuse, 28*, 1–21.

Jeynes, W. (2003a). A meta-analysis: the effects of parental involvement on minority children's academic achievement. *Education & Urban Society, 35*(2), 202–218.

Jeynes, W. (2003b). The effects of black and Hispanic twelfth graders living in intact families and being religious on their academic achievement. *Urban Education, 38*(1), 35–57.

Jeynes, W. (2005a). A meta-analysis of the relation of parental involvement to urban elementary school student academic achievement. *Urban Education, 40*(3), 237–269.

Jeynes, W. (2005b). Effects of parental involvement and family structure on the academic achievement of adolescents. *Marriage & Family Review, 37*(3), 99–116.

Jeynes, W. (2006a). Standardized tests and the true meaning of kindergarten and preschool. *Teachers College Record, 108*(10), 1937–1959.

Jeynes, W. (2006b). The impact of parental remarriage on children: A meta-analysis. *Marriage and Family Review, 40*(4), 75–102.

Jeynes, W. (2007). The relationship between parental involvement and urban secondary school student academic achievement: A meta-analysis. *Urban Education, 42*, 82–110.

Jeynes, W. (2010). The salience of the subtle aspects of parental involvement and encouraging that involvement: Implications for school-based programs. *Teachers College Record, 112*(3), 747–774.

Jeynes, W. (2011a). Help families by fostering parental involvement. *Phi Delta Kappan, 93*(3), 38–39.

Jeynes, W. (2011b). *Parental involvement & academic success.* New York: Taylor & Francis/Routledge.

Jeynes, W. (2012a). A meta-analysis on the effects and contributions of public, public charter, and religious schools on student outcomes. *Peabody Journal of Education, 87*(3), 265–305.

Jeynes, W. (2012b). A meta-analysis of the efficacy of different types of parental involvement programs for urban students. *Urban Education, 47*(4), 706–742.

Jeynes, W. (2015a). A meta-analysis on the factors that best reduce the achievement gap. *Education & Urban Society, 47*(5), 523–554.

Jeynes, W. (2015b). A meta-analysis: The relationship between father involvement and student academic achievement. *Urban Education, 50*(4), 387–423.

Jeynes, W. (2016). A meta-analysis: The relationship between parental involvement and African American school & behavioral outcomes. *Journal of Black Studies, 47*(3), 195–216.

Jeynes, W., & Littell, S. (2000). A meta-analysis of studies examining the effect of whole language instruction on the literacy of low-SES Students. *Elementary School Journal, 101*, 21–33.

Klein, A. (2007). *A class apart: Prodigies, pressure, and passion inside one of America's best high schools.* New York: Simon & Schuster.

Kyriakides, L., & Creemers, B. P. (2008). Using a multidimensional approach to measure the impact of classroom-level factors upon student achievement: A study testing the validity of the dynamic model. *School Effectiveness and School Improvement, 19*, 183–205.

Leithwood, K., Patten, S., & Jantzi, D. (2010). Testing a conception of how school leadership influences student learning. *Educational Administration Quarterly, 46*(5), 671–706.

Levine, M. (2012). *Teach your children well: Parenting for authentic success.* New York: Harper.

MacMillan, J. (2004). Learning the piano: A study of attitudes to parental involvement. *British Journal of Music Education, 21*(3), 295–311.

Mann, V. J. (2010). *Getting your share of the pie: The complete guide to finding grants*. Santa Barbara: Praeger.

Mapp, K. L., Johnson, V. R., Strickland, C. S., & Meza, C. (2008). High school family centers: Transformative spaces linking schools and families in support of student learning. *Marriage & Family Review, 43*(3/4), 338–368.

Mayne, L., & Ritchie, S. (2009). *Great teacher projects*. Erin: Boston Mills.

McLanahan, S., & Sandefur, G. (1994). *Growing up with a single parent: What hurts, what helps*. Cambridge, MA: Harvard University Press.

Meyer, J. (2009). *The love revolution*. New York: Faithwords.

Mincy, R. B., Jethwani, M., & Klempin, S. (2015). *Failing our fathers: Confronting the crisis of economically vulnerable, nonresident fathers*. New York: Oxford University Press.

Morgan, J. (1986). *Godly learning: Puritan attitudes towards religion, learning, and education*. New York: Cambridge University Press.

Morrison, C. (2005). *Women in the workforce*. St. Petersburg: Human Resource Institute.

National Academy of Sciences. (2005). *Facilitating interdisciplinary research*. Washington, DC: National Academic Press.

Norris, C. M. (1999). Parents and schools: The involvement, participation and expectations of parents in the education of their children. *Education Quarterly Review, 5*(4), 61.

Olds, J., & Schwartz, R. S. (2009). *The lonely American*. Boston: Beacon.

Osborne, S., & deOnis, A. (1997). Parent involvement in rural schools: Implications for educators. *Rural Educator, 19*(2), 20–29.

Pew Research Center. (2007). *As marriage and parenthood drift apart, public is concerned about social impact*. Washington, DC: Pew Research Center.

Phillips, R. (1988). *Untying the knot: A short history of divorce*. New York: Cambridge University Press.

Popenoe, D. (2009). Cohabitation, marriage & child well-being: A cross-national perspective. *Society, 46*(5), 429–436.

Potter, C., & Carpenter, J. (2008). Something in it for dads. Getting fathers involved in Sure Start. *Early Child Development & Care, 18*(7/8), 761–772.

Pratt, M. W., & Fiese, B. W. (2004). *Family stories and the life course: Across time and generations*. Mahwah: Erlbaum.

Reinking, D., & Bradley, B. A. (2008). *On formative and design experiments: Approaches to language and literacy research*. New York: Teachers College Press.

Risley, T., & Hart, B. (2006). Promoting early language development. In N. F. Watt, C. Ayoub, R. F. Bradley, J. E. Puma, & W. A. LeBeouf (Eds.), *The crisis in youth mental health: Critical issues and effective programs* (Vol. 4, pp. 83–88). Westport: Praeger.

Roberts, S. (2014). *Parents with price tags: Heal yourself of family dysfunction and love your children unconditionally*. Cork: BookBaby.

Robinson, K. (2014). *The broken compass*. Cambridge, MA: Harvard University Press.

Sax, L. (2009). *Boys adrift: The five factors that driving the growing epidemic of unmotivated boys and underachieving young men*. New York: Basic.

Shirakawa, T. (2010). Family structure and children's reading letracy: Academic achievement of children from single-parent families in Japan and the United States. *Sociological Theory & Methods, 25*(2), 249–265.

Smith, E. P., Atkins, J., & Connell, C. (2003). Family, school, and community factors and relationships to racial-ethnic attitudes and academic achievement. *American Journal of Community Psychology, 32*(1/2), 159–173.

Snyder, C. R., Lopez, S. R., & Petrotti, J. T. (2011). *Positive psychology: The scientific and practical explorations of human strength*. Thousand Oaks: Sage.

Steinberg, L. D. (2004). *Ten basic principles of good parenting*. New York: Simon & Schuster.

Stevenson, B., & Wolfers, J. (2007). *Marriage & divorce: Changes and their driving forces.* Cambridge, MA: Bureau of Economic Research.

Stipek, D. J., & Seal, K. (2001). *Motivated minds: Raising children to love learning.* New York: Holt & Co..

Thomas, R. M. (2005). *High stakes testing: Coping with collateral damage.* Mahwah: Erlbaum.

Turkat, I. D. (1995). Divorce-related malicious mother syndrome. *Journal of Family Violence, 10*(3), 253–264.

U.S. Department of Health & Human Services. (2012). *Statistical abstracts of the United States.* Washington, DC: Author.

United States Department of Justice. (1999). *Age-specific arrest rate and race-specific arrest rates for selected offenses 1965-1992.* Washington, DC: Author.

Vangelisti, A. L. (2004). *Handbook of family communication.* Mahweh: Erlbaum.

Wallerstein, J. S., Lewis, J., & Blakeslee, S. (2002). *The unexpected legacy of divorce: A 25 year landmark study.* New York: Hyperion.

Wartman, K. L., & Savage, M. (2008). *Parental involvement in higher education: Understanding the relationship among students, parents, and the institution.* San Francisco: Wiley/Jossey-Bass.

Weaver, J. M., & Schofield, T. J. (2015). Mediation and moderation of divorce effects on children's behavior problems. *Journal of Family Psychology, 29,* 39–48.

Winter, J. (2006). *Breakthrough parenting for children with special needs: Raising the bar of expectations.* San Francisco: Jossey-Bass.

Wolfinger, N. (2005). *Understanding the divorce cycle.* Cambridge: Cambridge University Press.

Chapter 15
Changing the Educational Culture of the Home to Increase Student Success at School

Kenneth Leithwood and Penny Patrician

Considerable evidence suggests that family background accounts for a substantial proportion of variation in student achievement (Coleman et al. 1966). Family background is a multi-dimensional concept including some features that are largely unalterable in the short to mid term such as family income and parental education. Some features associated with family background are alterable, however; together, these alterable features are often referred to as the family's "educational culture" (Leithwood and Jantzi 1999).

The educational culture of the home includes, for example, parenting style, parental expectations for children's work at school, direct instructional support for school learning (e.g., parents reading with their children at home), active parent interest in the school's curriculum, and the monitoring of children's engagement with their school work (Hattie 2009). These features of a child's home environment directly influence the social and intellectual capital students need to be successful at school (Epstein et al. 2002; Henderson and Mapp 2002; Ma et al. 2013).

A family's educational culture is often strongly associated with parental income, education, and other relatively hard-to-change family features. While some families with low incomes and modest parental education manage to develop very strong educational cultures in their homes, this is difficult to do and is clearly the exception without some kind of help from others. School staff members, research now demonstrates, are capable of being the "others" who assist parents to build strong educational cultures in their homes (Bolivar and Chrispeels 2011). Indeed, initiatives by school staff aimed at helping those families struggling to build productive educational cultures in their homes would appear to be a very promising strategy for closing achievement gaps between advantaged and disadvantaged students.

K. Leithwood (✉) • P. Patrician
Ontario Inst. for Studies in Education University of Toronto, University of Toronto, Toronto, ON, Canada
e-mail: kenneth.leithwood@utoronto.ca; penny.patrician@mail.utoronto.ca

Parent involvement in their children's learning is widely acknowledged as having a positive effect on student academic success (e.g., Fan and Chen 2001; Harris et al. 2009; Henderson and Mapp 2002; Hoover-Dempsey et al. 2009; Mapp 2002). Of particular relevance is the finding that while all students benefit from family involvement in education, the influence of parent engagement can mitigate differences in socioeconomic status (SES) and family background (Epstein and Dauber 1991; Henderson and Mapp 2002; Jeynes 2005).

The work described in this chapter, a quasi-experimental field study, originated from a series of discussions with directors of education (CEOs) in Ontario about finding manageable ways to close achievement gaps in their districts. Readings from a sample of the literature on parent engagement (e.g., Bolivar and Chrispeels 2011; Freeman-Loftis 2011) led directors to the view that a manageable approach to such gap closing might include developing an ongoing relationship, in schools serving significant numbers of "high needs" students, with a small sample of the most challenged parents and students along with their teachers, actively supported by one or more members of the school staff. The aim of these relationships would be to help parents further develop selected features of their "family educational cultures" conducive to student success at school; these relationships were to be enacted wherever it seemed most comfortable for the parents, possibly in the school but possibly in home or community environments also.

Directors in seven school districts each selected a small team to lead their district's participation in the project. Working with the project director and staff in several schools, the district teams helped schools develop strategies for enhancing a small number of the most promising features of home educational cultures, implement these strategies with a small number of families in their schools, monitor the implementation of the strategies (making appropriate mid-course refinements), and assess the effects of the strategies on family educational cultures. The design and conduct of the project included important features of both a quasi-experimental field study (described more fully below) and action research.

Reflecting a central feature of action research was adherence, in the design and conduct of the project, to strong preferences and beliefs of those enacting the project. In this case such preferences and beliefs took the form of three broad principles:

- *All students are capable of learning to relatively high levels given suitable opportunities and supports.* Many times during the initial project meeting, mention was made of a small but significant number of staff who, although they espouse this belief, did not act in accordance with it. In their study of school-family relations, Cooper et al. (2010) observed that, due to a lack of familiarity with the values, beliefs, and practices of diverse families, some educators make stereotypical assumptions about families and communities resulting in low expectations and other deficit-based practices. Because authentically held-high expectations for student success are so important to the improvement of student learning, this belief was considered to be a fundamental starting point for all staff members involved in the project (and a goal to work toward with all parents and students participating in the project).
- *All parents want the best for their children.* District team members noted a complete absence, in their experience, of parents not wanting the best for their children. That

said, there is considerable variation in terms of what "the best" actually means among parents. Such variation can be accounted for by differences, for example, in parents' own school experiences, the importance of education in parents' own employment and broader life opportunities, cultural and religious values, knowledge of possible futures for their children, and the like. So all parents have altruistic aspirations for their children, although those aspirations often look quite different. This belief directed project staff to focus their efforts on differences in what parents viewed as "the best" as opposed to whether or not parents wanted the best for their children.

- *All parents, and the home environments they create, include assets of significant value to the success of their children at school.* There are enormous differences, especially in the surface features, of children's home environments; these surface features are often a product of families' economic circumstances. Because this project was aimed at helping parents, many of whom were economically challenged, the surface features of some of their home environments were expected to include, for example, crowded physical spaces, uncertain housing arrangements, limited availability of education-related resources such as books, scarce opportunities for parent-child interaction because of work demands, and limited access to food high in nutritional value. These home features clearly do present indirect challenges to students' school success. But as Jeynes concluded from his meta-analysis of relevant research, "some of the most potent facets of parent involvement are among the more subtle aspects of family support" (2005, p. 262). Most notably, parental expectations and style each demonstrate strong relationships with scholastic outcomes. It was not, according to Jeynes' synthesis of research, particular actions by parents but "a general atmosphere of involvement [that] produced the greatest results" for students at school (p. 262). This belief discouraged project staff from adopting a deficit view of family environments unlike those they were used to and typically valued. Furthermore, schools often do not know what the assets specific to a given family are and/or how to build on them for the improvement of student learning. In addition to a "generally involved atmosphere," available to some children, no matter their economic circumstances, families involved in this project were likely to have unique cultures, traditions, and social networks that schools could build on in their efforts to help children make sense of the school curriculum. One of the challenges of the project was trying to identify those assets and determine how best to use them in the interests of helping children succeed at school. This belief encouraged project staff to seek out aspects of each family's environment that could be used to help build student success at school.

15.1 Objectives

Three sets of parent engagement goals were established for project schools; these goals directed project schools to the elements of "family educational culture" that contribute most to student success at school.

15.1.1 Fostering High Expectations Among Parents for Their Children's Success at School

Parental expectations were defined for purposes of this project as "The degree to which a student's parents [hold] high expectations of the student's promise of achieving at high levels" (Jeynes 2005, p. 246). Personally held and challenging but achievable goals (or expectations) are at the heart of most contemporary theories of human motivation (e.g., Bandura 1986); theories with application in many fields. Such theory and related evidence is reflected, for example, in the *Ontario Leadership Framework*, which points to the establishment of high expectations among staff and students as an essential leadership practice. Many people, whether children or adults, either rise or fall to the level of expectation that valued others have for them; their own goals and sense of confidence about what is possible for them are, to a great extent, socially constructed. Consistent with this theory, Jeynes' (2005) meta-analysis identified "parental expectations," among all forms of parental involvement in school, as having the greatest impact on student achievement by a large margin: a significant effect size of 0.58 (p. 253). A significant proportion of parents involved in this project had struggled at school themselves, did not perceive much real-life value from their own schooling experience, and had difficulty envisioning a future for their children that would depend on relatively high levels of school success (see Hornby and Lafaele 2011 for a discussion of barriers to parental involvement in their children's education). So an important set of tasks to be accomplished by those implementing the project in their schools was to identify the existing expectations parents had for their children's schooling, persuade parents that their children were capable of high levels of achievement, and extend parents' views of what was possible for their children when they were successful at school.

15.1.2 Creating Effective Communication Between Parents and Their Children in the Home

Schools typically spend considerable effort creating meaningful ways of communicating with parents (Epstein et al. 2002). Examples of such as efforts include school newsletters, curriculum nights at school, online messaging systems, and the like. While these communication efforts remain important, it is the communication between parents and their children that is of greatest concern to this project. Underlying most such communication is what the literature refers to as "parenting style." While it may seem presumptuous to view parenting style as something that might be influenced by school, the styles described in the literature are centrally defined by different approaches to communication between parents and their children. In his meta-analysis, Jeynes, (2005) defines parenting style as "The extent to which a parent demonstrates a supportive and helpful parenting approach" (p. 246). So creating effective parent/child communications necessarily entails clarifying with parents the advantages of adopting a supportive yet firm approach to interacting with their children, as compared with more extreme forms of either autocratic or laissez-faire approaches.

Overt, direct discussions of parenting styles between parents and school staff may go beyond the boundaries of what parents will accept from schools and what some staff members will feel is a legitimate part of their role. Creating effective parent/child communication about school-related matters, therefore, required project staff to focus on how productive parenting styles are applied to obviously school-relevant issues.

15.1.3 Building Families' Social and Intellectual Capital Related to Schooling

The basic concepts framing this project objective are reviewed by Bolivar and Chrispeels (2011), and explored by Lee and Bowen (2006), for example. "Social capital" is defined as the power and information present in parents' social relationships that can be used to leverage additional resources helpful in furthering children's success at school. Often considered key to the building of social capital are three mechanisms (Coleman 1988): trust, access to sources of information that promote the common good over individual self-interest, and norms and sanctions within a community that promote the common good over individual self-interest. According to Ferlazzo (2011): "The more people do for themselves, the larger community social capital will become, and the greater will be the dividends upon the social investment" (p. 11).

Intellectual capital is defined as the knowledge and capabilities of parents with the potential for collaborative action. Evidence from Hoover-Dempsey and Sandler's (1997) review of psychological theory and research about why parents become involved in their children's education shows that parent engagement is nurtured when parents believe they should be involved in their children's education and schooling, and have a positive sense of efficacy about the usefulness of their involvement (p. 27). Many low-income parents who were part of this project differed from middle-income parents in two ways that help explain differences in their children's potential for success at school (Bolivar and Chrispeels 2011). First, low-income parents are often unable to gain access to and benefit from the resources available in the school; they are less familiar with the "grammar of schooling" (Hattie 2009). In addition, they often do not have opportunities for forms of collective action which foster the exchange and development of collective knowledge or intellectual capital; working two or three jobs to "make ends meet" reduces the time available to interact with other parents, for example.

In order to build the social and intellectual capital of the parents who participated in this study, school staff provided structures for face-to-face meetings with parents to improve their understanding of the school's expectations for their children, as well as opportunities to discuss manageable ways in which they could help their children at home. While the content of experiences differed in response to unique parent group needs, common across all schools were opportunities for parents to learn more about general grade-level curriculum expectations, the school's assumptions about the school work that students do at home, teachers' general approaches to instruction, how student behavior is managed in the classroom and across the school, and different types of student testing.

This project objective was also pursued by creating and maintaining parent-peer networks (Johnson 2012; Lawson and Alameda-Lawson 2012). Most project schools provided parents with encouragement and opportunities to interact with other project parents about the challenges they faced in providing a productive family educational culture for their children, how those challenges might best be met, and what school personnel might do to help.

15.2 Framework

The project as a whole tested claims about the effects of the three different, but by no means mutually exclusive, approaches to improving the engagement and achievement of students in challenging circumstances as described above. These claims can be represented, in summary form, as a "theory of action," represented in Fig. 15.1, which also points to the types of data that would be necessary if all of the project's claims were to be tested. As Fig. 15.1 suggests, parent engagement initiatives implemented by project schools were intended to have a positive influence on two sets of conditions important for student success: family educational cultures (FEC: high expectations, social/intellectual capital, communication) and both school and classroom conditions (SCC) of those students selected to be in the project (as well as on the relationships between family and school)[1].

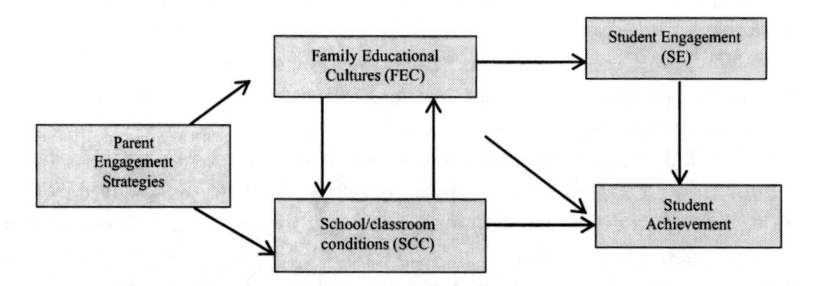

Fig. 15.1 The project's theory of action

---

[1] Based on Bronfenbremmer's (2005) bioecological model, Niehaus and Adelson (2014) these two sources of influence on children's achievement as microsystems and mesosystems which, together, account for most of the "potential risk and protective factors ....highly important to students' performance and well-being" (p. 812).

This framework indicates that a positive influence on both the FEC and the SCC should, in turn, enhance students' engagement (SE) with school, as well as their achievement. Some of the influence of family, school and classroom conditions will have direct effects on achievement, while some will have indirect effects that are mediated by student engagement[2]. Similarly, improvements in family educational cultures are expected to result in more fully engaged students through additional motivation to succeed, as well as improved student achievement as a result of increased parental expectations, communication, and the social and intellectual capital provided by families.

While school and classroom conditions were an important part of the framework for the study, as Figure 15.1 suggests, labor conditions in the province at the time of project implementation prevented all but one district from collecting data about this variable, and these data are not reported.

15.3 Methods

A pre-test/post-test control group design was used in each of the seven district projects, although there was considerable variation especially in the selection of parents and students to act as control groups[3]. The project on which this study is based was initiated jointly by directors of education of the participating districts. Each participating districts followed the ethical review procedures established in their own districts. Project funding was provided by the Ministry of Education, and the first author led the project team.

Sample This section outlines a set of modal decisions around which each district's sampling plan varied. Districts were asked to approximate, as best they could, the modal decisions described in this section and, with a few quite important exceptions, this was largely accomplished by the participating districts.

Grade Levels Each district was asked to include at least three children and one or both parents in each of three classrooms in each of about four schools (36 student/parent dyads). While, in principle, there was no restriction placed on the grades to be involved, two guidelines were provided to help ensure the availability of suitable data. First, district teams were asked to make sure that for whatever grades were selected, access to reliable information about achievement at both the beginning and at or near the end of the 12-month project period would be available. This guideline turned out to be difficult to follow, partly because the province's labor challenges unexpectedly delayed the start of most projects, and partly because of the minimal

---

[2] In this study of parent engagement, student engagement is one of three outcomes used to assess the effects of changes in three components of family educational culture. For a discussion of the influence of school and classroom practices on student engagement, see for example the research series of Dunleavyet al. (2012).

[3] The full report of results (Leithwood 2014) includes individual district reports. These individual reports provide more detail about samples and sample selection.

use that could be made of provincial test results given the grade levels of participating students and the schedule for reporting Ontario's Education Quality and Accountability Office (EQAO) student assessment results. Second, district teams were asked to avoid selecting grades for which only report card data about achievement was available. While such data may be considered very reliable in some schools, it is widely believed to be unreliable in many schools, and so would not provide convincing evidence of project effects on achievement. That said, report card data was to be included with the other data about achievement collected[4]. As it turned out, report card data (about subject achievement and learning skills) were the only achievement data available to most districts, and not all districts provided such data as part of their reports.

Student and Parent Background As much as possible, districts were asked to consider four criteria when selecting student/parent dyads for project participation:

- *Students are struggling academically.* This could mean that students had been achieving at levels 1 or 2 on at least several EQAO measures over multiple testing cycles without showing signs of improvement, for example.
- *Students are less engaged in school than is needed for success.* This could mean significantly below average attendance rates and/or unusually disruptive behavior in school, for example.
- *Parents are facing significant social and/or economic challenges.* Examples of social challenges include having limited formal education, being a single parent, and being a new immigrant without a support network in the community. Economic challenges could include, for example, having an income at or below the poverty line, having an occupation providing little time for engagement with children, and having unstable housing accommodation.
- *Parents have either low or no explicit expectations for their children's success at school.* These parental expectations may have been known by school staff as a result of their previous contact with parents.

Districts were asked to ensure the selection of student/parent dyads that met as many of these four criteria as possible based on credible sources of evidence, and profiles of each student/parent dyad were developed before the project began in each district. All districts were able to follow these four guidelines.

Control Student/Parent Dyads Participating districts were asked to address three important challenges when selecting control student/parent dyads, and they were largely successful in doing this. First, districts were asked to ensure comparability of the control dyads to the participant dyads on the selection criteria outlined above. Second, districts were asked to minimize the risk of "treatment contamination" or influence from project schools' parent engagement initiatives. Finally, districts were required to gain reasonable access to, and the cooperation of, the control student/parent dyads.

---

[4] As a result of his series of meta-analyses, Jeynes (2011) has observed that parent engagement initiatives typically have significantly larger effects on report card scores than on standardized achievement test results.

Measures

Student Survey The survey instrument used in the study provided the most direct evidence about achievement of the three project goals, and was used by all district teams. Appendix A describes items included in the survey, which was used to measure two dimensions of student engagement (behavioral and psychological) and the three components of family educational culture selected as key outcomes for the project. Many of these items were originally based on Finn's (1989) model of school engagement adapted for research on school leader effects on student engagement (see for example Leithwood and Jantzi 2000). Finn's model defines engagement as having both behavioral and psychological dimensions.

The behavioral dimension of Finn's model of school engagement comprises four "levels" of behavior: responding to requirements, engaging in class-related initiatives, participating in extra-curricular activities, and being involved in school decision making (through student councils and the like). However, previous evidence suggests that the fourth level has no effect on achievement, and so items measuring such engagement were not used by most districts. Students' psychological engagement or identification with school includes both a sense of belonging at school, and valuing school[5,6,7]. Some features of the survey were slightly modified (reduced numbers of items measuring some variables, simplified language) by several districts to accommodate unique local conditions.

Report Card Student Achievement Measures Achievement measures depended, in part, on the grade of the students selected for the project. Each district team was asked to specify which existing sets of achievement data would be used as their pre- and post-measure of achievement. However, despite initial guidelines about measures of achievement, several districts did not report achievement data at all, while the remainder relied exclusively on report card evidence about subject achievement (all schools in Ontario use a common report card developed by the province).

Report Card Student Learning Skills Measures The province's common report card also requires teachers to provide an assessment of each student's "learning skills" including collaboration, independent work, initiative, organization, responsibility, and self-regulation.

Parent Interviews Each school engaged in discussions with parents about their interest in participating in the project. Parents selected to be part of the study were interviewed at two points during the project (after three months and after six months). Interviews included the following questions:

---

[5] While scale reliabilities for this instrument could not be calculated from the data in this project, previous data sets have indicated reliabilities (Cronbach's Alpha) for all scales significantly above minimum acceptable levels (0.60).

[6] Also see Turner et al. 2014, for a comparable theoretical account of factors contributing to student engagement.

[7] For a discussion of the relationships between student engagement and family and school factors see Willms 2003.

- To this point, what does participating in your school's parent engagement project involve for you?
- Please describe how you have been involved in each aspect of the project.
- To what extent has each aspect of your project involvement been useful to you?
- In particular, what has this involvement meant for your relationships with your child's school?
- What has this involvement meant for you and your child's interactions about school in your home?
- What aspects of the project have been most and least helpful for you?
- Do you have any suggestions for changes to the project that would make it more useful for you?

Student Interviews As with parents, interviews with students selected to be part of the study also took place at two points during the project. Questions asked during student interviews included at least the following:

- Since you became part of your school's parent engagement project (some other designation may be needed for students) is anything different for you at school? If so, what?
- Do you and your parents approach your schoolwork any differently now than before? If yes, what is the difference?
- Do you and your teacher(s) approach your schoolwork any differently now than before? If yes, what is the difference?
- What else could be done by the school or by your parents to help you do better at school?

School Staff Interviews Interviews with school staff members who were part of each school's project implementation team were conducted during the same time period suggested for parents and students. Questions asked during staff interviews included:

- What challenges have you encountered while implementing your school's parent engagement project?
- How have you addressed the most significant of these challenges?
- Can you detect much difference in parental support for the students in your class/school who are participating in the project?
- Have you changed your approach to these students in your classroom practices? If so, how?
- What could the project do differently that would make it more effective in your view?

15.4 Results

Selected Ojectives Table 15.1 summarizes the objectives each district established for its project. Developing the social capital of parents related to schooling was selected by five of the seven districts, and improving communication in the home between parents and students was selected by three districts. Only D3 explicitly set out to

Table 15.1 Objectives selected by districts for their parent engagement interventions

Districts	Objectives			
	Increasing parental expectations for students' success at school	Developing the social capital of parents related to schooling	Improving communication between parents and students in the hme	Other
D1		√		√
D2		√		√
D3	√	√	√	√
D4			√	√
D5		√		√
D6		√	√	√
D7			√	√

increase parents' expectations for student success at school. All districts had additional objectives, mostly concerned with building awareness among staff about the importance of parent engagement and developing the capacities of staff needed to enhance parent engagement in their classrooms, schools, and in the homes of their students.

Selected Interventions The districts in the study and many of their schools exercised considerable autonomy in making decisions about the specific parent engagement strategies they used for their version of the project. However, project teams were provided with background literature about parent engagement strategies, and several districts had significant experience with many such strategies already. A summary of the strategies used by each district is provided in Table 15.2, below. Because of the fundamental nature of the project, all strategies were, by definition, "school driven" rather than "parent driven," a distinction discussed by Ma et al. (2013); strategies were also targeted at one or more of the three overall project outcomes as indicated in Table 15.1, above.

In a wide-ranging review of relevant research, Leithwood and Jantzi (2006) identified three broad categories (including thirteen specific forms) of parent engagement strategies. One of these categories encompasses seven specific forms of school-initiated parent engagement strategies, four of which were used by some project schools, including assisting parents in child rearing skills (e.g., D7), assisting parents in instructional skills (e.g., D2), advising parents on assisting child with homework (D4), and communicating with parents about school-related matters such as school programs, activities, and things studied in class (D1, D6).

Not used by any project schools were three school-initiated parent engagement strategies that most evidence suggests have little bearing on student outcomes in schools (Fan and Chen 2001): involving parents as school volunteers, involving parents in school-community collaborations, and involving parents in school decision-making through PTA, school councils, and the like.

A second category of parent engagement strategies – shared forms of school-parent engagement – includes just one strategy: communication between parents and school. This strategy was part of all districts' intervention strategies; it was especially central to initiatives undertaken in D6.

Table 15.2 Summary of interventions used by districts

Districts	Nature of project interventions
D1	Parent "how-to" guides, including questions to ask at parent-teacher interviews
	Teacher in-service
	Series of meetings in school with parents to address parent-identified needs
	Individual parent consultations by teacher to facilitate parent contact with school
	Multiple avenues used to keep parents informed of important school dates and other activities in which their children were involved
D2	*In three project schools:*
	Parents and students meet in school four or five times to explore learning strategies especially in math and literacy
	Summer program:
	Developing literacy and numeracy skills for students
	Helping parents with ways of assisting such learning in the home
	Instruction in native languages
D3	Develop and support parent-directed groups that met once or twice per week
D4	Creation and use of a communication book
	Face-to-face conversations with parents by staff
	Telephone conversations with parents by staff
	Formally scheduled classroom visits
D5	Responding to parent focus group
	In-service for educators
	Community evening family engagement group
	Literacy sessions
D6	Math, literacy, arts nights with parents
	BBQ
	Movie nights, games nights, community walk
	Personal phone calls/invitations to parents
	Use of social media to inform parents of student work
D7	Hire "student asset" coaches who meet for one hour and 30 min twice a week with parents in the home
	Meeting in school for all parents served by asset coaches (dinner, engage with children in "play" activity, free passes for selected community activities)

Parent-initiated types of engagement, a third category, includes five specific strategies. Although project schools (as opposed to parents) initiated all of the strategies studied, some of these initiatives aimed to prompt some forms of parent initiation, including: communicating with children about schooling including the frequency of parental talk with one's child about school, high school plans, post high school plans, help with homework and the like (e.g., D7); communicating with children about educational aspirations, such as how far in school parents want their children to go (e.g., D7); providing academic stimulation at home (not necessarily related to the school curriculum) (e.g., D6); supervising children's activities to ensure education as priority by setting guidelines about how often parent checks homework, limiting the frequency child is allowed to go out with friends, amounts of TV/Internet/video game/music time as well as how late they can be used (e.g., D4); and contacting the school about, for example, academic programs, children's behaviour, and/or children's school performance (e.g., D6).

In sum, schools in the project districts, as a group, implemented about two-thirds of the thirteen specific interventions described in previous research. Prior evidence (Fan and Chen 2001) indicates that most of the strategies not used in the study have little or no demonstrable effect on student outcomes. The choice of intervention strategies provided districts with a promising start in terms of accomplishing their chosen goals.

15.4.1 Parent, Student, and Teacher Interview Results

All districts collected interview evidence from parents, teachers, and students involved in their intervention efforts, typically at the mid-point and at the end of the intervention. Most of these interviews asked some close variation of the questions proposed in the overall design of the project, and the responses provided evidence for mid-course refinements of district interventions as well as evidence about outcomes. Most individual district reports included quite detailed responses to the interview questions and are a rich source of information about the experiences of parents, teachers, and students as each set of interventions was being implemented.

Of greatest salience to the project as a whole is what the interview results suggest about outcomes of the interventions. First, much of the evidence indicates that, at the point of being officially completed, many study participants believed that the value of the interventions was just beginning to be realized. This perception suggests that parent engagement strategies likely to be effective in nurturing student success at school need to engage parents and students deeply, either through their duration or intensity. A "light touch" does not seem likely to make much difference. More likely, the strategies implemented in the study should become a routine part of what schools do on a regular basis.

Second, parents and teachers who participated directly in the interventions often attributed greater value to the interventions than the more "objective" outcome data reported subsequently suggests. Furthermore, the significant weight awarded to these data by most districts in their individual reports exemplifies the well-documented claim that some types of evidence are considered more salient than others in terms of influencing decision making; qualitative data, for example, seem more meaningful to many than do quantitative data (Kahneman 2011). Knowing about this predictable bias in human decision making, future efforts to judge the value of parent engagement interventions should include multiple types of evidence.

15.4.2 Student Perceptions of Changes in Family Educational Cultures

Evidence from the student survey is the best indicator available of the impact of the project. The survey included multi-item scales measuring five variables. Two of these variables were dimensions of student engagement: behavioral engagement and psychological engagement or identification with school. The remaining variables measured by the survey were explicit goals to be achieved by the project: increasing parental expectations for their children's success at school, the social and intellectual capital of parents, and communication between parents and students. The survey measures align directly with project goals, provide evidence directly from students themselves, and are the only data common across all seven project districts.

Both treatment and control students in all schools responded to the survey near the beginning and at the end of their involvement in the project. Results of the survey are summarized in Table 15.3 (note that D2 had three sets of students included in its version of the project, hence three sets of data; the summary of results below refers to only the mean of the three scores for D2). All districts collected evidence about all five variables, even though not all of these variables were explicitly included among the goals selected for their projects.

Student Behavioral Engagement Treatment groups in five of the seven districts made at least modest average gains in the behavioral dimension of student engagement as indicated in the first two columns of data in Table 15.3. In only one district the results favored the control group students (D4). Of the three different intervention programs implemented by D2, the summer-school-only treatment group outperformed the other treatment and control groups with the in-school-only alternative producing negative results. Because this is the pattern of results across all variables measured by the survey, the remaining report of the survey results takes into account only D2's average ratings, clearly ratings that mask the noteworthy differences in the impact of D2's three intervention programs.

Student Psychological Engagement Treatment groups made at least modest average gains on the psychological dimension of student engagement in five of the seven districts. Negative "gains" by treatment groups were larger than control groups in one district (D1) and smaller in the other district (D2).

Parent Expectations Treatment groups in five districts made gains in parental expectations for student success at school while treatment groups in the two remaining districts made no change (D1 and D4). Treatment group changes also exceeded control group changes in five districts, while D4 and D6 control group changes exceeded treatment group changes.

Parents' Social and Intellectual Capital Five of the seven treatment groups gained on this goal; only D1 and D6 treatment groups did not, although the D6 treatment group's losses were not nearly as large as the control group. Treatment group changes exceeded control group changes in five districts.

15 Changing the Educational Culture of the Home to Increase Student Success at School   343

Table 15.3 Cross-district summary of student survey results

Districts	Behav. engage't T	Behav. engage't C	Psych. engage't T	Psych. engage't C	High expect'n T	High expect'n C	Social/int. capital T	Social/int. capital C	Parent/child comm. T	Parent/child comm. C	Mean change T	Mean change C
D1	−0.01	−0.14	−0.25	−0.08	0.00	−0.09	−0.07	−0.02	−0.02	−0.11	−0.07	−0.08
D2[a]												
A	0.06	−0.22	0.10	−0.26	−0.08	−0.13	0.06	−0.21	0.06	−0.48	0.04	−0.26
B	−0.17	−0.12	−0.16	−0.18	−0.24	−0.11	−0.13	−0.04	−0.27	−0.12	−0.19	−0.16
C	0.09	−0.15	0.04	−0.17	0.10	−0.15	0.18	−0.05	0.21	−0.17	0.12	−0.14
Mean	−0.01	−0.16	−0.01	−0.20	0.07	−0.13	0.04	−0.10	0.00	−0.26	−0.01	−0.18
D3	0.20	0.00	0.08	−0.07	0.02	−0.01	0.43	0.05	0.29	0.49	0.21	0.09
D4	0.26	0.39	0.11	NA	0.00	0.19	0.07	0.40	0.04	0.23	0.10	0.30
D5	0.31	−0.27	0.54	−0.13	0.50	−0.15	0.76	−0.22	0.57	−0.19	0.53	−0.30
D6	0.27	0.06	0.05	0.07	0.03	0.06	−0.02	−0.23	0.12	0.05	0.09	−0.01
D7	0.05	−0.04	0.15	0.08	0.22	−0.04	0.56	0.03	0.27	0.08	0.25	0.02

[a]Group A = in-school plus summer school; Group B = in-school program only; Group C = summer learning program only.
Mean change scores of treatment (T) and control (C) groups (4 point rating scales)

Parent-Child Communications Five of the seven treatment groups gained on this goal; only D1 and D2 treatment groups, on average, did not. Treatment group changes exceeded control group changes in five districts.

Across all districts, average results favored the treatment over the controls groups on 67% of the survey items, with D2 results offering a more complex picture of the consequences of treatment variation. D2's summer school treatment resulted in substantially better student engagement results than results of the other D2 student groupings.

This summary of student survey results supports the claim that, with one exception (D1), interventions by districts had, on average, positive effects; and all but one district (D4), were modestly more successful in achieving the central goals of the project with treatment students as compared with control students.

In the case of D1, as the far right column of Table 15.3 indicates, both treatment and control group ratings declined from pre- to post-test, and by almost identical amounts (−0.07 and −0.08). This was the only district working with a secondary school population, which may have presented both different and more significant challenges to the achievement of project goals than did elementary school populations[8]. Another plausible explanation for the decline, and one that would also apply to the weaker gains by D4's treatment as compared to control group results, is that the interventions implemented were largely "school driven," a category of interventions some previous evidence suggests has marginal effects on student outcomes (Ma et al. 2013). However, student achievement evidence, described in the next section, provides some support for the strategies used by D4.

Student Report Card Learning Skills Six learning skills are included on the provincial report cards used by all project schools. Table 15.4 compares average changes from pre- to post-test for all treatment and all control students in each of the four districts able to provide such evidence. The data from which these change scores are derived are based on numerical transformations of descriptive words or phrases used on report cards, where Excellent = 4, Good = 3, Satisfactory = 2, and Needs Improvement = 1.

Mean changes in ratings across all six learning skills in each of the four districts are found in the bottom row of Table 15.4. Data in this row indicate small improve-

Table 15.4 Changes in learning skills results by treatment (T) and control (C) students

Learning skills	D3 T	D3 C	D4 T	D4 C	D6 T	D6 C	D7 T	D7 C
Collaboration	1.8	0.00	0.20	0.0	0.55	−0.13	−0.11	0.00
Independent work	0.20	0.00	0.20	0.2	0.31	−0.13	0.05	−0.21
Initiative	0.05	0.20	0.00	0.0	−0.08	−0.19	−0.23	−0.06
Organization	0.10	0.16	0.20	0.2	0.27	−0.11	−0.18	0.00
Responsibility	0.01	−0.15	0.00	0.0	−0.13	0.03	−0.23	0.10
Self-regulation	−0.03	0.00	0.10	−0.2	0.25	−0.27	0.12	0.21
Mean	**0.35**	**0.04**	**0.12**	**0.03**	**−0.10**	**−0.30**	**−0.10**	**0.01**

---

[8] For an outline of these differences and challenges, see Hill and Tyson 2009.

ments in learning skills ratings for both treatment and control students in two districts (D3 and D4), declines in such ratings for both groups in D6 (a larger decline for the control than the treatment students, however), and declines for the treatment group and a very slight increase for the control group in D7. Nonetheless, ratings of treatment students' learning skills exceed ratings of control students in three of the four districts. Treatment students made the greatest gains, as compared with control students, for Collaboration and Independent Work in all but D7.

These results provide additional (albeit weak) support for claims about the impact of three of the four districts' parent engagement interventions. Although the student engagement results for D4, described in the previous section, generally favored control over treatment students, the learning skills data included in Table 15.4 favor that district's treatment group.

Student Report Card Subject Achievement Table 15.5 displays report card results in reading, writing (D6 reported a combined language score only), math, and science (D7 and D6 only) before and after the districts' interventions for both treatment and control groups. These data, from four of the seven districts in the project, are based on the numerical transformations of letter grades typically used to report achievement on elementary school report cards. Grades ranged from A+ to D−, a total of 12 possible grades. These letter grades were transformed to numbers by assigning A+ = 12, A = 11, A− = 10 and so on, with D− = 1. Results reported in Table 15.5 are average changes in these scores from pre- to post-test, usually a period of one term. This, admittedly, is a truncated description of report card subject achievement data, largely because subject classifications differed by district, due in part to the reporting requirements at different grade levels. So only data about reading, writing, and math are available across the four boards. Given these limitations, a very cautious interpretation of the data is warranted.

As the bottom row of Table 15.5 indicates, average changes in the subject achievement of treatment and control students was marginal in the four districts. However, these small changes favored the treatment groups in three of the four districts. The results therefore provide at least weak support for claims about the impact of the parent engagement interventions on student achievement implemented in all but D3.

Table 15.5 Changes in subject achievement by treatment (T) and control (C) students

	D3		D4		D6		D7	
Subjects	T	C	T	C	T	C	T	C
Reading	1.0	1.0	1.2	0.6			0.12	−0.1
Writing	1.0	0.0	0.3	−1.4			0.18	−0.21
Language					−0.08	0.24		
Math	−2.0	2.0	1.38[a]	−1.29	−0.02	−0.01	−0.53[b]	−0.55
Science					0.11	−0.49	0.12	−0.61
Mean	**0.0**	**1.0**	**0.96**	**0.70**	**0.03**	**−0.08**	**−0.03**	**−0.37**

[a] The math change scores reported in this table for D4 are the average of separate scores reported for number sense, measurement, geometry, patterning, and data management
[b] Number sense and numeration

15.5 Conclusions

The three types of student outcome evidence summarized in the previous section (student engagement, learning skills, and subject achievement) generally support a claim about the positive impact of the interventions implemented by project districts. Clearly, support for this claim is relatively weak, and for two of the three types of evidence, does not include all seven districts. However, the more fulsome accounts of interviews with parents, students, and teachers found in the individual district reports add some credence to a positive assessment of project effects.

Individual district reports included in the final project report (Leithwood 2014) are a rich source of detailed information about how each district developed its interventions, the challenges experienced as those interventions were unfolding, and the consequences of intervention implementation. These individual reports conclude with suggestions concerning "lessons" for future work, which are typically fairly detailed and appropriate to their chosen interventions. The reports, as a whole, also suggest eight larger, overlapping lessons of which other districts might take heed as they embark on their own parent engagement interventions[9].

The first lesson described by the project reports suggests that productively engaging parents as partners in the education of their children can be hard work. For many staff members, engaging parents is certainly a departure from their typical day-to-day routine. As Kruse and Louis (2006) observe: "deep-seated changes in the culture of schools are unlikely to occur without action to create more fundamental bonds with the community" (p. 7). Learning how to do this work well requires significant time and support. Schools and districts embarking on parent engagement efforts targeted at improving student outcomes should build in sufficient time and opportunity for staff learning, and sometimes for staff members to undergo significant shifts in their attitude toward the parents with whom they are likely to be working.

Second, efforts on the part of regular school staff to build parents' social and intellectual capital related to schooling work best when a relatively generous amount of time during meetings, at the outset, is allowed for trust building among parents and between parents and the school staff.

Third, and overlapping the previous lesson, a handful of meetings with parents, no matter how well planned and executed, are unlikely to be sufficiently intensive, sensitive to parent perspectives, or sustained to have much impact on student-related goals for parent engagement. Initiatives of this type, however, likely provide a good foundation for follow-up initiatives aimed directly, for example, at building parents' social capital, fostering higher expectations for their children's success at school, and nurturing productive communication between parents and children in the home. Such truncated initiatives provide the opportunities for learning, attitude change, and starting points for trust building needed to subsequently make a difference for students in partnership with parents, but are of little value by themselves.

---

[9] These lessons should be considered provisional, of course, because of the small size of the sample on which they are based.

Fourth, the duration of efforts to engage parents productively in the education of their children may be less important than the intensity and focus of those efforts. Intense efforts within a relatively short period can pay off when they occur either inside or outside the home, as long as they provide direct, practical help to parents in supporting their child's work at school. This lesson is most suitable for efforts that do not depend exclusively for their implementation on regular school staff. The importance of a sharp focus on how to be successful at school is mirrored in a significant amount of previous research. For example, Hill and Tyson's (2009) meta-analysis found stronger effects on student achievement of "academic socialization" approaches to parent engagement than a wide range of other approaches.

Fifth, within any of the broad approaches to parent engagement that might be chosen, effective implementation strategies are likely to be dynamic. To build productive partnerships with parents, a concept discussed by Ferlazzo (2011), schools must carefully plan their initial contact, but assume that plans are likely going to need changing as knowledge about parent and student needs grows. Flexibility is a critical quality for schools to bring to their parent engagement efforts.

Sixth, engaging parents of secondary students and developing partnerships with them in the interests of their children's success at school is typically more complicated – or at the very least, different – than it is with parents of elementary school children. But secondary teachers who are initially pessimistic about the feasibility of developing such partnerships may become strong advocates for the effort with a willingness to persist long enough to make significant progress. This lesson is also reflected in a significant amount of previous research on parent engagement, which takes account of differences in students' stage of development (see for example Hill and Tyson 2009).

Seventh, while many First Nations parents and children face huge challenges related to poverty and sometimes to location, many such parents are highly motivated to increase their social and intellectual capital related to the schooling of their children and readily build on opportunities to improve those conditions in the home which foster their children's success at school. In their comprehensive report of approaches to the improvement of education for indigenous peoples in Alberta, Gunn et al. (Gunn et al. 2011) discuss specific and effective strategies, including making communication with Aboriginal parents a priority, and paying substantial attention to creating a sense of belonging and enhancing cultural awareness. Understanding Aboriginal people and their traditional ways of life and culture help to create effective communication between staff and Aboriginal parents (Agbo 2007).

Finally, communication between parents and schools is central to productive parent-school partnerships, but there is no one form or even several forms that work well in all circumstances and with all parents. Schools should ask their parents what forms of communication work best for them and stay tuned for changes in the answers. As Ferlazzo (2011) notes: "A school striving for parent engagement… tends to lead with its ears – listening to what parents think, dream, and worry about. The goal of family engagement is not to serve clients but to gain partners" (p. 10).

Appendix A

	Student survey
Behavioral engagement	
Respond to requirements	
1	I rarely daydream in my classes
2	I rarely am late for school
3	I always finish my school work on time
4	I do all the homework that I am supposed to do
5	I respond whenever I am asked questions during class.
6	I rarely am absent for a whole day.
7	I rarely am sent to the office because of misbehaviour.
8	I rarely skip a class (without permission).
9	I rarely receive a detention.
10	I rarely stay home unless I am sick.
Class-related initiative	
11	I put a lot of energy into my schoolwork.
12	I enjoy giving my opinion during class discussions.
13	I frequently ask questions during class.
14	I frequently have discussions with my teacher about things I find interesting.
15	I frequently do extra schoolwork to find out more about something that interests me.
16	I do a lot of extra reading for my own benefit.
Psychological engagement	
Sense of belonging	
17	I feel that I "belong" at this school.
18	Most of my teachers are interested in me as a person.
19	I have made many friends in my school.
20	Most of my teachers treat me the same as other students.
21	Most of my teachers make me feel comfortable in class.
22	I have gotten to know other students in our school really well.
23	I get along with most other students I have met at school.
24	My teachers spend time just talking with me.
25	Most of my teachers seem to understand me.
26	I get along with most of my teachers.
	Student survey
Valuing school	
27	The most important things that happen to me usually happen at school.
28	I think schoolwork is really important.
29	It is really important to me that I gain knowledge and develop skills.
30	I am proud of my school.
31	I really enjoy school most of the time.
32	All people should get as much education as they can.
33	School spirit is very high in my school.

(continued)

High expectations	
34	My parents/guardians make sure I do my homework before having free time.
35	My parents/guardians always know whether or not I am at school.
36	My parents/guardians make sure that I get to school on time.
37	My parents/guardians make sure that I attend school unless I am sick.
38	My parents/guardians contact my school when I am having difficulty or when they are not sure of how they can help me.
39	My parents/guardians encourage me to participate in extracurricular activities.
40	Study aids that I have at home help me do better schoolwork.
41	I have my own work space at home that is fairly quiet for doing school work.
Social/Intellectual capital	
42	My parents/guardians usually go to parents' nights and special school events.
43	I often discuss my schoolwork with my parents/guardians.
44	My parents/guardians ensure that I have a healthy diet and enough sleep.
45	My parents/guardians often talk with other parents about what is happening at school
46	My parents/guardians often discuss my work at school with my teacher
Communication	
47	My parents/guardians always are willing to help me with my schoolwork.
48	I talk with my parents/guardians about what I am doing at school almost every day.
49	I have conversations about what is happening in my community and the wider world with my parents/guardians.
50	My parents/guardians listen to my ideas.
51	My parents/guardians encourage me to take responsibility for my own learning at school.
52	My parents/guardians encourage me not to give up when I am having difficulty at school.

References

Agbo, S. A. (2007). Addressing school-community relations in a cross-cultural context: A collaborative action to bridge the gap between First Nations and the school. *Journal of Research in Rural Education, 22*. Retrieved from http://jrre.vmhost.psu.edu/wp-content/uploads/2014/02/22-8.pdf

Bandura, A. (1986). *Social foundations of thought and action*. Englewood Cliffs: Prentice Hall.

Bolivar, J., & Chrispeels, J. (2011). Enhancing parent leadership through building social and intellectual capital. *American Educational Research Journal, 48*, 4–38.

Bronfenbrenner, U. (2005). Ecological models of human development. In *International encyclopedia of education* (Vol. 3, 2nd ed., pp. 1643–1647). Oxford: Elsevier.

Coleman, J. (1988). Social capital in the creation of human capital. *American Journal of Sociology, 94*, S95–S120.

Coleman, J., Campbell, E., Hobson, C., McPartland, J., Mood, A., Weinfeld, F., & York, R. (1966). *Equality of educational opportunity*. Washington, DC: U.S. Government Printing Office.

Cooper, C. W., Riehl, C. J., & Hasan, A. L. (2010). Leading and learning with diverse families in schools: Critical epistemology amid communities of practice. *Journal of School Leadership, 20*, 758–788.

Dunleavy, J., Willms, J. D., Milton, P., & Friesen, S. (2012). *What did you do in school today?* Toronto: Canadian Education Association Retrieved from http://cea-ace.ca/sites/cea-ace.ca/files/cea-2012-wdydist-report-1.pdf.

Epstein, J., & Dauber, S. (1991). School programs and teacher practices of parent involvement. *Elementary School Journal, 91*, 289–305.

Epstein, J., Sanders, M., Simon, B., Salinas, K., Jansorn, N., & Van Voorhis, F. (2002). *School, community, and community partnerships: Your handbook for action* (2nd ed.). Thousand Oaks: Corwin.

Fan, X., & Chen, M. (2001). Parent involvement and students' academic achievement: A meta-analysis. *Educational Psychology Review, 13*, 1–22.

Ferlazzo, L. (2011). Involvement or engagement? *ASCD Journal, 68*, 10–14.

Finn, J. (1989). Withdrawing from school. *Review of Educational Research, 59*, 117–143.

Freeman-Loftis, B. (2011). How to really listen to parents. *ASCD Journal, 8*. Available online: http://www.ascd.org/publications/educational-leadership/may11/vol68/num08/How-to-(Really)-Listen-to-Parents.aspx

Gunn, T. M., Pomahac, G., Striker, E. G., & Tailfeathers, J. (2011). First Nations, Metis, and Inuit education: The Alberta initiative for school improvement approach to improve Indigenous education in Alberta. *Journal of Educational Change, 12*, 323–345.

Harris, A., Andrew-Power, K., & Goodall, J. (2009). *Do parents know they matter? Raising achievement through parental engagement.* London: Continuum.

Hattie, J. (2009). *Visible learning: A Synthesis of over 800 meta-analyses relating to achievement.* London: Routledge.

Henderson, A., & Mapp, K. L. (2002). *A new wave of evidence: The impact of school, family, and community connections on student achievement (Annual synthesis).* Austin: National Center for Family & Community Connections with Schools.

Hill, N., & Tyson, D. (2009). Parental involvement in middle school: A meta-analytic assessment of the strategies that promise achievement. *Developmental Psychology, 45*, 740–763.

Hoover-Dempsey, K. V., & Sandler, H. M. (1997). Why do parents become involved in their children's education? *Review of Educational Research, 67*, 3–12.

Hoover-Dempsey, K. V., Walker, J. M. T., Sandler, H. M., Whetsel, D., Green, C. L., Wilkins, A. S., & Closson, K. (2009). Why do parents become involved? Research findings and implications. *Elementary School Journal, 106*, 105–130.

Hornby, G., & Lafaele, R. (2011). Barriers to parental involvement in education: An explanatory model. *Educational Review, 63*, 37–52.

Jeynes, W. (2005). A meta-analysis of the relation of parent involvement to urban elementary school student academic achievement. *Urban Education, 40*, 237–269.

Jeynes, W. (2011). *Parental involvement and academic success.* New York: Routledge.

Johnson, S. (2012). *Future perfect: The case for progress in networked age.* New York: Riverhead.

Kahneman, D. (2011). *Thinking fast and slow.* New York: Farrar, Straus and Giroux.

Kruse, S. D., & Louis, S. K. (2006). *Building strong school cultures: A guide to leading change.* Sage: Thousand Oaks.

Lawson, M. A., & Alameda-Lawson, T. A. (2012). Case study of school-linked, collective parent engagement. *American Educational Research Journal, 49*, 651–684.

Lee, J., & Bowen, N. (2006). Parent involvement, cultural capital and the achievement gap among elementary school children. *American Educational Research Journal, 43*, 193–218.

Leithwood, K. (2014). *Ontario Parent Engagement Project*, Final report of research for the Ontario Ministry of Education. Toronto: *Ontario Ministry of Education.*

Leithwood, K., & Jantzi, D. (1999). The relative effects of principal and teacher sources of leadership on student engagement with school. *Educational Administration Quarterly, 35*, 679–706.

Leithwood, K., & Jantzi, D. (2000). The effects of transformation leadership on student engagement with school. *Journal of Educational Administration, 38*, 112–129.

Leithwood, K., & Jantzi, D. (2006). *A critical review of the parent engagement literature*, Final report of research for the Ontario Ministry of Education. Toronto: *Ontario Ministry of Education.*

Ma, X., Shen, J., & Krenn, H. (2013). The relationships between parental involvement and adequate yearly progress among urban, suburban and rural schools. *School Effectiveness and School Improvement, 25*, 629–650.

Mapp, K. L. (2002, April). *Having their say: Parents describe how and why they are involved in their children's education.* Presented at the annual meeting of the American Educational Research Association, New Orleans.

Niehaus, K., & Adelson, J. (2014). School support, parent involvement and academic and social-emotional outcomes for English language learners. *American Journal of Educational Research, 51*, 810–844.

Turner, J., Christensen, A., Kackar-Cam, H., Turcano, M., & Fulmer, S. (2014). Enhancing students' engagement: Report of a 3-year intervention with middle school teachers. *American Educational Research Journal, 51*, 1195–1226.

Willms, J. D. (2003). *Student engagement at school: A sense of belonging and participation.* Paris: Organization for Economic Co-operation and Development.

Chapter 16
Conclusion

Kenneth Leithwood, Jingping Sun, and Katina Pollock

This concluding chapter provides a summary of the results reported in the book's chapters along with some reflections on those results. Also provided is a unique approach to helping practicing school leaders use the results of relevant research to guide their own decision making; this approach is illustrated using a recent, large-scale data set not yet reported elsewhere. Implications are identified for school leadership development and associations are noted between the expectations for leadership development reflected in one prominent set of school leadership standards and the contents of the book as a whole.

16.1 The Four Paths Framework as a Whole

As we argued in the first chapter, effective approaches to school leadership make important contributions to students' success at school; among the wide array of school conditions influencing students, school leadership is second only to classroom instruction. But leadership is not always effective and, even when it is, its influence on students is largely indirect (or mediated). Better understanding the

---

K. Leithwood (✉)
Ontario Inst. for Studies in Education University of Toronto, University of Toronto, Toronto, ON, Canada
e-mail: kenneth.leithwood@utoronto.ca

J. Sun
Educational Leadership, Policy and Technology Studies, The College of Education, University of Alabama, Box 870302, 301 Graves Hall, Tuscaloosa, AL 35487, USA
e-mail: jsun22@ua.edu

K. Pollock
Faculty of Education, Western University,
1137 Western Road, London, ON N6G 1G7, Canada
e-mail: kpolloc7@uwo.ca

nature of effective leadership and how the influence of such leadership "seeps through" families, schools and classrooms to students was the main goal of the book.

The largely indirect nature of school leadership has been acknowledged since at least the early 1980s (Bossert et al. 1982; Pitner 1988). Indeed, the concept of "paths" along which leadership "flows" is not unique to our Four Paths framework. Alluding to Pitner's (1988) taxonomy of approaches to the study of school leadership, Hallinger and Heck explained in 1998 that a "mediated effects framework… hypothesizes that leaders achieve their effect on school outcomes through indirect paths" (Hallinger and Heck 1998, p. 167).

While acknowledging the indirect or mediated effects of school leadership, by far the largest proportion of leadership research over the past 25 years has been focused on the discovery of effective leadership practices and has neglected much inquiry about (a) which paths are most likely to carry the influence of those practices or (b) the extent to which influencing different mediators depends on mediator-specific leadership practices. Those systematic attempts that have been carried out over this period to unpack the indirect effects of school leadership included such mediators of leadership as, for example, the educational expectations of staff, teachers' academic optimism, collaborative decision making, changes in teacher practices, teacher commitment to change and organizational learning (e.g., Mascall et al. 2008; Hallinger and Heck 1998; Geijsel et al. 2003). The Four Paths framework is the only attempt we are aware of, however, to codify mediators with a high probability of contributing to student success, as well as being susceptible to the influence of effective leadership practices. While such codification alone ignores the importance for school leaders of the context in which they find themselves, the Four Paths approach encourages school leaders to pick, from a menu of mediators on the Four Paths, those that seem most suitable for their own school improvement purposes.

16.1.1 Successful Leadership Practices (Part I)

Research methods inquiring about successful leadership provide evidence varying widely in the types of validity they address. For example, in-depth qualitative cases of individual leaders at work in their schools typically aim to provide evidence which meets high standards of internal validity but poorly reflects standards of external validity, whereas the opposite is the case for large scale quantitative studies of the effects of selected leadership practices on many schools, staffs and students. Mixed methods research aspire to evidence meeting high standards of both types of validity.

Naïve interpretations of research focused on providing high levels of internal validity encourage a "context is everything" claim about successful leadership; every school (classroom, teacher, student, leader, etc.) has unique features which demand unique responses by leaders. Extreme forms of this interpretation spin into ever more detailed features of the school and its inhabitants implying understandings of what will constitute successful leadership that are eventually not open to codification. In this extreme view, even detailed case study research has no contribution to make since every case will be different in some important way. From this view, the practical experiences of leaders will always be more valuable than the results of research except possibly "action research".

Naïve interpretations of research aiming at high levels of external validity nudge us toward a universalistic model of leadership practices effective in all contexts. Extreme forms of this interpretation suggest that successful leadership is not just learnable but what is learned transcends the context in which it is exercised requiring almost no thought about differences in context, no "local knowledge". Robust research results with high levels of external validity will always outweigh practical experience in this view; people highly skilled in the exercise of externally validated successful leadership practices will be effective no matter the organizational circumstances or domain.

We hold a nuanced view about the relative value of practical experience and the results of research in the framing of leadership practices that are successful in context. Our view awards considerable importance – but not dominance – to the guidance provided by research about effective leadership practices. As Christensen and Demski (2002) argue, the usefulness of theory and research is found in the guidance it provides to organizing our thinking about some phenomenon. More specifically, our position reflected in this book, is that leadership success in most school contexts requires locally sensitive adaptations of a set of core leadership practices that are generally effective in most circumstances. Chaps. 2 and 3 of Part I of the book provide a closely related set of such "core practices". These core practices are derived from considerable amounts of evidence gathered in many different contexts. Each of the core practices is associated with one of four domains or categories of leadership including setting directions, developing people, re-designing the organization and improving the instructional program. The *Ontario Leadership Framework* summarized in Chap. 3 includes, in addition to the four sets of core practices, an additional category entitled Securing Accountability; this is in recognition of the policy contexts in which very large proportions of school leaders now find themselves.

The most important assumption on which our position about the relative contribution of research and experience to successful practice rests is that those exercising leadership are capable of taking key features of their own organizational contexts into account when they are deciding how best to adapt, for that context, leadership practices known to be successful in many organizational circumstances. Sometimes these leaders will need help: coaching might be useful from time-to-time; professional development undoubtedly will be valuable occasionally. But these leaders are, on the whole, astute professionals and deserve enough autonomy to do the right thing. Figuring out what the right thing is and doing it is also their responsibility.

The position we have adopted on the role of context, however, remains open to evidence about variation within "contextual categories" that warrant significant differences in the responses of large groups of leaders. By contextual categories we mean unique sets of socio-cultural beliefs, norms and values influencing approaches to leadership that have been so comprehensively documented in the massive Globe project (e.g., Chhokar et al. 2007; House et al. 2004). Contextual categories will sometimes also include distinctly different sets of organizing principles adopted by districts (e.g., degree of centralized decision making), demographic features of families and communities served by schools (e.g., high or low SES families) and characteristics of educational policies with widely different consequences for schools and their leaders (e.g., policies shaping how schools will be held accountable).

Hallinger (2016) has provided a comprehensive review of many such contextual categories and their consequences for leadership with which we largely agree. There is a productive role for leadership research in clarifying those contexts and clarifying what those contexts mean for leaders' adaptations of core practices, as well as the enactment of context-specific approaches to leadership.

16.1.2 Rational Path (Part II)

The Rational Path includes a large handful of variables or conditions with important consequences for students, some located in classrooms and some across the school, as a whole. Instructional leadership models perseverate on a sub-set of these conditions (those in classrooms), at least by implication. Of all the experiences students have at school, most published evidence indicates that what happens in classrooms matters most (Scheerens et al. 1989: Reetzig and Creemers 2005). While a reasonable corpus of empirical evidence indicates that leadership influences classroom instruction, little evidence is available about *how* that occurs. Spillane's chapter (Chap. 4) provides one of the few sources of conceptual guidance in response to this question. Adopting a "distributed perspective", Spillane's conceptual explanation centers on the interactions among those in many roles providing leadership and both the situations in which they find themselves and those directly responsible for students' experiences in the classroom.

There is also a surprisingly small amount of evidence assessing the *relative* effects on students of instruction in comparison with other variables on the Rational Path. As we report below, results of some very recent research with this comparative potential are surprising and counter-intuitive, to say the least. So how school leaders improve instruction in schools -- the technical core of their business - and with what consequences for students - is still something of a "black box".

The Rational Path also includes extra – classroom conditions, conditions that influence students' experiences not only in the classroom but across the school, as a whole. As Part II of the book indicates, considerable evidence recommends leaders' attention to the status of both Academic Press or emphasis and Disciplinary Climate in their schools. Malloy and Leithwood's chapter (Chap. 5) illustrates the extent to which Academic Press can influence student learning and the value of one coordinated form of distributed leadership in providing this influence. While the impact of a school's Disciplinary Climate on students is well documented, there is little evidence about how leaders might influence it. Furthermore, we know little about the impact of other extra-classroom conditions, potentially situated on the Rational

Path, that school leaders might reasonably expect would significantly influence student learning in response to their interventions. Beverborg and his colleagues (Chap. 6), however, provide a compelling evidence suggesting that, whatever changes might be needed in the classroom and school to improve student learning, at least one set of well-documented leadership practices is likely to foster the types of teacher reflection that will contribute to the increased teacher self-efficacy and learning needed to discover and enact those changes. These leadership practices, among the core practices included in transformational leadership models, include vision building, individualized consideration and intellectual stimulation; they are encompassed in the leadership framework summarized in Chap. 2.

16.1.3 Emotional Path (Part III)

Variables or conditions on the Emotional Path are among the most frequently researched variables on all four paths. Chapters in Part III suggest at least four especially powerful teacher emotions mediating the influence of school leadership on student learning including teacher trust, collective teacher efficacy, teacher commitment, and teachers' organization citizenship behavior (which we treat as a function of "commitment"). Results reported in Part III chapters indicate that these teachers' emotions matter as much to student learning as teachers' instructional skills and practices. As a whole, the evidence in Part III recommends that school leaders pay as much attention to nurturing teachers' psychological states and well-being as to directly improving teachers' instructional practices.

The chapters in this section also indicate, not surprisingly, that some practices associated with transformational approaches to leadership are helpful for improving the status of variables on the Emotional Path. We say "not surprisingly" because transformational leadership is explicitly designed to provide the support needed to improve the quality of one's work. Tshannen-Moran and her colleagues (Chap. 8) suggest that teacher trust in leaders, "cultivates", or helps prepare, the school culture for improving student achievement; it does this, in part, by making it more possible to improve the status of other variables on the Emotional Path (e.g., collective teacher efficacy) as well as on other paths (e.g., Academic Press, Teacher Professionalism) carrying leaders influence on students. Edge and her colleagues (Chap. 9) demonstrate the considerable importance teachers attribute to their leaders' ability and willingness to care about their staff, not only about their work in schools, but also about their lives outside of school. Such care or benevolence is one of a small handful of indicators leading teachers to attribute trustworthiness to their leaders, others including indications of vulnerability, honesty, openness, competence and reliability (Handford and Leithwood 2013). Building trusting relationships with staff is clearly a key successful leadership practice.

While Part III positions teachers' inner states as mediators of leaders' influence on student learning, they are more precisely conceptualized as mediators of leaders' influence on teachers' classroom practices. It seems likely that these emotional states have a positive influence on teachers' willingness to experiment with new forms of instruction, for example. It is also likely that these emotional states influence more subtle aspects of what students experience in their relationships with teachers such as supportive interactions, a ready willingness to help students outside the normal boundaries of classroom work, and an "upbeat" and optimistic disposition toward working with students. These more subtle aspects of teachers' behavior contribute in quite fundamental ways to the quality of teacher-student relationships so critical to student motivation (Lazowski and Hulleman 2016), engagement (Roorda et al. 2011), well-being (Neihaus and Adelson 2014) and achievement (Ahnert et al. 2013).

16.1.4 Organizational Path (Part IV)

For many years, a common focus of school leaders was focused on instruction and school organizational culture or effectiveness (primarily those on the Rational and Organizational Paths), however, very few constructs have been developed that capture the essential features of school conditions conducive to student learning. A number of concepts have been developed, such as: professional community, organizational learning, corporative learning, and healthy schools. Yet, the association of these variables with student learning is moderate, based on limited quantitative research evidence so far. Murphy's review, for example, identifies dynamic cultural and well-entrenched structural barriers that make the realization of effective professional community problematic. More significant evidence is needed regarding the conceptual, technical, and statistical constructs on student learning. In addition, there is limited research evidence illustrating the relationship and mediating roles of these variables with student learning, though their positive impacts on student learning have been documented in some research studies.

16.1.5 Family Path (Part V)

Our own experience working with schools suggests that the majority of teachers and school administrators feel uncomfortable working with parents outside the relatively narrow confines of the school's walls. This is the case in spite of a long line of research making the case for greater collaboration between schools and families (e.g., Jeynes 2011) and greater attention to families by school leaders (Goldring and Rallis 2000).

While significant attention is given by many schools to such in-school initiatives as communicating to parents about school expectations and activities, arranging events that parents are expected to attend and developing parent volunteer programs, few of these school-driven activities have much impact on student learning, although they do serve other important purposes). Yet variables or conditions in the home explain an equal or larger proportion of variation in student achievement across schools, as compared with many better known school-based variables and conditions (Coleman 1998; Jeynes 2011). In Chap. 1, for example, we reported that our initial test of the Four Paths Framework found effects on student math and language achievement of variables on the Family Path to be about the same as, or slightly larger than, the effects of variables on the Rational and Emotional Paths and greater than variables on the Organizational Path. With substantial effects on student success at school but as-yet limited attention by schools, influencing key variables on the Family Path should be considered "low hanging fruit" for leaders' school improvement initiatives (big effects without big costs).

The two chapters in this section of the book clarify which features of the home are likely to be the most productive focus for schools to nurture. Elements of a broader family educational culture, these features include parent expectations for their students' success at school, parents' social and intellectual capital about schooling and forms of child-parent communications in the home. In Chap. 14, Jeynes provided a comprehensive synthesis of evidence about the impact of each of these three family conditions and others while Chap. 15 provides evidence from a large-scale quasi-experimental field study about the ability of schools to significantly influence these conditions specifically in families struggling to provide supportive educational cultures for their children. To be clear, leaders' efforts to influence key conditions on the Family Path need not and should not target all families in any school and in some schools very few families may be in need of the school's support in the home. Identifying families that could benefit from school support and providing this support is an important contribution to achieving equity across a school's student population.

16.1.6 *Using Evidence from Research to Help Guide Leaders' Decisions*

We return here to our earlier argument that a primary responsibility of leadership research is to identify successful practices with high levels of generalizability or "external validity" and that a primary responsibility of practicing school leaders is to adapt and enact those externally valid practices in ways that are "ecologically valid", that is, in ways that reflect the nature and demands of their own schools' context. This general argument has two important caveats.

The first caveat acknowledges that if available research results comprehensively addressed the myriad circumstances, problems and interactions faced by practicing leaders, our argument would seem to privilege research-based knowledge over local knowledge in practicing leaders' decision making. But research results are actually available to serve as guides for only a minor portion of those decisions. So our first caveat is that, for those decisions about which there is relevant robust research evidence, practicing leaders should use such evidence as one source of guidance in making their decisions; they should certainly avoid making decisions that fly in the face of robust research evidence. On decisions about which there is little relevant research evidence – a very large proportion of their decisions - leadership practitioners' existing expertise and local knowledge should "carry the day".

The second caveat to our general argument acknowledges that a great deal of research evidence potentially relevant to practicing leaders' decision making is extremely difficult to use well. This caveat is not about interpreting technically complex statistical analyses or arcane theoretical frameworks, as challenging as that may be. Rather, it is about determining the most promising focus of leadership efforts, *all things equal* (that is, temporarily leaving aside considerations about the unique features of the leaders' context). For example, the chapters in this book as a whole provide a considerable amount of high quality evidence about both successful leadership practices and characteristics of schools, classrooms and families that contribute significantly to the success of students. But identifying the relative effects of these characteristics on student success, given the concerted efforts of leaders, remains a tenuous business at best. *All other things equal, should I focus on building trust among staff, parents and students or improving the disciplinary climate across my school or nurturing my colleagues collective sense of efficacy or working more closely with some parents to enhance the educational culture of their homes or ...... etc.* Evidence in the book to this point has provided no direct way of reliably answering this question. So in this final section of this final chapter we illustrate one way of making the results of relevant research a more transparent and useable source of guidance for school leaders.

This illustration uses a large, quantitative data set collected through surveys of teachers and school leaders in more than 100 elementary and secondary schools whose leaders were associated with the Rice University Entrepreneurship Program (REEP) in Texas. Collected through a collaboration between REEP staff (Lawrence Kohn) and two editors of this book (Leithwood and Sun), and explicitly guided by the Four Paths framework, these data provided evidence about most of the variables describe in earlier sections of the book. The main purpose for collecting the data was to provide individual schools with evidence about the status of the Four Path variables in their schools and the association between those variables and student achievement in each of the schools. These results were then used by school leaders and teachers as part of their ongoing school improvement work.

Evidence of student achievement in each school was provided by the state's testing program, the *Texas STAAR Percentage at Phase-in Satisfactory Standard or Above*, combing all subjects and all grades. The measure of school leadership practices included in the teacher survey was based on the *Ontario Leadership Framework* summarized in Chap. 3. Variables on each of the Four Paths, 14 in total, were measured with surveys of both teachers and school leaders in each of the participating schools. Appropriate controls for student disadvantage were included as part of the data collection.

For the purpose of illustrating how to make relevant research a more transparent and usable source of guidance for school leaders, the full REEP data set were used

Table 16.1 The power idex

Paths and variables	Impact of leadership on each variable	Impact of each variable on student learning	Power index
Rational path			
Classroom instruction	.47	.02	**.01**
Use of instructional time in the classroom	.41	.42	**.17**
Academic press	.71	.42	**.30**
Disciplinary climate	.56	.56	**.31**
Emotional path			
Teacher trust in others	.80	.50	**.40**
Collective teacher efficacy	.69	.52	**.36**
Teacher commitment	.69	.30	**.21**
Organizational citizenship behavior	.32	.39	**.15**
Organizational path			
Safe and orderly environment	.76	.44	**.33**
Collaborative structures & cultures	.78	.25	**.20**
Organization of planning. & instructional time	.77	.24	**.18**
Family path			
Parental expectations for child's school success	.47	.64	**.30**
Parents social & intellectual capital about schooling	.43	.68	**.29**
Forms of communication between parents and child	.45	.61	**.27**

to calculate a "power index". First, the correlation between the measure of leadership and the measures of each of the Four Path variables were calculated. Then correlations between each of the Four Path Variables and student achievement were calculated. These two sets of correlations were combined (multiplied) to represent a power index as reported in Table 16.1.

A comparison of indices across combinations of leadership practices and Four Path variables serves as a form of guidance for one critical set of school leader decisions. For example, the power index suggests that leaders' engagement in efforts to improve *Teacher Trust* and *Teacher Collective Efficacy* in their schools may be the most powerful paths to improved student achievement whereas, surprisingly, leaders' engagement in efforts to improve *Classroom Instruction* may have almost no impact on student achievement. This result prompted considerable further exploration about how to explain these results among those in schools providing the data, although there was little quarrel that the survey measured a legitimate conception of effective classroom instruction (those teacher survey items appear in the box below).

> My teaching is explicitly guided by the goals that I intend to accomplish with my students.
>
> I constantly monitor my students' progress to make sure that they are actively engaged in meaningful learning
>
> I provide prompt, informative feedback to my students.
>
> I analyze my students' achievement results and provide differentiated instruction.
>
> My instructional strategies enable students to construct their own knowledge
>
> My students have significant opportunities to learn collaboratively.
>
> I use data to identify weaknesses in my students' academic skills and develop interventions to remediate or reteach
>
> I supplement my face-to-face instruction in schools with technology-facilitated assignments reinforcing what has been learned in class interventions to remediate or reteach
>
> I supplement my face-to-face instruction in schools with technology-facilitated assignments reinforcing what has been learned in class

This power index does not, of course, take account of other contingencies legitimately influencing school leaders' choices such as degree of environmental turbulence, organizational size or the demands of specific policies. But it is a precise way of helping leaders understand the nature of the guidance provided by research relevant to their school improvement decisions. As we argued earlier, absent something comparable to the calculation of a power index, a large proportion of available research is difficult to use by school leaders wanting to be evidence informed.

16.1.7 Some Implications for Leadership Development

Leadership development programs, especially principal preparation programs, have come under intense criticism over the past 15 years. These criticisms have included, for example, issues concerning context, the recruitment and selection of candidates, curriculum content, the qualifications and experience of those providing instruction, types of pedagogy used, program organization, and student assessment practices (Crow and Whiteman 2016). During this same period, however, considerable effort has been made, especially in the U.S. to identify the characteristics of exemplary leadership development programs (Young 2015; Jacobson et al. 2015). Particularly relevant to the Four Paths framework explored in this book is the conclusion of a major study of exemplary programs by Darling-Hammond and her colleagues. This study "found that along with research-based content 'curricular coherence linking goals, learning activities, and assessments around a set of shared values, beliefs and knowledge about effective organizational practice was evident in exemplary programs" (quoted in Crow and Whiteman 2016, p. 126).

The Four Paths framework, including the core leadership practices summarized in Part I of this book, provide coherent curriculum content for that portion of a school leader preparation program concerned with school improvement and student success at school. While effective leadership practices in Part I have been organized around four categories of core leadership practices, most of these practices are also included, for example, in the new U.S. *Professional Standards for Educational Leaders* (2015) used to guide the many principal preparation programs offered by U.S. universities. One section of the new U.S. standards entitled "What is the link between educational leadership and student learning?" explains that:

The 2015 Standards embody a research- and practice-based understanding of the relationship between educational leadership and student learning. Improving student learning takes a holistic view of leadership. In all realms of their work, educational leaders must focus on how they are promoting the learning, achievement, development, and well-being of each student. The 2015 Standards reflect interdependent domains, qualities and values of leadership work that research and practice suggest are integral to student success:

1. Mission, Vision, and Core Values
2. Ethics and Professional Norms
3. Equity and Cultural Responsiveness
4. Curriculum, Instruction and Assessment
5. Community of Care and Support for Students
6. Professional Capacity of School Personnel
7. Professional Community for Teachers and Staff
8. Meaningful Engagement of Families and Community
9. Operations and Management
10. School Improvement

Of these ten standards and their more detailed specification, only number 2 (*Ethics and Professional Norms*) is not fully reflected in the core practices described in Part II of the book. This standard, however, includes six more detailed expectations, of which three are also part of the core practices described in Part II of the book:

(b) Act according to and promote the professional norms of integrity, fairness, transparency, trust, collaboration, perseverance, learning, and continuous improvement.
(c) Place children at the center of education and accept responsibility for each student's academic success and well-being.
(e) Lead with interpersonal and communication skill, social-emotional insight, and understanding of all students' and staff members' backgrounds and cultures. (page 10)

The account of how leadership influences student learning in the new U.S. standards (Please see Figure 1 on page 5) reflects a "direct effects" model of school leadership influence, a conception clearly inconsistent with the now very large body of evidence about the indirect effects of most school leadership influence and the systematic outline of leadership mediators as described in our Four Paths model.

The Four Paths model, then, encompasses almost all of the new U.S. standards and provides considerable additional guidance about how the leadership practices identified by the standards might actually be enacted by school leaders to influence student learning, guidance largely absent from the U.S. standards themselves. Knowledge about variables on each of the four paths would help prepare candidates for both diagnosing school needs and designing effective school improvement processes. Chapters included in each section of the book could be used to deepen candidates' understandings about each of the conditions or variables on the Four Paths and the more specific leadership practices likely to improve those conditions.

While the genesis of the Four Paths framework was a large-scale project aimed at further developing the capacities of existing school principals, we recommend this framework as a partial solution to some of the central problems associated with the initial preparation of school principals, as well as the further education of all those - no matter official role - who find themselves exercising leadership in their schools.

References

Ahnert, L., Milatz, A., Kappler, G., Schneiderwind, J., & Fischer, R. (2013). The impact of teacher-child relationships on child cognitive performance as explored by a priming paradigm. *Developmental Psychology, 49*(3), 554–567.

Bossert, S. T., Dwyer, D. C., Rowan, B., & Lee, G. V. (1982). The instructional management role of the principal. *Educational Administration Quarterly, 18*, 34–64.

Chhokar, J., Brodbeck, F., & House, R. (2007). *Culture and leadership across the world.* New York: Lawrence Erlbaum.

Christensen, P. O., & Demski, J. S. (2002). Accounting policies in agencies with moral hazard and renegotiation. *Journal of Accounting Research, 40*(4), 1071–1090.

Coleman, J. S. (1988). Social capital in the creation of human capital. *American Journal of Sociology, 94*, S95–S120.

Crow, G., & Whiteman, R. (2016). Effective program features: A literature review. *Journal of Research on Leadership Education, 11*, 120–148.

Geijsel, F., Sleegers, P., Leithwood, K., & Jantzi, D. (2003). Transformational leadership effects on teacher commitment and effort toward school reform. *Journal of Educational Administration, 41*(3), 228–256.

Goldring, E., & Rallis, S. (2000). *Principals of dynamic schools: Taking charge of change* (2nd ed.). Newbury Park: Corwin/Sage.

Hallinger, P. (2016). *Building a global knowledge base in educational leadership and management: Bringing context out of the shadows of leadership.* Paper presented at the annual meeting of the British Educational Leadership and Management Society (BELMAS), Chester, UK.

Hallinger, P., & Heck, R. H. (1998). Exploring the principal's contribution to school effectiveness: 1980-1995. *School Effectiveness and School Improvement, 9*(2), 157–191.

Handford, T., & Leithwood, K. (2013). Why teachers trust leaders. *Journal of Educational Administration, 51*(2), 194–212.

Heck, R. H., & Hallinger, P. (2009). Assessing the contribution of distributed leadership to school improvement and growth in math achievement. *American Educational Research Journal, 46*, 659–689.

Heck, R., & Hallinger, P. (2014). Modeling the longitudinal effects of school leadership on teaching and learning. *Journal of Educational Administration, 52*, 653–681.

House, R., Hanges, P., Javidan, M., Dorfman, P., & Gupta, V. (2004). *Culture, leadership and organizations: The Globe study of 62 societies.* Thousand Oaks: Sage.

Jacobson, S., McCarthy, M., & Pounder, D. (2015). What makes a leadership preparation program exemplary? *Journal of Research on Leadership Education, 10*, 63–76.

Jeynes, W. (2011). *Parental involvement and academic success.* New York: Routledge.

Lazowski, R., & Hulleman, C. (2016). Motivation interventions in education: A meta-analytic review. *Review of Educational Research, 86*(2), 602–640.

Marzano, R. J., Waters, T., & McNulty, B. (2005). *School leadership that works: From research to results.* Aurora: ASCD and McREL.

Mascall, B., Leithwood, K., Strauss, T., & Sacks, R. (2008). The relationship between distributed leadership and teachers' academic optimism. *Journal of Educational Administration, 46*(2), 214–228.

Neihaus, K., & Adelson, J. (2014). School support, parent involvement, and academic and socio-emotional outcomes for English language learners. *American Journal of Educational Research, 51*(4), 810–844.

National Policy Board for Educational Administration. (2015). *Professional standards for educational leaders.* Reston: Author.

Pitner, N. (1988). The study of administrator effects and effectiveness. In N. Boyan (Ed.), *Handbook of research on educational administration* (pp. 99–122). New York: Longman.

Reetzig, G., & Creemers, B. (2005). A comprehensive framework for effective school improvement. *School Effectiveness and School Improvement, 16*(4), 407–424.

Robinson, V., Hohepa, M., & Lloyd, C. (2009). *School leadership and student outcomes: Identifying what works and why: Best evidence synthesis iteration [BES].* Wellington: Ministry of Education.

Roorda, D. L., Koomen, H. M. Y., Spilt, J. L., & Oort, F. J. (2011). The influence of affective teacher–student relationships on students' school engagement and achievement. *Review of Educational Research, 8*(4), 493–529.

Scheerens, J., Vermeulen, C., & Pelgrum, W. (1989). Generalizability of instructional and school effectiveness indicators across nations. *International Journal of Educational Research, 13*(7), 691–706.

Young, M. (2015). Effective leadership preparation: What it looks like and what it can do. *Journal of Research on Leadership Education, 10*, 3–10.